THE FUNCTION OF THE NIPH'AL IN BIBLICAL HEBREW

PAUL D. SANSONE, O.F.M.

STUDIA SEMITICA NEERLANDICA

For publications in the series see page 209

P.A. Siebesma

The function of the niph'al in Biblical Hebrew

in relationship to other passive-reflexive verbal stems and to the pu'al and hoph'al in particular

1991
VAN GORCUM, ASSEN/MAASTRICHT, THE NETHERLANDS

CIP-GEGEVENS KONINKLIJKE BIBLIOTHEEK, DEN HAAG

Siebesma, P.A.

The function of the niph'al in biblical Hebrew: in relationship to other passive-reflexive verbal stems and to the pu'al and hoph'al in particular/P.A. Siebesma. - Assen [etc.]: Van Gorcum. -
(Studia Semitica Neerlandica: nr. 28, ISSN 0081-6914);
Met lit. opg., reg.
NUGI 941
Trefw.: Hebreeuwse taal; grammatica/bijbel.

ISBN 90 232 2594 5

Printed in The Netherlands by Van Gorcum, Assen

This edition represents a slightly revised version of my doctoral dissertation which was first published in 1988. The publication of the original was made possible due to a two-year grant from the Ministry of Education and Sciences in 1980. The revision mainly consists of the addition of certain comments made by the examining committee. Translation into English has been realized thanks to the generous supply of funds by the Netherlands Organization for Scientific Research, NWO. Furthermore, I express my gratitude for financial assistance provided by the J.E. Jurriaanse Foundation and the Dr. Hendrik Muller's Vaderlandsch Fonds Foundation, which have supported the publication of this book.

After much effort and considerable set-backs the work has finally been published. It would not have come about but for the help of many. It is impossible to give credit to all who were involved.

I appreciate the meticulous care with which the translation of the Dutch text was carried out by drs. Jan Chris Pennekamp. Moreover, I am thankful for the valuable comments of Dr. Ellis Brotzman of Tyndale Theological Seminary in Badhoevedorp who read the draft version of the English manuscript.

Special thanks are due to my wife Marianne whose encouragement and perceptive comments have been of great value during the days of this project. Moreover, I wish to give thanks to the LORD God who gave me the talents and strength to complete this book. (Ps. 127:1).

Transcription of Hebrew Alphabet

א	=	A
ב	=	B
ג	=	G
ד	=	D
ה	=	H
ו	=	W
ז	=	Z
ח	=	Ḥ
ט	=	Ṭ
י	=	J
כ	=	K
ל	=	L
מ	=	M
נ	=	N
ס	=	S
ע	=	ᶜ
פ	=	P
צ	=	Ṣ
ק	=	Q
ר	=	R
שׂ	=	Ś
שׁ	=	Š
ת	=	T

Lowercase characters in transcriptions of Hebrew verb forms indicate Masoretic vocalization.

Table of contents

Introduction

In recent decades, various studies have appeared on the function of the so-called 'perfect' and 'imperfect' in Biblical Hebrew. Questions about the origin of these forms, as well as about their usage, function, and relationship to the so-called 'consecutive' forms, have been widely discussed. The issues have been dealt with from various perspectives. However, much less attention was devoted to verbal stems in Biblical Hebrew and their mutual relationships. Since the beginning of this century only two comprehensive studies on verbal stems have been published.

In the first place, the article of M. Lambert, "L'emploi du niph'al en hébreu", must be mentioned. It was published in REJ 41, 196-214, in 1900. In this article the author presents extensive lists of niph'al forms which, according to him, have a reflexive or passive relationship to the qal, pi'el or hiph'il. In the second place we mention the book by E. Jenni *Das hebräische Pi'el*, Basel, 1968, which, as the title indicates, contains an extensive study of the pi'el.

Lambert developed his presuppositions, method, and conclusions exclusively out of those of the traditional Gesenius-Kautzsch grammar. Yet Jenni opted for a totally different approach in his study of the pi'el. His work is based on findings which had been commonly accepted in Akkadian grammar. Thus his presuppositions are different from those of the traditional grammars before him.

The topic of our dissertation is the niph'al in Biblical Hebrew. Since the appearance of the above-mentioned article of Lambert in 1900 hardly anything new has been published on this verbal stem. By means of this publication I hope to spur on the study of passive-reflexive verbal stems in Biblical Hebrew. My study is arragned as follows:

The first chapter offers a survey of the study of verbal stems in Biblical Hebrew. Due to the importance of Jenni's research on the pi'el I have chosen his book as a starting point. Since the niph'al is the topic of my study, I will deal with Jenni's presuppositions and methods of research in particular and discuss the ways in which these differ from those applied in grammatical studies published before his. Next, I will compare Jenni's insights into the niph'al and the mutual relationships between the verbal stems with those of grammars which preceded his. In the second half of the chapter I will examine the question how far Jenni's ideas have permeated later publications. Critical views will also be dealt with. Moreover, I will present my own critique especially where Jenni's presuppositions and method of research are concerned. The purpose of the chapter is to lay a foundation for the scientific study of the niph'al.

The second chapter offers an account of the method which I have adopted in the research of the niph'al. One of my main conclusions is that the niph'al cannot be studied in isolation but that it must only be studied in relation to the other passive-reflexive verbal stems.

The third chapter consists mainly of tables. It presents an overview of all verbal roots of which niph'al forms occur in Biblical Hebrew. The material is subdivided into three groups: prose, poetry, and prophecy. Apart from giving the scripture references of the niph'al forms, it also supplies the corresponding forms of other passive-reflexive verbal stems (pu'al, hoph'al, hitpa'el and the passive qal-participle). The list forms the basis for the following research. The advantage of the enumeration is that the reader can check the observations and conclusions of the fourth chapter by himself. Some might disagree with me in regard to certain conclusions. This is almost unavoidable in a study of thousands of verbal forms. Even so, the list may serve as a basis for further research.

In the fourth chapter I will deal with the relationship between the niph'al and the other passive-reflexive verbal stems and discuss in what way the niph'al differs morphologically as well as semantically from these. The other verbal stems will only be studied in their relationship to the niph'al. This approach was chosen for two reasons. First, the study is primarily geared to obtaining a better understanding of the function of the niph'al and not to presenting a description of passive-reflexive verbal stems as a whole. Secondly, the issues are fairly complex. Therefore, it is useful to limit our study to the niph'al. Because of this other verbal stems will only be discussed in as far as they are related to the topic. I will deal especially with the relationship between niph'al and pu'al or hoph'al respectively. According to traditional grammars a number of pu'al and hoph'al forms are remainders of the passive qal which was lost in Biblical Hebrew. I will investigate to what extent my own findings support this theory. The relationship between niph'al and hitpa'el and the passive-qal participle will be treated briefly.

The final conclusions are presented in the fifth and last chapter.

I Survey of the study of verbal stems in Biblical Hebrew

1.1 Introduction

In 1968 the Swiss Hebrew scholar Ernst Jenni published *Das hebräische Pi'el*, a study on the pi'el in Biblical Hebrew, subtitled *Syntaktisch-semasiologische Untersuchung einer Verbalform im Alten Testament*.[1] Its publication may be regarded as quite extraordinary because it is the first book in which a single verbal stem of OT Hebrew is discussed in an extensive and thorough manner.[2] In Hebrew grammar prior to 1968 much attention had been given to the so called 'tempora', the 'tenses' of the verb, and related issues. Much was written on the origins of the forms of the perfect and imperfect and on their development from Proto-Semitic to their present form.[3]

Moreover, a considerable amount of research had been devoted to the function of the perfect and the imperfect and their mutual relationship. Also, questions about the true nature of the waw-consecutive had been frequently discussed as well as the issue whether 'tenses' should be referred to as temporal concepts.[4] The study of verbal stems in Biblical Hebrew, however, had progressed to a much lesser extent and publications were scarce. Apart from what could be derived from grammars on the subject--most being based largely on the standard works of W. Gesenius and H. Ewald--the study of verbal stems relied heavily on comparative grammars of Semitic languages and a few articles on Semitic verbal stems.[5] Concerning the study of the individual verbal stems, publications focused primarily on the ni. and the hitp. in Biblical Hebrew.[6] Practically no research at all had been devoted to other verbal stems. Therefore, Jenni's publication on the pi. was an important step forwards in the study of Hebrew verbal stems.

In this chapter we present a survey of the literature of the last one and a half centuries concerning the study of verbal stems in Biblical Hebrew. As a starting date, I chose the year 1813 when the first edition of Gesenius' Hebrew Grammar was published. Gesenius is generally regarded as the founding father of Hebrew linguistics; his lexicon and grammar (29th edition) are still respected as standard works in spite of all progress in the field of Hebrew studies.[7] Basing my approach on Jenni's book, I have dealt with the following questions: What are his views on verbal stems in general and on pi. and ni. in particular? What are his presuppositions? To what extent is his work innovative in respect to preceding grammars?

The chapter is organized as follows: first, Jenni's views on the pi. are compared to those of the standard grammars of Gesenius, Ewald, Joüon and Bauer-Leander.[8] In my research I also refer to a number of other grammars dating from 1813 to 1968. Subsequently, in the same way Jenni's views on the ni. will be compared with other grammatical studies. Again, I will investigate to what extent Jenni's classification of the verbal stems differs from those of the standard grammars. In the second part of this chapter I will trace the influence of Jenni's views on grammatical studies after 1968.

1.2 Jenni's observations on the pi'el

For Jenni's observations on the pi. and other verbal stems we first consult *Das hebräische Pi'el*. In addition, we may refer to his article preceding it: "Faktitiv und Kausativ von **ABD** 'zu grunde gehen'", in which he discusses the difference in meaning and function between the pi. and hi. of this stem.[9] Much information on his views on verbal stems in general may be gleaned from the summary of a lecture on the function of the passive-reflexive verbal stems which he gave about one year after the publication of his book on the pi.[10] Additional information may be found in his completely revised version of the Hollenberg-Budde school grammar.[11] Although the grammar book was published about ten years after *Das hebräische Pi'el*, it corroborates the fact that his ideas on verbal stems essentially remain unchanged. Finally, we must refer to his article on the difference between nominal and verbal sentences.[12]

In *Das hebräische Pi'el* Jenni attempts to offer a new evaluation of the semantic function of the pi. He considers the treatment of the pi. in traditional grammars insufficient and unsatisfactory. So, he points out some shortcomings of the above-mentioned grammars in his introduction.

Obviously, there is a considerable difference of opinion between Jenni and traditional grammarians. The latter derive all verbal stems from one, the qal, referred to as the 'simple' or 'main verbal stem'.[13] Jenni rejects the presupposition. For although he does not state his rejection *in expressis verbis* it may be inferred from his conclusions.[14] Jenni assumes that the verbal stems of qal, pi. and hi., and their related passive-reflexive counterparts ni., pu., ho. and hitp., originally formed a closed system of grammatical categories. He does not question whether or not the qal was a basis for the other verbal stems. In the system each of the seven verbal stems had, morphologically and semantically, a clearly defined function distinct from that of others. Each verbal stem stood, in form and meaning, in distinctive opposition to each of the other verbal stems. According to Jenni, this presupposition is not only a given fact from the earliest linguistic history of OT Hebrew, but it also applies for Masoretic OT Hebrew. In stating his opinion, he abandons the view that the qal should be the basic form for all other verbal stems.[15]

The Gesenius-Kautzsch grammar supposes that verbal stems, in form and function, do not relate to each other but to the qal. Its findings are based on its view of the 'word stem': "Die Wortstämme der hebr. wie der übrigen sem. Sprachen haben die Eigentümlichkeit, dass sie weitaus der Mehrzahl nach aus drei Konsonanten bestehen. An diesen letzteren haftet zugleich wesentlich die Bedeutung, während die wechselnden Vokale mehr zum Ausdruck der verschiedenen Modifikationen des Begriffs dienen."[16]

Gesenius quotes the root **'MQ** as an example here, which may occur as a verb form (**'āMaQ** or **'āMōQ,** 'be deep'), as a noun (**'ōMeQ** 'deep' and **'ēMeQ** 'plain'), as well as an adjective (**'āMoQ** 'deep'). A word stem may adopt the form of a verbal and a substantival form. They often occur side by side.

The above may lead to the conclusion that Gesenius-Kautzsch assumes a basic word root, consisting of three radicals, from which all nominal and verbal forms are derived. Yet, Gesenius does not hold the view that the word stem, from which stem derivatives are formed, is identical to the root of the stem. He rejects the historical explanation which allows derivatives to be derived from the consonantal word stem:[17] "Andere haben die drei Stammkonsonanten in dem Sinn als Wurzel bezeichnet, dass sie--vokallos und unaussprechbar gedacht--die gemeinsame Grundlage für den daraus entwickelten Verbal- und Nominalstamm repräsentiere, wie im Pflanzenreiche (dem der bildliche Ausdruck entlehnt ist) die Stämme aus der unsichtbaren Würzel hervorgehen... Für die Erforschung des historischen Bestands der Sprache ist jedoch diese Annahme unaussprechbarer, ihrer Bedeutung nach indifferenter Würzeln ohne Belang".[18]

The Gesenius-Kautzsch grammar cannot avoid introducing a basic concept for its word stem. For this purpose it reserves the qal: "Aus praktischen Gründen ist es jedoch von Alters her üblich, dass man die dritte Person Sing. Perfekti Qal, als eine der einfachsten, durch keinerlei Bildungszusätze vermehrten Verbalformen als Wortstamm aufstellt und ihr nicht nur die übrigen Bildungen des Verbums selbst, sondern auch die Nominalformen und damit zugleich die vom Nomen ausgehende Mehrzahl der Partikeln anreiht".[19] For practical reasons, Gesenius-Kautzsch takes the third person perfect qal as the basic stem from which all other forms are derived, including the nominal.[20]

Based on these presuppositions, Gesenius-Kautzsch postulates its division of verb stems.[21] They are distinguished as: a) the *verba primitiva*, b) the *derivativa verbalia*, and c) the *verba denominativa*. The *verba primitiva* are the verb stems which render the stem without any affix, viz. in the qal. The *derivativa verbalia* are the verb stems derived from the qal, viz. the other verbal stems. The *verba denominativa* are the stems that are derived from nouns or particles. They may occur as *verba primitiva* as well as *verba derivativa*. Furthermore, Gesenius-Kautzsch expresses the conviction that the original verb roots, from which the *verba denominativa* have been derived, may still be present in Hebrew.[22]

The equation of the basic form of the verb to the 3rd pers. perf. qal results in difficulties for which Gesenius-Kautzsch fails to provide adequate solutions. The forms of the perf. and the part. are derived from the 3rd pers. sing. perf. qal, yet the impf. and impv. forms are derived from a different basic form.[23] The grammar does not mention any existing connection between these two basic forms nor does it provide any information about the relationship between the last basic form and the forms of the impf. and the impv.

of the other verbal stems. It adopts for every verbal stem the 3rd pers. sing. perf. as the 'representative' from which all other forms may be derived analogously to the qal of qatal. Gesenius-Kautzsch concludes about these verbal stems: "Vom reinen Stamm oder qal werden nach feststehender Analogie die Derivativstämme gebildet, in welchen sich der Stammbegriff je nach der veränderten Form in den verschiedensten Nuancierungen darstellt (intensiv, frequentativ, privativ, causativ, reflexiv, reziprok, zum Teil mit Passivbildungen)".[24]

The view that the qal would be the 'pure' or 'primitive' form of which all other conjugations are derived may be found in all grammars of Biblical Hebrew of the last one and a half centuries.[25] Although they express different views on the exact nature of the relationship between qal and e.g. pi., hi., or the ni., yet they accept the existence of this relationship as a fact.

The Gesenius-Kautzsch grammar describes the pi. as follows: "Der Grundbegriff des Pi'el, auf welchem alle die mannigfaltigen Nuancierungen in der Bedeutung dieser Konjug. zurückgeführt werden können, ist, sich angelegentlich mit der im Stammbegriff enthaltenen Handlung beschäftigen".[26] Here, a close relationship is acknowledged between the verbal stem form (strengthening and doubling of the middle radical of the qal-form) and its meaning (to be zealously and intensively involved in the action expressed by the qal-form).[27] From this basic concept all meanings of the pi. are derived: the intensive, the iterative and also the causative. Analogous to this, the so called denominative pi.-forms of the nouns are formed.[28]

Other grammars, dated prior to 1968, consider pi. to be primarily an intensive. According to Joüon it is the basic meaning of the pi.[29] Also, the pi. may convey causative or declarative-estimative meaning. The historical grammar of Bauer-Leander ranks the pi. under the intensive verbal stems. However, Bauer-Leander assumes pi. to have have received its causative meaning in Proto-Semitic. The reason for this is unclear. The intensive meaning is only a historical fact for this grammar; in practice, intensive and causative meaning of pi. coexist as equals.[30]

The views, as found in these grammars, present certain problems to Jenni.[31] He doubts whether doubling of the middle radical of pi. actually translates symbolically into intensification of the action. According to him, it is impossible to explain the apparent causative meaning of the pi. in this way. Nor is it clear why pi. represents a causative when another causative verbal stem, hi., exists. Also, according to Jenni, other grammarians fail to provide adequate explanation for the occurring change from intensive to causative. Aside from this, Jenni contends, no explanation is given for the apparent agreement in meaning of certain verb stems among forms of the qal and the pi., or between forms of a causative hi. and a causative pi.

We concluded above that Jenni wants to base his approach on a difference in function and meaning between the qal and pi. and between the pi. and hi. Jenni, does not want to base his approach on traditional Hebrew and Arabic grammar, but on the insights into the D-stem which have beem commonly accepted in Akkadian grammar.

These views, as found e.g. in W. von Soden's grammar, all refer to an article by the Assyriologist A. Goetze.[32] In his article on the intensive in Semitic languages, Goetze studies the relationship between the G-stem (comparable to the qal) and the D-stem (the doubling stem, comparable to pi.) in Akkadian. First, he questions whether the supposition that *qaṭala*, the hypothetical form of the 3rd pers. sing. qal in Proto-Semitic, is the basic form from which all other verbal stems are derived as modifications.[33] He proves that it does not apply for the D-stem in Akkadian. The D-stem cannot be derived from the fientive forms of the G-stem but must be derived from the so-called 'stative' of the G-stem.[34] The stative is a kind of verb tense representing a condition; it does not express any temporal aspect, but it depends on the tense of the whole sentence.[35]

Goetze discerns three kinds of statives and studies their semantic relationship to the D-stem. The first group is that of the so-called 'durative statives', i.e. statives expressing a quality peculiar to a person or thing.[36] The D-stems related to these statives have a factitive function, i.e. they put a person or thing into the condition expressed by the stative.[37] The second group of statives is that of the so-called 'perfect statives' which express a condition resulting from an action performed by the subject.[38] The D-stem related to this group of statives may have two meanings. When the stative is transitive, the D-stem indicates 'allow someone to have something'. When the stative is intransitive the related D-stem may convey the meaning of 'put someone or something in the specific situation' expressed by the stative.[39] The third group of statives is formed by the so-called 'passive statives', i.e. statives with a passive meaning.[40] Contrary to the first group, this group contains transitive verbs. The D-stem also represents the factitive meaning.[41] Sometimes, hardly any difference can be noticed between the G- and D- stems. The G-stem refers to the completion of an action, whereas the D-stem emphasizes the result of the action.[42]

Von Soden develops these ideas on the D-stem further. He does not discuss the intensive meaning, yet he refers to the factitive of the stative of the G-stem as the main meaning of the D-stem.[43] Also, it may have a declarative meaning with respect to the stative, or even a non-factitive meaning.[44] Goetze's and W. von Soden's views on the D-stem are copied by almost all Akkadian lexicons and grammars.[45] Goetze enunciates that the findings of his research apply for the Western-Semitic area as well. However, the original function of the pi. has become uncertain due to the fact that the stative in Western-Semitic is lost.[46] In this respect, Goetze and later Akkadian grammarians diverge principally from their traditional Hebrew and Arabic precursors. First, Goetze relates the stative of the G-stem to the D-stem instead of relating the 3rd pers. sing. qal and the D-stem. Secondly, and because of that, the function of the D-stem is primarily factitive and not intensive.[47]

Jenni wants to test these views on the pi. A major part of his book has been devoted to proving the thesis that the pi. is primarily a factitive.[48] In agreement with Goetze, Jenni distinguishes between the stems with a transitive meaning in the qal and those whith an intransitive meaning. The main part of his book consists of three sections. In the first part (pp. 20-123) he studies the pi. stems for which intransitive qal-forms exist. Jenni exhaustively treats this topic since it is often hard to distinguish clearly in meaning between the pi. and the hi. He contrasts apparently similar verses in numbered pairs and studies the difference between the pi. and hi. The second part (pp. 123-229) is devoted to pi.-stems of which certain forms occur with a transitive meaning in the qal. Here, Jenni discusses the difference in meaning between qal and pi. According to the grammars and lexicons, the distinction qal-pi. leads to problems for a number of these stems. In the third part (pp. 230-274) Jenni discusses pi.-stems for which no forms occur in the qal. In these cases, he assumes a hypothetical qal which he constructs in analogy to identical stems in other Semitic languages with forms in the basic stem. In the final part (pp. 275-278) Jenni concludes that the outcome of his study of the D-stem in Akkadian applies for the pi.-stem in Hebrew as well.

The function and meaning of the pi. is not that of an intensive or a causative of the qal. The pi. describes much more the bringing about of that condition which is expressed by the adjective in the basic stem or by the form of the pass. pt. of the qal-stem.[49] Since classical Hebrew does not have a stative, contrary to Akkadian, Jenni opts for the form of the adjective corresponding most to the form of the stative, namely, the adjective formed from the same root as the verb stem or the pass.-qal pt.[50] When the qal has an intransitive meaning the pi is a factitive in that it brings about the condition expressed by the adjective related to the qal without paying attention to the progress of the action and while the object remains totally passive.[51] Whenever the qal of a verb stem is transitive, the pi describes the achievement of the result expressed by the adjective related to the qal. In this case, the adjective is usually the pass.-qal pt.[52] For this pi.-form the the result of the action is emphasized, yet for the transitive qal the action itself is emphasized. Jenni refers to this as an *actualis*. The difference is often not expressed in translation for Western languages do not allow for these categories. This accounts for the impression among Western Europeans that the pi. and transitive qal may have the same meaning.[53] The described view adequately fits those verbal stems of which pi.-forms exist but which have no qal forms, and the denominative pi.-stems. When an intransitive meaning is adopted for the hypothetical qal, the pi. has a factitive meaning, and when the hypothetical qal is transitive the pi. is resultative.

From Jenni's conclusions it is clear that there is an obvious difference in function and meaning of pi. and qal on the one hand and of pi. and the hi. on the other. The hi. conveys causative meaning, i.e. the subject causes the object to carry out the action expressed by the qal or the subject causes the object to be in the condition expressed by the qal.[54] Jenni illustrates the difference between the factitive pi. and the causative hi. in the German translation *machen* (make) and *lassen*, *veranlassen* (let, cause). A factitive pi. is properly translated by *machen*; this allows for a totally passive object which does not cooperate in the action and which is brought into a new condition. In the hi. the object remains at the same time the logical subject of the event described by the basic stem.[55]

In summary, it may be said of Jenni's treatment of pi. that he transferred the results of Akkadian grammar in their entirety to Hebrew grammar. We note in this respect that he follows W. von Soden's grammar as a guideline according to its ideas as well as its terminology, whereas in certain instances he elaborates upon it. Thus, Jenni presents an explanation for certain apparent overlaps in meaning of the D-stem and the Š-stem in Akkadian in order to support his own theories on the pi.[56] In his study of the pi. Jenni opts for an approach completely different from that of earlier Hebrew grammarians.[57] He is one of the first to make use of Akkadian grammar in the study of Hebrew verbal stems.[58]

1.3 Jenni's views on the niph'al

Jenni's views on the pi. have also influenced his approach to the study of the niph'al. Jenni bases his approach on the assumption that verbal stems formed a system within which each verbal stem had a clearly defined semantic function and meaning distinct from that of others. As in his treatment of the pi., he is dissatisfied with the traditional classification of the ni. as found in e.g. the Gesenius-Kautzsch grammar.[59]

According to Gesenius-Kautzsch the ni. appears to be somewhat like the Greek middle voice as far as its meaning is concerned. Gesenius-Kautzsch mentions the reflexive of the qal as the first meaning (e.g. **NSTR** 'to hide oneself', **NGAL** 'to redeem oneself'). It also classifies under this heading the forms of the ni. representing a certain mood (e.g. **NANḤ** 'sigh'), as well as the forms of the so-called 'tolerative ni'. (the toleration of certain actions, e.g. **NMṢA** 'allow oneself to be found'). Secondly, the ni. may express the reciprocal idea of the qal (e.g. **NŠPṬ** 'judge with one another'). Thirdly, the ni. may express a middle voice for the qal, just like the hitp., e.g. an active with the affix *sibi*, meaning '(one)-self' (e.g. **NŠAL** 'ask for oneself'). Finally, the ni. may function as the passive of the qal (e.g. **NQBR** 'be buried'). Here, the ni. has replaced the original passive of the qal. In those cases where the qal has an intransitive meaning, or where it is not evident, the ni. functions as the passive of the pi. or the hi. (e.g. **NKḤD** pass. of the pi. as well as of the hi.).

Jenni assumes that the ni. occurs in direct opposition to the qal, but asserts that it expresses a single uniform category of meaning.[60] He presents this definition of the ni.: "The ni. expresses an event which happens with respect to the subject or it expresses the completion of an action, irrespective of the manner in which or the measure to which the subject cooperates with the action".[61] This definition allows both for a passive as well as for a reflexive or tolerative translation of the ni. form, depending on the context in which the event occurs. It is not relevant whether the subject undergoes the event or action passively or whether it cooperates with it.

We are forced to translate the ni. in different ways because we are unable to express this category of meaning in our Western languages in a single manner. According to Jenni, the variety of meanings listed in Gesenius' grammar are largely due to the fact that it is impossible for us to translate the ni. by one concept in a Western language. On the basis of this definition one may understand that, in the immediate context of ni. which are considered to be passives, the person performing the action (the agent) is almost always absent and almost never mentioned explicitly. Neither do we find anywhere a purely transitive action expressed among ni. that are considered to be reflexives where the reflexive pronoun '(one)-self' might be regarded as an accusative, according to Jenni.[62] Comparative analysis of the definitions of the ni. in Jenni and in preceding grammars reveals the following differences:

1.3.1 First, it is striking that Jenni does not even mention the historically primary function of the ni., as presented in other grammars, in his definition. To him, the question is not essential. He presents a description of this function which fits a passive as well as a reflexive translation.

On the contrary, most grammarians assume that the reflexive embodied the primary and original function and meaning of the ni. Only in a later stage, after the pass. qal forms had become obsolete, the ni. is thought to have replaced the pass. qal by having become the pass. of the qal. It is true that the passive is mentioned as the first meaning of the ni. in older editions of Gesenius, because predominantly the ni. is used passively and because the ni. has totally replaced the original passive qal.[63] The original meaning, however, was that of the reflexive. In support of this claim Gesenius' grammar adduces the following arguments:[64]

a) With respect to its outward appearance the ni. shows little agreement with the other passive verbal stems, such as pu., ho. and pass. qal-participles. (It has no 'obscure' vowels).

b) We observe traces of an original passive of the qal.[65]

c) In Arabic the verbal stem that is related to the ni. in its form (the 7th verbal stem) has its own passive.

d) There may be traces of a possible passive of the ni. (Isa. 59:3, Lam. 4:14). Later editions of Gesenius' grammar have completely abandoned this view.[66] The historical Bauer-Leander grammar adduces another argument, namely that a development has occurred in various Indo-european languages. Because of this development the reflexive pronoun of the verb has turned into an exponent of the passive at a given point in time.[67]

The grammars of Ewald, Bergsträsser, Bauer-Leander, Joüon, and many others besides follow Gesenius' grammar in its views on the original reflexive function of the ni.[68] The extensive grammatical study of the ni. by M. Lambert supports the theory as well.[69] Only a handful of grammars assume that originally the niph'al was not a reflexive but that it had a passive or non-reflexive function.[70] Thus, I. Nordheimer's grammar, in opposition to Ewald's views about the original meaning of the ni., presents the following arguments in favour of a passive function of the ni.:[71]

a) It is obviously more appropriate to derive the reflexive from the passive than vice versa. Indeed, the reflexive is a part of the passive: it expresses the undergoing of a certain action in which the person undergoing the action is also the agent of the action. In this respect, Nordheimer indicates the difference in meaning between the ni. and hitp. In an attempt to prove that the hitp. puts more emphasis on those performing the action, he offers Gen. 3:8 and 3:10, where a hitp. and a ni. of the stem **ḤBA** occur. Yet in case of the ni. the emphasis is directed more toward the action itself or toward the undergoing of the action. Nordheimer remarks that reflexive verbs may be regarded as passives; the reverse is not the case (the ni. of **KTB** can only be translated as a passive: 'be written' and not as a reflexive).

b) If the ni. is considered to be a passive of the qal, each active verbal stem will have its corresponding passive verbal stem.

c) A third argument of Nordheimer's is that the original meaning of the 7th verbal stem in Arabic was that of the passive. In Syrian and other Aramaic dialects, the reflexive is also expressed by the passive. His argument is debated today but finds no adherents.[72] Jenni considers the issue of the original passive or reflexive function of the ni. to be non-essential, as stated above.

1.3.2 A second difference between Jenni and preceding grammars is that, according to his definition, the ni. can only occur in oppositional relationship to the qal. The ni. may, therefore, not be regarded as a passive or reflexive of the pi. or hi. even if qal forms do not exist.[73] Jenni refutes the above-mentioned article of M. Lambert "L'emploi du niph'al en hébreu". It documents extensive lists of ni.-forms that, according to Lambert, have a semantic relationship to pi. or hi. be it passive or reflexive.[74] Moreover, there are many grammars which assume that the ni. may have a semantic relationship to pi. or hi.[75] Yet the exact nature of the relationship is a debatable issue. Gesenius-Kautzsch states that in cases where the qal has an intransitive meaning, or where it does not exist, the ni. serves as the passive of pi. or hi, e.g. the stem **KBD**, for which ni. and pu. are passives of the pi.[76] A number of more recent grammars follow Lambert's opinion that the ni. can be used as a passive as well as a reflexive of the pi. or hi.[77]

1.3.3 A third difference is that Jenni does not accept the idea that the ni. meaning may be synonymous to that of the qal. At the most, he concedes that it is impossible to adequately express the differences in meaning among qal and ni. in Western languages in the cases under discussion. In this respect he differs from Lambert who lists 38 roots of which the ni. meaning is identical to that of the qal, one root of which ni. and pu. are identical in meaning, and five roots of which ni. and hi. meanings are identical.[78] (Although, as will be observed later, a number of these cases are disputable they represent 44 of a total of 428 roots, or about 10 %, of all roots of which ni. occur).[79] Gesenius-Kautzsch mentions only one root with identical ni. and qal meanings.[80] Joüon and Bauer-Leander do not mention this aspect of the ni.

Jenni does not agree with these views of Lambert. He observes that verbs have an intransitive meaning in the qal in almost all cases in which grammars and dictionaries agree that ni. and qal are synonymous in meaning. Yet, obviously there is a clear difference in meaning between qal and ni. The qal-form expresses a general rendering of the condition of the subject or of the action performed by the subject. The ni., on the contrary, expresses the 'emerging' or 'becoming manifest' of the condition of the subject, or of the action performed on the subject. According to Jenni the emphasis lies on what he calls the *sich als etwas erweisen*.[81] An example in this respect is the root **HJH** ('be, become'), which in the ni. may mean 'occur, happen' (Ex. 11:6; Deut. 4:32; Dan. 12:1, etc.).[82]

It should be noticed that the comparison with Akkadian does not apply with respect to the root **HJH**. For the G-stem of *bašum* ('be') the present *ibašši* is used to express a condition: 'it is'; the stative of this stem does not occur. The N-stem, however, does express the ingressive, fientive meaning ('originate'). Jenni admits that in some cases it is hard to recognize the difference between the qal and ni. He does not elaborate on his views on the ni. in his article on the passive-reflexive verbal stems.

Jenni's views on the ni. show agreement with those of Akkadian grammars in another respect. W. von Soden states that the main function of the N-stem is that of the passive of the G-stem. Verb forms in the N-stem with a reflexive or a reciprocal meaning occur only very rarely. Akkadian uses a peculiar stem form with a t-infix for this. Von Soden claims that the N-stem may only be very rarely in oppositional relationship to a stem different from the G-stem.[83] This observation has become outdated now. Edzard discovered that the N-stem in Old Babylonian could be in opposition to the Dt- and the Št1-stem.[84]

We note von Soden's observations on the N-stem of verbs of condition (somewhat comparable to Hebrew intransitive verbs). According to his perception, the N-stem of this category expresses an ingressive (lit. the 'occurrence' of the condition conveyed by the G-stem).[85] Yet Jenni stresses the aspect of 'becoming manifest'.

1.4 Jenni's views on verbal stems

Jenni's views on the pi. and, particularly his views on the differences in function and meaning between pi. and qal and between pi. and hi., have led him to adopt a classification of verbal stems totally different from that of grammars before him. First of all he distinguishes two groups of verbal stems: group I, that of the *actualis*--verb forms of these stems express ongoing action--and group II, that of the resultative, which describe the action from the point of view of the result irrespective of the course of the action.[86] Group I includes the qal with its ni. pass.-reflexive and the hi. causative of the qal with its ho. pass. Group II includes the pi., its pu. pass., and its hitp. reflexive. Jenni apparently assumes that this applies for verb stems of which the basic stem is transitive as well as for verbs of which it is intransitive.[87] Jenni's view comprises a closed system in which each verbal stem has its own unchangeable function.

To Jenni, the difference between the ni. and pu. is not only that the ni. as passive-reflexive is related to the qal and that the pu. serves as passive of the pi. but also that the ni. puts more emphasis on the happening itself and on the non-definitive aspect, whereas the pu. puts more emphasis on the definitive, eventual aspect.[88] According to Jenni, this explains why the percentage of occurrence of pu.-participles in the OT is twice that (c. 40 %) of the number of ni.-participles (c. 20 %).[89]

Within the two groups Jenni applies yet other distinctions. He puts the qal with the ni. in opposition to the hi. and the ho. in group I, the *actualis*.[90] The hi. expresses causative meaning with respect to the qal, e.g. the subject of the hi. causes an object to perform the happening or action expressed by the qal.[91] The ho. functions as the passive of the hi. The difference from the other passive forms lies in the fact that the subject of the ho.-form is brought into an event, by an unmentioned agent, an event in which it is actively--almost never passively--involved. Jenni does not develop this notion any further.[92]

In group II, the resultative, the pi. stands in opposition to the pu., the passive of the pi., and to the hitp., the reflexive (and at times the reciprocal) of the pi. While the qal is in opposition to a verbal stem with both a passive as well as a reflexive function, the pi. stands in opposition to two clearly distinct verbal stems. In Jenni's classification, the pass. qal-participle adopts a position in between the actual and the resultative. This form expresses the result of an action which is taking place. Jenni's classification may be represented as follows:

I.ACTUAL			II.RESULTATIVE	
Qal	Niph'al	Pass. qal partic.		Pu'al
			Pi'el	
Hiph'il	Hoph'al			Hithpa'el

Jenni observes that the distinction between actual and resultative eventually may be traced back to the distinction between the verbal and nominal sentence in Hebrew grammar.[93]

The way in which Jenni classifies verbal stems of Biblical Hebrew, is fundamentally different from that applied by grammars preceding his. Since these grammars differ in their individual approach to the subject, we will present first an overview of the various methods of classification employed by them. Subsequently, we will discuss differences with respect to Jenni's classification.

1.4.1 The first manner of classification is that which is found in the grammar of Gesenius-Kautzsch.[94] This offers a division into the verbs and the passive verbal stems. Passive verbal stems, which may be distinguished from the active verbal stems by their obscure vowels, belong to the largely obsolete passive of the qal, the pu., the ho., and the rare hotp. Gesenius-Kautzsch schematically presents the classification as follows:

ACTIVE	PASSIVE
1. Qal	(Pass.Qal)
2. Niph'al	
3. Pi'el	4. Pu'al
5. Hiph'il	6. Hoph'al
7. Hithpa'el	(Hothpa'el)

This classification does not agree with the phase of the language of the text of the OT but it represents a situation in an earlier phase of the language. According to the Gesenius-Kautzsch grammar, the ni. may serve as a passive of the qal, having replaced the passive qal, due to a weakening command of the language.[95] In the same way, the ni. of certain stems functions as the passive of the pi. and the hi., and even the hitp. may function as a passive.[96]

The classification may be found in the older editions of Gesenius' grammar and in those of e.g. Böttcher, Stade and Lambert.[97] These grammars agree that both the ni. as well as the qal and hitp. must have had their own passive. Consequently, attempts were made to discover the remnants of these forms in the OT.[98] Hence, it is assumed that, originally, the system of the verbal stems must have been closed.

A similar classification is found in certain English grammars in which the ni. is treated as a qal-passive. Because of this, the verbal stem has been classified under the passive verbal stems.[99] The system of Gesenius and the other grammars may be regarded as a classification on purely formal grounds; the passives are distinguished from the corresponding actives by changes in vowels. This refers back to the classifications applied in Arabic grammar.

1.4.2 A second manner of classification is found in some older grammars of Biblical Hebrew.[100] They have opted for a classification system with main verbal stems and reflexive-medial verbal stems subdivided into active and passive verbal stems as far as they occur in Hebrew. Schematically this may be represented as:[101]

MAIN VERBAL STEMS		REFLEXIVE VERBAL STEMS	
ACTIVES	PASSIVES	ACTIVES	PASSIVES
Qal	-	Niph'al	-
Pi'el	Pu'al	Hithpa'el	Hothpa'el
Hiph'il	Hoph'al	-	-

This differs from the preceding classification in that the actives and passives have been grouped under two headings.

1.4.3 Joüon moves one step further in his grammar. His classification almost approaches that of Jenni's in that he attempts to come to a closed system as far as possible. He divides the stems into three basic forms: qal, pi. and hi., each of which may occur in three forms, namely, active, passive, and reflexive. He presents it schematically in the following diagram [in French]:[102]

VOIX	ACTIVE	PASSIVE	REFLéCHIE
Action Simple	Qal	-	Niph'al
Action Intensive	Pi'el	Pu'al	Hithpa'el
Action Causative	Hiph'il	Hoph'al	-

This classification is found in quite a number of grammars.[103] It is striking that the passive qal and the reflexive of the hi. are lacking in the diagram. In general, these grammars assume that certain forms of the pass.-qal remain in Biblical Hebrew.[104] Hence, attempts were made to recover remains of the reflexive of the hi.[105]

1.4.4 Ewald's grammar and the historical grammar of Bauer-Leander are the last that need mentioning in this survey. These grammars differ from those mentioned before in that they do not present a classification of verbal stems according to formal or semantic criteria. Their presentation features a historical description of the origins and development of verbal stems. In this respect, we note Ewald's statement that the verbal stems did not necessarily originate from the qal.[106] Although Bauer-Leander assumes such to be the case, it does not include a classification of verbal stems.[107]

1.4.5 A comparison of the above-mentioned systems to Jenni's reveals certain differences. Prior to the publication of Jenni's grammar, classifications are based on formal, (Gesenius), or semantic criteria. The criteria differ from Jenni's: Roorda distinguishes main verbal stems as opposed to reflexive verbal stems, actives and passives. Joüon distinguishes between active, passive and reflexive. Yet Jenni's system offers a different perspective. He applies a new semantic criterion which yields the actual and the resultative. Thus, verbal stems expressing an action which is taking place are put in opposition to those expressing completed action. The formal criteria are of less importance to him, and the diachronic aspect of the Hebrew language is not important at all. Another difference between Jenni's grammar and others is that they, except for Ewald, take the qal to be the basic form for all verbal stems.

Jenni's classification of verbal stems differs from that of Akkadian grammars. W. von Soden offers a classification based on purely formal grounds. He distinguishes four main verbal stems: the G, D, Š, and H stem. From each stem stems may be derived with iterative or habitative meaning (GTN, DTN, ŠTN, and NTN) by addition of the -tan-infix. Stems with different meanings result (Gt, Dt, and Št) by the addition of the -ta/t-infix.[108] Moreover, there are fundamental differences between Hebrew and Akkadian verbal stems. Hebrew does not have a reflexive of the qal, such as the Gt, nor does pi. allow for derivation of a reflexive stem. In this survey we have skipped rare verbal stems, (such as po'lel, pilpel, etc.), because Jenni purposely ignores these in his discussion.

1.5 Evaluation of Jenni's views on the pi'el

1.5.1 Jenni's book *Das hebräische Pi'el* was discussed in a great number of book reviews.[110] The majority of reviewers merely offer a concise summary of its content. Little criticism, if any, is given. Some give it an outstanding evaluation. T.A. Lambdin asserts being much impressed by its logical organization and exhaustive approach. He calls it one of the best treatments available on a distinct issue of the Hebrew and Semitic verb system.[111] Hospers considers the argumentation to be convincing; to his mind Jenni is completely successful in achieving his aims.[112] Other reviews express praise as well.[113]

However, not all reviewers agree. Degen calls Jenni's attempt to apply notions from Akkadian grammar to Hebrew a complete failure.[114] Fokkelman insists that Jenni's work should be redone.[115]

We will return to this later. First, we will examine a number of points which the reviewers praised.

1) Jenni is right in observing that traditional views on the pi. function are insufficient, so new solutions must be found.[116] To my mind, the reviewers are right in this respect. The traditional view of the pi. as intensive does not apply for a great number of stems. Moreover, it does not explain the (seemingly) causative meaning of the pi. and the mutual relationship between pi. and the hi. remains unclear.

2) Jenni was correct in applying notions about the D-stem in Akkadian, as formulated by Goetze and developed by von Soden, as a basis for Hebrew and West-Semitic grammar.[117] Later we will return to this issue which received a recommendation in Hospers' review. Not all reviewers agree that this starting point is correct.[118]

3) A third point for which Jenni was frequently commended was the fact that he succeeded in developing a complete picture of the pi'el. The pi. has a uniform factitive function which is clearly distinct from that of the qal or hiph'il.[119] The topic will be dealt with later.

4) Jenni's method of research receives praise for various reasons: his study includes all 415 stems of which pi. forms exist. He studies his examples as much as possible in their contexts.[120] He compares parallel verses, in which a pi. and a hi. occur or, respectively, a qal and pi, which appear to have the same meaning. Verb stems are divided in transitives and intransitives and both groups are divided again into subgroups with similar meanings. Brockington put it this way in his review: "it makes us look again at the different forms of the Hebrew verb and realize that they were not used arbitrarily but with nuances that in other languages have to be obtained by the use of auxiliary verbs, or adverbs, or other complementary words".[121] We will deal with this later.

1.5.2 The majority of grammars that have appeared after 1968 have been influenced by Jenni's ideas to a greater or lesser extent. Just a few grammars treat the pi. like that of Gesenius-Kautzsch by listing a number of meanings of the pi. of which the intensive is the most important, e.g. Krinetzki and LaSor.[122] The grammar of Sawyer lacks any trace of Jenni's views.[123]

A few grammars are clearly influenced by Jenni's theories without copying those entirely. An example of this is Blau. On the pi. he states that: "**QiṬṬeL** denotes intensity, both of quality (...) and particularly of quantity (...). Especially when derived from stative verbs, it is used in factitive sense (...), then also as a causative (...); further also as a resultative (...). Besides it is quite often denominative, (...), as so it may be declarative (...) and privative".[124] Although Blau mentions the factitive and resultative meaning of the pi, for which he refers to Jenni's work, in general, his enumeration of the functions of the pi. differs little from that of Gesenius-Kautzsch.[125] He accepts the intensive function of the pi., and mentions the factitive and the resultative as new functions. He does not discuss the relationship between the new functions and those known from earlier grammars. The same ambivalence is found in the grammars by Lettinga and Lambdin.[126] They too affirm the intensive function of the pi. without defining the relationship between the intensive and the factitive.

The syntax of Williams deserves to be mentioned separately.[127] He describes the factitive as the first meaning of the pi., yet he does not refer to Jenni's work but to that of Goetze's.[128] Williams does not mention the resultative meaning of the pi'el. He presents a list much like that of e.g. Gesenius-Kautzsch, the only difference being that the intensive function is replaced by the factitive. Only very few grammars have adopted Jenni's views in full, such as Richter, Irsigler, and Welzel.[129] Finally, Schweitzer's grammar must be mentioned. It does not include verbal stems at all. It maintains a very cautious position with respect to the pi.[130]

In summary, we may state that the majority of grammars discussed here are informed of Jenni's views on the pi. Only a small number of German grammars have adopted these views entirely, whereas others mention the function of the pi. in a type of treatment showing little difference from that of Gesenius-Kautzsch.

The work of the Arabist F. Leemhuis bears clear impressions of Jenni's views on the pi.[131] Leemhuis bases his research on Jenni and to a lesser extent on Ryder in his dissertation *The D and H stems in Koranic Arabic*.[132] Leemhuis' study shows resemblances to that of Jenni's where his method of research and his conclusions are concerned. Leemhuis studies the D-stem in its context by contrasting various passages in which D-forms of certain stems occur with apparently similar H- or G-forms of the same stem.[133] According to Leemhuis, the D-stem may be distinguished as the factitive of the causative H-stem, as in Biblical Hebrew. In this context, the D-stem is a transformation of a nominal sentence and the H-stem is a transformation of a verbal sentence.[134] As far as my research has shown, only Leemhuis published an extensive study of the D-stem in a Semitic language other than Hebrew and Akkadian in which he incorporated Jenni's findings on the pi.[135]

1.5.3 Not all reviews of *Das hebräische Pi'el* were completely favorable. Both his approach as well as the elaboration on his theory were criticized. Below, I will list especially the issues criticized in the methodology which he adopted. My own criticism will also be included.

1.5.3.1 An important critical issue is presented by Claassen in his review of Jenni's article "Faktitiv und Kausativ von **ABD** 'zugrunde gehen'".[136] He questions whether it is permissible to transfer the Akkadian factitive and causative categories and to apply them to Hebrew. Claassen considers such a transfer unacceptable.[137] According to him it is not permissible to transfer verbal categories that apply to one language into another language. The distinction factitive-causative, as observed in the D and Š stem in Akkadian, does not have to apply a priori to the Hebrew pi. and hi. It is recognized that there are agreements between Hebrew and Akkadian, but the differences between the verb systems of the two languages are much more numerous; e.g. the Hebrew language does not have a stative. Akkadian operates with a system of stem forms different from that in Hebrew (e.g. G, Gt, Gtn, Dt, etc.). Therefore, Claassen maintains that: "There are always some correspondences between these two languages, but these correspondences are not inevitable and therefore this way of argumentation carries no cogency. If two languages show but one difference in their verbal systems, then the semantic load of any verbal category will not be the same as in the other language".[138]

In my view, Claassen is right when he questions the validity of such a transfer. It will only be valid and permissible when the results are good, and when it appears that these verbal categories do apply for the other language. It is permissible to apply the verbal categories of one language to another language in a working hypothesis, as long as these categories are not enforced rigidly, and provided that one is willing to abandon the working hypothesis once it is disproved.[139] [It should be noted, however, that, Jenni is more careful in the formulation of his theory than what Claassen assumes. Jenni states that: "Im ganzen sind aber die Ergebnisse der assyriologischen Arbeit von so grosser Folgerichtigkeit, dass es sich lohnen dürfte, sie 25 bzw. 15 Jahre nach ihrer Veröffentlichung einmal als Anstoss zu einer Überprüfung der hebräische Grammatik dienen zu lassen".[140] Jenni refers to his research as a first step towards a review of Hebrew grammar (in this respect). In practice, his approach is mainly deductive].

1.5.3.2 A second point of criticism is the fact that Jenni based his research on the vocalized Textus Receptus. Some reviewers wonder to what extent this Tiberian vocalization can be trusted.[141] In the Qumran texts and in the Greek transcription of the Hebrew text in Origen's Hexapla quite often qal-forms are used instead of the Tiberian pi. and vice versa.[142] Jenni opted for the Tiberian vocalization for methodical and practical reasons--a simplification which is understandable in view of the extent of his work.[143] For, indeed, it is not easy to distinguish a pi'el and a qal form on the basis of the consonantal text. In my opinion, the consonantal text, because it offers too few indications, does not allow for the development of a complete description of the system of verbal stems. Here, one has to rely on language tradition. Yet, we should be cautioned by the fact that the Qumran texts and the Greek transcription of the Hebrew text in Origen's Hexapla differ occasionally from the Masoretic vocalization. It is remarkable that Jenni does not always stick to his premises with the same consistency, for, in some cases, he changes the Tiberian vocalization.[144]

1.5.3.3 A third point of criticism concerns the method which Jenni applies in practice. He assumes that the text of the Old Testament is a synchronous whole. Hence, we note the following consequences with respect to his methodology:

a) Jenni treats the pi. from a purely synchronic point of view without paying attention to a possible diachronic development in the various stages of Biblical Hebrew. We may wonder whether or not the function of the pi. has evolved or whether it has undergone changes in the course of time. Does the pi. in a young book, such as Dan. or Chron., *a priori* have the same function as in Gen.?[145] Jenni does not deal with these questions. Yet he contrasts books from different periods in his discussion of pi.- and hi.-forms.[146] It is not always possible to arrive at a precise and justifiable classification of OT texts, due to the wide variety of opinions on the subject. Yet, we think it is possible to adopt a tentative classification which may serve as a basis of investigation of the extent of the function of the pi. in the various elements.

b) Jenni does not distinguish between the different genres of texts. Prose and poetry are the main genres of the OT. When the function of the perf. and imperf. of the qal in poetry differs from that in prose, then perhaps it is also (theoretically) possible for the pi. Moreover, in poetic texts one should also consider semasiological phenomena, as well as metre, sound, parallellism and other poetic phenomena.[147]

c) Neither does Jenni, in his research, take into consideration which form of a verbal stem is used. This appears to indicate that it has no effect on the outcome. E.g. he contrasts very different verb forms in his discussion of verses where the meaning of pi. and hi. are seemingly alike.[158] In my view, this is methodically incorrect.[149] One should not reject beforehand the possibility that a change in form might correspond to a change in verbal stem. My research has proved it to be true in certain instances with respect to the function of the ni. Jenni himself points out that it must not be excluded for the pi. either. In his discussion of the root **ŠḤT**, he remarks that the distribution of the verbal forms over the pi. and hi. is very striking. Primarily forms of the perf. occur in the pi. of this stem, whereas mostly the imperf. and the participles occur in the hi. Jenni uses this fact as an argument for his theory.[150] It is debated how the distribution over the verb forms of other stems may be accounted for--where pi.-forms occur which apparently have the same meaning as forms of qal or hi. It is not sure whether such research will yield any positive evidence.

d) Jenni pays little attention to the linguistic development of Hebrew in times prior to the recording the consonantal text. He fails to discuss the various theories on the origins of the perf. and the imperf. In my view, these matters are vital elements in the discussion of the pi'el. Meyer, in his grammar, argues that the Hebrew imperf. of the qal originally must have had two paradigms: a punctual **yaQṬuLu** and a durative **yaQaṬṬaLu.**[151] The latter form with the second doubled radical shows remarkable resemblance to the Akkadian durative *iparras*. In the course of time this Hebrew durative may have disappeared, or it may have merged secondarily into the pi. This might explain the apparent similarity of certain verb stems among the qal and pi'el. If the theory is correct, this may have affected the function of the pi. It could be an explanation for the apparent similarity of the qal and pi. of certain verb stems. Jenni did not consider this in his study because of his presuppositions which we discussed under 1) and 2).[152]

1.5.3.4 A fourth point of criticism concerns Jenni's presuppositions that there can be no mutual overlap in meaning and function between the various verbal stems and that each verbal stem has its own individual morphological and semantic function. Jenni presents this as a conclusion, yet actually these are presuppositions.[153] As such, they still need to be established by proven facts. Moreover, it is conceivable that the function of a certain verb stem evolved in the course of time and that there is a difference between the forms in earlier and later texts. It is possible that forms of two verbal stems, which had different functions originally, developed gradually a certain overlap or that they became supplementary to one another as e.g. the stem **ŠḤT.**[154] Therefore, it is necessary to investigate whether or not the pi. and hi. of this stem supplement one another instead of making forced attempts to find differences for these verbal stems.[155] In this respect we must mention Mettinger's critical remark. He says that Jenni failed to apply the linguistic concepts 'marked' and 'unmarked'.[156] Especially where he discusses the various *Aktionsarten* of the pi. and hi. this difference might applied profitably.

1.5.3.5 Another point of criticism is that Jenni does not provide an adequate definition of the concepts 'transitivity' and 'intransitivity'.[157] Yet much of his argumentation is based on the usage of these terms. Jenni calls verbs 'intransitive' which, in their basic meaning (e.g. the qal), do not allow for an accusative object.[158] He is not consistent in this respect for he classifies many stems as intransitive verbs which allow for an accusative object in the qal; e.g. **SBB**, **JRA**, **MLA**, **ALP**, and **LMD.** The latter two stems occur almost always with an accusative object. However, Jenni classifies them as intransitives for both stems have an 'a' instead of an 'o' in the imperf. of the qal and because of the fact that this corresponds to the treatment of similar verbs in other Semitic languages.[159] Yet he classifies certain verb stems, expressing movement or the making of a certain sound, as transitives. Thus, Jenni gives the concept 'transitivity' a broad application. He says about this: "Es wird sich im zweiten Hauptkapitel zeigen, dass die strenge Definition von transitiv und intransitiv, je nachdem ob das Verbum eine akkusativischen Konstruktion aufweist oder nicht, einer extensiven Auffassung des Begriffes transitiv Raum lassen muss, da wir dort u.a. auch gewisse Verben der Bewegung und der Lautaüsserung, die im Deutschen normalerweise intransitiv sind, unterzubringen haben (gehen = einen Gang tun, springen = einen Sprung tun, schreien = einen Schrei ausstossen usw.)".[160] Hence, the roots **HLK** (go), **Ṣ'Q** (cry), and **ṢḤQ** / **ŚḤQ** (laugh), are transitive according to Jenni even if they occur rarely if ever with an accusative object.[161] Jenni does not define the concepts *transitivum* and *intransitivum* according to strict formal and/or semantic principles, but according to the premise that the qal must be regarded as transitive when it is 'logically' conceivable.[162] 'Logical', in this case, is not a narrowly defined concept. Moreover, it is more related to German than to the Hebrew language. In my opinion this is not scientifically justified.[163] The person who wishes to use these concepts should first define them properly.

1.5.3.6 Claassen also discusses which percentage of cases should match the proposed theory for it to be accepted as proven.[164] Jenni is satisfied with 90 %. Claassen prefers a higher percentage or even a total agreement with the proposed theory.[165] In my opinion, Jenni is correct when he refers to this by remarking that one should always take into consideration exceptions or incidental developments in a living language.[166]

More critical remarks can be made with respect to Jenni's book, especially where certain details are involved.[167] However, most of these issues relate to the methodical presuppositions dealt with above In conclusion, we may affirm that Jenni does not ground his method sufficiently. This has affected the reliability of his premises. He attempted too much to prove his theory deductively instead of basing himself on the text and working inductively. He studied the pi. synchronically but did not pay attention to the development of the function of the pi. within the texts of the OT.

1.5.4 Lastly, we present a short discussion of other literature with respect to the pi. The earlier-mentioned book of Ryder *The D-stem in western Semitic*, a dissertation which was written more or less simultaneously with Jenni's study.[168] There are remarkable similarities between this work and Jenni's. Ryder's approach is also based on Akkadian grammar, especially on the studies of Poebel, Goetze, and von Soden mentioned above.[169] Moreover, Ryder considers the intensive function of the D-stem to be a debatable issue. He is not so sure of the presupposition that all other verbal stems have been derived from the basic stem. He suggests three presuppositions and examines whether they do apply indeed:

"(1) The D-stem has a single point of origin and a basic function.
(2) The D-stem is 'derived' from the B-stem, and must therefore have a meaning distinct from that of the B-stem.
(3) That meaning connotes 'intensity' or 'plurality' of the root concept, embodied in the B-stem".[170]

Ryder concludes that the first presupposition applies but that the latter two do not. With respect to the first he agrees with Jenni's conclusions.[171] He assumes that the D-stem has a factitive/denominative origin and presents the following definition for this: "The D-stem denotes and embodies the process by which one person (the subject) brings another person or some other entity (the object) into a state of being implicit in the nominal form (noun or adjective) to which the verbal form is related. The D-stem itself may not be derived from any other stem, nor dependent upon the existence of any other for its own existence; rather, like most elementary verbal forms, it may be derived directly from a nominal form, and constitutes one of the several alternate and coordinate stems of the Semitic verbal system. Finally, it is quadriliteral in structure; this structure is integral to its function and is to some extent an outcome thereof".[172] This definition agrees with Jenni's definition of the pi. Yet methodologically, Ryder's approach differs greatly from that of Jenni's. This relates e.g. to the area which Ryder covers: he wishes to present an overview of the function of the D-stem in the Western-Semitic language area, yet Jenni restricts himself to Biblical Hebrew. Ryder devotes much attention to the morphological aspects of the D-stem and to its origin and development.[173] In his discussion of the D-stem in the individual languages such as Biblical Hebrew and Koranic Arabic, however, he argues his thesis on the basis of the verb meanings as he finds them in dictionaries or translations.[174] At this point, he is methodically weaker than Jenni who studies forms in their context. However, this is inevitable due to the design of his work.

Two other publications with respect to the pi. are Boonstra's dissertation about newer theories on verb stems in the Semitic language area and an article by Weingreen on the pi.[175] Boonstra presents a general bibliography in which he discusses e.g. Goetze, Jenni, Ryder and Leemhuis. He mostly limits himself to presenting a summary of the content of these theories, but one can read between the lines where Boonstra's preference lies. He is quite impressed by Jenni's study on the pi. and contests criticism by others leveled against it.[176]

Weingreen made an important contribution to the discussion in his article "The pi'el in biblical Hebrew: a suggested new concept". In it, he gives a short survey of the various views on the function of the pi. He makes three comments on this:[177]

(1) The so-called 'intensive' function of the pi. may also be described as an 'extensive'.[178]
(2) There must be a single basic concept, which comprises everything, from which all the various functions of the pi. may be derived.
(3) No distinction is made between verbs of action and verbs of non-action within the various views on the function of the pi.

The author develops the last point more fully in his article. The Gesenius-Kautzsch-Cowley grammar divides the qal verb stems into transitives (with a pataḥ in the second syllable) and intransitives (with a ṣerē and ḥōlem in the second syllable). According to Weingreen, it would be better to replace these two categories by those of the action verbs ('active verbs', e.g. **HLK**, **NPL**, **JRD**) and those of the non-action verbs ('stative verbs', e.g. **ŠKḤ**, **ḤMD**, **ZKR**).[179] The view of the Gesenius-Kautzsch-Cowley grammar is correct in that the basic idea of the pi. is expressed as 'to occupy oneself eagerly with the action indicated by the stem'.[180] This description applies only for action verbs. For the non-action verbs the pi. expresses 'the active promotion of the state, condition or situation indicated by the Qal'. Weingreen quotes the following examples: "**QDŠ** 'promoted the state of holiness', i.e. 'hallowed, sanctified'; **KBD** 'promoted the honoured state', i.e. 'gave honour to'; **LMD** 'promoted the state of learning', i.e. 'taught'".[181] Weingreen develops the thesis further by means of the non-action verb **HJH**. In this, he often makes use of rabbinical commentaries.

Thus, Weingreen pleads the case for a return to the old view on the function of the pi. His division into verbs of action and non-action is not as new as its application with respect to the function determination of the pi.[182] In agreement with Jenni he separates the pi. and the causative hi. I wonder whether there is any distinction between Jenni's factitive and the 'active promotion of state' by Weingreen. The distinction between these two new categories is problematic. It is not always easy to determine to which category certain verb stems belong.[183] We will return to this in our discussion of the ni.

1.6 Evaluation of Jenni's views on the niph'al

1.6.1 Now, I will examine in what way Jenni's views on the ni. have influenced Hebrew grammatical studies after 1973.[184] Jenni's approach to the function of the ni. differs in three respects from that of his predecessors:[185]

1. Jenni is not interested in the original function of the ni. (reflexive or passive). He presents a description of the ni. within which fits a reflexive as well as a passive function.
2. The ni. may only be in oppositional relationship to the qal, but not to one of the other active verbal stems such as pi. or hi.
3. The ni. meaning may not be synonymous to that of the qal.

It is striking that the treatment of the ni. in grammars has been affected hardly or not at all by these views.[186] The reason for this may be that the article in which he launched his ideas on the ni. is relatively unknown. Moreover, he presented his ideas in a very succinct manner. The majority of grammars adheres to the traditional classification of Gesenius-Kautzsch or to one similar to it.[187] Some grammars possibly contain traces of Jenni's views, but it is hard to ascertain because they are fairly succinct in their treatment of the ni.[188]

1.6.2 In as far as my research has discovered, there are no critical reviews devoted to Jenni's views on the ni. My own criticism will be discussed in the next chapter in which I will especially deal with his proposition that the ni. may only occur in oppositional relationship to the qal and not to the pi. or hi. In my view, this proposition needs to be proved first.

1.6.3 Since 1973 relatively little literature of importance has appeared on the function of the ni. in Biblical Hebrew. J. Margain's article is worth mentioning.[189] He proves that the pi. and hi. may possess a so-called 'tolerative function'. He treats the tolerative as a weakening of the causative function of these verbal stems.[190] In this context, it is a remarkable challenge to Bergsträsser who argues that the tolerative function of the ni. was derived from the passive function.[191] However, it is more likely that the tolerative ni. should be related to the tolerative pi. or hi.[192] We will deal with this view in the next chapter; it diametrically opposes Jenni's thesis that the ni. may only occur in oppositional relationship to the qal.

Another important issue is Bean's dissertation on the hitpa'el in the OT.[193] The hitp. is a verbal stem which, like the ni., is translated reflexively and, to a lesser degree, passively. Bean's dissertation shows certain resemblances to Jenni's study of the pi.[194] In the preface he states: "No study has been made to determine if patterns of usage exist or to determine a rationale for the usage of the Hithpa'el form. No overall view of the stem has been offered by the scholars. . . ..[195]" In this respect the situation is comparable to that of the study of the pi. The traditional grammars list a great number of hitp. functions, some of which overlap with those of the ni.[196] The author makes use of what he refers to as a phenomenological methodology. He offers as a definition: "The stem is isolated as a focus of study, and the usage of the Hithpa'el is considered from several stances in order that new understandings of the verb-stem may develop. Each occurrence of the Hithpa'el is analyzed, considered, and categorized, that a view of the whole may evolve." The first step, then, is the presentation of a morphological description of the hitp.[197] Bean, in agreement with Jenni, excludes from his description forms which do not fit the norm, such as hitpo'el, hitpilpel, etc. Nor does he compare the hitp. with similar verbal stems in other Semitic languages or research its origins and development.[198] Contrary to Jenni, Bean does not discuss the relationship between the hitp. and other verbal stems, such as e.g. the ni. This is the weak spot of his dissertation. His study is limited to superficial observations because he isolated the hitp. from other verbal stems, and because he did not pay attention to a comparison with e.g. the ni. He investigates the distribution of the hitp.-forms in the individual books of the OT and he calculates the percentage of forms per book. He makes such calculations according to differences in date and, if ascertainable, according to differences in place of origin of the concerned text. He also discusses form critical, semantic, and syntactic aspects of hitp. usage.

Bean's conclusions are negative: "The Hithpa'el is not restricted to a specific sentence usage, and its usage is not tied exclusively to a time, place, type of literature, or life-setting".[199] These (negative) conclusions primarily resulted from the phenomenological methodology that Bean applies. Therefore, this method is less advanced than Jenni's study in which the pi. is discussed in its relationship to other verbal stems.

1.7 Evaluation of Jenni's views on verbal stems

1.7.1 We must answer the question negatively as to whether Jenni's analysis of the mutual relationship of verbal stems has been copied by other Hebrew grammars. One of the few grammars that present a classification of verbal stems, Lettinga's agrees to that of Joüon.[200] Irsigler's grammar presents a classification that differs from Jenni's on semantic grounds.[201] Other grammars do not include a classification. It is remarkable that Jenni's fails to provide a systematized account of the mutual relationship of verbal stems.[202]

1.7.2 The article by Goshen-Gottstein on verbal stems in classical Semitic languages is of special importance in recent literature on the subject.[203] He also wants to arrive at a new classification of verbal stems; different from that of Jenni's, his is based on morphological characteristics. He divides verbal stems into three groups:

a) verbal stems with a consonant-nucleus affix
b) verbal stems with a lengthened phoneme or a half-vowel
c) verbal stems with changes in the vowel model (internal passives).

He puts these three groups in a diagram. Due to its complexity this classification has not been included in recent grammars.

II Methodological presuppositions and principles for the study of the niph'al

2.1 Introduction

In the first chapter a tentative critical survey was presented of the various methods and points of origin for the study of verbal stems. The survey was based on Jenni's studies of the pi. and other verbal stems.

In this chapter I will defend my own method of approach for the study of the ni. I will refer back to critical remarks made with respect to the various approaches in the previous chapter. I will describe schematically how I have developed my method and discuss the critical questions I dealt with. Moreover, I will attempt to provide answers to these questions. At the end of the chapter I will elucidate the manner in which my research and its results have been incorporated in this dissertation.

2.2 Definition and delimitation of the notion niph'al

The question raises itself as to how the ni.-form should be defined and in what way it may be distinguished from other verbal stems. The question may be answered from a morphological, functional, or syntactic viewpoint. Morphologically, the ni. may be distinguished from other verbal stems by two important characteristics: by the prefix ***Na**, which is put before the stem in the perf., the partic. and (sometimes) the inf. abs. Moreover, the ni. may also be distinguished by the infix ***iN** which is placed before the stem in the imperf., the imper., the inf. cs., and (sometimes) the inf. abs.[204] In forms of the imperf. the nun of the infix ***iN** is assimilated into the first stem consonant which then is doubled and which is indicated by a dageš forte in Masoretic punctuation. The forms of the imper., inf. cs. and (sometimes) the inf. abs. are preceded by a prefix -hi., apart from the assimilation of the nun. The above-mentioned characteristics apply also for the weak verb in as far as no changes have occurred due to linguistic developments. It would lead beyond the scope of this study to deal with this here. The ni. is described adequately in various grammars.[205] All forms which have the above-mentioned characteristics may be regarded as ni.-forms, according to Masoretic punctuation as found in the B.H.S.

The first objective of my research was the collection of all forms which complied with the above-mentioned criteria. The basis for this was the concordance of Mandelkern. In a second phase, materials were checked against the various editions of the Köhler-Baumgartner lexicon the latest edition of which was consulted as much as possible. I also consulted other lexicons such as the Gesenius and the Brown-Driver-Briggs-Ges. The last-mentioned will only be referred to when they differ from HAL and Mandelkern.[206]

According to my calculations the Masoretic text of the OT contains 4143 niph'al forms, distributed over 428 verb roots.[207] However, various different Hebrew grammars and dictionaries differ in opinion in certain respects as to which verb forms may be counted as ni. and which may not. This became clear especially in the comparison of the Mandelkern concordance and the Köhler-Baumgartner Lexicon. Mandelkern treats certain forms as ni., where HAL does not and vice versa. It also appeared that they have skipped certain ni.-forms at times. HAL distinguishes various homonymic roots where Mandelkern does not. In my list as many ni.-forms as possible have been included, unless they evidently were not ni.-forms, and I have based myself on the Mandelkern concordance. Next I list the main differences between Mandelkern and HAL:

2.2.1 The following forms and roots of the ni. are included in our collection; they are mentioned by HAL, but not by Mandelkern:

AWH : Ps. 93:5; Song 1:10; Isa. 52:7.
These forms are treated as pa'lel forms of **NAH** by MANDELKERN, GESENIUS 1915 and some of the older grammars, e.g. KÖNIG 1881, 603. According to GESENIUS-KAUTZSCH 1909, &75x, BAUER-LEANDER 1922, 1965, 422t'' and HAL; these are ni. of **AWH.**

DḤH : 2 Sam. 14:14: **JiDDaḤ.**
Thus GESENIUS 1915 and HAL. MANDELKERN and BROWN-DRIVER-BRIGGS-GES. treat this form as the ni. of **NDḤ.**

ZLL : Judg. 5:5: **NāZĕLu**
According to MANDELKERN it is a qal of **NZL**; according to GESENIUS-KAUTZSCH 1909, &67dd (under Aramaic influence); BAUER-LEANDER 1922, 1965, 431t and KBL regard it as a ni. (cf. the other forms of **ZLL**: Isa. 63:19; 64:2).

NDḤ : Isa. 11:12; 56:8; Ps. 147:2.
This is how GESENIUS 1915 and HAL regard the form; MANDELKERN however, includes it under the ni. of **DḤH.**

NṢH : According to GESENIUS and HAL; yet MANDELKERN thinks these are ni. forms of **JṢT/ṢWT.**

PWṢ : Isa. 11:12 :**NĕPōṢōT.**
According to MANDELKERN a pass. partic. qal of **NPS.**

QBR : 1 Kin. 11:43.
Supplement to MANDELKERN

QRA I: Jer. 4:20.
MANDELKERN mistakenly classifies this form under the root **QRA** II.

ŚTR : 1 Sam. 5:9.
MANDELKERN lists this text under the root **STR.**

2.2.2 Roots and forms of the ni. which are mentioned by Mandelkern but which are not included in HAL or in our collection:

DḤH : Isa. 11:12; 56:8; Ps. 147:2
See 2.2.1 :**NDḤ.**

DLL : Judg. 6:6; Isa. 17:4
GESENIUS 1915 and HAL categorize these as qals of **DLL.**

DMM : Jer. 8:14 :**NiDDěMā.**
According to GESENIUS 1915 and HAL it is a qal of **DMM.**

JṢT/ṢWT: Jer. 2:15; 9:11; 46:19.
See 2.2.1 :**NṢH.**

MLL : Ps. 37:2; Job 14:2; 18:6; 24:24.
GESENIUS 1915 and HAL regard these forms as qals.

NDḤ : 2 Sam. 14:14.
See 2.2.1 :**DḤH.**

NZL : Jdg. 5:5.
See 2.2.1. :**ZLL.**

RKK : Deut. 20:3; Isa. 7:4; Jer. 51:46.
Hal regards these forms as qals.

STR : 1 Sam. 5:9.
See 2.2.1 **ŚTR.**

QRAII: Jer. 4:20.
See 2.2.1 **QRA**I.

2.2.3 Roots and forms of the ni. which are not mentioned by Mandelkern and Hal but which are listed in our collection.

ḤNN : Jer. 22:23 :**NěḤaNT**
GESENIUS 1915 and HAL 1967 want to derive this form from the root **ANH** and read **NeAeḤaNT.** In my opinion this is unnecessary. See the KÖNIG 1922 and KÖNIG 1881 lexicons, &68:14c, which translate *zu bemitleiden, mitleidswürdig sein.* He refers to Phoenician where, in the inscription of 'Esmun'azar of Sidon (KAI 14:12) a ni.-form of this root occurs. SEGERT, COOKE, GIBSON and FRIEDRICH-RÖLLIG agree to this. In Misjnaic Hebrew the ni. of **ḤNN** is also attested (see JASTROW, 484) This verse might be translated as follows: "How shalt thou be pitied if...".

ṬMH : Lev. 11:43; Job 18:3. HAL includes these under the root **ṬMA.** Perhaps these are variants of **ṬMA**, yet they are listed as different roots in my collection.

MWL : Gen. 17:11.
GESENIUS 1915 and HAL list it under the root **MLL.**

NSK : Prov. 8:23.
HAL takes this form as a ni. of **SKK** 'weave', this is less likely in view of the context.

PLH : Ps. 139:14.
GESENIUS 1915 and HAL list this form at the root **PLA.** Although it is a possible variant of **PLA**, I list it as a separate root.

RMM : Num. 17:10; Ezek. 10:15, 17, 19.
According to HAL it is a qal; according to GESENIUS-KAUTZSCH 1909, &67t it is a ni.

RṢH : Lev. 22:23.
Supplement to HAL.

ŠBR : Ps. 37:17.
Supplement to HAL.

2.2.4 Debatable Issues. There are certain forms which defy adequate classification. The problem is compounded because Masoretic punctuation and context allow for more than one interpretation. For the sake of completeness I list them below. Apart from the last form, all are included in my collection.

AWR : 2 Sam. 2:32 :**WaJJeAōR.**
GESENIUS-KAUTZSCH 1909, &72r, GESENIUS 1915 and HAL describe the form as qal; MANDELKERN and BROWN-DRIVER-BRIGGS-GESENIUS 1951 as a ni.

NKP : Job 19:26.
The form may be seen as a ni. or a pi. Most likely, it is a ni. cf. JENNI 1968, 237.

ŚB' : Job 31:31 :**NiŚBa'.**
qal imperf. 1st pl.: MANDELKERN, GORDIS 1978 or ni. partic.: GESENIUS 1915, HAL.

PRŞ : 1 Chron. 13:2 :**NiPRĕŞā.**
qal imperf. 1st pl. :GESENIUS 1915, HAL or ni. perf. 3rd pl. fem. :MANDELKERN.

ŠWH : Prov. 27:5 :**NiŠtāWā.**
hitpa'el according to MANDELKERN or ni. According to GESENIUS- KAUTZSCH 1909, &75x, GESENIUS 1915 and HAL: a ni. The first possibility seems most probable to me. Therefore, I did not include this form in my collection.

2.2.5 Hybrid forms. We also include the so-called hybrid forms:

BZH : 1 Sam. 15:9 :**NiMBĕZā.**
GESENIUS-KAUTZSCH 1909, &75y describe it as a hybrid form of pt. fem. of the ni. (**NiBZā**) and ho. (**MūBZā**).

GAL : Isa. 59:3; Lam. 4:14
See note 66.

ŠAR : Ezek. 9:8 : **WĕNēAŠaAaR**
According to GESENIUS-KAUTZSCH 1909, &51k it is a hybrid form of the pt. ni. (**WeNiŠAaR**) and impf. cs. ni. (**WeAeŠŠaAeR**).

NDP : Ps. 68:3: **KēHiNDōP**
According to GESENIUS-KAUTZSCH 1909, &51k it is a hybrid form of inf. ni. (**HiNNāDēP**) and inf. qal (**NēDōP**).

2.3 Delimitation of material

As was discussed above, in most cases identification of ni.-forms in the vocalized text of the Masoretes is fairly straightforward. In this context the two following questions must be answered. First, we must decide whether we base ourselves on the unvocalized text. Secondly, we must decide to what extent we should incorporate extra-biblical material into our research.

2.3.1 The identification of ni.-forms in the unvocalized text is problematic. The prefix ***Na-** allows clear distinction of the forms of the perf., partic. and the inf. cs. of the strong verb as opposed to forms of other verbal stems. Although the nun-prefix may serve to indicate a 1st pers. plur. imperf. qal (**NQTL: NiQṬoL**), in practice the context will serve to ascertain the form in question. Identification is not as clear cut for the forms of the imperf of the strong verb and for the verb forms of most weak verbs. In the unvocalized text the imperf. of the ni. cannot be distinguished from the forms of the imperf. of the qal, pi., pu. or ho. (**JQṬL**). Neither may the forms of the imper. sg. 2nd masc. and the inf. abs. and cs. be distinguished from those of the hi. When the hi.-forms are written defectively, the perf. 3rd sing. and plural of the hi. cannot be distinguished from the ni.-forms.

For the irregular verb, it is even more complicated. For the pe nun verbs there is no difference to be observed between the qal and ni. of the pt. though there is a difference between the forms of the imperf. Yet confusion may arise over determination of the forms of the ni. imperf. and pi. imperf (cf. the above-mentioned texts of **NQP**, Isa. 10:34 and Job 19:26). Moreover, it should be taken into consideration that these forms may be derived from another root. E.g. the root **NQM** occurs in Lev. 19:18 in the form **TiQQŌM** meaning "thou shalt not be vindictive". On the basis of the unvocalized text one might also read **TāQŪM** "thou shalt (not) act inimically", cf. Jdg. 9:18; 2Sam. 18:32; Gen. 4:8, etc). The case is even more complex for the double 'ayin verbs. Here, even in vocalized text, determination of ni.-forms is fairly complicated.[208] Some forms may be derived from other roots. With respect to other irregular verbs one is faced with similar problems. For the above-mentioned reasons I, therefore, will stick to the Masoretic punctuation.

2.3.2 For my study of the ni. I have opted to draw from epigraphic material. However, in as far as could be ascertained, there are only a small number of forms in these texts. The following six forms were discovered:[209]

Samaria ostracon no. c1101	(GIBSON, 14),	1.3:	**JMNH** (?)[210]
Siloam-inscription	(GIBSON, 22),	1.2:	**LHN[QB]** inf.
Siloam-inscription	(KAI, 189),	1.3:	**[NŠM]'** perf.(?)
Yavneh Yam	(GIBSON, 28),	1.11:	**NQTJ** perf.
Lachish III	(GIBSON, 38),	1.21:	**HŠMR** imper
Lachish IX	(GIBSON, 47),	1.3:	**NŠLḤ** perf.(?)

It is impossible to ascertain whether the forms in Lachish IX and the Siloam-inscription are ni., but, it is quite likely that the form in the Samaria-ostracon is a ni.

Epigraphic material after the 2nd Century BC, and later texts, such as that of Qumran and Mishnah, will not be dealt with. The debate continues on the relationship between these texts and classical Hebrew. Some scholars do not count them among classical Hebrew.[211] Moreover, we will not discuss the forms of the N-stem which occur in the Hebrew-related languages from the North-Western Semitic language area.

2.4 Classification of material

In the previous chapter one of the main critical arguments against Jenni's study of the pi. was that he did not take into consideration diachronic aspects but that he treated his material as a whole. Bean, however, discusses diachronic aspects in his dissertation on the hitp. Moreover, he classifies his material according to different aspects, such as the canonical and the geographical, though only from a numerical point of view. We observed that Bean analyses meticulously how many hitp.-forms occur in each book. He also calculates the ratio of the number of hitp.-forms to the number of lines per book. The method provides quite few results for the hitp.[212] In my opinion such calculations are inconsequential if one does not study the ratio of other verbal stems (i.e. those which agree most with the hitp. in function, such as the ni.). Only then it is possible to draw relevant conclusions from such statistical evidence.

Bean's classification according to geographical aspects fails to result in anything important.[213] There is much difference of opinion as to how the classification of material ought to be conducted. Therefore, I do not consider it useful to classify the material according to Bean's principles. A classification on the basis of diachronic aspects is also problematic. This approach has not met with unanimous approval either.[214]

Therefore, we have decided to classify the textual material into three groups in agreement with Hoftijzer: prose, poetry, and prophecy.[215] Such a classification is mainly based on practical considerations. I have attempted to incorporate all data into one diagram; for this purpose a threefold division is more appropriate than a classification with a great numer of groups. It ought not to be more than a rough classification. It is especially difficult to make a clear distinction between poetry and prophecy in each instance. In many cases prophetic texts are pure poetry whereas the other texts should be ranged somewhere in between prose and poetry. The same reservation applies for what I refer to as prose in Ezekiel, Jeremiah, Daniel, or Ecclesiasticus. Here, it is not always easy to make the distinction between prose and poetry. Thus, this classification should not be regarded as completely fixed or prescriptive. It is a rough classification which should be applied with reserve: its form is determined mainly by practical considerations. The following texts are considered to be prose: Gen. (except 49:1b-27), Ex. (except 15:1b-21), Num. (except 23:7b-10, 18b-24; 24:3b-9, 15b-24), Deut. (except 32; 33:2b-29), Josh., Judges (except 5:2-31a), 1 Sam. (except 2:1b-10), 2Sam. (except 1:19-27; 3:33b-34; 22:2-23:7), 1Kin., 2Kin. (except 19: 21b-28), Isa. 36-39 (except 38:9-20), Jer. 19:1-20:6; 26-45; 52, Ezek. (except 17:1-9, 25- 36; 19; 28:11-19; 32:2-15), Jonah (except 2:3-10), Job 1; 2; 42:7-17; Ruth, Eccl., Esther, Daniel, Ezra, Neh., 1Chron. (except 16:8-36; 29:10-19) and 2Chron. The following texts are classified as poetry; in the Pentateuch: Jacob's words of blessing (Gen. 49: 1b-27), the song at the Sea of Reeds (Ex. 15:1b-21), the song of Israel (Num. 21:17b-18), the oracles of Balaam (Num. 23:7b-10, 18b-24; 24:3b-9, 15b-24), the song of Moses (Deut. 32) and the Mosaic blessing (Deut. 33:2b-29). Moreover, Deborah's song (Judg. 5:2-31a), various songs of David (2 Sam. 1:19-27; 3: 33b-34; 22:2-23:7), Hannah's song (1Sam. 2:1b-10), Ps., Job (except the introduction and the epilogue: 1; 2; 42:7-17), Pro., Song, Lam. and 1Chron. 16: 8-36 (Psalm of David). The following texts are classified as prophecy: Isa. (except 36-39, apart from 38:9-20); Jer. (except 19: 1-20: 6; 26-45; 52), Ezek. 19; 27:1-9, 25-36; 28:12-19; 32:2-15, Hos., Joel, Amos, Ob., Jon. 2:3-10, Mic., Nah., Hab., Zeph., Hag., Zech. and Mal.

Hoftijzer, in his book *A Search for Method*, offers a further classification of prose texts. He classifies Pentateuch material according to sources (J, P and D), and he deals with the lists separately. The books of Judges and Kings are dealt with as a whole since a further subdivision would result in too many problems. The other prose texts are discussed book by book.

My own classification differs from Hoftijzer's in the following respects, due to mostly practical reasons. The purpose of this study is the description and study of the ni. in relation to the other 'passive' verbal stems (pass. qal, pu., ho. and hitp.). It is not useful to adhere to a classification in very small units since the number of forms under discussion is limited. Therefore, I will treat the Hexateuch, and Judges up to and including Kings, as a whole. Moreover, I will deal with the prose texts as individual units in the prophetic books and the post-exilic writings (Esther, Dan., Ezra and Neh., etc). If at all possible, the material will be classified in more detail. Tentatively, the poetic material is classified as follows: a) poetic texts of the Pentateuch, Deborah's song and Hannah's song; b) the Psalms and the various songs of David; c) the other texts. Wherever it is possible I will classify the texts in more detail. The prophetic material is discussed as a whole and if possible it is differentiated by book.

2.5 The function of the niph'al

In chapter 1.3 we found that classical grammars, in their discussion of the niph'al verbal stem, mention a number of meanings for it which may differ considerably. The Gesenius-Kautzsch grammar mentions the reflexive of the qal as its first meaning. Apart from that--according to Gesenius Kautzsch--the ni. may have a reciprocal, a middle (such as the hitp.) and a passive meaning (both of the qal as well as of the pi. and hi). The ni. may agree with the qal in the cases where the qal has intransitive meaning.[216]

Moreover, the grammar of Joüon mentions a number of meanings of the ni. which agree with those supplied by Gesenius-Kautzsch. The difference is that Joüon makes separate mention of the tolerative (where the Gesenius-Kautzsch grammar assumes that it is a part of the reflexive). Additionally, Joüon attests that the ni. may serve as a reflexive of the pi. and the hi.[217]

The most extensive enumerations are found in the article of M. Lambert "L'emploi du niph'al en hébreu" and in the grammar of Bergsträsser which is fairly similar to Lambert's discussion of the ni.[218] Thus, Lambert presents extensive lists in his article of the forms of which the ni. serves as the reflexive and passive of the qal, pi., and hi. respectively. He also lists ni.-forms that are the reflexive of a factitive, which does not occur in the OT, comparable to the tolerative. Moreover, he presents a list of ni.-forms whose meaning is synonymous to that of the qal, pi. or hi. Finally, Lambert sums up the ni.-forms that are used in a certain 'tense' (perf. or imperf), with the understanding that the qal occurs only in the other 'tense' (imperf. or perf.), and he lists the ni.-forms of which no forms of other verbal stems occur. Jenni, on the other hand, wishes to adopt a single function for the ni. He describes the function in such a way that it accommodates all the above-mentioned meanings.[219] Below I will discuss two issues in detail:

1) May we indeed formulate one function for the ni. within which all the above-mentioned meanings fit?

2) Is Jenni's presupposition correct that the ni. occurs in a passive-reflexive relationship only with respect to the qal but not with respect to the pi.?

2.5.1 I want to discuss these two questions by means of examples of ni. usage in the book of Ruth. I want to state first and foremost that the usage of the ni. in Ruth need not be normative for that in the rest of the OT. Here it is merely used as illustrative material. Since the book of Ruth is restricted in content, since it contains only a few ni.-forms, and since it consists of homogenous material it is suitable for our research. In the book Ruth we find 12 ni.-forms of 9 roots. I list them together with their NIV translations for easy understanding:

1: 3 **WaTTiŚŚāAēR** (**ŚAR**) - she was left
1: 5 **WaTTiŚŚaAēR** (**ŚAR**) - she was left
1:13 **Te'āGēNā** (**'GN**) - would you wait
1:17 **eQQāBēR** (**QBR**) - I will be buried
1:19 **WaTTĕHōM** (**HWM**) - and (the whole town) was stirred
2: 5 **HaNNīṢṢaB** (**NṢB**) - the foreman--(lit.) who was put in charge of
2: 6 **HaNNīṢṢaB** (**NṢB**) - ibid.
3: 3 **AaL-TiWWāDé'i** (**JD'**) - do not let (him) know you are there
3: 8 **WaJJiLLāPēT** (**LPT**) - and he turned
3:14 **AaL-JiWWāDā** (**JD'**) - don't let it be known
4:10 **JiKKāRēT** (**KRT**) - (so that his name) will (not) disappear
4:14 **WaJJiQQāRéA** (**QRA**) - may he become famous

2.5.1.1 The first notion that strikes us is that most forms (9 out of 12) are translated as a passive. In the above-mentioned grammars some of these ni.-stems are also classified as passive (Gesenius-Kautzsch: **QBR**, pass. of qal; Lambert: **JD'** and **QRA**, pass. qal; **KRT**, pass. of hi.[220] Lambert treats the ni. of **ŚAR** as a hi.-passive **HiŚAiR** (leave), as in the NIV 'was left', yet the Dutch Bible Society translates it as an active 'stay behind'. This view fits the general notion of the ni. in the OT. My calculation has brought to light that more than 270 roots may be translated passively of the total of 428 roots containing ni.-forms. The notion 'passivity' in this instance need not be indicated grammatically. In relation to this it is important to ascertain which definition one should give to the notion 'passive verb form'. I define it as follows: a passive verb form is a verb form of which the grammatical subject undergoes a certain action, (or of which the grammatical subject is the object of that action), expressed by the verb form. The agent, i.e. the person performing the action, or from whom the action proceeds, need not be mentioned. In the context of the so-called 'passive' ni.-forms in Ruth the agent is nowhere mentioned explicitly. This agrees with the general view of the ni. Other examples of pass. ni.-forms are: **BRA** (Gen. 2:4, 5:2; Isa. 48: 7, etc.); (Neh. 7: 1; 1 Kin. 3:2, 6:7 (3x)); **BḤN** (Gen. 42:15, 16); **GNB** (Ex. 22:11, etc.).

2.5.1.2 The second feature that strikes us is that not a single ni.-form in Ruth is translated reflexively. The form **WaJJiLLāPēT** (Ruth 3:8) may be regarded as a reflexive in agreement with the manner in which Gesenius' dictionary translates it as: *sich vorbeugen od. umdrehen* (cf. the other ni.-form in Job 6:18).[221] It is difficult to assess the character of the relationship between the qal and the ni. since the qal occurs only once (Judg. 16:29). My definition of a reflexive verb form is the following: a verb form of which the grammatical subject undergoes a certain action, (or, of which the grammatical subject is the object of the action), expressed by the verb and where the grammatical subject agrees with the agent, i.e. the person who performs or who causes the action. Whereas reflexivity of the verb form in Western languages is indicated by an addition, [Du.: *zich*, (one)self, transl.], such an addition is lacking in Hebrew.[222] Therefore, one can only decide whether a form has passive or reflexive meaning on the basis of the interpretation of meaning and context of the respective form. In this instance exegetical presuppositions may come into play as well. The number of ni.-stems that is to be translated reflexively is much smaller than the number of ni.-stems that requires a passive translation; according to my calculation it concerns more than seventy roots. We cite the following examples of reflexive usage, according to the definition of the ni. given above: **ṬMA** (Lev. 18: 24); **GAL** (Lev. 25:49); **ṬMN** (Isa. 2:10).

2.5.1.3 One may ask to what extent Biblical Hebrew allows for the distinction reflexive/passive for the ni., such as may be observed in Western languages. Does the distinction apply for Hebrew? For ni. reflexive and passive cannot be distinguished formally, as in e.g. Dutch where a difference is observed between *zich* and *worden* ['(one-) self' and 'become', transl]. The ni.-form does not indicate the distinction reflexive-passive grammatically. We may adduce the following:

a) It is sometimes difficult to determine whether one should translate a ni. reflexively, passively, or reciprocally; to a major extent it depends on semantic and theological interpretation e.g.:

AHB (2 Sam 1:23: pass., refl. or reciprocal?).
PTḤ (Gen. 7:11: pass. or refl. depending on whether God opens doors or whether they open by themselves?)
BRK (Gen. 12:3; 18:8; 28:29: pass., refl. or reciprocal depending on whether this refers to 'shall be blessed', or

to 'shall wish blessing to one another'.

Thus, the form **TeA3GeNā** in Ruth 1:13 might be translated reflexively instead of passively: 'should you therefore refrain yourself'. Thus, the distinction reflexive/passive, such as Lambert suggests in his lists, is not always obvious. At times, it seems as if his decisions were based more on French than on Hebrew, e.g.:

ASB: *s'affliger* - be/become sad (Gen. 45:5)
SPK: *s'épancher* - be poured out (1 Kin. 13:3, 5)
BNH: *s'édifier* - be built (Gen. 16:2; 30:3)

If one assumes that Biblical Hebrew lacked the distinction passive/reflexive it would account for the fact that various nuances may occur in one verb root. A few examples may illustrate this:

ASP: Num. 11:22 (passive) vs. Num. 11:30 (reflexive).
GAL: Lev. 25:54 (passive) vs. Lev. 25:49 (reflexive).

b) The question raises itself in what way the so-called 'tolerative' differs from a 'passive'. The Gesenius-Kautzsch grammar defines the tolerative as follows: "Handlungen die jemand an sich geschehen, auf sich wirken lässt". As an example it mentions among others the root **DRŠ**, ni. *sich erfragen lassen*, Isa. 65:1; Ezek. 14: 3. Lambert calls this a factitive and mentions also as examples the root **MWL** 'to allow oneself to be circumcised', Gen. 17:10; **ŠPṬ** 'to allow oneself to be judged', Josh. 8:15 and **NG'** 'to allow oneself to be beaten', 1 Sam. 12:7; Isa. 43:26 etc. The tolerative fits almost completely in the definition of the passive which we determined above: In this case the grammatical subject undergoes passively a certain action or it may be the object of that action. Just as in the case of the passive the agent is not mentioned explicitly. The tolerative ni.-forms, therefore, may be translated passively just as well, e.g.:

MWL: Gen. 17:10 'be circumcized'
NG': Josh. 8:15 'be defeated'
DRŠ: Isa. 65:1 'be consultable'

Logically it is possible to make a distinction between a passive and a tolerative: the tolerative is a passive with an extra specification, namely to condone a certain action passively. Formally, however, Hebrew cannot express this distinction. The grammars are not always consistent in determining the tolerative ni.-forms. E.g. forms of the root **QBR** ('allow oneself to be buried') etc. could be regarded as toleratives on the basis of their definition.

We saw that Jenni offered the following definition of the ni.[223]: The ni. expresses the occurring of an event, or the occurring of an action on the subject independent of the fact whether the subject participates voluntarily or involuntarily, to a greater or lesser extent, or whether it cooperates in the event. This definition suffices for at least 75 % of the number of ni.-stems. We may doubt, together with Jenni, to what extent a classification such as reflexive versus reciprocal or passive versus tolerative may be established on other than logical grounds. This logical-functional classification does not have to correspond to form features and does not do that in Hebrew. For a number of roots the definition does not apply. The classical example of this is **NLḤM** 'fight', of which certain occurring qal forms also have the meaning of 'to fight'.

2.5.2 Jenni assumes that the ni. occurs only in an oppositional relationship to the qal but not to the pi. or hi.[224] The classical grammars, however, assume that there is a relationship between ni. and pi. or hi. Since Jenni fails to present arguments for his assumption I have not accepted it as a given fact, but I have investigated to what extent a relationship to the other verbal stems may be possible.

I want to illustrate this by means of certain examples from the book of Ruth. According to Lambert the ni. of the root **KRT** (Ruth 4:10) should be regarded as a passive of the hi. This root does occur in the qal 132 times, with the meanings 'cut off' (e.g. of the edge of a robe 1Sam. 24:5, 6 etc.), 'cut down' (e.g. of a forest or of trees, Jer. 46:23 etc., or of the Asheras, Ex. 34:13 etc.), and its meaning in the expression **KRT BĕRĪT** (to make a covenant, Gen. 21:27 etc.). The hi. which occurs 78 times has the meaning of 'to extirpate', 'to destroy' (mainly with people as its object, 1Kin. 18:4, or a name, Josh. 7:9). This meaning does not occur in the qal; the form is only used to express the cutting off of certain parts of the body (foreskin, Ex. 4:25 etc. or head, 1Sam. 17:51 etc.). In Ruth 4:10, the ni.-form **JiKKāRēT**, (to be destroyed, said of the name of the deceased), can be more appropriately related to the hi. (cf. Josh. 7:9) than to the qal. If we accept this, the question raises itself how the ni. relates to the ho. and what relationship there is between the ni. and the ho. (once in Joel 1:9). What is the relationship between the ni. and pu. (twice, the pi. does not occur)? How do the passive qal partic. forms fit in the whole system?

Lambert also regards the ni.-forms of the root **ŚAR** (Ruth 1:3, 5) as passives of the hi. The hi. (36 times) has the meaning 'leave' (Ex. 10:12 etc.). According to him the ni. should be translated as 'be left over, i.e. remain'. The qal occurs only once, as 'leave' in 1Sam. 16:11. If we accept that Lambert is correct in this case, we are left with the issue of what the difference is between this qal-form and the ni. (e.g. Gen. 42:38).

Finally, we would like to discuss the form **AaL-TiWWāDé'i** in Ruth 3:3, which is translated by the NIV as 'do not let him know you are there'. According to Lambert this form is a reflexive of the hi., contrary to other ni.-forms of **JD'** which may be regarded as passives of the qal, and he translates it as *se faire connaître*. This form might be translated as 'do not let yourself be known, do not make yourself known'. This is possible and would be adequate considering the context. (Boaz has seen Ruth, but she has not introduced herself to him). There are more examples in the OT of an agent introduced by **Lĕ** e.g. Ruth 2:20; Gen. 25:21. However, this ni. may also be regarded as a passive of the qal. Lambert mentions other examples of a reflexive of the hi.: Ex. 6:3; Isa. 19:21; 56:16; Ps. 9:17, etc. These examples, to my mind, are less convincing than those of the roots **KRT** and **ŚAR.** The fact that it is hard to provide an accurate Dutch translation ('you will not be known by the man') may not be a reason for rejecting the possibility.

Also in this case it is helpful to obtain a clear understanding of the relationship between the ni. and other 'passive' verbal stems. The root **JD'** is accounted for in all seven verbal stems. Therefore it provides an example for further research into the mutual relationships between the pass. qal, ni., pu., ho. and hitpa'el. Hence, I will not base my research on Jenni's presupposition that the ni. can only occur in oppositional relationship to the qal, but I will adopt the notion that the ni. may also occur in an oppositional relationship to other 'active' verbal stems.

2.6 Conclusions

The methodological presuppositions on which I based my study of the ni. are different from those of Jenni's and other authors in the following respects:

a) This research is concerned not only with the ni.-forms that are declined according to the normal paradigm, but anomalous forms are taken into consideration as well. Only those instances have been ignored in which a form occurs which is evidently not a ni. Moreover, this study also makes use of epigraphical material, even though it is scarce.

b) Textual material is divided into three genres: prose, poetry, and prophecy; wherever it is possible and justifiable a further sub-categorization is applied.

c) This research assumes that, possibly, the ni. occurs not only in a semantic relationship to the qal but also to one of the other active verbal stems.

2.7 Focus and purpose of research

For above-mentioned reasons studying the ni. in isolation is insufficient, i.e. without considering its relationship to other verbal stems. Such a method, as applied by Bean for the study of the hitp., will not yield satisfactory results. In my opinion the ni. should preferably be studied in comparison with other verbal stems. Traditional grammars always describe the ni. in relationship to the qal, or to the pi. and the hi. In my research, I want to start on different premises and study the usage of the ni. in the OT in relation to the other passive-reflexive verbal stems, passive qal-partic., pu., ho. and hitp. If the ni. serves according to general opinion as passive/reflexive of the qal, then what is its relationship to the pass. qal, in as far as these forms are accounted for? Are the pass. qal-partic. and the ni. supplementary to one another, or are there clear differences to be observed? These questions will be dealt with in relation to the ni.-forms which are regarded as a passive/reflexive of the pi. and which occur next to pu.-forms. For these stems, what is the relationship between, if at all, the passive qal-partic. and the ni., and between the ni. and hitp., the reflexive of the pi.? In the same way we shall discuss the relationship between the ni. and the ho. We will do this in particular for those stems of which the ni. is regarded as a passive/reflexive of the hi. Finally, we will investigate what the relationship is between ni. and pass. qal-partic. and between ni. and hitp.

Having presented satisfactory clarification of the mutual

relationship of the passive-reflexive verbal stems, we will give a scientifically justified answer to questions about the relationship between the ni. and the 'active' verbal stems.

A collection of verb forms was made and categorized in order to answer the above-mentioned questions adequately; we collected all stems of which ni. forms occur, and also all other forms of the verbal stems, in as far as they exist. The result is presented in the tables on following pages.

III The niph'al in Biblical Hebrew: A survey of all roots of which niph'al forms occur in Biblical Hebrew

3.1 Introduction to the tables

In the first column under the heading ROOT all roots are listed alphabetically of which ni.-forms are found in Biblical Hebrew. There are 428 roots in total.

The second column is reserved for the MEANING, i.e. the semantic value of the root that is mentioned in the first column, and, if necessary, all distinct meanings derived from it. Since space is restricted not all semantic nuances could be included. The purpose of this column is to provide the user of these tables with a first insight in the semantic value of the ni.-stem. It is not our intention to provide exhaustive information of all possible semantic nuances.

Below that, in the same column textual references are listed for the places where the ni.-forms of the root occur. Note that the place and order of the texts corresponds to the columns 'G' and "NIPH'AL". For an explanation of these columns see below. E.g. at number 11 the root **ALM**; it occurs eight times in the OT, four times in prose (corresponding to row A), three times in poetry (corresponding to row B), and one time in prophecy (corresponding to row C). The order of texts mentioned under the heading 'MEANING' corresponds to the numbers included in the column "NIPH'AL". E.g. in the rows of **ALM**, 1. 2, the first three texts are perfects and the fourth and last text are imperfects. Row B is similar: Ps. 39:3 and 10 are perfects and Ps. 31:19 is an imperfect. They have been separated by double brackets. The advantage of this notation of texts is that one can see at a glance which texts contain pt., perf. imperf. or other forms.

Since the number of ni.-forms is too numerous to be included in the table 'MEANING', we refer to the list of ni.-forms in 3.3 (see e.g. number 13: **AMN** II).

At times, the second column lists semantic values different from the main value of the ni. We refer to the text by means of an asterisk: cf. number 28 **BWK**. The form in Ez. 14:3 has the meaning 'roam', see also under number 46 **GAL** or number 51 **GZR**. An asterisk after the root number refers to the notes in paragraph 3.4 (cf. number 4: **AWH**).

In the third column the 'DIVISION' (abbreviated as DIV) is given. The roots have been divided into three groups: I, II, and

III. Group I is comprised of the ni.-stems occurring in oppositional semantic relationship (passive, reflexive and/ or reciprocal) toward the qal (indicated as Iq) or toward the pi. (indicated as Ip) or toward the hi. (indicated as Ih). In this column more possibilities may be mentioned. When the meaning of the ni. is synonymous to, or where it appears to be synonymous to, that of the qal, pi., or hi., it is indicated by means of =, cf. number 85 **ZWR.** In group II, roots are classified of which no semantic relationship could be detected between the forms of the ni. on the one hand and those of the qal, pi. or hi. on the other. Group III contains the roots of which ni.-forms occur but of which no forms of qal, pi. or hi. exist. For these roots it is impossible to state the relationship between the ni. and the active verbal stems.

The fourth column 'GENRE' (abbreviated as G) contains the abbreviation 'TOT' (of 'TOTAL') and the letters A, B and C which correspond to the numbers that are mentioned in the adjoining columns. As stated before, A stands for prose, B for poetry, and C for prophecy.

In the fifth column under the heading "NIPH'AL" a number of ni.-forms are summed up (under TOT). Moreover they are divided according to two criteria; they are divided according to GENRE: A, B, or C, and according to FORM: participle (PT), perfect (PF), imperfect (IMPF), inf. cs and inf.abs (INF) and imperative (IMPV). Similarly, the following columns are divided up: passive qal participle (PQ), PU'AL, HOPH'AL and HITPA'EL. In these columns the inf. and impv. have been included under the heading O (other forms).

The last column is reserved for the number of qal, pi. and hi.forms of other verbal stems which are classified according to GENRE and not according to FORM. If there are many forms of the qal, pi. or hi. (about 100 or more) this has been indicated by 'M' for 'many' since it does not seem useful to supply the accurate figures in such cases.

3.2 Tables

The tables containing the roots are found on pages 41-78.

3.3 List of Niph'al forms

9 **AKL** A PT: Lev. 11:47 PF: Ex. 22:5 IMPF: Gen. 6:21/ Ex. 12:16, 46/ 13:3, 7/ 21:28/ 29:34/ Lev. 6:9, 16, 19, 23/ 7:6, 15, 16(2x), 18, 19/ 11:13, 34, 41, 47/ 17:13/ 19:6, 7, 23/ 22:30/ Num. 28:17/ 12:12/ Deut. 12:22/ 14:19/ Jer. 29:17/ 30:16/ Ez. 23:25/ 45:21 INF: Lev. 7:18/ 19:7

B IMPF: Job 6:6

C IMPF: Jer. 24:2, 3, 8/ Zeph. 1:18/ 3:8/ Zech. 9:4.

(continued on p. 79)

	ROOT	MEANING	DIV	G	NIPH'AL TOT	PT	PF	IMPF	INF	IMPV	PQ	PU'AL TOT	PT	PF	IMPF	O	HOPH'AL TOT	PT	PF	IMPF	O	HITPA'EL TOT	PT	PF	IMPF	O	QAL	PI	HI	O	G
1	ABQ	wrestle with	III	TOT	2	-	-	1	1	-	-	-	-	-	-	-	-	-	-	-	-	-	-	-	-	-	-	-	-	-	TOT
		Gen.32:25/32:26		A	2	-	-	1	1	-	-	-	-	-	-	-	-	-	-	-	-	-	-	-	-	-	-	-	-	-	A
2	ADR	glorious	II	TOT	2	2	-	-	-	-	-	-	-	-	-	-	-	-	-	-	-	-	-	-	-	-	-	-	1	-	TOT
		Ex.15:6,11		B	2	2	-	-	-	-	-	-	-	-	-	-	-	-	-	-	-	-	-	-	-	-	-	-	-	-	B
				C	-	-	-	-	-	-	-	-	-	-	-	-	-	-	-	-	-	-	-	-	-	-	-	-	1	-	C
3	AHB	beloved	Iq	TOT	1	-	-	-	-	-	5	-	-	-	-	-	-	-	-	-	-	-	-	-	-	-	M	16	-	-	TOT
				A	-	-	-	-	-	-	4	-	-	-	-	-	-	-	-	-	-	-	-	-	-	-	M	7	-	-	A
		2Sam.1:23		B	1	1	-	-	-	-	-	-	-	-	-	-	-	-	-	-	-	-	-	-	-	-	M	1	-	-	B
				C	-	-	-	-	-	-	1	-	-	-	-	-	-	-	-	-	-	-	-	-	-	-	M	8	-	-	C
4*	AWH	be lovely	II	TOT	3	-	3	-	-	-	-	-	-	-	-	-	-	-	-	-	-	15	7	3	5	-	-	11	-	-	TOT
				A	-	-	-	-	-	-	-	-	-	-	-	-	-	-	-	-	-	6	2	1	3	-	-	5	-	-	A
		Ps.93:5/Song1:10		B	2	-	2	-	-	-	-	-	-	-	-	-	-	-	-	-	-	7	4	1	2	-	-	4	-	-	B
		Isa.52:7		C	1	-	1	-	-	-	-	-	-	-	-	-	-	-	-	-	-	2	1	1	-	-	-	2	-	-	C
5*	AWR	be lit/be lighted up	I=q?	TOT	3	1	-	1	1	-	-	-	-	-	-	-	-	-	-	-	-	-	-	-	-	-	6	-	34	-	TOT
		2Sam.2:32		A	1	-	-	1	-	-	-	-	-	-	-	-	-	-	-	-	-	-	-	-	-	-	4	-	12	-	A
		Ps.76:5//Job33:10		B	2	1	-	-	1	-	-	-	-	-	-	-	-	-	-	-	-	-	-	-	-	-	1	-	18	-	B
				C	-	-	-	-	-	-	-	-	-	-	-	-	-	-	-	-	-	-	-	-	-	-	1	-	4	-	C
6*	AWT	oblige/grant	III	TOT	4	-	-	4	-	-	-	-	-	-	-	-	-	-	-	-	-	-	-	-	-	-	-	-	-	-	TOT
		Gen.34:15/:22/:33/2Kin.12:9		A	4	-	-	4	-	-	-	-	-	-	-	-	-	-	-	-	-	-	-	-	-	-	-	-	-	-	A
7	AZR	girded up	Iq	TOT	1	1	-	-	-	-	1	-	-	-	-	-	-	-	-	-	-	3	-	1	-	2	6	6	-	-	TOT
				A	-	-	-	-	-	-	1	-	-	-	-	-	-	-	-	-	-	-	-	-	-	-	1	-	-	-	A
		Ps.65:7		B	1	1	-	-	-	-	-	-	-	-	-	-	-	-	-	-	-	1	-	1	-	-	4	4	-	-	B
				C	-	-	-	-	-	-	-	-	-	-	-	-	-	-	-	-	-	2	-	-	-	2	1	2	-	-	C
8	AḤZ	1) be kept/be imprisoned	Iq	TOT1	2	1	1	-	-	-	9	-	-	-	-	-	1	1	-	-	-	-	-	-	-	-	58	1	-	-	TOT
		2) occupy/establish oneself	II	TOT2	5	-	2	1	-	2																					
		1) Gen.22:13//Eccl.9:12		A1)	2	1	1	-	-	-	7	-	-	-	-	-	1	1	-	-		-	-	-	-	-	27	-	-	-	A
		2) Num.32:30/Josh.22:9//Gen.		A2)	5	-	2	1	-	2																					
		47:27//34:10/Josh.22:19		B	-	-	-	-	-	-	2	-	-	-	-	-	-	-	-	-	-	-	-	-	-	-	25	1	-	-	B
				C	-	-	-	-	-	-	-	-	-	-	-	-	-	-	-	-	-	-	-	-	-	-	6	-	-	-	C
9	AKL	be eaten/be consumed	Iq	TOT	45	1	1	41	2	-	-	5	1	3	1	-	-	-	-	-	-	-	-	-	-	-	M	-	20	-	TOT
		see 3.3		A	38	1	1	34	2	-	-	3	1	2	-	-	-	-	-	-	-	-	-	-	-	-	M	-	12	-	A
				B	1	-	-	1	-	-	-	-	-	-	-	-	-	-	-	-	-	-	-	-	-	-	M	-	3	-	B
				C	6	-	-	6	-	-	-	2	-	1	1	-	-	-	-	-	-	-	-	-	-	-	M	-	5	-	C
10	ALH	be corrupted	III	TOT	3	1	2	-	-	-	-	-	-	-	-	-	-	-	-	-	-	-	-	-	-	-	-	-	-	-	TOT
		Job15:6//Ps.14:3/53:4		B	3	1	2	-	-	-	-	-	-	-	-	-	-	-	-	-	-	-	-	-	-	-	-	-	-	-	B
11	ALM	be dumb	II	TOT	8	-	6	2	-	-	-	-	-	-	-	-	-	-	-	-	-	-	-	-	-	-	-	1	-	-	TOT
		Ezek.3:26/33:22/Dan.10:15//		A	4	-	3	1	-	-	-	-	-	-	-	-	-	-	-	-	-	-	-	-	-	-	-	1	-	-	A
		Ezek.24:27																													
		Ps.39:3,10//31:19		B	3	-	2	1	-	-	-	-	-	-	-	-	-	-	-	-	-	-	-	-	-	-	-	-	-	-	B
		Isa.53:7		C	1	-	1	-	-	-	-	-	-	-	-	-	-	-	-	-	-	-	-	-	-	-	-	-	-	-	C
12	AMN	I be carried	Iq	TOT	1	-	-	1	-	-	1	-	-	-	-	-	-	-	-	-	-	-	-	-	-	-	8	-	-	-	TOT
				A	-	-	-	-	-	-	-	-	-	-	-	-	-	-	-	-	-	-	-	-	-	-	6	-	-	-	A
				B	-	-	-	-	-	-	1	-	-	-	-	-	-	-	-	-	-	-	-	-	-	-	1	-	-	-	B
		Isa.60:4		C	1	-	-	1	-	-	-	-	-	-	-	-	-	-	-	-	-	-	-	-	-	-	1	-	-	-	C
13	AMN	II be trustworthy/ be	Ihi	TOT	45	32	5	8	-	-	-	-	-	-	-	-	-	-	-	-	-	-	-	-	-	-	-	-	51	-	TOT

	ROOT	MEANING	DIV	G	NIPH'AL TOT	NIPH'AL PT	NIPH'AL PF	NIPH'AL IMPF	INF	IMPV	PQ	PU'AL TOT	PU'AL PT	PU'AL PF	PU'AL IMPF	PU'AL O	HOPH'AL TOT	HOPH'AL PT	HOPH'AL PF	HOPH'AL IMPF	HOPH'AL O	HITPA'EL TOT	HITPA'EL PT	HITPA'EL PF	HITPA'EL IMPF	HITPA'EL O	QAL	PI	HI	O	G
		steadfast/ be confirmed																													
				A	21	13	1	7	-	-	-	-	-	-	-	-	-	-	-	-	-	-	-	-	-	-	-	-	24	-	A
		see 3.3		B	12	9	3	-	-	-	-	-	-	-	-	-	-	-	-	-	-	-	-	-	-	-	-	-	19	-	B
				C	12	10	1	1	-	-	-	-	-	-	-	-	-	-	-	-	-	-	-	-	-	-	-	-	8	-	C
14	**AMR**	be said/ be told	Iq	TOT	21	-	1	20	-	-	1	-	-	-	-	-	-	-	-	-	-	1	-	-	-	1	M	-	2	-	TOT
		See 3.3		A	7	-	1	6	-	-	-	-	-	-	-	-	-	-	-	-	-	-	-	-	-	-	M	-	2	-	A
				B	2	-	-	2	-	-	-	-	-	-	-	-	-	-	-	-	-	1	-	-	-	1	M	-	-	-	B
				C	12	-	-	12	-	-	1	-	-	-	-	-	-	-	-	-	-	-	-	-	-	-	M	-	-	-	C
15	**ANḤ**	sigh	III	TOT	12	5	3	3	-	1	-	-	-	-	-	-	-	-	-	-	-	-	-	-	-	-	-	-	-	-	TOT
		Ezek.9:4/21:12//21:11/		A	5	2	-	2	-	1	-	-	-	-	-	-	-	-	-	-	-	-	-	-	-	-	-	-	-	-	A
		Ex.2:23//Ezek.21:11																													
		Lam.1:4,11,21//1:8//Pro.29:2		B	5	3	1	1	-	-	-	-	-	-	-	-	-	-	-	-	-	-	-	-	-	-	-	-	-	-	B
		Joel1:18/Isa.24:7		C	2	-	2	-	-	-	-	-	-	-	-	-	-	-	-	-	-	-	-	-	-	-	-	-	-	-	C
16*	**ANQ**	groan (during mourning)	I=q	TOT	2	1	-	-	-	1	-	-	-	-	-	-	-	-	-	-	-	-	-	-	-	-	2	-	-	-	TOT
		Ezek.9:4//24:17		A	2	1	-	-	-	1	-	-	-	-	-	-	-	-	-	-	-	-	-	-	-	-	1	-	-	-	A
				C	-	-	-	-	-	-	-	-	-	-	-	-	-	-	-	-	-	-	-	-	-	-	1	-	-	-	C
17	**ANŠ**	become ill	Iq	TOT	1	-	-	1	-	-	8	-	-	-	-	-	-	-	-	-	-	-	-	-	-	-	8	-	-	-	TOT
		2Sam.12:15		A	1	-	-	1	-	-	2	-	-	-	-	-	-	-	-	-	-	-	-	-	-	-	2	-	-	-	A
				B	-	-	-	-	-	-	1	-	-	-	-	-	-	-	-	-	-	-	-	-	-	-	1	-	-	-	B
				C	-	-	-	-	-	-	5	-	-	-	-	-	-	-	-	-	-	-	-	-	-	-	5	-	-	-	C
18	**ASP**	be gathered/be taken away	Iq	TOT	82	4	28	40	3	7	1	5	1	4	-	-	-	-	-	-	-	1	-	-	-	1	M	8	-	-	TOT
		see 3.3		A	58	2	19	32	3	2	1	1	1	-	-	-	-	-	-	-	-	-	-	-	-	-	M	5	-	-	A
				B	7	-	4	2	-	1	-	-	-	-	-	-	-	-	-	-	-	1	-	-	-	1	M	-	-	-	B
				C	17	2	5	6	-	4	-	4	-	4	-	-	-	-	-	-	-	-	-	-	-	-	M	3	-	-	C
19	**ASR**	be bound/be captured	Iq	TOT	5	-	-	4	-	1	16	2	-	2	-	-	-	-	-	-	-	-	-	-	-	-	65	-	-	-	TOT
		Gen.42:19/Judg.16:6,10,13/		A	5	-	-	4	-	1	11	-	-	-	-	-	-	-	-	-	-	-	-	-	-	-	52	-	-	-	A
		Gen.42:16		B	-	-	-	-	-	-	3	-	-	-	-	-	-	-	-	-	-	-	-	-	-	-	9	-	-	-	B
				C	-	-	-	-	-	-	2	2	-	2	-	-	-	-	-	-	-	-	-	-	-	-	4	-	-	-	C
20	**APH**	be baked	Iq	TOT	3	-	-	3	-	-	-	-	-	-	-	-	-	-	-	-	-	-	-	-	-	-	22	-	-	-	TOT
		Lev.6:10/7:9/23:17		A	3	-	-	3	-	-	-	-	-	-	-	-	-	-	-	-	-	-	-	-	-	-	18	-	-	-	A
				C	-	-	-	-	-	-	-	-	-	-	-	-	-	-	-	-	-	-	-	-	-	-	4	-	-	-	C
21	**AṢL**	be taken away	Iq	TOT	1	-	1	-	-	-	-	-	-	-	-	-	-	-	-	-	-	-	-	-	-	-	4	-	-	-	TOT
		Ezek.42:6		A	1	-	1	-	-	-	-	-	-	-	-	-	-	-	-	-	-	-	-	-	-	-	3	-	-	-	A
				B	-	-	-	-	-	-	-	-	-	-	-	-	-	-	-	-	-	-	-	-	-	-	1	-	-	-	B
22	**AṢR**	be heaped up	Iq	TOT	1	-	-	1	-	-	-	-	-	-	-	-	-	-	-	-	-	-	-	-	-	-	3	-	1	-	TOT
				A	-	-	-	-	-	-	-	-	-	-	-	-	-	-	-	-	-	-	-	-	-	-	2	-	1	-	A
		Isa.23:18		C	1	-	-	1	-	-	-	-	-	-	-	-	-	-	-	-	-	-	-	-	-	-	1	-	-	-	C
23	**ARR**	be cursed	Iq	TOT	1	1	-	-	-	-	40	-	-	-	-	-	1	-	-	1	-	-	-	-	-	-	53	7	-	-	TOT
				A	-	-	-	-	-	-	32	-	-	-	-	-	1	-	-	1	-	-	-	-	-	-	40	7	-	-	A
				B	-	-	-	-	-	-	1	-	-	-	-	-	-	-	-	-	-	-	-	-	-	-	2	-	-	-	B
		Mal.3:9		C	1	1	-	-	-	-	7	-	-	-	-	-	-	-	-	-	-	-	-	-	-	-	9	-	-	-	C
24*	**AŠM**	suffer guilt/punishment	Iq	TOT	1	-	1	-	-	-	-	-	-	-	-	-	-	-	-	-	-	-	-	-	-	-	34	-	1	-	TOT
				A	-	-	-	-	-	-	-	-	-	-	-	-	-	-	-	-	-	-	-	-	-	-	21	-	-	-	A
				B	-	-	-	-	-	-	-	-	-	-	-	-	-	-	-	-	-	-	-	-	-	-	10	-	1	-	B
		Jo.1:18		C	1	-	1	-	-	-	-	-	-	-	-	-	-	-	-	-	-	-	-	-	-	-	3	-	-	-	C

	ROOT	MEANING	DIV	G	NIPH'AL TOT	PT	PF	IMPF	INF	IMPV	PQ	PU'AL TOT	PT	PF	IMPF	O	HOPH'AL TOT	PT	PF	IMPF	O	HITPA'EL TOT	PT	PF	IMPF	O	QAL	PI	HI	O	G
25	**BAS**	make oneself odious	Ih	TOT	3	-	3	-	-	-	-	-	-	-	-	-	-	-	-	-	-	1	-	1	-	-	5	-	8	-	TOT
		1Sam.13:4/2Sam.10:6/16:21		A	3	-	3	-	-	-	-	-	-	-	-	-	-	-	-	-	-	1	-	1	-	-	4	-	5	-	A
				B	-	-	-	-	-	-	-	-	-	-	-	-	-	-	-	-	-	-	-	-	-	-	-	-	3	-	B
				C	-	-	-	-	-	-	-	-	-	-	-	-	-	-	-	-	-	-	-	-	-	-	1	-	-	-	C
26	**BDL**	separate oneself/be separated	Ih	TOT	10	2	2	4	-	2	-	-	-	-	-	-	-	-	-	-	-	-	-	-	-	-	-	-	32	-	TOT
		Ezra6:21/Neh.10:29//Ezra9:1/1		A	10	2	2	4	-	2	-	-	-	-	-	-	-	-	-	-	-	-	-	-	-	-	-	-	29	-	A
		Chr.12:8//Ezra10:8,16/Neh.9:2/																													
		1Chr.23:13//Num.16:21/Ezra10:11																													
				C	-	-	-	-	-	-	-	-	-	-	-	-	-	-	-	-	-	-	-	-	-	-	-	-	3	-	C
27	**BHL**	be frightened/be(come)	Ip	TOT	24	3	13	8	-	-	-	2	2	-	-	-	-	-	-	-	-	-	-	-	-	-	-	10	3	-	TOT
		confused. See 3.3		A	7	-	4	3	-	-	-	1	1	-	-	-	-	-	-	-	-	-	-	-	-	-	-	5	2	-	A
				B	13	2	6	5	-	-	-	1	1	-	-	-	-	-	-	-	-	-	-	-	-	-	-	5	1	-	B
				C	4	1	3	-	-	-	-	-	-	-	-	-	-	-	-	-	-	-	-	-	-	-	-	-	-	-	C
28	**BWK**	be(come) confused//wander*	III	TOT	3	1	2	-	-	-	-	-	-	-	-	-	-	-	-	-	-	-	-	-	-	-	-	-	-	-	TOT
		Ex.14:3*//Esth.3:18		A	2	1	1	-	-	-	-	-	-	-	-	-	-	-	-	-	-	-	-	-	-	-	-	-	-	-	A
		Jo.1:18		C	1	-	1	-	-	-	-	-	-	-	-	-	-	-	-	-	-	-	-	-	-	-	-	-	-	-	C
29	**BZH**	despise (despicable)	Iq	TOT	10	10	-	-	-	-	4	-	-	-	-	-	-	-	-	-	-	-	-	-	-	-	31	1	-	-	TOT
		1Sam.15:9/Dan.11:21		A	2	2	-	-	-	-	-	-	-	-	-	-	-	-	-	-	-	-	-	-	-	-	17	1	-	-	A
		Ps.15:4/119:141		B	2	2	-	-	-	-	2	-	-	-	-	-	-	-	-	-	-	-	-	-	-	-	10	-	-	-	B
		Isa.53:3(2x)/Jer.22:28/		C	6	6	-	-	-	-	2	-	-	-	-	-	-	-	-	-	-	-	-	-	-	-	4	-	-	-	C
		Mal.1:7, 12/2:9																													
30	**BZZ**	be plundered	Iq	TOT	3	-	1	1	1	-	1	1	-	1	-	-	-	-	-	-	-	-	-	-	-	-	39	-	-	-	TOT
				A	-	-	-	-	-	-	-	-	-	-	-	-	-	-	-	-	-	-	-	-	-	-	28	-	-	-	A
				B	-	-	-	-	-	-	-	-	-	-	-	-	-	-	-	-	-	-	-	-	-	-	1	-	-	-	B
		Am.3:11//Isa.24:3//24:3		C	3	-	1	1	1	-	1	1	-	1	-	-	-	-	-	-	-	-	-	-	-	-	10	-	-	-	C
31	**BḤN**	be tried/proved	Iq	TOT	3	-	-	3	-	-	-	2	-	2	-	-	-	-	-	-	-	-	-	-	-	-	25	-	-	-	TOT
		Gen.42:15,16		A	2	-	-	2	-	-	-	1	-	1	-	-	-	-	-	-	-	-	-	-	-	-	-	-	-	-	A
		Job34:36		B	1	-	-	1	-	-	-	-	-	-	-	-	-	-	-	-	-	-	-	-	-	-	15	-	-	-	B
				C	-	-	-	-	-	-	-	1	-	1	-	-	-	-	-	-	-	-	-	-	-	-	10	-	-	-	C
32	**BḤR**	be chosen/be elected	Iq	TOT	7	6	1	-	-	-	18	-	-	-	-	-	-	-	-	-	-	-	-	-	-	-	M	1	-	-	TOT
				A	-	-	-	-	-	-	14	-	-	-	-	-	-	-	-	-	-	-	-	-	-	-	M	-	-	-	A
		Pro.8:10,19/10:20/16:16/		B	6	6	-	-	-	-	2	-	-	-	-	-	-	-	-	-	-	-	-	-	-	-	M	1	-	-	B
		21:3/22:1																													
		Jer.8:3		C	1	-	1	-	-	-	2	-	-	-	-	-	-	-	-	-	-	-	-	-	-	-	M	-	-	-	C
33*	**BJN**	be intelligent/have under-	II	TOT	22	21	1	-	-	-	-	-	-	-	-	-	-	-	-	-	-	22	-	4	15	3	13	-	M	1	TOT
		standing		A	7	7	-	-	-	-	-	-	-	-	-	-	-	-	-	-	-	2	-	-	2	-	5	-	M	-	A
		See 3.3		B	9	9	-	-	-	-	-	-	-	-	-	-	-	-	-	-	-	13	-	2	10	1	7	-	M	1	B
				C	6	5	1	-	-	-	-	-	-	-	-	-	-	-	-	-	-	7	-	2	3	2	1	-	M	-	C
34	**BL'**	be devoured/be swallowed up	Iq	TOT	2	-	2	-	-	-	-	3	1	-	2	-	-	-	-	-	-	1	-	-	1	-	20	22	-	-	TOT
				A	-	-	-	-	-	-	-	1	-	-	1	-	-	-	-	-	-	-	-	-	-	-	9	3	-	-	A
				B	-	-	-	-	-	-	-	1	-	-	1	-	-	-	-	-	-	1	-	-	1	-	8	13	-	-	B
		Isa.28:7/Hos.8:8		C	2	-	2	-	-	-	-	1	1	-	-	-	-	-	-	-	-	-	-	-	-	-	3	6	-	-	C
35	**BNH**	be (re-)built	Iq	TOT	30	1	11	14	4	-	4	-	-	-	-	-	-	-	-	-	-	-	-	-	-	-	M	-	-	-	TOT
		See 3.3		A	17	1	9	5	2	-	2	-	-	-	-	-	-	-	-	-	-	-	-	-	-	-	M	-	-	-	A
				B	5	-	-	5	-	-	2	-	-	-	-	-	-	-	-	-	-	-	-	-	-	-	M	-	-	-	B

ROOT	MEANING	DIV	G	NIPH'AL TOT	PT	PF	IMPF	INF	IMPV	PQ	PU'AL TOT	PT	PF	IMPF	O	HOPH'AL TOT	PT	PF	IMPF	O	HITPA'EL TOT	PT	PF	IMPF	O	QAL	PI	HI	O	G
			C	8	-	2	4	2	-	-	-	-	-	-	-	-	-	-	-	-	-	-	-	-	-	M	-	-	-	C
36* **B'H**	be searched//be bent forward*	Iq/II	TOT	2	1	1	-	-	-	-	-	-	-	-	-	-	-	-	-	-	-	-	-	-	-	3	-	-	-	TOT
	Isa.30:6*//Ob.6		C	2	1	1	-	-	-	-	-	-	-	-	-	-	-	-	-	-	-	-	-	-	-	3	-	-	-	C
37 **B'L**	be married	Iq	TOT	2	-	-	2	-	-	4	-	-	-	-	-	-	-	-	-	-	-	-	-	-	-	14	-	-	-	TOT
			A	-	-	-	-	-	-	2	-	-	-	-	-	-	-	-	-	-	-	-	-	-	-	6	-	-	-	A
	Pro.30:23		B	1	-	-	1	-	-	-	-	-	-	-	-	-	-	-	-	-	-	-	-	-	-	-	-	-	-	B
	Isa.62:4		C	1	-	-	1	-	-	2	-	-	-	-	-	-	-	-	-	-	-	-	-	-	-	8	-	-	-	C
38 **B'R**	be dumb/stupid	I=q	TOT	4	1	3	-	-	-	-	-	-	-	-	-	-	-	-	-	-	-	-	-	-	-	3	-	-	-	TOT
			A	-	-	-	-	-	-	-	-	-	-	-	-	-	-	-	-	-	-	-	-	-	-	1	-	-	-	A
			B	-	-	-	-	-	-	-	-	-	-	-	-	-	-	-	-	-	-	-	-	-	-	1	-	-	-	B
	Isa.19:11//Jer.10:14,21/51:17		C	4	1	3	-	-	-	-	-	-	-	-	-	-	-	-	-	-	-	-	-	-	-	1	-	-	-	C
39 **B'T**	be frightened/terrified	Ip	TOT	3	-	3	-	-	-	-	-	-	-	-	-	-	-	-	-	-	-	-	-	-	-	-	13	-	-	TOT
	Esth.7:6/Dan.8:17/1Chr.21:30		A	3	-	3	-	-	-	-	-	-	-	-	-	-	-	-	-	-	-	-	-	-	-	-	2	-	-	A
			B	-	-	-	-	-	-	-	-	-	-	-	-	-	-	-	-	-	-	-	-	-	-	-	10	-	-	B
			C	-	-	-	-	-	-	-	-	-	-	-	-	-	-	-	-	-	-	-	-	-	-	-	1	-	-	C
40 **BṢR**	be impossible	II	TOT	2	-	-	2	-	-	26	-	-	-	-	-	-	-	-	-	-	-	-	-	-	-	34	2	-	-	TOT
	Gen.11:6		A	1	-	-	1	-	-	19	-	-	-	-	-	-	-	-	-	-	-	-	-	-	-	23	-	-	-	A
	Job42:2		B	1	-	-	1	-	-	-	-	-	-	-	-	-	-	-	-	-	-	-	-	-	-	1	-	-	-	B
			C	-	-	-	-	-	-	7	-	-	-	-	-	-	-	-	-	-	-	-	-	-	-	10	2	-	-	C
41* **BQ'**	be split/tear	Iq/p	TOT	15	-	6	8	1	-	-	3	2	-	1	-	1	-	1	-	-	2	-	1	1	-	16	12	2	-	TOT
	Gen.7:11/2Chr.25:12//Ex.14:21/Num.16:31/1Kin.1:4/2Kin.25:4/Jer.52:7//Ezek.30:16		A	8	-	2	5	1	-	-	2	2	-	-	-	1	-	1	-	-	1	-	1	-	-	8	7	1	-	A
	Pro.3:20/Job26:8//32:19		B	3	-	2	1	-	-	-	-	-	-	-	-	-	-	-	-	-	-	-	-	-	-	4	3	-	-	B
	Isa.35:6/Zech.14:4//Isa.58:8/59:5		C	4	-	2	2	-	-	-	1	-	-	1	-	-	-	-	-	-	1	-	-	1	-	4	2	1	-	C
42 **BQQ**	be destroyed/be emptied	Iq	TOT	3	-	1	1	1	-	-	-	-	-	-	-	-	-	-	-	-	-	-	-	-	-	5	-	-	1	TOT
			A	-	-	-	-	-	-	-	-	-	-	-	-	-	-	-	-	-	-	-	-	-	-	1	-	-	-	A
	Isa.19:3//24:3//24:3		C	3	-	1	1	1	-	-	-	-	-	-	-	-	-	-	-	-	-	-	-	-	-	4	-	-	1	C
43 **BRA**	be created	Iq	TOT	10	1	4	1	4	-	-	-	-	-	-	-	-	-	-	-	-	-	-	-	-	-	34	4	-	-	TOT
	Ex.34:10/Ez.21:35//Gen.2:4/5:2		A	4	-	2	-	2	-	-	-	-	-	-	-	-	-	-	-	-	-	-	-	-	-	11	4	-	-	A
	Ps.148:5//102:19//104:30		B	3	1	1	1	-	-	-	-	-	-	-	-	-	-	-	-	-	-	-	-	-	-	4	-	-	-	B
	Isa.48:7//Ezek.28:13,15		C	3	-	1	-	2	-	-	-	-	-	-	-	-	-	-	-	-	-	-	-	-	-	19	-	-	-	C
44 **BRK**	bless oneself/bless each other	Ip	TOT	3	-	3	-	-	-	71	12	6	-	6	-	-	-	-	-	-	7	1	4	2	-	74	M	-	-	TOT
	Gen.12:3/18:18/28:14		A	3	-	3	-	-	-	42	4	2	-	2	-	-	-	-	-	-	3	-	3	-	-	44	M	-	-	A
			B	-	-	-	-	-	-	24	8	4	-	4	-	-	-	-	-	-	1	-	-	1	-	25	M	-	-	B
			C	-	-	-	-	-	-	5	-	-	-	-	-	-	-	-	-	-	3	1	1	1	-	5	M	-	-	C
45* **BRR**	purify oneself/keep oneself pure	Iq/p	TOT	3	2	-	-	-	1	7	-	-	-	-	-	-	-	-	-	-	3	-	-	3	-	10	1	2	-	TOT
			A	-	-	-	-	-	-	4	-	-	-	-	-	-	-	-	-	-	1	-	-	1	-	5	1	-	-	A
	2Sam.22:27/Ps.18:27		B	2	2	-	-	-	-	1	-	-	-	-	-	-	-	-	-	-	2	-	-	2	-	3	-	-	-	B
	Isa.52:11		C	1	-	-	-	-	1	2	-	-	-	-	-	-	-	-	-	-	-	-	-	-	-	2	-	2	-	C

	ROOT	MEANING	DIV	G	NIPH'AL TOT	NIPH'AL PT	NIPH'AL PF	NIPH'AL IMPF	NIPH'AL INF	NIPH'AL IMPV	PQ	PU'AL TOT	PU'AL PT	PU'AL PF	PU'AL IMPF	PU'AL O	HOPH'AL TOT	HOPH'AL PT	HOPH'AL PF	HOPH'AL IMPF	HOPH'AL O	HITPA'EL TOT	HITPA'EL PT	HITPA'EL PF	HITPA'EL IMPF	HITPA'EL O	QAL	PI	HI	O	G
46	**GAL**	I be redeemed/redeem oneself*	Iq	TOT	8	-	1	7	-	-	5	-	-	-	-	-	-	-	-	-	-	-	-	-	-	-	92	-	-	-	TOT
		Lev.25:49*//25:30,54/27:20, 27,28,33		A	7	-	1	6	-	-	-	-	-	-	-	-	-	-	-	-	-	-	-	-	-	-	50	-	-	-	A
				B	-	-	-	-	-	-	4	-	-	-	-	-	-	-	-	-	-	-	-	-	-	-	16	-	-	-	B
		Isa.52:3		C	1	-	-	1	-	-	1	-	-	-	-	-	-	-	-	-	-	-	-	-	-	-	26	-	-	-	C
47*	**GAL**	II be defiled/be contaminated	Ip	TOT	3	1	2	-	-	-	-	4	2	-	2	-	-	-	-	-	-	2	-	-	2	-	-	1	1	-	TOT
				A	-	-	-	-	-	-	-	2	-	-	2	-	-	-	-	-	-	2	-	-	2	-	-	-	-	-	A
		Lam.4:14		B	1	-	1	-	-	-	-	-	-	-	-	-	-	-	-	-	-	-	-	-	-	-	-	-	-	-	B
		Zeph.3:1//Isa.59:3		C	2	1	1	-	-	-	-	2	2	-	-	-	-	-	-	-	-	-	-	-	-	-	-	1	1	-	C
48	**GD'**	be cut off/be smashed	Iq	TOT	7	-	7	-	-	-	1	1	-	1	-	-	-	-	-	-	-	-	-	-	-	-	5	9	-	-	TOT
		Judg.21:6/Ezek.6:6		A	2	-	2	-	-	-	-	-	-	-	-	-	-	-	-	-	-	-	-	-	-	-	1	6	-	-	A
				B	-	-	-	-	-	-	-	-	-	-	-	-	-	-	-	-	-	-	-	-	-	-	1	2	-	-	B
		Isa.14:12/22:25/Jer.48:25/ 50:23/Am.3:14		C	5	-	5	-	-	-	1	1	-	1	-	-	-	-	-	-	-	-	-	-	-	-	3	1	-	-	C
49	**GZZ**	be shorn (off)	Iq	TOT	1	-	1	-	-	-	-	-	-	-	-	-	-	-	-	-	-	-	-	-	-	-	14	-	-	-	TOT
				A	-	-	-	-	-	-	-	-	-	-	-	-	-	-	-	-	-	-	-	-	-	-	11	-	-	-	A
		Nah.1:12		C	1	-	1	-	-	-	-	-	-	-	-	-	-	-	-	-	-	-	-	-	-	-	3	-	-	-	C
50	**GZL**	be taken away	Iq	TOT	1	-	1	-	-	-	5	-	-	-	-	-	-	-	-	-	-	-	-	-	-	-	29	-	-	-	TOT
				A	-	-	-	-	-	-	2	-	-	-	-	-	-	-	-	-	-	-	-	-	-	-	15	-	-	-	A
		Pro.4:16		B	1	-	1	-	-	-	-	-	-	-	-	-	-	-	-	-	-	-	-	-	-	-	8	-	-	-	B
				C	-	-	-	-	-	-	3	-	-	-	-	-	-	-	-	-	-	-	-	-	-	-	6	-	-	-	C
51	**GZR**	be cut off/be announced*	Iq	TOT	6	-	6	-	-	-	-	-	-	-	-	-	-	-	-	-	-	-	-	-	-	-	7	-	-	-	TOT
		Ezek.37:11/Esth.2:1*/2Chr.		A	3	-	3	-	-	-	-	-	-	-	-	-	-	-	-	-	-	-	-	-	-	-	3	-	-	-	A
		26:21Ps.88:6/Lam.3:54		B	2	-	2	-	-	-	-	-	-	-	-	-	-	-	-	-	-	-	-	-	-	-	2	-	-	-	B
		Isa.53:8		C	1	-	1	-	-	-	-	-	-	-	-	-	-	-	-	-	-	-	-	-	-	-	2	-	-	-	C
52*	**GLH**	be revealed/be uncovered/ reveal oneself	Iq/p	TOT	32	2	15	9	5	1	6	2	1	1	-	-	6	1	5	-	-	2	-	-	1	1	50	53	39	-	TOT
				A	18	2	7	5	4	-	4	-	-	-	-	-	5	1	4	-	-	1	-	-	1	-	26	34	34	-	A
		see 3.3		B	4	-	1	3	-	-	2	1	1	-	-	-	-	-	-	-	-	1	-	-	1	-	7	9	1	-	B
				C	10	-	7	1	1	1	-	1	-	1	-	-	1	-	1	-	-	-	-	-	-	-	17	10	4	-	C
53	**GLL**	roll up oneself	Iq	TOT	2	-	1	1	-	-	-	1	1	-	-	-	-	-	-	-	-	3	1	1	-	1	10	1	1	1	TOT
				A	-	-	-	-	-	-	-	-	-	-	-	-	-	-	-	-	-	2	1	-	-	1	5	-	1	-	A
				B	-	-	-	-	-	-	-	-	-	-	-	-	-	-	-	-	-	-	-	-	-	-	5	-	-	-	B
		Isa.34:4//Am.5:1		C	2	-	1	1	-	-	-	1	1	-	-	-	-	-	-	-	-	1	-	1	-	-	-	1	-	1	C
54	**GML**	be weaned	Iq	TOT	3	-	-	2	1	-	4	-	-	-	-	-	-	-	-	-	-	-	-	-	-	-	34	-	-	-	TOT
		Gen.21:8/1Sam.1:22//Gen.21:8		A	3	-	-	2	1	-	-	-	-	-	-	-	-	-	-	-	-	-	-	-	-	-	12	-	-	-	A
				B	-	-	-	-	-	-	2	-	-	-	-	-	-	-	-	-	-	-	-	-	-	-	14	-	-	-	B
				C	-	-	-	-	-	-	2	-	-	-	-	-	-	-	-	-	-	-	-	-	-	-	8	-	-	-	C
55	**GNB**	be stolen	Iq	TOT	1	-	-	1	-	-	3	4	-	2	1	1	-	-	-	-	-	2	-	-	2	-	30	2	-	-	TOT
		Ex.22:11		A	1	-	-	1	-	-	3	3	-	2	-	1	-	-	-	-	-	2	-	-	2	-	21	1	-	-	A
				B	-	-	-	-	-	-	-	1	-	-	1	-	-	-	-	-	-	-	-	-	-	-	5	-	-	-	B
				C	-	-	-	-	-	-	-	-	-	-	-	-	-	-	-	-	-	-	-	-	-	-	4	1	-	-	C
56*	**G'L**	be defiled	II	TOT	1	-	1	-	-	-	-	-	-	-	-	-	-	-	-	-	-	-	-	-	-	-	8	-	1	-	TOT
				A	-	-	-	-	-	-	-	-	-	-	-	-	-	-	-	-	-	-	-	-	-	-	7	-	-	-	A

	ROOT	MEANING	DIV	G	NIPH'AL TOT	NIPH'AL PT	NIPH'AL PF	NIPH'AL IMPF	INF	IMPV	FQ	PU'AL TOT	PU'AL PT	PU'AL PF	PU'AL IMPF	PU'AL O	HOPH'AL TOT	HOPH'AL PT	HOPH'AL PF	HOPH'AL IMPF	HOPH'AL O	HITPA'EL TOT	HITPA'EL PT	HITPA'EL PF	HITPA'EL IMPF	HITPA'EL O	QAL	PI	HI	O	G
		2Sam.1:21		B	1	-	1	-	-	-	-	-	-	-	-	-	-	-	-	-	-	-	-	-	-	-	-	-	1	-	B
				C	-	-	-	-	-	-	-	-	-	-	-	-	-	-	-	-	-	-	-	-	-	-	1	-	-	-	C
57	GRZ	be cut off (cf. 51)	III	TOT	1	-	1	-	-	-	-	-	-	-	-	-	-	-	-	-	-	-	-	-	-	-	-	-	-	-	TOT
		Ps.31:23		B	1	-	1	-	-	-	-	-	-	-	-	-	-	-	-	-	-	-	-	-	-	-	-	-	-	-	B
58	GR'	be taken away	Iq	TOT	7	1	2	4	-	-	2	-	-	-	-	-	-	-	-	-	-	-	-	-	-	-	14	1	-	-	TOT
		Ex.5:11//Lev.27:18/Num.36:3 //9:7/27:4/36:3,4		A	7	1	2	4	-	-	-	-	-	-	-	-	-	-	-	-	-	-	-	-	-	-	8	-	-	-	A
				B	-	-	-	-	-	-	-	-	-	-	-	-	-	-	-	-	-	-	-	-	-	-	4	1	-	-	B
				C	-	-	-	-	-	-	2	-	-	-	-	-	-	-	-	-	-	-	-	-	-	-	2	-	-	-	C
59	GRŠ	be rejected//be stirred up	Iq/II	TOT	3	-	3	-	-	-	5	2	-	1	1	-	-	-	-	-	-	-	-	-	-	-	7	35	-	-	TOT
				A	-	-	-	-	-	-	5	1	-	1	-	-	-	-	-	-	-	-	-	-	-	-	6	27	-	-	A
				B	-	-	-	-	-	-	-	1	-	-	1	-	-	-	-	-	-	-	-	-	-	-	-	5	-	-	B
		Isa.57:20*/Am.8:8*/Jon.2:5		C	3	-	3	-	-	-	-	-	-	-	-	-	-	-	-	-	-	-	-	-	-	-	1	3	-	-	C
60	DBR	discuss with each other	Ip	TOT	4	1	3	-	-	-	1	2	1	-	1	-	-	-	-	-	-	4	4	-	-	-	41	M	-	-	TOT
		Ezek.33:30		A	1	1	-	-	-	-	-	-	-	-	-	-	-	-	-	-	-	4	4	-	-	-	13	M	-	-	A
		Ps.119:23		B	1	-	1	-	-	-	1	2	1	-	1	-	-	-	-	-	-	-	-	-	-	-	12	M	-	-	B
		Mal.3:13,16		C	2	-	2	-	-	-	-	-	-	-	-	-	-	-	-	-	-	-	-	-	-	-	16	M	-	-	C
61*	DGL	to provide with a banner	Iq	TOT	2	2	-	-	-	-	1	-	-	-	-	-	-	-	-	-	-	-	-	-	-	-	2	-	-	-	TOT
		Song6:4,10		B	2	2	-	-	-	-	1	-	-	-	-	-	-	-	-	-	-	-	-	-	-	-	2	-	-	-	B
62	DHM	astounded/defeated	III	TOT	1	1	-	-	-	-	-	-	-	-	-	-	-	-	-	-	-	-	-	-	-	-	-	-	-	-	TOT
		Jer.14:9		C	1	1	-	-	-	-	-	-	-	-	-	-	-	-	-	-	-	-	-	-	-	-	-	-	-	-	C
63	DWŠ/ DJŠ	be trodden down	Iq	TOT	2	-	1	-	1	-	-	-	-	-	-	-	1	-	-	1	-	-	-	-	-	-	13	-	-	-	TOT
				A	-	-	-	-	-	-	-	-	-	-	-	-	-	-	-	-	-	-	-	-	-	-	4	-	-	-	A
				B	-	-	-	-	-	-	-	-	-	-	-	-	-	-	-	-	-	-	-	-	-	-	1	-	-	-	B
		Isa.25:10//25:10		C	2	-	1	-	1	-	-	-	-	-	-	-	1	-	-	1	-	-	-	-	-	-	8	-	-	-	C
64	DḤH	be thrust down	Iq	TOT	1	-	-	1	-	-	1	1	-	1	-	-	-	-	-	-	-	-	-	-	-	-	5	-	-	-	TOT
		Pro.14:32		B	1	-	-	1	-	-	1	1	-	1	-	-	-	-	-	-	-	-	-	-	-	-	5	-	-	-	B
65	DḤḤ	stumble (variant of 64?)	III	TOT	1	-	-	1	-	-	-	-	-	-	-	-	-	-	-	-	-	-	-	-	-	-	-	-	-	-	TOT
		Jer.23:12		C	1	-	-	1	-	-	-	-	-	-	-	-	-	-	-	-	-	-	-	-	-	-	-	-	-	-	C
66	DḤP	hurry	Iq	TOT	2	-	2	-	-	-	2	-	-	-	-	-	-	-	-	-	-	-	-	-	-	-	2	-	-	-	TOT
		Esth.6:12/2Chr.26:20		A	2	-	2	-	-	-	2	-	-	-	-	-	-	-	-	-	-	-	-	-	-	-	2	-	-	-	A
67	DWN/ DJN	to fight with each other	Iq	TOT	1	1	-	-	-	-	-	-	-	-	-	-	-	-	-	-	-	-	-	-	-	-	24	-	-	-	TOT
		2Sam.19:10		A	1	1	-	-	-	-	-	-	-	-	-	-	-	-	-	-	-	-	-	-	-	-	4	-	-	-	A
				B	-	-	-	-	-	-	-	-	-	-	-	-	-	-	-	-	-	-	-	-	-	-	15	-	-	-	B
				C	-	-	-	-	-	-	-	-	-	-	-	-	-	-	-	-	-	-	-	-	-	-	5	-	-	-	C
68	DKA	be shattered (cf. 69)	Ip	TOT	1	1	-	-	-	-	-	4	2	1	1	-	-	-	-	-	-	2	-	-	2	-	-	11	-	-	TOT
				A	-	-	-	-	-	-	-	1	-	1	-	-	-	-	-	-	-	-	-	-	-	-	-	-	-	-	A
				B	-	-	-	-	-	-	-	1	-	-	1	-	-	-	-	-	-	2	-	-	2	-	-	9	-	-	B
		Isa.57:15		C	1	1	-	-	-	-	-	2	2	-	-	-	-	-	-	-	-	-	-	-	-	-	-	2	-	-	C
69	DKH	be shattered/be broken	Ip	TOT	2	1	1	-	-	-	-	-	-	-	-	-	-	-	-	-	-	-	-	-	-	-	1	2	-	-	TOT
		Ps.51:19//38:9		B	2	1	1	-	-	-	-	-	-	-	-	-	-	-	-	-	-	-	-	-	-	-	1	2	-	-	B
70*	DMH	be destroyed/annihilated	Iq	TOT	13	1	11	-	1	-	-	-	-	-	-	-	-	-	-	-	-	1	-	-	1	-	20	14	-	-	TOT
				A	-	-	-	-	-	-	-	-	-	-	-	-	-	-	-	-	-	-	-	-	-	-	4	4	-	-	A
		Ps.49:13,21		B	2	-	2	-	-	-	-	-	-	-	-	-	-	-	-	-	-	-	-	-	-	-	11	4	-	-	B
		Hos.10:7//Isa.6:5/15:1(2x)/Jer.		C	11	1	9	-	1	-	-	-	-	-	-	-	-	-	-	-	-	1	-	-	1	-	5	6	-	-	C

ROOT	MEANING	DIV	G	NIPH'AL TOT	PT	PF	IMPF	INF	IMPV	PQ	PU'AL TOT	PT	PF	IMPF	O	HOPH'AL TOT	PT	PF	IMPF	O	HITPA'EL TOT	PT	PF	IMPF	O	QAL	PI	HI	O	G
	47:5/Ezek.32:2/Hos.4:6/10:15/																													
	Ob.5/Zeph.1:11//Hos.10:15																													
71* **DMM**	be shattered	Iq	TOT	5	1	-	4	-	-	-	-	-	-	-	-	-	-	-	-	-	-	-	-	-	-	22	-	1	1	TOT
			A	-	-	-	-	-	-	-	-	-	-	-	-	-	-	-	-	-	-	-	-	-	-	5	-	-	-	A
	1Sam.2:9		B	1	-	-	1	-	-	-	-	-	-	-	-	-	-	-	-	-	-	-	-	-	-	13	-	-	1	B
	Jer.25:37//49:26/50:30/51:6		C	4	1	-	3	-	-	-	-	-	-	-	-	-	-	-	-	-	-	-	-	-	-	4	-	1	-	C
72* **D'K**	be dried up	Iq	TOT	1	-	1	-	-	-	-	1	-	1	-	-	-	-	-	-	-	-	-	-	-	-	8	-	-	-	TOT
	Job6:17		B	1	-	1	-	-	-	-	1	-	1	-	-	-	-	-	-	-	-	-	-	-	-	8	-	-	-	B
73 **DQR**	be pierced	Iq	TOT	1	-	-	1	-	-	-	3	3	-	-	-	-	-	-	-	-	-	-	-	-	-	7	-	-	-	TOT
			A	-	-	-	-	-	-	-	1	1	-	-	-	-	-	-	-	-	-	-	-	-	-	5	-	-	-	A
			B	-	-	-	-	-	-	-	1	1	-	-	-	-	-	-	-	-	-	-	-	-	-	-	-	-	-	B
	Isa.13:15		C	1	-	-	1	-	-	-	1	1	-	-	-	-	-	-	-	-	-	-	-	-	-	2	-	-	-	C
74 **DRŠ**	be sought/be searched	Iq	TOT	8	1	2	4	1	-	2	-	-	-	-	-	-	-	-	-	-	-	-	-	-	-	M	-	-	-	TOT
	Gen.42:22//1Chr.26:31/Ezek.		A	7	1	1	4	1	-	-	-	-	-	-	-	-	-	-	-	-	-	-	-	-	-	M	-	-	-	A
	14:3/20:3,31/36:37//14:3																													
			B	-	-	-	-	-	-	1	-	-	-	-	-	-	-	-	-	-	-	-	-	-	-	M	-	-	-	B
	Isa.65:1		C	1	-	1	-	-	-	1	-	-	-	-	-	-	-	-	-	-	-	-	-	-	-	M	-	-	-	C
75 **HDR**	be honoured	Iq	TOT	1	-	1	-	-	-	2	-	-	-	-	-	-	-	-	-	-	1	-	-	1	-	5	-	-	-	TOT
			A	-	-	-	-	-	-	-	-	-	-	-	-	-	-	-	-	-	-	-	-	-	-	3	-	-	-	A
	Lam.5:12		B	1	-	1	-	-	-	-	-	-	-	-	-	-	-	-	-	-	1	-	-	1	-	-	-	-	-	B
			C	-	-	-	-	-	-	2	-	-	-	-	-	-	-	-	-	-	-	-	-	-	-	2	-	-	-	C
76 **HMM/**	be stirred/resound	II	TOT	3	-	-	3	-	-	-	-	-	-	-	-	-	-	-	-	-	-	-	-	-	-	15	-	2	-	TOT
HMM	1Sam.4:5/1Kin.1:45/Ruth1:19		A	3	-	-	3	-	-	-	-	-	-	-	-	-	-	-	-	-	-	-	-	-	-	9	-	-	-	A
			B	-	-	-	-	-	-	-	-	-	-	-	-	-	-	-	-	-	-	-	-	-	-	4	-	1	-	B
			C	-	-	-	-	-	-	-	-	-	-	-	-	-	-	-	-	-	-	-	-	-	-	2	-	1	-	C
77* **HJH**	be done / happen	Iq	TOT	21	1	20	-	-	-	-	-	-	-	-	-	-	-	-	-	-	-	-	-	-	-	M	-	-	-	TOT
	see 3.3		A	15	-	15	-	-	-	-	-	-	-	-	-	-	-	-	-	-	-	-	-	-	-	M	-	-	-	A
			B	1	1	-	-	-	-	-	-	-	-	-	-	-	-	-	-	-	-	-	-	-	-	M	-	-	-	B
			C	5	-	5	-	-	-	-	-	-	-	-	-	-	-	-	-	-	-	-	-	-	-	M	-	-	-	C
78 **HLH**	removed	III	TOT	1	1	-	-	-	-	-	-	-	-	-	-	-	-	-	-	-	-	-	-	-	-	-	-	-	-	TOT
	Mi.4:7		C	1	1	-	-	-	-	-	-	-	-	-	-	-	-	-	-	-	-	-	-	-	-	-	-	-	-	C
79 **HLK**	go (away)	I=q	TOT	1	-	1	-	-	-	-	-	-	-	-	-	-	-	-	-	-	64	10	18	26	10	M	25	46	-	TOT
			A	-	-	-	-	-	-	-	-	-	-	-	-	-	-	-	-	-	32	7	13	9	3	M	2	27	-	A
	Ps.109:23		B	1	-	1	-	-	-	-	-	-	-	-	-	-	-	-	-	-	24	3	3	14	4	M	21	9	-	B
			C	-	-	-	-	-	-	-	-	-	-	-	-	-	-	-	-	-	8	-	2	3	3	M	2	10	-	C
80 **HFK**	be turned (over)	Iq	TOT	34	2	24	7	1	-	2	-	-	-	-	-	1	-	1	-	-	4	3	-	1	-	55	-	-	-	TOT
	see 3.3		A	17	1	12	3	1	-	-	-	-	-	-	-	-	-	-	-	-	2	2	-	-	-	28	-	-	-	A
			B	11	1	9	1	-	-	1	-	-	-	-	-	1	-	1	-	-	2	1	-	1	-	15	-	-	-	B
			C	6	-	3	3	-	-	1	-	-	-	-	-	-	-	-	-	-	-	-	-	-	-	12	-	-	-	C
81 **HRG**	be killed	Iq	TOT	3	-	-	2	1	-	8	2	-	2	-	-	-	-	-	-	-	-	-	-	-	-	M	-	-	-	TOT
	Ezek.26:6,//15		A	2	-	-	1	1	-	2	-	-	-	-	-	-	-	-	-	-	-	-	-	-	-	M	-	-	-	A
	Lam.2:20		B	1	-	-	1	-	-	1	1	-	1	-	-	-	-	-	-	-	-	-	-	-	-	M	-	-	-	B
			C	-	-	-	-	-	-	5	1	-	1	-	-	-	-	-	-	-	-	-	-	-	-	M	-	-	-	C
82 **HRS**	be destroyed/be torn down	Iq	TOT	10	2	5	3	-	-	1	-	-	-	-	-	-	-	-	-	-	-	-	-	-	-	30	3	-	-	TOT
	Ezek.36:35,36//30:4/38:20//		A	5	2	2	1	-	-	1	-	-	-	-	-	-	-	-	-	-	-	-	-	-	-	16	2	-	-	A

	ROOT	MEANING	DIV	G	NIPH'AL TOT	NIPH'AL PT	NIPH'AL PF	NIPH'AL IMPF	NIPH'AL INF	NIPH'AL IMPV	PQ	PU'AL TOT	PU'AL PT	PU'AL PF	PU'AL IMPF	PU'AL O	HOPH'AL TOT	HOPH'AL PT	HOPH'AL PF	HOPH'AL IMPF	HOPH'AL O	HITPA'EL TOT	HITPA'EL PT	HITPA'EL PF	HITPA'EL IMPF	HITPA'EL O	QAL	PI	HI	O	G
		Jer.31:40																													
		Pro.24:31//Ps.11:3/Pro.11:11		B	3	-	1	2	-	-	-	-	-	-	-	-	-	-	-	-	-	-	-	-	-	-	8	-	-	-	B
		Jer.50:15/Jo.1:17		C	2	-	2	-	-	-	-	-	-	-	-	-	-	-	-	-	-	-	-	-	-	-	6	1	-	-	C
83	**ZHR**	be warned	Ih	TOT	7	1	4	-	1	1	-	-	-	-	-	-	-	-	-	-	-	-	-	-	-	-	-	-	14	-	TOT
		Ezek.3:21/33:4,5,6//		A	6	-	4	-	1	1	-	-	-	-	-	-	-	-	-	-	-	-	-	-	-	-	-	-	14	-	A
		Eccl.4:13/12:12																													
		Ps.19:12		B	1	1	-	-	-	-	-	-	-	-	-	-	-	-	-	-	-	-	-	-	-	-	-	-	-	-	B
84	**ZWḤ/**	come loose/move	III	TOT	2	-	-	2	-	-	-	-	-	-	-	-	-	-	-	-	-	-	-	-	-	-	-	-	-	-	TOT
	ZḤḤ	Ex.28:28/39:21		A	2	-	-	2	-	-	-	-	-	-	-	-	-	-	-	-	-	-	-	-	-	-	-	-	-	-	A
85	**ZWR**	turn oneself away	I=q	TOT	2	-	2	-	-	-	-	-	-	-	-	-	1	1	-	-	-	-	-	-	-	-	4	-	-	-	TOT
		Ezek.14:15		A	1	-	1	-	-	-	-	-	-	-	-	-	-	-	-	-	-	-	-	-	-	-	-	-	-	-	A
				B	-	-	-	-	-	-	-	-	-	-	-	-	1	1	-	-	-	-	-	-	-	-	4	-	-	-	B
		Isa.1:4		C	1	-	1	-	-	-	-	-	-	-	-	-	-	-	-	-	-	-	-	-	-	-	-	-	-	-	C
86*	**ZKR**	be reminded of	Iq	TOT	19	1	1	16	1	-	1	-	-	-	-	-	-	-	-	-	-	-	-	-	-	-	M	-	41	-	TOT
		Esth.9:28//Num.10:9//Ezek.3:		A	10	1	1	7	1	-	-	-	-	-	-	-	-	-	-	-	-	-	-	-	-	-	M	-	23	-	A
		20/18:22,24/21:37/25:10/33:																													
		13,16//21:29																													
		Ps.83:5/109:4/Job24:20/28:18		B	4	-	-	4	-	-	1	-	-	-	-	-	-	-	-	-	-	-	-	-	-	-	M	-	8	-	B
		Isa.23:16/65:17/Jer.11:19/		C	5	-	-	5	-	-	-	-	-	-	-	-	-	-	-	-	-	-	-	-	-	-	M	-	10	-	C
		Hos.2:19/Zech.13:2																													
87	**ZLL**	quake	II	TOT	3	-	3	-	-	-	-	-	-	-	-	-	-	-	-	-	-	-	-	-	-	-	6	-	1	-	TOT
		Judg.5:5		A	1	-	1	-	-	-	-	-	-	-	-	-	-	-	-	-	-	-	-	-	-	-	1	-	-	-	A
				B	-	-	-	-	-	-	-	-	-	-	-	-	-	-	-	-	-	-	-	-	-	-	4	-	1	-	B
		Isa.63:19/64:2		C	2	-	2	-	-	-	-	-	-	-	-	-	-	-	-	-	-	-	-	-	-	-	1	-	-	-	C
88	**ZMR**	be pruned	Iq	TOT	1	-	-	1	-	-	-	-	-	-	-	-	-	-	-	-	-	-	-	-	-	-	2	-	-	-	TOT
				A	-	-	-	-	-	-	-	-	-	-	-	-	-	-	-	-	-	-	-	-	-	-	2	-	-	-	A
		Isa.5:6		C	1	-	-	1	-	-	-	-	-	-	-	-	-	-	-	-	-	-	-	-	-	-	-	-	-	-	C
89*	**Z'K**	be dried up/burnt out	III	TOT	1	-	1	-	-	-	-	-	-	-	-	-	-	-	-	-	-	-	-	-	-	-	-	-	-	-	TOT
		Job17:1		B	1	-	1	-	-	-	-	-	-	-	-	-	-	-	-	-	-	-	-	-	-	-	-	-	-	-	B
90	**Z'M**	be indignant	Iq	TOT	1	1	-	-	-	-	2	-	-	-	-	-	-	-	-	-	-	-	-	-	-	-	11	-	-	-	TOT
				A	-	-	-	-	-	-	-	-	-	-	-	-	-	-	-	-	-	-	-	-	-	-	1	-	-	-	A
		Pro.25:22		B	1	1	-	-	-	-	1	-	-	-	-	-	-	-	-	-	-	-	-	-	-	-	6	-	-	-	B
				C	-	-	-	-	-	-	1	-	-	-	-	-	-	-	-	-	-	-	-	-	-	-	4	-	-	-	C
91	**Z'Q**	be called up/be summoned	Ih	TOT	6	-	2	4	-	-	-	-	-	-	-	-	-	-	-	-	-	-	-	-	-	-	57	-	7	-	TOT
		Judg.18:22,23//Josh.8:16/		A	6	-	2	4	-	-	-	-	-	-	-	-	-	-	-	-	-	-	-	-	-	-	33	-	5	-	A
		Judg.6:34,35/1Sam.14:20																													
				B	-	-	-	-	-	-	-	-	-	-	-	-	-	-	-	-	-	-	-	-	-	-	7	-	1	-	B
				C	-	-	-	-	-	-	-	-	-	-	-	-	-	-	-	-	-	-	-	-	-	-	17	-	1	-	C
92	**ZRH**	be scattered	Ip	TOT	2	-	-	1	1	-	-	5	1	3	1	-	-	-	-	-	-	-	-	-	-	-	8	27	-	-	TOT
		Ezek.36:19//6:8		A	2	-	-	1	1	-	-	-	-	-	-	-	-	-	-	-	-	-	-	-	-	-	4	12	-	-	A
				B	-	-	-	-	-	-	-	3	1	1	1	-	-	-	-	-	-	-	-	-	-	-	-	7	-	-	B
				C	-		-	-	-	-	-	2	-	2	-	-	-	-	-	-	-	-	-	-	-	-	4	8	-	-	C
93	**ZR'**	be sown	Iq	TOT	6	-	2	4	-	-	2	1	-	1	-	-	-	-	-	-	-	-	-	-	-	-	44	3	-	-	TOT
		Num.5:28/Ezek.36:9//		A	5	-	2	3	-	-	-	-	-	-	-	-	-	-	-	-	-	-	-	-	-	-	20	3	-	-	A
		Lev.11:37/Deut.21:4/29:22																													

	ROOT	MEANING	DIV	G	NIPH'AL TOT	NIPH'AL PT	NIPH'AL PF	NIPH'AL IMPF	NIPH'AL INF	NIPH'AL IMPV	PQ	PU'AL TOT	PU'AL PT	PU'AL PF	PU'AL IMPF	PU'AL O	HOPH'AL TOT	HOPH'AL PT	HOPH'AL PF	HOPH'AL IMPF	HOPH'AL O	HITPA'EL TOT	HITPA'EL PT	HITPA'EL PF	HITPA'EL IMPF	HITPA'EL O	QAL	PI	HI	O	G
				B	-	-	-	-	-	-	1	-	-	-	-	-	-	-	-	-	-	-	-	-	-	-	9	-	-	-	B
		Nah.1:14		C	1	-	-	1	-	-	1	1	-	1	-	-	-	-	-	-	-	-	-	-	-	-	15	-	-	-	C
94	ḤBA/	be hidden/hide oneself	Ih	TOT	19	3	7	4	5	-	-	1	-	1	-	-	1	-	1	-	-	10	5	1	4	-	1	-	6	-	TOT
	ḤBH	see 3.3		A	14	3	5	2	4	-	-	-	-	-	-	-	-	-	-	-	-	9	5	1	3	-	-	-	5	-	A
				B	3	-	2	1	-	-	-	1	-	1	-	-	-	-	-	-	-	1	-	-	1	-	-	-	-	-	B
				C	2	-	-	1	1	-	-	-	-	-	-	-	1	-	1	-	-	-	-	-	-	-	1	-	1	-	C
95	ḤBṬ	be threshed	Iq	TOT	1	-	-	1	-	-	-	-	-	-	-	-	-	-	-	-	-	-	-	-	-	-	4	-	-	-	TOT
				A	-	-	-	-	-	-	-	-	-	-	-	-	-	-	-	-	-	-	-	-	-	-	3	-	-	-	A
		Isa.28:27		C	1	-	-	1	-	-	-	-	-	-	-	-	-	-	-	-	-	-	-	-	-	-	1	-	-	-	C
96	ḤBL	be pledged	Iq	TOT	1	-	-	1	-	-	-	-	-	-	-	-	-	-	-	-	-	-	-	-	-	-	11	-	-	-	TOT
				A	-	-	-	-	-	-	-	-	-	-	-	-	-	-	-	-	-	-	-	-	-	-	5	-	-	-	A
		Pro.13:13		B	1	-	-	1	-	-	-	-	-	-	-	-	-	-	-	-	-	-	-	-	-	-	5	-	-	-	B
				C	-	-	-	-	-	-	-	-	-	-	-	-	-	-	-	-	-	-	-	-	-	-	1	-	-	-	C
97*	ḤLH	be ill	I=q	TOT	10	7	3	-	-	-	-	1	-	1	-	-	3	-	3	-	-	3	-	-	1	2	35	18	4	-	TOT
		Jer.30:12/Ezek.34:4,21 //		A	4	3	1	-	-	-	-	-	-	-	-	-	3	-	3	-	-	3	-	-	1	2	24	9	-	-	A
		Dan. 8:27																													
				B	-	-	-	-	-	-	-	-	-	-	-	-	-	-	-	-	-	-	-	-	-	-	6	5	1	-	B
		Isa.17:11/Jer.10:19/14:17/		C	6	4	2	-	-	-	-	1	-	1	-	-	-	-	-	-	-	-	-	-	-	-	5	4	3	-	C
		Nah.3:19//Jer.12:13/Am.6:6																													
98	ḤLL	be polluted/defile oneself	Ip	TOT	10	-	3	3	4	-	-	1	1	-	-	-	1	-	1	-	-	-	-	-	-	-	-	67	2	-	TOT
		Ezek.7:24/22:16/25:3/Lev.		A	9	-	3	2	4	-	-	1	1	-	-	-	1	-	1	-	-	-	-	-	-	-	-	50	2	-	A
		21:9/Ezek.22:26//20:9,14,																													
		22/Lev.21:4																													
				B	-	-	-	-	-	-	-	-	-	-	-	-	-	-	-	-	-	-	-	-	-	-	-	6	-	-	B
		Isa.48:11		C	1	-	-	1	-	-	-	-	-	-	-	-	-	-	-	-	-	-	-	-	-	-	-	11	-	-	C
99	ḤLṢ	be equipped//be saved*	Iq/p*	TOT	7	-	1	5	-	1	18	-	-	-	-	-	-	-	-	-	-	-	-	-	-	-	22	14	1	-	TOT
		Num.32:17,20//31:3		A	3	-	-	2	-	1	17	-	-	-	-	-	-	-	-	-	-	-	-	-	-	-	18	2	-	-	A
		Pro.11:8*//Ps.60:7/108:7/		B	4	-	1	3	-	-	-	-	-	-	-	-	-	-	-	-	-	-	-	-	-	-	1	12	-	-	B
		Pro.11:9*																													
				C	-	-	-	-	-	-	1	-	-	-	-	-	-	-	-	-	-	-	-	-	-	-	3	-	1	-	C
100	ḤLQ	be divided/divide oneself	Ip	TOT	6	-	-	6	-	-	-	3	-	2	1	-	-	-	-	-	-	1	-	1	-	-	18	28	1?	-	TOT
		Gen.14:15/Num.26:53,55,56/		A	5	-	-	5	-	-	-	-	-	-	-	-	-	-	-	-	-	1	-	1	-	-	13	12	1	-	A
		1Kin.16:21																													
		Job38:24		B	1	-	-	1	-	-	-	-	-	-	-	-	-	-	-	-	-	-	-	-	-	-	4	7	-	-	B
				C	-	-	-	-	-	-	-	3	-	2	1	-	-	-	-	-	-	-	-	-	-	-	1	9	-	-	C
101	ḤMD	desirable	Iq	TOT	4	4	-	-	-	-	3	-	-	-	-	-	-	-	-	-	-	-	-	-	-	-	16	1	-	-	TOT
		Gen.2:9/3:6		A	2	2	-	-	-	-	-	-	-	-	-	-	-	-	-	-	-	-	-	-	-	-	6	-	-	-	A
		Ps.19:11/Pro.21:20		B	2	2	-	-	-	-	2	-	-	-	-	-	-	-	-	-	-	-	-	-	-	-	6	1	-	-	B
				C	-	-	-	-	-	-	1	-	-	-	-	-	-	-	-	-	-	-	-	-	-	-	4	-	-	-	C
102	ḤMM	warm oneself by	I=q	TOT	1	1	-	-	-	-	-	-	-	-	-	-	-	-	-	-	-	1	-	-	1	-	26	1	-	-	TOT
				A	-	-	-	-	-	-	-	-	-	-	-	-	-	-	-	-	-	-	-	-	-	-	14	-	-	-	A
				B	-	-	-	-	-	-	-	-	-	-	-	-	-	-	-	-	-	1	-	-	1	-	5	1	-	-	B
		Isa.57:5		C	1	1	-	-	-	-	-	-	-	-	-	-	-	-	-	-	-	-	-	-	-	-	7	-	-	-	C
103	ḤMS	suffer violence	Iq	TOT	1	-	1	-	-	-	-	-	-	-	-	-	-	-	-	-	-	-	-	-	-	-	7	-	-	-	TOT
				A	-	-	-	-	-	-	-	-	-	-	-	-	-	-	-	-	-	-	-	-	-	-	1	-	-	-	A

	ROOT	MEANING	DIV	G	NIPH'AL TOT	PT	PF	IMPF	INF	IMPV	PQ	PU'AL TOT	PT	PF	IMPF	O	HOPH'AL TOT	PT	PF	IMPF	O	HITPA'EL TOT	PT	PF	IMPF	O	QAL	PI	HI	O	G
				B	-	-	-	-	-	-	-	-	-	-	-	-	-	-	-	-	-	-	-	-	-	-	4	-	-	-	B
		Jer.13:22		C	1	-	1	-	-	-	-	-	-	-	-	-	-	-	-	-	-	-	-	-	-	-	2	-	-	-	C
104	ḤNN	be lamented	Iq	TOT	1	-	1	-	-	-	-	-	-	-	-	-	2	-	-	2	-	17	-	6	9	2	54	1	2	-	TOT
				A	-	-	-	-	-	-	-	-	-	-	-	-	-	-	-	-	-	11	-	6	3	2	12	-	-	-	A
				B	-	-	-	-	-	-	-	-	-	-	-	-	1	-	-	1	-	5	-	-	5	-	35	1	2	-	B
		Jer.22:23		C	1	-	1	-	-	-	-	-	-	-	-	-	1	-	-	1	-	1	-	-	1	-	7	-	-	-	C
105	ḤNQ	hang oneself/strangle oneself	Ip	TOT	1	-	-	1	-	-	-	-	-	-	-	-	-	-	-	-	-	-	-	-	-	-	-	1	-	-	TOT
		2Sam.17:23		A	1	-	-	1	-	-	-	-	-	-	-	-	-	-	-	-	-	-	-	-	-	-	-	-	-	-	A
				C	-	-	-	-	-	-	-	-	-	-	-	-	-	-	-	-	-	-	-	-	-	-	-	1	-	-	C
106	ḤSN	be heaped up	III	TOT	1	-	-	1	-	-	-	-	-	-	-	-	-	-	-	-	-	-	-	-	-	-	-	-	-	-	TOT
		Isa.23:18		C	1	-	-	1	-	-	-	-	-	-	-	-	-	-	-	-	-	-	-	-	-	-	-	-	-	-	C
107*	ḤPH	covered, overlaid	Ip	TOT	1	1	-	-	-	-	2	-	-	-	-	-	-	-	-	-	-	-	-	-	-	-	6	5	-	-	TOT
				A	-	-	-	-	-	-	2	-	-	-	-	-	-	-	-	-	-	-	-	-	-	-	4	5	-	-	A
		Ps.68:14		B	1	1	-	-	-	-	-	-	-	-	-	-	-	-	-	-	-	-	-	-	-	-	-	-	-	-	B
				C	-	-	-	-	-	-	-	-	-	-	-	-	-	-	-	-	-	-	-	-	-	-	2	-	-	-	C
108	ḤPZ	hurry (away)	I=q	TOT	4	1	1	1	1	-	-	-	-	-	-	-	-	-	-	-	-	-	-	-	-	-	6	-	-	-	TOT
		1Sam.23:26//2Kin.7:15(K)		A	2	1	-	-	1	-	-	-	-	-	-	-	-	-	-	-	-	-	-	-	-	-	3	-	-	-	A
		Ps.48:6//104:7		B	2	-	1	1	-	-	-	-	-	-	-	-	-	-	-	-	-	-	-	-	-	-	3	-	-	-	B
109	ḤPŚ	be searched	Iq	TOT	1	-	1	-	-	-	-	2	1	-	1	-	-	-	-	-	-	8	-	1	5	2	4	8	-	-	TOT
				A	-	-	-	-	-	-	-	-	-	-	-	-	-	-	-	-	-	7	-	1	4	2	-	5	-	-	A
				B	-	-	-	-	-	-	-	2	1	-	1	-	-	-	-	-	-	1	-	-	1	-	4	1	-	-	B
		Ob.6		C	1	-	1	-	-	-	-	-	-	-	-	-	-	-	-	-	-	-	-	-	-	-	-	2	-	-	C
110	ḤṢB	be cut out	Iq	TOT	1	-	-	1	-	-	-	1	-	1	-	-	-	-	-	-	-	-	-	-	-	-	22	-	1	-	TOT
				A	-	-	-	-	-	-	-	-	-	-	-	-	-	-	-	-	-	-	-	-	-	-	14	-	-	-	A
		Job19:24		B	1	-	-	1	-	-	-	-	-	-	-	-	-	-	-	-	-	-	-	-	-	-	2	-	-	-	B
				C	-	-	-	-	-	-	-	1	-	1	-	-	-	-	-	-	-	-	-	-	-	-	6	-	1	-	C
111	ḤṢH	be divided/divide oneself	Iq	TOT	4	-	-	4	-	-	-	-	-	-	-	-	-	-	-	-	-	-	-	-	-	-	11	-	-	-	TOT
		2Kin.2:8,14/Ezek.37:22/ Dan.11:4		A	4	-	-	4	-	-	-	-	-	-	-	-	-	-	-	-	-	-	-	-	-	-	8	-	-	-	A
				B	-	-	-	-	-	-	-	-	-	-	-	-	-	-	-	-	-	-	-	-	-	-	2	-	-	-	B
				C	-	-	-	-	-	-	-	-	-	-	-	-	-	-	-	-	-	-	-	-	-	-	1	-	-	-	C
112	ḤQR	be searched out	Iq	TOT	4	-	2	2	-	-	-	-	-	-	-	-	-	-	-	-	-	-	-	-	-	-	22	1	-	-	TOT
		1Kin.7:47/2Chr.4:18// Jer.31:37		A	3	-	2	1	-	-	-	-	-	-	-	-	-	-	-	-	-	-	-	-	-	-	7	-	-	-	A
				B	-	-	-	-	-	-	-	-	-	-	-	-	-	-	-	-	-	-	-	-	-	-	14	1	-	-	B
		Jer.46:23		C	1	-	-	1	-	-	-	-	-	-	-	-	-	-	-	-	-	-	-	-	-	-	1	-	-	-	C
113	ḤRB	I uninhabited/deserted	Iq	TOT	2	2	-	-	-	-	-	-	-	-	-	-	3	1	1	-	1	-	-	-	-	-	16	-	13	-	TOT
		Ezek.26:19/30:7		A	2	2	-	-	-	-	-	-	-	-	-	-	3	1	1	-	1	-	-	-	-	-	5	-	4	-	A
				B	-	-	-	-	-	-	-	-	-	-	-	-	-	-	-	-	-	-	-	-	-	-	2	-	-	-	B
				C	-	-	-	-	-	-	-	-	-	-	-	-	-	-	-	-	-	-	-	-	-	-	9	-	9	-	C
114	ḤRB	II attack each other/fight	Iq	TOT	1	-	1	-	-	-	-	-	-	-	-	-	-	-	-	-	-	-	-	-	-	-	2	-	-	-	TOT
		2Kin.3:23		A	1	-	1	-	-	-	-	-	-	-	-	-	-	-	-	-	-	-	-	-	-	-	-	-	-	-	A
				B	-	-	-	-	-	-	-	-	-	-	-	-	-	-	-	-	-	-	-	-	-	-	-	-	-	-	B
				C	-	-	-	-	-	-	-	-	-	-	-	-	-	-	-	-	-	-	-	-	-	-	2	-	-	-	C
115	ḤRH	be angry with	II	TOT	3	2	1	-	-	-	-	-	-	-	-	-	-	-	-	-	-	4	-	-	4	-	81	-	2	2	TOT

	ROOT	MEANING	DIV	G	NIPH'AL TOT	NIPH'AL PT	NIPH'AL PF	NIPH'AL IMPF	NIPH'AL INF	NIPH'AL IMPV	PQ	PU'AL TOT	PU'AL PT	PU'AL PF	PU'AL IMPF	PU'AL O	HOPH'AL TOT	HOPH'AL PT	HOPH'AL PF	HOPH'AL IMPF	HOPH'AL O	HITPA'EL TOT	HITPA'EL PT	HITPA'EL PF	HITPA'EL IMPF	HITPA'EL O	QAL	PI	HI	O	G
				A	-	-	-	-	-	-	-	-	-	-	-	-	-	-	-	-	-	-	-	-	-	-	69	-	1	-	A
		Song1:6		B	1	-	1	-	-	-	-	-	-	-	-	-	-	-	-	-	-	4	-	-	4	-	5	-	1	-	B
		Isa.41:11/45:24		C	2	2	-	-	-	-	-	-	-	-	-	-	-	-	-	-	-	-	-	-	-	-	8	-	-	2	C
116	ḤRP	submitted	III	TOT	1	1	-	-	-	-	-	-	-	-	-	-	-	-	-	-	-	-	-	-	-	-	-	-	-	-	TOT
		Lev.19:20		A	1	1	-	-	-	-	-	-	-	-	-	-	-	-	-	-	-	-	-	-	-	-	-	-	-	-	A
117	ḤRṢ	be determined/decreed	Iq	TOT	5	5	-	-	-	-	3	-	-	-	-	-	-	-	-	-	-	-	-	-	-	-	7	-	-	-	TOT
		Dan.9:26,27/11:36		A	3	3	-	-	-	-	1	-	-	-	-	-	-	-	-	-	-	-	-	-	-	-	5	-	-	-	A
				B	-	-	-	-	-	-	1	-	-	-	-	-	-	-	-	-	-	-	-	-	-	-	1	-	-	-	B
		Isa.10:23/28:22		C	2	2	-	-	-	-	1	-	-	-	-	-	-	-	-	-	-	-	-	-	-	-	1	-	-	-	C
118*	ḤRR	be burnt/scorched	Iq	TOT	6	-	4	2	-	-	-	-	-	-	-	-	-	-	-	-	-	-	-	-	-	-	3	-	-	1	TOT
		Ezek.15:4//15:5/24:10		A	3	-	1	2	-	-	-	-	-	-	-	-	-	-	-	-	-	-	-	-	-	-	1	-	-	-	A
		Ps.69:4/102:4		B	2	-	2	-	-	-	-	-	-	-	-	-	-	-	-	-	-	-	-	-	-	-	1	-	-	1	B
		Jer.6:29		C	1	-	1	-	-	-	-	-	-	-	-	-	-	-	-	-	-	-	-	-	-	-	1	-	-	-	C
119	ḤRŠ	be ploughed	Iq	TOT	2	-	-	2	-	-	1	-	-	-	-	-	-	-	-	-	-	-	-	-	-	-	23	-	1	-	TOT
		Jer.26:18		A	1	-	-	1	-	-	-	-	-	-	-	-	-	-	-	-	-	-	-	-	-	-	6	-	1	-	A
				B	-	-	-	-	-	-	-	-	-	-	-	-	-	-	-	-	-	-	-	-	-	-	10	-	-	-	B
		Mi.3:12		C	1	-	-	1	-	-	1	-	-	-	-	-	-	-	-	-	-	-	-	-	-	-	7	-	-	-	C
120	ḤŠB	be counted/considered	Iq	TOT	30	3	13	14	-	-	-	-	-	-	-	-	-	-	-	-	-	1	-	-	1	-	77	16	-	-	TOT
		see 3.3		A	14	2	4	8	-	-	-	-	-	-	-	-	-	-	-	-	-	-	-	-	-	-	35	8	-	-	A
				B	8	-	5	3	-	-	-	-	-	-	-	-	-	-	-	-	-	1	-	-	1	-	21	6	-	-	B
				C	8	1	4	3	-	-	-	-	-	-	-	-	-	-	-	-	-	-	-	-	-	-	21	2	-	-	C
121	ḤŚK	be saved, be repayed	Iq	TOT	2	-	-	2	-	-	-	-	-	-	-	-	-	-	-	-	-	-	-	-	-	-	26	-	-	-	TOT
				A	-	-	-	-	-	-	-	-	-	-	-	-	-	-	-	-	-	-	-	-	-	-	9	-	-	-	A
		Job16:6/21:30		B	2	-	-	2	-	-	-	-	-	-	-	-	-	-	-	-	-	-	-	-	-	-	13	-	-	-	B
				C	-	-	-	-	-	-	-	-	-	-	-	-	-	-	-	-	-	-	-	-	-	-	4	-	-	-	C
122	ḤŠL	weak/exhausted	III	TOT	1	1	-	-	-	-	-	-	-	-	-	-	-	-	-	-	-	-	-	-	-	-	-	-	-	-	TOT
		Deut.25:18		A	1	1	-	-	-	-	-	-	-	-	-	-	-	-	-	-	-	-	-	-	-	-	-	-	-	-	A
123	ḤTK	be determined	III	TOT	1	-	1	-	-	-	-	-	-	-	-	-	-	-	-	-	-	-	-	-	-	-	-	-	-	-	TOT
		Dan.9:24		A	1	-	1	-	-	-	-	-	-	-	-	-	-	-	-	-	-	-	-	-	-	-	-	-	-	-	A
124	ḤTM	be sealed	Iq	TOT	2	-	1	-	1	-	10	-	-	-	-	-	-	-	-	-	-	-	-	-	-	-	22	1	1	-	TOT
		Esth.3:12//8:8		A	2	-	1	-	1	-	5	-	-	-	-	-	-	-	-	-	-	-	-	-	-	-	12	-	1	-	A
				B	-	-	-	-	-	-	3	-	-	-	-	-	-	-	-	-	-	-	-	-	-	-	6	1	-	-	B
				C	-	-	-	-	-	-	2	-	-	-	-	-	-	-	-	-	-	-	-	-	-	-	4	-	-	-	C
125	ḤTT	be frightened/cast down	I=q/	TOT	30	-	1	29	-	-	-	-	-	-	-	-	-	-	-	-	-	-	-	-	-	-	15	2	5	-	TOT
		see 3.3	p*	A	14	-	-	14	-	-	-	-	-	-	-	-	-	-	-	-	-	-	-	-	-	-	-	-	-	-	A
				B	3	-	-	3	-	-	-	-	-	-	-	-	-	-	-	-	-	-	-	-	-	-	2	1	1	-	B
				C	13	-	1	12	-	-	-	-	-	-	-	-	-	-	-	-	-	-	-	-	-	-	13	1	4	-	C
126	TBL	be immersed	Iq	TOT	1	-	1	-	-	-	-	-	-	-	-	-	-	-	-	-	-	-	-	-	-	-	15	-	-	-	TOT
		Josh.3:15		A	1	-	1	-	-	-	-	-	-	-	-	-	-	-	-	-	-	-	-	-	-	-	13	-	-	-	A
				B	-	-	-	-	-	-	-	-	-	-	-	-	-	-	-	-	-	-	-	-	-	-	2	-	-	-	B
127	TWḤ	be plastered/be spread over	Iq	TOT	2	-	-	-	2	-	-	-	-	-	-	-	-	-	-	-	-	-	-	-	-	-	9	-	-	-	TOT
		Lev.14:43,48		A	2	-	-	-	2	-	-	-	-	-	-	-	-	-	-	-	-	-	-	-	-	-	9	-	-	-	A
128*	TMA	defile oneself	Ip	TOT	18	2	16	-	-	-	-	1	1	-	-	-	-	-	-	-	-	15	-	-	15	-	75	49	-	1	TOT
		Lev.11:43/18:24//Num.5:13,		A	15	2	13	-	-	-	-	1	1	-	-	-	-	-	-	-	-	14	-	-	14	-	71	45	-	1	A
		14(2x),20,27,28,29/Ezek.20:																													

					NIPH'AL						PQ	PU'AL					HOPH'AL					HITPA'EL					QAL	PI	HI	O	
	ROOT	MEANING	DIV	G	TOT	PT	PF	IMPF	INF	IMPV		TOT	PT	PF	IMPF	O	TOT	PT	PF	IMPF	O	TOT	PT	PF	IMPF	O					G
		30(2x),31,43/23:7,13																													
				B	-	-	-	-	-	-	-	-	-	-	-	-	-	-	-	-	-	-	-	-	-	-	1	4	-	-	B
		Jer.2:23/Hos.5:3/6:10		C	3	-	3	-	-	-	-	-	-	-	-	-	-	-	-	-	-	1	-	-	1	-	3	1	-	-	C
129*	JMH	defile oneself/be defiled	III	TOT	2	-	2	-	-	-	-	-	-	-	-	-	-	-	-	-	-	-	-	-	-	-	-	-	-	-	TOT
		Lev.11:43		A	1	-	1	-	-	-	-	-	-	-	-	-	-	-	-	-	-	-	-	-	-	-	-	-	-	-	A
		Job18:13		B	1	-	1	-	-	-	-	-	-	-	-	-	-	-	-	-	-	-	-	-	-	-	-	-	-	-	B
130	JMN	hide oneself	Iq	TOT	1	-	-	-	-	1	7	-	-	-	-	-	-	-	-	-	-	-	-	-	-	-	28	-	2	-	TOT
				A	-	-	-	-	-	-	2	-	-	-	-	-	-	-	-	-	-	-	-	-	-	-	7	-	2	-	A
				B	-	-	-	-	-	-	5	-	-	-	-	-	-	-	-	-	-	-	-	-	-	-	16	-	-	-	B
		Isa.2:10		C	1	-	-	-	-	1	-	-	-	-	-	-	-	-	-	-	-	-	-	-	-	-	5	-	-	-	C
131	JRP	be torn	Iq	TOT	2	-	-	2	-	-	-	2	-	2	-	-	-	-	-	-	-	-	-	-	-	-	20	-	1	-	TOT
		Ex.22:12		A	1	-	-	1	-	-	-	2	-	2	-	-	-	-	-	-	-	-	-	-	-	-	5	-	-	-	A
				B	-	-	-	-	-	-	-	-	-	-	-	-	-	-	-	-	-	-	-	-	-	-	8	-	1	-	B
		Jer.5:6		C	1	-	-	1	-	-	-	-	-	-	-	-	-	-	-	-	-	-	-	-	-	-	7	-	-	-	C
132	JAL	act foolishly	III	TOT	4	-	4	-	-	-	-	-	-	-	-	-	-	-	-	-	-	-	-	-	-	-	-	-	-	-	TOT
		Num.12:11		A	1	-	1	-	-	-	-	-	-	-	-	-	-	-	-	-	-	-	-	-	-	-	-	-	-	-	A
		Isa.19:13/Jer.5:4/50:36		C	3	-	3	-	-	-	-	-	-	-	-	-	-	-	-	-	-	-	-	-	-	-	-	-	-	-	C
133*	JAŠ	despair	II	TOT	5	4	1	-	-	-	-	-	-	-	-	-	-	-	-	-	-	-	-	-	-	-	-	1	-	-	TOT
		1Sam.27:1		A	1	-	1	-	-	-	-	-	-	-	-	-	-	-	-	-	-	-	-	-	-	-	-	-	-	-	A
		Job6:26		B	1	1	-	-	-	-	-	-	-	-	-	-	-	-	-	-	-	-	-	-	-	-	-	1	-	-	B
		Isa.57:10/Jer.2:25/18:12		C	3	3	-	-	-	-	-	-	-	-	-	-	-	-	-	-	-	-	-	-	-	-	-	-	-	-	C
134	JGH	grieved	Ih	TOT	2	2	-	-	-	-	-	-	-	-	-	-	-	-	-	-	-	-	-	-	-	-	-	1	5	-	TOT
		Lam.1:4		B	1	1	-	-	-	-	-	-	-	-	-	-	-	-	-	-	-	-	-	-	-	-	-	1	4	-	B
		Zeph.3:18		C	1	1	-	-	-	-	-	-	-	-	-	-	-	-	-	-	-	-	-	-	-	-	-	-	1	-	C
135*	JD'	be known/be instructed	Iq/h?	TOT	41	3	21	16	1	-	3	8	8	-	-	-	3	1	2	-	-	2	-	-	1	1	M	1	71	1	TOT
		See 3.3		A	25	1	14	9	1	-	2	2	2	-	-	-	2	-	2	-	-	2	-	-	1	1	M	-	31	1	A
				B	11	2	3	6	-	-	-	5	5	-	-	-	-	-	-	-	-	-	-	-	-	-	M	1	28	-	B
				C	5	-	4	1	-	-	1	1	1	-	-	-	1	1	-	-	-	-	-	-	-	-	M	-	12	-	C
136*	JḤL	wait	I=p/h	TOT	2	-	1	1	-	-	-	-	-	-	-	-	-	-	-	-	-	-	-	-	-	-	-	24	14	-	TOT
		Ezek.19:5//Gen.8:12		A	2	-	1	1	-	-	-	-	-	-	-	-	-	-	-	-	-	-	-	-	-	-	-	1	4	-	A
				B	-	-	-	-	-	-	-	-	-	-	-	-	-	-	-	-	-	-	-	-	-	-	-	20	9	-	B
				C	-	-	-	-	-	-	-	-	-	-	-	-	-	-	-	-	-	-	-	-	-	-	-	3	1	-	C
137	JKḤ	fight with each other/	II	TOT	3	1	1	1	-	-	-	-	-	-	-	-	1	-	1	-	-	1	-	-	1	-	-	-	54	-	TOT
		be set right*																													
		Gen.20:16*		A	1	-	1	-	-	-	-	-	-	-	-	-	-	-	-	-	-	-	-	-	-	-	-	-	13	-	A
		Job23:7		B	1	1	-	-	-	-	-	-	-	-	-	-	1	-	1	-	-	-	-	-	-	-	-	-	32	-	B
		Isa.1:18		C	1	-	-	1	-	-	-	-	-	-	-	-	-	-	-	-	-	1	-	-	1	-	-	-	9	-	C
138	JLD	be born	Iq	TOT	38	7	9	19	3	-	6	26	1	25	-	-	3	-	-	-	3	1	-	-	1	-	M	10	M	-	TOT
		see 3.3		A	28	6	9	11	2	-	3	18	1	17	-	-	3	-	-	-	3	1	-	-	1	-	M	10	M	-	A
				B	8	1	-	7	-	-	3	5	-	5	-	-	-	-	-	-	-	-	-	-	-	-	M	-	3	-	B
				C	2	-	-	1	1	-	-	3	-	3	-	-	-	-	-	-	-	-	-	-	-	-	M	-	6	-	C
139	JSD	be founded/conspire*	* Iq/	TOT	4	-	1	1	2	-	-	7	3	4	-	-	3	1	2	-	-	-	-	-	-	-	19	10	-	-	TOT
		Ex.9:18	II*	A	1	-	-	-	1	-	-	4	2	2	-	-	2	-	2	-	-	-	-	-	-	-	2	6	-	-	A
		Ps.2:2*//31:14*		B	2	-	1	-	1	-	-	1	1	-	-	-	-	-	-	-	-	-	-	-	-	-	9	1	-	-	B
		Isa.44:28		C	1	-	-	1	-	-	-	2	-	2	-	-	1	1	-	-	-	-	-	-	-	-	8	3	-	-	C

	ROOT	MEANING	DIV	G	NIPH'AL TOT	PT	PF	IMPF	INF	IMPV	PQ	PU'AL TOT	PT	PF	IMPF	O	HOPH'AL TOT	PT	PF	IMPF	O	HITPA'EL TOT	PT	PF	IMPF	O	QAL	PI	HI	O	G
140	**JSP**	be added/add oneself	Iq	TOT	6	2	4	-	-	-	-	-	-	-	-	-	-	-	-	-	-	-	-	-	-	-	31	-	M	-	TOT
		Ex.1:10/Num.36:3,4/Jer.36:32		A	4	-	4	-	-	-	-	-	-	-	-	-	-	-	-	-	-	-	-	-	-	-	26	-	M	-	A
		Pro.11:24		B	1	1	-	-	-	-	-	-	-	-	-	-	-	-	-	-	-	-	-	-	-	-	-	-	M	-	B
		Isa.15:19		C	1	1	-	-	-	-	-	-	-	-	-	-	-	-	-	-	-	-	-	-	-	-	5	-	M	-	C
141	**JSR**	be corrected/chastened	Iq	TOT	5	-	-	3	-	2	-	-	-	-	-	-	-	-	-	-	-	-	-	-	-	-	3	32	1	1	TOT
		Lev.26:23/Jer.31:18		A	2	-	-	2	-	-	-	-	-	-	-	-	-	-	-	-	-	-	-	-	-	-	-	15	-	1	A
		Pro.29:19//Ps.2:10		B	2	-	-	1	-	1	-	-	-	-	-	-	-	-	-	-	-	-	-	-	-	-	2	11	-	-	B
		Jer.31:18		C	1	-	-	-	-	1	-	-	-	-	-	-	-	-	-	-	-	-	-	-	-	-	1	6	1	-	C
142*	**J'D**	assemble/gather oneself	II	TOT	19	5	6	8	-	-	-	-	-	-	-	-	2	2	-	-	-	-	-	-	-	-	5	-	3	-	TOT
		Num.14:35/16:11/27:3/1Kin.8:5 /2Chr.5:6//Ex.25:22/19:43/Num. 10:3,4//Ex.29:42/30:6,36/Num. 17:19/Josh.11:5/Neh.6:2.10		A	16	5	4	7	-	-	-	-	-	-	-	-	1	1	-	-	-	-	-	-	-	-	3	-	-	-	A
		Ps.48:5//Job2:11		B	2	-	1	1	-	-	-	-	-	-	-	-	-	-	-	-	-	-	-	-	-	-	-	-	1	-	B
		Am.3:3		C	1	-	1	-	-	-	-	-	-	-	-	-	1	1	-	-	-	-	-	-	-	-	2	-	2	-	C
143	**J'Z**	impudent/shameless	III	TOT	1	1	-	-	-	-	-	-	-	-	-	-	-	-	-	-	-	-	-	-	-	-	-	-	-	-	TOT
		Isa.33:19		C	1	1	-	-	-	-	-	-	-	-	-	-	-	-	-	-	-	-	-	-	-	-	-	-	-	-	C
144	**J'Ṣ**	consult with/take counsel	Iq	TOT	22	5	3	14	-	-	1	-	-	-	-	-	-	-	-	-	-	1	-	-	1	-	59	-	-	-	TOT
		1Kin.12:6,9/2Chr.10:6,9//1Kin. 12:6,8,28/2Kin.6:8/1Chr.13:1/ 2Chr.10:6,8/20:21/25:17/30:2, 23/32:3/Neh.6:7		A	17	4	-	13	-	-	-	-	-	-	-	-	-	-	-	-	-	-	-	-	-	-	26	-	-	-	A
		Pro.13:10//Ps.71:10/83:6		B	3	1	2	-	-	-	-	-	-	-	-	-	-	-	-	-	-	1	-	-	1	-	10	-	-	-	B
		Isa.40:14//45:21		C	2	-	1	1	-	-	1	-	-	-	-	-	-	-	-	-	-	-	-	-	-	-	23	-	-	-	C
145	**JṢR**	be formed	Iq	TOT	1	-	1	-	-	-	-	1	-	1	-	-	1	-	-	1	-	-	-	-	-	-	58	-	-	-	TOT
				A	-	-	-	-	-	-	-	-	-	-	-	-	-	-	-	-	-	-	-	-	-	-	9	-	-	-	A
				B	-	-	-	-	-	-	-	1	-	1	-	-	-	-	-	-	-	-	-	-	-	-	9	-	-	-	B
		Isa.43:10		C	1	-	1	-	-	-	-	-	-	-	-	-	1	-	-	1	-	-	-	-	-	-	40	-	-	-	C
146*	**JṢT/ ṢWT**	be burned/burn	Iq	TOT	9	-	9	-	-	-	-	-	-	-	-	-	-	-	-	-	-	-	-	-	-	-	4	-	-	-	TOT
		2Kin.22:13,17/Neh.1:3/2:17		A	4	-	4	-	-	-	-	-	-	-	-	-	-	-	-	-	-	-	-	-	-	-	-	-	-	-	A
				B	-	-	-	-	-	-	-	-	-	-	-	-	-	-	-	-	-	-	-	-	-	-	-	-	-	-	B
		Jer.2:15(2x)/9:9,11/46:19		C	5	-	5	-	-	-	-	-	-	-	-	-	-	-	-	-	-	-	-	-	-	-	4	-	-	-	C
147*	**JQŠ/ QWŠ**	be caught	Iq	TOT	5	-	4	1	-	-	-	-	-	-	-	-	1	1	-	-	-	-	-	-	-	-	4	-	17	-	TOT
		Deut.7:25		A	1	-	-	1	-	-	-	-	-	-	-	-	1	1	-	-	-	-	-	-	-	-	-	-	9	-	A
		Ps.9:17/Pro.6:2		B	2	-	2	-	-	-	-	-	-	-	-	-	-	-	-	-	-	-	-	-	-	-	2	-	1	-	B
		Isa.8:15/28:13		C	2	-	2	-	-	-	-	-	-	-	-	-	-	-	-	-	-	-	-	-	-	-	2	-	7	-	C
148	**JRA**	fearful/be feared	Iq	TOT	45	44	-	1	-	-	-	-	-	-	-	-	-	-	-	-	-	-	-	-	-	-	M	5	-	-	TOT
		see 3.3		A	16	16	-	-	-	-	-	-	-	-	-	-	-	-	-	-	-	-	-	-	-	-	M	5	-	-	A
				B	19	18	-	1	-	-	-	-	-	-	-	-	-	-	-	-	-	-	-	-	-	-	M	-	-	-	B
				C	10	10	-	-	-	-	-	-	-	-	-	-	-	-	-	-	-	-	-	-	-	-	M	-	-	-	C
149	**JRH**	be shot through (by arrows)	Iq	TOT	1	-	-	1	-	-	-	-	-	-	-	-	-	-	-	-	-	-	-	-	-	-	15	-	17	-	TOT
		Ex.19:13		A	1	-	-	1	-	-	-	-	-	-	-	-	-	-	-	-	-	-	-	-	-	-	10	-	12	-	A
				B	-	-	-	-	-	-	-	-	-	-	-	-	-	-	-	-	-	-	-	-	-	-	5	-	3	-	B
				C	-	-	-	-	-	-	-	-	-	-	-	-	-	-	-	-	-	-	-	-	-	-	-	-	2	-	C
150	**JRŠ**	be empoverished	II	TOT	4	-	-	4	-	-	-	-	-	-	-	-	-	-	-	-	-	-	-	-	-	-	M	2	66	-	TOT

ROOT		MEANING	DIV	G	NIPH'AL TOT	PT	PF	IMPF	INF	IMPV	PQ	PU'AL TOT	PT	PF	IMPF	O	HOPH'AL TOT	PT	PF	IMPF	O	HITPA'EL TOT	PT	PF	IMPF	O	QAL	PI	HI	O	G
		Gen.45:11		A	1	-	-	1	-	-	-	-	-	-	-	-	-	-	-	-	-	-	-	-	-	-	M	2	61	-	A
		Pro.20:13/23:21/30:9		B	3	-	-	3	-	-	-	-	-	-	-	-	-	-	-	-	-	-	-	-	-	-	M	-	4	-	B
				C	-	-	-	-	-	-	-	-	-	-	-	-	-	-	-	-	-	-	-	-	-	-	M	-	1	-	C
151	**JŠB**	be inhabited	Iq	TOT	9	4	5	-	-	-	-	-	-	-	-	-	2	-	1	1	-	-	-	-	-	-	M	1	37	-	TOT
		Ex.16:35/Ezek.12:20/26:17/ 38:12//26:19/36:10		A	6	4	2	-	-	-	-	-	-	-	-	-	-	-	-	-	-	-	-	-	-	-	M	1	25	-	A
				B	-	-	-	-	-	-	-	-	-	-	-	-	-	-	-	-	-	-	-	-	-	-	M	-	8	-	B
		Jer.6:8/22:6(2x)		C	3	-	3	-	-	-	-	-	-	-	-	-	2	-	1	1	-	-	-	-	-	-	M	-	4	-	C
152	**JŠN**	become old	III	TOT	3	2	1	-	-	-	-	-	-	-	-	-	-	-	-	-	-	-	-	-	-	-	-	-	-	-	TOT
		Lev.13:11/26:10//Deut.4:25		A	3	2	1	-	-	-	-	-	-	-	-	-	-	-	-	-	-	-	-	-	-	-	-	-	-	-	A
153	**JŠ'**	be saved/delivered	Ih	TOT	21	2	4	14	-	1	-	-	-	-	-	-	-	-	-	-	-	-	-	-	-	-	-	-	M	-	TOT
		Num.10:9//Jer.30:7/33:16		A	3	-	1	2	-	-	-	-	-	-	-	-	-	-	-	-	-	-	-	-	-	-	-	-	M	-	A
		Ps.33:16//Deut.33:29//2Sam.22: 4/Ps.18:4/80:4,8,20/119:117/ Pro.28:18		B	9	1	1	7	-	-	-	-	-	-	-	-	-	-	-	-	-	-	-	-	-	-	-	-	M	-	B
		Zech.9:9//Jer.8:20/Isa.45:17// 30:15/64:4/Jer.4:14/17:14/23: 6//Isa.45:22		C	9	1	2	5	-	1	-	-	-	-	-	-	-	-	-	-	-	-	-	-	-	-	-	-	M	-	C
154	**JTR**	be left over	Ih	TOT	81	51	18	12	-	-	-	-	-	-	-	-	-	-	-	-	-	-	-	-	-	-	-	-	24	-	TOT
		see 3.3		A	71	48	15	8	-	-	-	-	-	-	-	-	-	-	-	-	-	-	-	-	-	-	-	-	21	-	A
				B	2	-	1	1	-	-	-	-	-	-	-	-	-	-	-	-	-	-	-	-	-	-	-	-	2	-	B
				C	8	3	2	3	-	-	-	-	-	-	-	-	-	-	-	-	-	-	-	-	-	-	-	-	1	-	C
155	**K'H**	be terrified/deterred	II	TOT	2	1	1	-	-	-	-	-	-	-	-	-	-	-	-	-	-	-	-	-	-	-	-	-	1	-	TOT
		Dan.11:30		A	1	-	1	-	-	-	-	-	-	-	-	-	-	-	-	-	-	-	-	-	-	-	-	-	1	-	A
		Ps.109:16		B	1	1	-	-	-	-	-	-	-	-	-	-	-	-	-	-	-	-	-	-	-	-	-	-	-	-	B
156	**KBD**	be honoured/glorify oneself	Ip	TOT	31	17	4	7	2	1	3	1	-	2	-	-	-	-	-	-	-	3	1	-	-	2	22	37	17	-	TOT
		see 3.3		A	19	10	2	4	2	1	-	-	-	-	-	-	-	-	-	-	-	-	-	-	-	-	12	18	11	-	A
				B	3	3	-	-	-	-	2	-	-	2	-	-	-	-	-	-	-	1	1	-	-	-	7	12	1	-	B
				C	9	4	2	3	-	-	1	1	-	-	-	-	-	-	-	-	-	2	-	-	-	2	3	7	5	-	C
157	**KBŠ**	be subjected	Iq	TOT	5	1	4	-	-	-	-	-	-	-	-	-	-	-	-	-	-	-	-	-	-	-	8	1	1	-	TOT
		Neh.5:5//Num.32:22,29/Josh. 18:1/1Chr.22:18		A	5	1	4	-	-	-	-	-	-	-	-	-	-	-	-	-	-	-	-	-	-	-	6	1	1	-	A
				C	-	-	-	-	-	-	-	-	-	-	-	-	-	-	-	-	-	-	-	-	-	-	2	-	-	-	C
158	**KWH**	be burned	III	TOT	2	-	-	2	-	-	-	-	-	-	-	-	-	-	-	-	-	-	-	-	-	-	-	-	-	-	TOT
		Pro.6:28		B	1	-	-	1	-	-	-	-	-	-	-	-	-	-	-	-	-	-	-	-	-	-	-	-	-	-	B
		Isa.43:2		C	1	-	-	1	-	-	-	-	-	-	-	-	-	-	-	-	-	-	-	-	-	-	-	-	-	-	C
159	**KWN**	be fixed/arranged	Ip(h?)	TOT	68	37	3	25	-	3	-	-	-	-	-	-	6	2	4	-	-	4	-	-	4	-	-	M	29	-	TOT
		see 3.3		A	29	18	2	7	-	2	-	-	-	-	-	-	1	1	-	-	-	1	-	-	1	-	-	M	3	-	A
				B	35	16	1	18	-	-	-	-	-	-	-	-	1	1	-	-	-	2	-	-	2	-	-	M	22	-	B
				C	4	3	-	-	-	1	-	-	-	-	-	-	4	-	4	-	-	1	-	-	1	-	-	M	4	-	C
160	**KZB**	be deceived/be regarded as	Ip	TOT	2	-	2	-	-	-	-	-	-	-	-	-	-	-	-	-	-	-	-	-	-	-	1	12	1	-	TOT
				A	-	-	-	-	-	-	-	-	-	-	-	-	-	-	-	-	-	-	-	-	-	-	-	2	-	-	A
		Pro.30:6/Job41:1		B	2	-	2	-	-	-	-	-	-	-	-	-	-	-	-	-	-	-	-	-	-	-	1	6	1	-	B
				C	-	-	-	-	-	-	-	-	-	-	-	-	-	-	-	-	-	-	-	-	-	-	-	4	-	-	C
161	**KḤD**	be destroyed/be concealed	Ip	TOT	11	3	5	3	-	-	-	-	-	-	-	-	-	-	-	-	-	[illegible]	[illegible]	[illegible]	[illegible]	[illegible]	[illegible]	[illegible]	[illegible]	[illegible]	[illegible]

	ROOT	MEANING	DIV	G	NIPH'AL TOT	NIPH'AL PT	NIPH'AL PF	NIPH'AL IMPF	NIPH'AL INF	NIPH'AL IMPV	PQ	PU'AL TOT	PU'AL PT	PU'AL PF	PU'AL IMPF	PU'AL O	HOPH'AL TOT	HOPH'AL PT	HOPH'AL PF	HOPH'AL IMPF	HOPH'AL O	HITPA'EL TOT	HITPA'EL PT	HITPA'EL PF	HITPA'EL IMPF	HITPA'EL O	QAL	PI	HI	O	G
		Ex.9:15/2Sam.18:13		A	2	-	-	2	-	-	-	-	-	-	-	-	-	-	-	-	-	-	-	-	-	-	-	7	3	-	A
		Job15:28//Ps.69:6/139:15/ Job4:7/22:20		B	5	1	4	-	-	-	-	-	-	-	-	-	-	-	-	-	-	-	-	-	-	-	-	5	2	-	B
		Zech.11:9,16//Hos.5:3// Zech.11:9		C	4	2	1	1	-	-	-	-	-	-	-	-	-	-	-	-	-	-	-	-	-	-	-	2	1	-	C
162	**KḤŠ**	cringe (hypocritically)	Ip	TOT	1	-	-	1	-	-	-	-	-	-	-	-	-	-	-	-	-	1	-	-	1	-	1	19	-	-	TOT
				A	-	-	-	-	-	-	-	-	-	-	-	-	-	-	-	-	-	1	-	-	1	-	-	7	-	-	A
		Deut.33:29		B	1	-	-	1	-	-	-	-	-	-	-	-	-	-	-	-	-	-	-	-	-	-	1	6	-	-	B
				C	-	-	-	-	-	-	-	-	-	-	-	-	-	-	-	-	-	-	-	-	-	-	-	6	-	-	C
163	**KLA**	restrain/be stopped	Ih	TOT	3	-	-	3	-	-	2	-	-	-	-	-	-	-	-	-	-	-	-	-	-	-	14	1	-	-	TOT
		Gen.8:2/Ex.31:15/36:6		A	3	-	-	3	-	-	1	-	-	-	-	-	-	-	-	-	-	-	-	-	-	-	6	1	-	-	A
				B	-	-	-	-	-	-	1	-	-	-	-	-	-	-	-	-	-	-	-	-	-	-	3	-	-	-	B
				C	-	-	-	-	-	-	-	-	-	-	-	-	-	-	-	-	-	-	-	-	-	-	5	-	-	-	C
164	**KLM**	be embarrassed/be humiliated	Ih	TOT	26	5	9	9	2	1	-	-	-	-	-	-	2	-	2	-	-	-	-	-	-	-	-	-	10	-	TOT
		see 3.3		A	13	4	6	2	-	1	-	-	-	-	-	-	1	-	1	-	-	-	-	-	-	-	-	-	4	-	A
				B	5	1	-	4	-	-	-	-	-	-	-	-	-	-	-	-	-	-	-	-	-	-	-	-	5	-	B
				C	8	-	3	3	2	-	-	-	-	-	-	-	1	-	1	-	-	-	-	-	-	-	-	-	1	-	C
165	**KMR**	grow warm/tender	III	TOT	4	-	4	-	-	-	-	-	-	-	-	-	-	-	-	-	-	-	-	-	-	-	-	-	-	-	TOT
		Gen.43:30/1Kin.3:26		A	2	-	2	-	-	-	-	-	-	-	-	-	-	-	-	-	-	-	-	-	-	-	-	-	-	-	A
		Lam.5:10		B	1	-	1	-	-	-	-	-	-	-	-	-	-	-	-	-	-	-	-	-	-	-	-	-	-	-	B
		Hos.11:8		C	1	-	1	-	-	-	-	-	-	-	-	-	-	-	-	-	-	-	-	-	-	-	-	-	-	-	C
166	**KN'**	humble/subject oneself	Ih	TOT	25	-	7	15	3	-	-	-	-	-	-	-	-	-	-	-	-	-	-	-	-	-	-	-	11	-	TOT
		see 3.3		A	24	-	7	14	3	-	-	-	-	-	-	-	-	-	-	-	-	-	-	-	-	-	-	-	7	-	A
				B	1	-	-	1	-	-	-	-	-	-	-	-	-	-	-	-	-	-	-	-	-	-	-	-	3	-	B
				C	-	-	-	-	-	-	-	-	-	-	-	-	-	-	-	-	-	-	-	-	-	-	-	-	1	-	C
167	**KNP**	hide oneself	III	TOT	1	-	-	1	-	-	-	-	-	-	-	-	-	-	-	-	-	-	-	-	-	-	-	-	-	-	TOT
		Isa.30:20		C	1	-	-	1	-	-	-	-	-	-	-	-	-	-	-	-	-	-	-	-	-	-	-	-	-	-	C
168	**KSH**	be covered	Ip	TOT	2	-	1	-	1	-	1	7	2	2	3	-	-	-	-	-	-	9	3	-	6	-	3	M	-	-	TOT
		Ezek.24:8		A	1	-	-	-	1	-	-	4	2	-	2	-	-	-	-	-	-	7	3	-	4	-	-	M	-	-	A
				B	-	-	-	-	-	-	1	3	-	2	1	-	-	-	-	-	-	1	-	-	1	-	3	M	-	-	B
		Jer.51:42		C	1	-	1	-	-	-	-	-	-	-	-	-	-	-	-	-	-	1	-	-	1	-	-	M	-	-	C
169	**KSP**	long greatly/unashamed*	I=q	TOT	4	2	2	-	1	-	-	-	-	-	-	-	-	-	-	-	-	-	-	-	-	-	2	-	-	-	TOT
		Gen.31:30//31:30	/II*	A	2	-	1	-	1	-	-	-	-	-	-	-	-	-	-	-	-	-	-	-	-	-	-	-	-	-	A
		Ps.84:3		B	1	1	-	-	-	-	-	-	-	-	-	-	-	-	-	-	-	-	-	-	-	-	2	-	-	-	B
		Zeph.2:1*		C	1	1	-	-	-	-	-	-	-	-	-	-	-	-	-	-	-	-	-	-	-	-	-	-	-	-	C
170	**KPL**	be doubled	Iq	TOT	1	-	-	1	-	-	2	-	-	-	-	-	-	-	-	-	-	-	-	-	-	-	3	-	-	-	TOT
		Ezek.21:19		A	1	-	-	1	-	-	2	-	-	-	-	-	-	-	-	-	-	-	-	-	-	-	3	-	-	-	A
171	**KPP**	bow oneself	Iq	TOT	1	-	-	1	-	-	2	-	-	-	-	-	-	-	-	-	-	-	-	-	-	-	4	-	-	-	TOT
				B	-	-	-	-	-	-	2	-	-	-	-	-	-	-	-	-	-	-	-	-	-	-	3	-	-	-	B
		Mi.6:6		C	1	-	-	1	-	-	-	-	-	-	-	-	-	-	-	-	-	-	-	-	-	-	1	-	-	-	C
172	**KRH**	be dug	Iq	TOT	1	-	-	1	-	-	-	-	-	-	-	-	-	-	-	-	-	-	-	-	-	-	13	-	-	-	TOT
				A	-	-	-	-	-	-	-	-	-	-	-	-	-	-	-	-	-	-	-	-	-	-	5	-	-	-	A
		Ps.94:13		B	1	-	-	1	-	-	-	-	-	-	-	-	-	-	-	-	-	-	-	-	-	-	6	-	-	-	B
				C	-	-	-	-	-	-	-	-	-	-	-	-	-	-	-	-	-	-	-	-	-	-	2	-	-	-	C
173	**KRT**	be exterminated/lack	Iq	TOT	72	-	35	35	2	-	3	2	-	2	-	-	1	-	1	-	-	-	-	-	-	-	M	-	78	-	TOT

	ROOT	MEANING	DIV	G	NIPH'AL TOT	PT	PF	IMPF	INF	IMPV	PQ	PU'AL TOT	PT	PF	IMPF	O	HOPH'AL TOT	PT	PF	IMPF	O	HITPA'EL TOT	PT	PF	IMPF	O	QAL	PI	HI	O	G
		see 3.3		A	43	-	24	18	1	-	2	2	-	2	-	-	-	-	-	-	-	-	-	-	-	-	M	-	47	-	A
				B	10	-	2	7	1	-	1	-	-	-	-	-	-	-	-	-	-	-	-	-	-	-	M	-	5	-	B
				C	19	-	9	10	-	-	-	-	-	-	-	-	1	-	1	-	-	-	-	-	-	-	M	-	26	-	C
174	**KŠL**	stumble	I=q	TOT	24	2	3	17	2	-	-	-	-	-	-	-	1	1	-	-	-	-	-	-	-	-	30	1	9	-	TOT
		Dan.11:14,19,33//11:35,41/Jer. 31:9/Ezek.33:12//Dan.11:34		A	8	-	3	4	1	-	-	-	-	-	-	-	-	-	-	-	-	-	-	-	-	-	3	1	4	-	A
		1Sam.2:4//Ps.9:4/Pro.4:12, 19/24:16//24:17		B	6	1	-	4	1	-	-	-	-	-	-	-	-	-	-	-	-	-	-	-	-	-	8	-	3	-	B
		Zech.12:8//Isa.40:30/63:13/ Jer.6:15/8:12/20:11/Hos.5:5/ 14:10/Nah.2:6/3:3		C	10	1	-	9	-	-	-	-	-	-	-	-	1	1	-	-	-	-	-	-	-	-	19	-	2	-	C
175	**KTB**	be written down	Iq	TOT	17	1	2	14	-	-	112	-	-	-	-	-	-	-	-	-	-	-	-	-	-	-	M	2	-	-	TOT
		Esth.8:8//3:12/9:32//Ezek.13: 9/Esth.1:19/2:23/3:9,12/8:5,9 /Ezra8:34		A	11	1	2	8	-	-	104	-	-	-	-	-	-	-	-	-	-	-	-	-	-	-	M	-	-	-	A
		Ps.69:29/102:19/139:16/ Job19:23		B	4	-	-	4	-	-	3	-	-	-	-	-	-	-	-	-	-	-	-	-	-	-	M	-	-	-	B
		Jer.17:13/Mal.3:16		C	2	-	-	2	-	-	5	-	-	-	-	-	-	-	-	-	-	-	-	-	-	-	M	2	-	-	C
176	**KTM**	defiled/stained	III	TOT	1	1	-	-	-	-	-	-	-	-	-	-	-	-	-	-	-	-	-	-	-	-	-	-	-	-	TOT
		Jer.2:22		C	1	1	-	-	-	-	-	-	-	-	-	-	-	-	-	-	-	-	-	-	-	-	-	-	-	-	C
177*	**LAH**	tire oneself/become tired	Iq	TOT	10	-	10	-	-	-	-	-	-	-	-	-	-	-	-	-	-	-	-	-	-	-	3	-	6	-	TOT
		Ex.7:18		A	1	-	1	-	-	-	-	-	-	-	-	-	-	-	-	-	-	-	-	-	-	-	1	-	1	-	A
		Ps.68:10/Pro.26:15		B	2	-	2	-	-	-	-	-	-	-	-	-	-	-	-	-	-	-	-	-	-	-	2	-	1	-	B
		Isa.1:14/16:12/47:13/Jer.6: 11/9:4/15:16/20:9		C	7	-	7	-	-	-	-	-	-	-	-	-	-	-	-	-	-	-	-	-	-	-	-	-	4	-	C
178	**LBB**	receive a heart	II	TOT	1	-	-	1	-	-	-	-	-	-	-	-	-	-	-	-	-	-	-	-	-	-	-	2	-	-	TOT
		Job11:12		B	1	-	-	1	-	-	-	-	-	-	-	-	-	-	-	-	-	-	-	-	-	-	-	2	-	-	B
179	**LBṬ**	be thrown down/fall	III	TOT	3	-	-	3	-	-	-	-	-	-	-	-	-	-	-	-	-	-	-	-	-	-	-	-	-	-	TOT
		Pro.10:8,10		B	2	-	-	2	-	-	-	-	-	-	-	-	-	-	-	-	-	-	-	-	-	-	-	-	-	-	B
		Hos.4:14		C	1	-	-	1	-	-	-	-	-	-	-	-	-	-	-	-	-	-	-	-	-	-	-	-	-	-	C
180	**LWH**	join with	Iq	TOT	11	2	7	2	-	-	-	-	-	-	-	-	-	-	-	-	-	-	-	-	-	-	1	-	-	-	TOT
		Esth.9:27//Num.18:4/		A	5	1	2	2	-	-	-	-	-	-	-	-	-	-	-	-	-	-	-	-	-	-	-	-	-	-	A
		Ps.83:9		B	1	-	1	-	-	-	-	-	-	-	-	-	-	-	-	-	-	-	-	-	-	-	1	-	-	-	B
		Isa.56:6//14:1/56:3/		C	5	1	4	-	-	-	-	-	-	-	-	-	-	-	-	-	-	-	-	-	-	-	-	-	-	-	C
181*	**LWZ**	crooked/wrong	II	TOT	4	4	-	-	-	-	-	-	-	-	-	-	-	-	-	-	-	-	-	-	-	-	1	-	1	-	TOT
		Pro.2:15/3:32/14:2		B	3	3	-	-	-	-	-	-	-	-	-	-	-	-	-	-	-	-	-	-	-	-	1	-	1	-	B
		Isa.30:11		C	1	1	-	-	-	-	-	-	-	-	-	-	-	-	-	-	-	-	-	-	-	-	-	-	-	-	C
182	**LWN**	murmur (rebel)	I=h	TOT	8	-	-	8	-	-	-	-	-	-	-	-	-	-	-	-	-	-	-	-	-	-	-	-	11	-	TOT
		Ex.15:24/16:2/16:7(Q)/Num.14:2, 36(K)/16:11(K)/17:6/Josh.9:18		A	8	-	-	8	-	-	-	-	-	-	-	-	-	-	-	-	-	-	-	-	-	-	-	-	10	-	A
				B	-	-	-	-	-	-	-	-	-	-	-	-	-	-	-	-	-	-	-	-	-	-	-	-	1	-	B
183	**LḤM**	fight/wage war	II	TOT	164	22	37	52	48	5	-	-	-	-	-	-	-	-	-	-	-	-	-	-	-	-	4	-	-	-	TOT
		see 3.3		A	146	20	27	49	45	5	-	-	-	-	-	-	-	-	-	-	-	-	-	-	-	-	-	-	-	-	A
				B	3	-	2	1	-	-	-	-	-	-	-	-	-	-	-	-	-	-	-	-	-	-	4	-	-	-	B
				C	15	2	8	2	3	-	-	-	-	-	-	-	-	-	-	-	-	-	-	-	-	-	-	-	-	-	C

	ROOT	MEANING	DIV	G	NIPH'AL TOT	NIPH'AL PT	NIPH'AL PF	NIPH'AL IMPF	NIPH'AL INF	NIPH'AL IMPV	PQ	PU'AL TOT	PU'AL PT	PU'AL PF	PU'AL IMPF	PU'AL O	HOPH'AL TOT	HOPH'AL PT	HOPH'AL PF	HOPH'AL IMPF	HOPH'AL O	HITPA'EL TOT	HITPA'EL PT	HITPA'EL PF	HITPA'EL IMPF	HITPA'EL O	QAL	PI	HI	O	G
184	**LHṢ**	press oneself against	Iq	TOT	1	-	-	1	-	-	-	-	-	-	-	-	-	-	-	-	-	-	-	-	-	-	18	-	-	-	TOT
		Num.22:25		A	1	-	-	1	-	-	-	-	-	-	-	-	-	-	-	-	-	-	-	-	-	-	14	-	-	-	A
				B	-	-	-	-	-	-	-	-	-	-	-	-	-	-	-	-	-	-	-	-	-	-	2	-	-	-	B
				C	-	-	-	-	-	-	-	-	-	-	-	-	-	-	-	-	-	-	-	-	-	-	2	-	-	-	C
185	**LKD**	be taken/be captured	Iq	TOT	35	1	16	18	-	-	-	-	-	-	-	-	-	-	-	-	-	2	-	-	2	-	82	-	-	-	TOT
		see 3.3		A	13	1	3	9	-	-	-	-	-	-	-	-	-	-	-	-	-	-	-	-	-	-	71	-	-	-	A
				B	6	-	3	3	-	-	-	-	-	-	-	-	-	-	-	-	-	2	-	-	2	-	4	-	-	-	B
				C	16	-	10	6	-	-	-	-	-	-	-	-	-	-	-	-	-	-	-	-	-	-	7	-	-	-	C
186	**L'G**	stammering	II	TOT	1	1	-	-	-	-	-	-	-	-	-	-	-	-	-	-	-	-	-	-	-	-	12	-	5	-	TOT
				A	-	-	-	-	-	-	-	-	-	-	-	-	-	-	-	-	-	-	-	-	-	-	1	-	3	-	A
				B	-	-	-	-	-	-	-	-	-	-	-	-	-	-	-	-	-	-	-	-	-	-	10	-	2	-	B
		Isa.33:19		C	1	1	-	-	-	-	-	-	-	-	-	-	-	-	-	-	-	-	-	-	-	-	1	-	-	-	C
187	**LPT**	grab around oneself	II	TOT	2	-	-	2	-	-	-	-	-	-	-	-	-	-	-	-	-	-	-	-	-	-	1	-	-	-	TOT
		Ruth3:8		A	1	-	-	1	-	-	-	-	-	-	-	-	-	-	-	-	-	-	-	-	-	-	1	-	-	-	A
		Job.6:18		B	1	-	-	1	-	-	-	-	-	-	-	-	-	-	-	-	-	-	-	-	-	-	-	-	-	-	B
188	**LQḤ**	be taken (away)	Iq	TOT	10	-	4	3	3	-	1	9	1	8	-	-	6	-	-	6	-	2	2	-	-	-	M	-	-	-	TOT
		1Sam.4:11,17,22/Ezek.33:6// 2Kin.2:9/Esth.2:8,16//1Sam. 4:19,21/21:7		A	10	-	4	3	3	-	-	6	1	5	-	-	3	-	-	3	-	2	2	-	-	-	M	-	-	-	A
				B	-	-	-	-	-	-	1	-	-	-	-	-	1	-	-	1	-	-	-	-	-	-	M	-	-	-	B
				C	-	-	-	-	-	-	-	3	-	3	-	-	2	-	-	2	-	-	-	-	-	-	M	-	-	-	C
189	**MAS**	I be rejected	Iq	TOT	3	2	-	1	-	-	-	-	-	-	-	-	-	-	-	-	-	-	-	-	-	-	71	-	-	-	TOT
				A	-	-	-	-	-	-	-	-	-	-	-	-	-	-	-	-	-	-	-	-	-	-	26	-	-	-	A
		Ps.15:4		B	1	1	-	-	-	-	-	-	-	-	-	-	-	-	-	-	-	-	-	-	-	-	23	-	-	-	B
		Jer.6:30//Isa.54:6		C	2	1	-	1	-	-	-	-	-	-	-	-	-	-	-	-	-	-	-	-	-	-	22	-	-	-	C
190	**MAS**	II perish	III	TOT	2	-	-	2	-	-	-	-	-	-	-	-	-	-	-	-	-	-	-	-	-	-	-	-	-	-	TOT
		Ps.58:8/Job7:5		B	2	-	-	2	-	-	-	-	-	-	-	-	-	-	-	-	-	-	-	-	-	-	-	-	-	-	B
191	**MDD**	be measured	Iq	TOT	3	-	-	3	-	-	-	-	-	-	-	-	-	-	-	-	-	1	-	-	1	-	42	5	-	1	TOT
		Jer.31:37/33:22		A	2	-	-	2	-	-	-	-	-	-	-	-	-	-	-	-	-	1	-	-	1	-	39	2	-	-	A
				B	-	-	-	-	-	-	-	-	-	-	-	-	-	-	-	-	-	-	-	-	-	-	-	3	-	-	B
		Hos.2:1		C	1	-	-	1	-	-	-	-	-	-	-	-	-	-	-	-	-	-	-	-	-	-	3	-	-	1	C
192	**MHR**	hurry/be quickened	II	TOT	4	3	1	-	-	-	-	-	-	-	-	-	-	-	-	-	-	-	-	-	-	-	-	60	-	-	TOT
				A	-	-	-	-	-	-	-	-	-	-	-	-	-	-	-	-	-	-	-	-	-	-	-	45	-	-	A
		Job5:13		B	1	-	1	-	-	-	-	-	-	-	-	-	-	-	-	-	-	-	-	-	-	-	-	5	-	-	B
		Isa.32:4/35:4/Hab.1:4		C	3	3	-	-	-	-	-	-	-	-	-	-	-	-	-	-	-	-	-	-	-	-	-	10	-	-	C
193	**MWG**	be tossed to and fro (melt	Iq	TOT	8	1	7	-	-	-	-	-	-	-	-	-	-	-	-	-	-	3	-	1	2	-	4	-	-	2	TOT
		away) Josh.2:9,24/1Sam.14:16		A	3	-	3	-	-	-	-	-	-	-	-	-	-	-	-	-	-	-	-	-	-	-	1	-	-	-	A
		Ps.75:4//Ex.15:15		B	2	1	1	-	-	-	-	-	-	-	-	-	-	-	-	-	-	1	-	-	1	-	1	-	-	2	B
		Isa.14:31/Jer.49:23/Nah.2:7		C	3	-	3	-	-	-	-	-	-	-	-	-	-	-	-	-	-	2	-	1	1	-	2	-	-	-	C
194	**MWṬ**	be shaken	Iq	TOT	23	-	1	22	-	-	-	-	-	-	-	-	-	-	-	-	-	1	-	1	-	-	15	-	2	-	TOT
				A	-	-	-	-	-	-	-	-	-	-	-	-	-	-	-	-	-	-	-	-	-	-	1	-	-	-	A
		Ps.17:5//10:6/13:5/15:5/16:8/21: 8/30:7/46:1/62:3,7/82:5/93:1/96: 10/104:5/112:6/125:1/140:11/Job 41:15/Pro.10:30/12:3/1Chr.16:30		B	21	-	1	20	-	-	-	-	-	-	-	-	-	-	-	-	-	1	-	1	-	-	11	-	2	-	B

	ROOT	MEANING	DIV	G	NIPH'AL TOT	PT	PF	IMPF	INF	IMPV	FQ	PU'AL TOT	PT	PF	IMPF	O	HOPH'AL TOT	PT	PF	IMPF	O	HITPA'EL TOT	PT	PF	IMPF	O	QAL	PI	HI	O	G
		Isa. 40:20/41:7		C	2	-	-	2	-	-	-	-	-	-	-	-	-	-	-	-	-	-	-	-	-	-	3	-	-	-	C
195	MWL	be circumcised	Iq	TOT	19	1	3	5	9	1	2?	-	-	-	-	-	-	-	-	-	-	-	-	-	-	-	13	-	3	-	TOT
		Gen.34:22//17:11,26,27//17:		A	18	1	3	5	9	-	1?	-	-	-	-	-	-	-	-	-	-	-	-	-	-	-	12	-	-	-	A
		12,13,14/34:24/Lev.12:3//Gen.																													
		17:10,13,24,25/34:15,17,22/																													
		Ex.12:48/Josh.5:8																													
				B	-	-	-	-	-	-	-	-	-	-	-	-	-	-	-	-	-	-	-	-	-	-	-	-	3	-	B
		Jer.4:4		C	1	-	-	-	-	1	1?	-	-	-	-	-	-	-	-	-	-	-	-	-	-	-	1	-	-	-	C
196	MWR	be changed	Ih	TOT	1	-	1	-	-	-	-	-	-	-	-	-	-	-	-	-	-	-	-	-	-	-	-	-	12	-	TOT
				A	-	-	-	-	-	-	-	-	-	-	-	-	-	-	-	-	-	-	-	-	-	-	-	-	5	-	A
				B	-	-	-	-	-	-	-	-	-	-	-	-	-	-	-	-	-	-	-	-	-	-	-	-	3	-	B
		Jer.48:11		C	1	-	1	-	-	-	-	-	-	-	-	-	-	-	-	-	-	-	-	-	-	-	-	-	4	-	C
197	MḤH	be wiped out/destroyed	Iq	TOT	9	-	1	8	-	-	-	-	-	-	-	-	-	-	-	-	-	-	-	-	-	-	22	-	3	-	TOT
		Ezek.6:6//Gen.7:23/		A	5	-	1	4	-	-	-	-	-	-	-	-	-	-	-	-	-	-	-	-	-	-	15	-	1	-	A
		Dt.25:6/Judg.21:17/Neh.3:3																													
		Ps.69:29/109:13,14/Pro.6:33		B	4	-	-	4	-	-	-	-	-	-	-	-	-	-	-	-	-	-	-	-	-	-	4	-	1	-	B
				C	-	-	-	-	-	-	-	-	-	-	-	-	-	-	-	-	-	-	-	-	-	-	3	-	1	-	C
198	MṬR	be rained upon	II	TOT	1	-	-	1	-	-	-	-	-	-	-	-	-	-	-	-	-	-	-	-	-	-	-	-	16	-	TOT
				A	-	-	-	-	-	-	-	-	-	-	-	-	-	-	-	-	-	-	-	-	-	-	-	-	7	-	A
				B	-	-	-	-	-	-	-	-	-	-	-	-	-	-	-	-	-	-	-	-	-	-	-	-	5	-	B
		Am.4:7		C	1	-	-	1	-	-	-	-	-	-	-	-	-	-	-	-	-	-	-	-	-	-	-	-	4	-	C
199	MKK	sag (sink?)	Iq	TOT	1	-	-	1	-	-	-	-	-	-	-	-	1	-	1	-	-	-	-	-	-	-	1	-	-	-	TOT
		Eccl.10:18		A	1	-	-	1	-	-	-	-	-	-	-	-	1	-	1	-	-	-	-	-	-	-	1	-	-	-	A
200	MKR	be sold/sell oneself	Iq	TOT	19	1	11	6	1	-	-	-	-	-	-	-	-	-	-	-	-	4	-	2	1	1	57	-	-	-	TOT
		Neh.5:8//Lev.25:39,47,48/27:27/		A	16	1	8	6	1	-	-	-	-	-	-	-	-	-	-	-	-	4	-	2	1	1	43	-	-	-	A
		Ex.22:2/Neh.5:8/Esth.7:4(2x)//																													
		Lev.25:23,34,42/27:28/Dt.15:12/																													
		Jer.34:14//Lev.25:50/Ps.105:17		B	1	-	1	-	-	-	-	-	-	-	-	-	-	-	-	-	-	-	-	-	-	-	4	-	-	-	B
		Isa.50:1/52:3		C	2	-	2	-	-	-	-	-	-	-	-	-	-	-	-	-	-	-	-	-	-	-	10	-	-	-	C
201*	MLA	full/filled/be satisfied	Iq	TOT	35	1	-	34	-	-	-	1	1	-	-	-	-	-	-	-	-	1	-	-	1	-	M	M	-	-	TOT
		see 3.3		A	17	-	-	17	-	-	-	-	-	-	-	-	-	-	-	-	-	-	-	-	-	-	M	M	-	-	A
				B	9	1	-	8	-	-	-	1	1	-	-	-	-	-	-	-	-	1	-	-	1	-	M	M	-	-	B
				C	9	-	-	9	-	-	-	-	-	-	-	-	-	-	-	-	-	-	-	-	-	-	M	M	-	-	C
202	MLḤ	be scattered	III	TOT	1	-	1	-	-	-	-	-	-	-	-	-	-	-	-	-	-	-	-	-	-	-	-	-	-	-	TOT
		Isa.51:6		C	1	-	1	-	-	-	-	-	-	-	-	-	-	-	-	-	-	-	-	-	-	-	-	-	-	-	C
203	MLṬ	escape/flee	Ip	TOT	62	3	17	36	3	3	-	-	-	-	-	-	-	-	-	-	-	2	-	-	2	-	-	27	2	-	TOT
		see 3.3		A	41	2	12	22	3	2	-	-	-	-	-	-	-	-	-	-	-	-	-	-	-	-	-	8	-	-	A
				B	11	-	5	6	-	-	-	-	-	-	-	-	-	-	-	-	-	2	-	-	2	-	-	11	-	-	B
				C	10	1	-	8	-	1	-	-	-	-	-	-	-	-	-	-	-	-	-	-	-	-	-	8	2	-	C
204	MLK	consult with oneself	III	TOT	1	-	-	1	-	-	-	-	-	-	-	-	-	-	-	-	-	-	-	-	-	-	-	-	-	-	TOT
		Neh.5:7		A	1	-	-	1	-	-	-	-	-	-	-	-	-	-	-	-	-	-	-	-	-	-	-	-	-	-	A
205	MLL	let oneself be circumsized	Iq	TOT	1	-	1	-	-	-	-	-	-	-	-	-	-	-	-	-	-	-	-	-	-	-	1	-	-	-	TOT
		Gen.17:11 (cf. 195)		A	1	-	1	-	-	-	-	-	-	-	-	-	-	-	-	-	-	-	-	-	-	-	1	-	-	-	A
206	MLṢ	be soft/smooth	III	TOT	1	-	1	-	-	-	-	-	-	-	-	-	-	-	-	-	-	-	-	-	-	-	-	-	-	-	TOT
		Ps.119:103		B	1	-	1	-	-	-	-	-	-	-	-	-	-	-	-	-	-	-	-	-	-	-	-	-	-	-	B

	ROOT	MEANING	DIV	G	NIPH'AL TOT	PT	PF	IMPF	INF	IMPV	PQ	PU'AL TOT	PT	PF	IMPF	O	HOPH'AL TOT	PT	PF	IMPF	O	HITPA'EL TOT	PT	PF	IMPF	O	QAL	PI	HI	O	G
207	MNH	be counted	Iq	TOT	6	-	1	4	1	-	-	1	1	-	-	-	-	-	-	-	-	-	-	-	-	-	12	9	-	-	TOT
		Gen.13:16/1Kin.3:8/8:5/2Chr.		A	5	-	-	4	1	-	-	1	1	-	-	-	-	-	-	-	-	-	-	-	-	-	8	7	-	-	A
		5:6//Eccl.1:15/																													
				B	-	-	-	-	-	-	-	-	-	-	-	-	-	-	-	-	-	-	-	-	-	-	3	2	-	-	B
		Isa.53:12		C	1	-	1	-	-	-	-	-	-	-	-	-	-	-	-	-	-	-	-	-	-	-	1	-	-	-	C
208	MN'	be restrained	Iq	TOT	4	-	1	3	-	-	-	-	-	-	-	-	-	-	-	-	-	-	-	-	-	-	25	-	-	-	TOT
		Num.22:16		A	1	-	-	1	-	-	-	-	-	-	-	-	-	-	-	-	-	-	-	-	-	-	10	-	-	-	A
		Job38:15		B	1	-	-	1	-	-	-	-	-	-	-	-	-	-	-	-	-	-	-	-	-	-	11	-	-	-	B
		Jo.1:13//Jer.3:3		C	2	-	1	1	-	-	-	-	-	-	-	-	-	-	-	-	-	-	-	-	-	-	4	-	-	-	C
209*	MSS	be weak/melt/weaken	II	TOT	19	3	6	8	2	-	-	-	-	-	-	-	-	-	-	-	-	-	-	-	-	-	1	-	1	-	TOT
		1Sam.15:9//Ex.16:21/Ez.21:12		A	10	1	2	6	1	-	-	-	-	-	-	-	-	-	-	-	-	-	-	-	-	-	-	-	1	-	A
		//Deut.20:8/Judg.15:14/Josh.																													
		2:11/5:1/7:5/2Sam.17:10//17:10																													
		Ps.22:5//97:5/112:10//68:3		B	4	1	2	-	1	-	-	-	-	-	-	-	-	-	-	-	-	-	-	-	-	-	-	-	-	-	B
		Nah.2:11//Isa.34:3/Mi.1:4//		C	5	1	2	2	-	-	-	-	-	-	-	-	-	-	-	-	-	-	-	-	-	-	1	-	-	-	C
		Isa.13:7/19:1																													
210	MSR	be supplied	II	TOT	1	-	-	1	-	-	-	-	-	-	-	-	-	-	-	-	-	-	-	-	-	-	1	-	-	-	TOT
		Num.31:5		A	1	-	-	1	-	-	-	-	-	-	-	-	-	-	-	-	-	-	-	-	-	-	1	-	-	-	A
211*	MṢA	be found/be located	Iq	TOT	141	41	49	49	2	-	-	-	-	-	-	-	-	-	-	-	-	-	-	-	-	-	M	-	7	-	TOT
		see 3.3		A	107	39	30	37	1	-	-	-	-	-	-	-	-	-	-	-	-	-	-	-	-	-	M	-	4	-	A
				B	9	-	5	4	-	-	-	-	-	-	-	-	-	-	-	-	-	-	-	-	-	-	M	-	2	-	B
				C	25	2	14	8	1	-	-	-	-	-	-	-	-	-	-	-	-	-	-	-	-	-	M	-	1	-	C
212	MṢH	be drained	Iq	TOT	3	-	1	2	-	-	-	-	-	-	-	-	-	-	-	-	-	-	-	-	-	-	4	-	-	-	TOT
		Lev.1:15//5:9		A	2	-	1	1	-	-	-	-	-	-	-	-	-	-	-	-	-	-	-	-	-	-	2	-	-	-	A
		Ps.73:10		B	1	-	-	1	-	-	-	-	-	-	-	-	-	-	-	-	-	-	-	-	-	-	1	-	-	-	B
				C	-	-	-	-	-	-	-	-	-	-	-	-	-	-	-	-	-	-	-	-	-	-	1	-	-	-	C
213	MQQ	rot away/waste away	II	TOT	9	1	4	4	-	-	-	-	-	-	-	-	-	-	-	-	-	-	-	-	-	-	-	-	1	-	TOT
		Ez.33:10//4:17/24:23//		A	5	1	2	2	-	-	-	-	-	-	-	-	-	-	-	-	-	-	-	-	-	-	-	-	-	-	A
		Lev.26:39(2x)																													
		Ps.38:6		B	1	-	1	-	-	-	-	-	-	-	-	-	-	-	-	-	-	-	-	-	-	-	-	-	-	-	B
		Isa.34:4//Zech.14:12(2x)		C	3	-	1	2	-	-	-	-	-	-	-	-	-	-	-	-	-	-	-	-	-	-	-	-	1	-	C
214	MRṬ	become bold	Iq	TOT	2	-	-	2	-	-	3	5	3	2	-	-	-	-	-	-	-	-	-	-	-	-	7	-	-	-	TOT
		Lev.13:40,41		A	2	-	-	2	-	-	3	3	1	2	-	-	-	-	-	-	-	-	-	-	-	-	6	-	-	-	A
				C	-	-	-	-	-	-	-	2	2	-	-	-	-	-	-	-	-	-	-	-	-	-	1	-	-	-	C
215	MRṢ	be grieved/be painful	II	TOT	3	2	1	-	-	-	-	-	-	-	-	-	-	-	-	-	-	-	-	-	-	-	-	-	1	-	TOT
		1Kin.2:8		A	1	1	-	-	-	-	-	-	-	-	-	-	-	-	-	-	-	-	-	-	-	-	-	-	-	-	A
		Job6:25		B	1	-	1	-	-	-	-	-	-	-	-	-	-	-	-	-	-	-	-	-	-	-	-	-	1	-	B
		Mi.2:8		C	1	1	-	-	-	-	-	-	-	-	-	-	-	-	-	-	-	-	-	-	-	-	-	-	-	-	C
216	MŠḤ	be anointed	Iq	TOT	5	-	1	-	4	-	6	-	-	-	-	-	-	-	-	-	-	-	-	-	-	-	64	-	-	-	TOT
		1Chr.14:18//Lev.6:13/Num.																													
		7:10,84,88		A	5	-	1	-	4	-	6	-	-	-	-	-	-	-	-	-	-	-	-	-	-	-	58	-	-	-	A
				B	-	-	-	-	-	-	-	-	-	-	-	-	-	-	-	-	-	-	-	-	-	-	2	-	-	-	B
				C	-	-	-	-	-	-	-	-	-	-	-	-	-	-	-	-	-	-	-	-	-	-	4	-	-	-	C
217	MŠK	be postponed/be prolonged	Iq	TOT	3	-	-	3	-	-	-	3	3	-	-	-	-	-	-	-	-	-	-	-	-	-	30	-	-	-	TOT
		Ezek.12:25,28		A	2	-	-	2	-	-	-	-	-	-	-	-	-	-	-	-	-	-	-	-	-	-	15	-	-	-	A

	ROOT	MEANING	DIV	G	NIPH'AL						PQ	PU'AL					HOPH'AL					HITPA'EL					QAL	PI	HI	O	G
					TOT	PT	PF	IMPF	INF	IMPV		TOT	PT	PF	IMPF	O	TOT	PT	PF	IMPF	O	TOT	PT	PF	IMPF	O					
				B	-	-	-	-	-	-	-	1	1	-	-	-	-	-	-	-	-	-	-	-	-	-	10	-	-	-	B
		Isa.13:22		C	1	-	-	1	-	-	-	2	2	-	-	-	-	-	-	-	-	-	-	-	-	-	5	-	-	-	C
218	**MŠL**	be/become equal	II	TOT	5	-	5	-	-	-	-	-	-	-	-	-	-	-	-	-	-	1	-	-	1	-	9	1	1	-	TOT
				A	-	-	-	-	-	-	-	-	-	-	-	-	-	-	-	-	-	-	-	-	-	-	8	1	-	-	A
		Ps.28:1/49:13,21/143:7		B	4	-	4	-	-	-	-	-	-	-	-	-	-	-	-	-	-	1	-	-	1	-	1	-	-	-	B
		Isa.14:10		C	1	-	1	-	-	-	-	-	-	-	-	-	-	-	-	-	-	-	-	-	-	-	-	-	1	-	C
219	**NBA**	prophesy	III	TOT	84	23	19	10	7	25	-	-	-	-	-	-	-	-	-	-	-	27	10	3	13	1	-	-	-	-	TOT
		see 3.3		A	61	16	14	3	4	24	-	-	-	-	-	-	-	-	-	-	-	25	9	2	13	1	-	-	-	-	A
				B	-	-	-	-	-	-	-	-	-	-	-	-	-	-	-	-	-	-	-	-	-	-	-	-	-	-	B
				C	23	7	5	7	3	1	-	-	-	-	-	-	-	-	-	-	-	2	1	1	-	-	-	-	-	-	C
220	**NG'**	be defeated	Iq	TOT	1	-	-	1	-	-	2	1	-	-	1	-	-	-	-	-	-	-	-	-	-	-	M	3	38	-	TOT
		Josh.8:15		A	1	-	-	1	-	-	-	-	-	-	-	-	-	-	-	-	-	-	-	-	-	-	M	3	21	-	A
				B	-	-	-	-	-	-	1	1	-	-	1	-	-	-	-	-	-	-	-	-	-	-	M	-	9	-	B
				C	-	-	-	-	-	-	1	-	-	-	-	-	-	-	-	-	-	-	-	-	-	-	M	-	8	-	C
221	**NGP**	be defeated	Iq	TOT	23	4	6	11	2	-	-	-	-	-	-	-	-	-	-	-	-	1	-	-	1	-	24	-	-	-	TOT
		see 3.3		A	23	4	6	11	2	-	-	-	-	-	-	-	-	-	-	-	-	-	-	-	-	-	17	-	-	-	A
				B	-	-	-	-	-	-	-	-	-	-	-	-	-	-	-	-	-	-	-	-	-	-	3	-	-	-	B
				C	-	-	-	-	-	-	-	-	-	-	-	-	-	-	-	-	-	1	-	-	1	-	4	-	-	-	C
222	**NGR**	be poured out	Ih	TOT	4	2	2	-	-	-	-	-	-	-	-	-	1	1	-	-	-	-	-	-	-	-	-	-	5	-	TOT
		2Sam.14:14		A	1	1	-	-	-	-	-	-	-	-	-	-	-	-	-	-	-	-	-	-	-	-	-	-	1	-	A
		Job20:28//Ps.77:3/Lam.3:49		B	3	1	2	-	-	-	-	-	-	-	-	-	-	-	-	-	-	-	-	-	-	-	-	-	2	-	B
				C	-	-	-	-	-	-	-	-	-	-	-	-	1	1	-	-	-	-	-	-	-	-	-	-	2	-	C
223	**NGŚ**	be hard pressed/be pressed together	Iq	TOT	4	-	4	-	-	-	-	-	-	-	-	-	-	-	-	-	-	-	-	-	-	-	19	-	-	-	TOT
		1Sam.13:6/14:24		A	2	-	2	-	-	-	-	-	-	-	-	-	-	-	-	-	-	-	-	-	-	-	9	-	-	-	A
				B	-	-	-	-	-	-	-	-	-	-	-	-	-	-	-	-	-	-	-	-	-	-	2	-	-	-	B
		Isa.3:5/53:7		C	2	-	2	-	-	-	-	-	-	-	-	-	-	-	-	-	-	-	-	-	-	-	8	-	-	-	C
224*	**NGŠ**	approach	I=q	TOT	17	1	16	-	-	-	-	-	-	-	-	-	2	1	1	-	-	1	-	-	-	1	67	-	36	-	TOT
		Ex.19:22//Gen.33:7/Ex.20:21/24:2/34:32/Deut.20:2/21:5/25:1,9/1Kin.20:13/1Sam.7:10/2Sam.11:20,21/Jer.30:21/Ezra9:1		A	15	1	14	-	-	-	-	-	-	-	-	-	-	-	-	-	-	-	-	-	-	-	59	-	24	-	A
				B	-	-	-	-	-	-	-	-	-	-	-	-	1	-	1	-	-	-	-	-	-	-	3	-	1	-	B
		Isa.29:13//Am.9:13		C	2	-	2	-	-	-	-	-	-	-	-	-	1	1	-	-	-	1	-	-	-	1	5	-	11	-	C
225	**NDḤ**	be rejected/be expelled	Ih	TOT	24	17	7	-	-	-	-	1	1	-	-	-	1	1	-	-	-	-	-	-	-	-	2	-	27	-	TOT
		see 3.3		A	13	8	5	-	-	-	-	-	-	-	-	-	-	-	-	-	-	-	-	-	-	-	2	-	15	-	A
				B	2	1	1	-	-	-	-	-	-	-	-	-	-	-	-	-	-	-	-	-	-	-	-	-	3	-	B
				C	9	8	1	-	-	-	-	1	1	-	-	-	1	1	-	-	-	-	-	-	-	-	-	-	9	-	C
226	**NDP**	be blown about/be expelled	Iq	TOT	6	4	1	-	1	-	-	-	-	-	-	-	-	-	-	-	-	-	-	-	-	-	3	-	-	-	TOT
		Lev.26:23		A	1	1	-	-	-	-	-	-	-	-	-	-	-	-	-	-	-	-	-	-	-	-	-	-	-	-	A
		Job13:25/Pro.21:6//Ps.68:30		B	3	2	-	-	1	-	-	-	-	-	-	-	-	-	-	-	-	-	-	-	-	-	3	-	-	-	B
		Isa.41:2//19:7		C	2	1	1	-	-	-	-	-	-	-	-	-	-	-	-	-	-	-	-	-	-	-	-	-	-	-	C
227	**NHH**	go mourning after	II	TOT	1	-	-	1	-	-	-	-	-	-	-	-	-	-	-	-	-	-	-	-	-	-	2	-	-	-	TOT
		1Sam.7:2		A	1	-	-	1	-	-	-	-	-	-	-	-	-	-	-	-	-	-	-	-	-	-	1	-	-	-	A
				C	-	-	-	-	-	-	-	-	-	-	-	-	-	-	-	-	-	-	-	-	-	-	1	-	-	-	C

	ROOT	MEANING	DIV	G	NIPH'AL TOT	PT	PF	IMPF	INF	IMPV	FQ	PU'AL TOT	PT	PF	IMPF	O	HOPH'AL TOT	PT	PF	IMPF	O	HITPA'EL TOT	PT	PF	IMPF	O	QAL	PI	HI	O	G
228	NWN/	be proclaimed(?)	Iq	TOT	1	-	-	1	-	-	-	-	-	-	-	-	-	-	-	-	-	-	-	-	-	-	1	-	-	-	TOT
	NUN	Ps.72:17Q		B	1	-	-	1	-	-	-	-	-	-	-	-	-	-	-	-	-	-	-	-	-	-	1	-	-	-	B
229	NW'	be shaken	Ih	TOT	2	-	-	2	-	-	-	-	-	-	-	-	-	-	-	-	-	-	-	-	-	-	25	-	14	-	TOT
				A	-	-	-	-	-	-	-	-	-	-	-	-	-	-	-	-	-	-	-	-	-	-	7	-	5	-	A
				B	-	-	-	-	-	-	-	-	-	-	-	-	-	-	-	-	-	-	-	-	-	-	8	-	6	-	B
		Am.9:9//Nah.3:12		C	2	-	-	2	-	-	-	-	-	-	-	-	-	-	-	-	-	-	-	-	-	-	10	-	3	-	C
230	NZR	dedicate oneself/ abstain from	I=h	TOT	4	-	-	3	1	-	-	-	-	-	-	-	-	-	-	-	-	-	-	-	-	-	-	-	6	-	TOT
		Lev.22:2/Ezek.14:7		A	2	-	-	2	-	-	-	-	-	-	-	-	-	-	-	-	-	-	-	-	-	-	-	-	6	-	A
		Hos.9:10//Zech.7:3		C	2	-	-	1	1	-	-	-	-	-	-	-	-	-	-	-	-	-	-	-	-	-	-	-	-	-	C
231	NḤM	repent	Ip	TOT	48	3	20	19	4	2	-	2	-	1	1	-	-	-	-	-	-	7	1	1	4	1	48	-	-	-	TOT
		see 3.3		A	30	1	11	15	2	1	-	-	-	-	-	-	-	-	-	-	-	4	1	1	1	1	13	-	-	-	A
				B	5	-	1	2	1	1	-	-	-	-	-	-	-	-	-	-	-	3	-	-	3	-	20	-	-	-	B
				C	13	2	8	2	1	-	-	2	-	1	1	-	-	-	-	-	-	-	-	-	-	-	15	-	-	-	C
232	NḤT	come down	Iq	TOT	1	-	1	-	-	-	-	-	-	-	-	-	-	-	-	-	-	-	-	-	-	-	4	3	1	-	TOT
		Ps.38:3		B	1	-	1	-	-	-	-	-	-	-	-	-	-	-	-	-	-	-	-	-	-	-	3	3	-	-	B
				C	-	-	-	-	-	-	-	-	-	-	-	-	-	-	-	-	-	-	-	-	-	-	1	-	-	-	C
233	NṬH	be streched out/extended	Iq	TOT	3	-	1	2	-	-	30	-	-	-	-	-	2	2	-	-	-	-	-	-	-	-	135	75	-	-	TOT
				A	-	-	-	-	-	-	17	-	-	-	-	-	1	1	-	-	-	-	-	-	-	-	83	29	-	-	A
		Num.24:6		B	1	-	1	-	-	-	4	-	-	-	-	-	-	-	-	-	-	-	-	-	-	-	25	28	-	-	B
		Jer.6:4/Zech.1:16		C	2	-	-	2	-	-	9	-	-	-	-	-	1	1	-	-	-	-	-	-	-	-	27	18	-	-	C
234	NṬ'	be planted	Iq	TOT	1	-	1	-	-	-	2	-	-	-	-	-	-	-	-	-	-	-	-	-	-	-	59	-	-	-	TOT
				A	-	-	-	-	-	-	2	-	-	-	-	-	-	-	-	-	-	-	-	-	-	-	26	-	-	-	A
				B	-	-	-	-	-	-	-	-	-	-	-	-	-	-	-	-	-	-	-	-	-	-	14	-	-	-	B
		Isa.40:24		C	1	-	1	-	-	-	-	-	-	-	-	-	-	-	-	-	-	-	-	-	-	-	19	-	-	-	C
235	NṬŠ	be abandoned/scatter oneself	Iq	TOT	6	-	3	3	-	-	2	1	-	1	-	-	-	-	-	-	-	-	-	-	-	-	32	-	-	-	TOT
		Judg.15:9/2Sam.5:18,22		A	3	-	-	3	-	-	1	-	-	-	-	-	-	-	-	-	-	-	-	-	-	-	16	-	-	-	A
				B	-	-	-	-	-	-	-	-	-	-	-	-	-	-	-	-	-	-	-	-	-	-	7	-	-	-	B
		Isa.16:8/33:23/Am.5:2		C	3	-	3	-	-	-	1	1	-	1	-	-	-	-	-	-	-	-	-	-	-	-	9	-	-	-	C
236	NKA	be scourged out of	III	TOT	1	-	1	-	-	-	-	-	-	-	-	-	-	-	-	-	-	-	-	-	-	-	-	-	-	-	TOT
		Job30:8		B	1	-	1	-	-	-	-	-	-	-	-	-	-	-	-	-	-	-	-	-	-	-	-	-	-	-	C
237	NKH	be beaten	Ih	TOT	1	-	1	-	-	-	2	-	2	-	-	16	6	8	2	-	-	-	-	-	-	-	-	M	-	-	TOT
		2Sam.11:5		A	1	-	1	-	-	-	2	-	2	-	-	10	4	5	1	-	-	-	-	-	-	-	-	M	-	-	A
				B	-	-	-	-	-	-	-	-	-	-	-	1	-	1	-	-	-	-	-	-	-	-	-	M	-	-	B
				C	-	-	-	-	-	-	-	-	-	-	-	5	2	2	1	-	-	-	-	-	-	-	-	M	-	-	C
238	NKR	feign*/be recognized	Ip*/h	TOT	2	-	1	1	-	-	-	-	-	-	-	-	-	-	-	-	-	4	2	-	2	-	5	39	-	-	TOT
				A	-	-	-	-	-	-	-	-	-	-	-	-	-	-	-	-	-	3	2	-	1	-	2	25	-	-	A
		Lam.4:8//Pro.26:24*		B	2	-	1	1	-	-	-	-	-	-	-	-	-	-	-	-	-	1	-	-	1	-	3	11	-	-	B
				C	-	-	-	-	-	-	-	-	-	-	-	-	-	-	-	-	-	-	-	-	-	-	-	3	-	-	C
239	NSḤ	be destroyed	Iq	TOT	1	-	1	-	-	-	-	-	-	-	-	-	-	-	-	-	-	-	-	-	-	3	-	-	-	-	TOT
		Deut.28:63		A	1	-	1	-	-	-	-	-	-	-	-	-	-	-	-	-	-	-	-	-	-	-	-	-	-	-	A
				B	-	-	-	-	-	-	-	-	-	-	-	-	-	-	-	-	-	-	-	-	-	3	-	-	-	-	B
240	NSK	be installed	Iq	TOT	1	-	1	-	-	-	-	-	-	-	-	-	2	-	-	2	-	-	-	-	-	-	7	1	14	-	TOT
				A	-	-	-	-	-	-	-	-	-	-	-	-	2	-	-	2	-	-	-	-	-	-	1	1	12	-	A
		Pro.8:23		B	1	-	1	-	-	-	-	-	-	-	-	-	-	-	-	-	-	-	-	-	-	-	1	-	1	-	B

No.	ROOT	MEANING	DIV	G	NIPH'AL TOT	PT	PF	IMPF	INF	IMPV	PQ	PU'AL TOT	PT	PF	IMPF	O	HOPH'AL TOT	PT	PF	IMPF	O	HITPA'EL TOT	PT	PF	IMPF	O	QAL	PI	HI	O	G
				C	-	-	-	-	-	-	-	-	-	-	-	-	-	-	-	-	-	-	-	-	-	-	5	-	1	-	C
241	**NS'**	be demolished/taken away	Iq	TOT	2	-	2	-	-	-	-	-	-	-	-	-	-	-	-	-	-	-	-	-	-	-	M	-	8	-	TOT
		Isa.38:12		A	1	-	1	-	-	-	-	-	-	-	-	-	-	-	-	-	-	-	-	-	-	-	M	-	3	-	A
		Job4:21		B	1	-	1	-	-	-	-	-	-	-	-	-	-	-	-	-	-	-	-	-	-	-	-	-	5	-	B
				C	-	-	-	-	-	-	-	-	-	-	-	-	-	-	-	-	-	-	-	-	-	-	3	-	-	-	C
242	**N'R**	shake oneself free/be shaken	Iq	TOT	3	-	1	2	-	-	1	-	-	-	-	-	-	-	-	-	-	1	-	-	-	1	4	3	-	-	TOT
		Judg.16:20		A	1	-	-	1	-	-	1	-	-	-	-	-	-	-	-	-	-	-	-	-	-	-	2	2	-	-	A
		Ps.109:23//Job38:13		B	2	-	1	1	-	-	-	-	-	-	-	-	-	-	-	-	-	-	-	-	-	-	-	1	-	-	B
				C	-	-	-	-	-	-	-	-	-	-	-	-	-	-	-	-	-	1	-	-	-	1	2	-	-	-	C
243	**NPŠ**	catch one's breath	III	TOT	3	-	-	3	-	-	-	-	-	-	-	-	-	-	-	-	-	-	-	-	-	-	-	-	-	-	TOT
		Ex.23:12/31:17/2Sam.16:14		A	3	-	-	3	-	-	-	-	-	-	-	-	-	-	-	-	-	-	-	-	-	-	-	-	-	-	A
244*	**NṢB**	stand up/take up space	Ih	TOT	51	43	8	-	-	-	-	-	-	-	-	-	3	2	1	-	-	-	-	-	-	-	-	-	21	-	TOT
		see 3.3		A	40	34	6	-	-	-	-	-	-	-	-	-	2	2	-	-	-	-	-	-	-	-	-	-	14	-	A
				B	6	4	2	-	-	-	-	-	-	-	-	-	-	-	-	-	-	-	-	-	-	-	-	-	6	-	B
				C	5	5	-	-	-	-	-	-	-	-	-	-	1	-	1	-	-	-	-	-	-	-	-	-	1	-	C
245*	**NṢH**	fight each other/	Ih/q*	TOT	12	3	5	4	-	-	-	-	-	-	-	-	-	-	-	-	-	-	-	-	-	-	2	-	3	-	TOT
		be destroyed*																													
		Ex.2:3/2Kin.19:25*/Isa.37:26*		A	7	3	-	4	-	-	-	-	-	-	-	-	-	-	-	-	-	-	-	-	-	-	-	-	2	-	A
		//Ex.21:22/Lev.24:10/Deut.																													
		25:11/2Sam.14:16																													
				B	-	-	-	-	-	-	-	-	-	-	-	-	-	-	-	-	-	-	-	-	-	-	1	-	1	-	B
		Jer.2:15(2x)/9:9,11/46:19		C	5	-	5	-	-	-	-	-	-	-	-	-	-	-	-	-	-	-	-	-	-	-	1	-	-	-	C
246	**NṢḤ**	continuing/perpetual	II	TOT	1	1	-	-	-	-	-	-	-	-	-	-	-	-	-	-	-	-	-	-	-	-	-	64	-	-	TOT
				A	-	-	-	-	-	-	-	-	-	-	-	-	-	-	-	-	-	-	-	-	-	-	-	8	-	-	A
				B	-	-	-	-	-	-	-	-	-	-	-	-	-	-	-	-	-	-	-	-	-	-	-	55	-	-	B
		Jer.8:5		C	1	1	-	-	-	-	-	-	-	-	-	-	-	-	-	-	-	-	-	-	-	-	-	1	-	-	C
247	**NṢL**	be saved/escape	Ih	TOT	15	-	1	10	2	2	-	-	-	-	-	-	2	2	-	-	-	1	-	-	1	-	-	4	M	-	TOT
		Gen.32:31/Deut.23:16/2Kin.19:		A	6	-	-	6	-	-	-	-	-	-	-	-	-	-	-	-	-	1	-	-	1	-	-	4	M	-	A
		11/Isa.37:11/Ezek.14:16,18																													
		Ps.69:15/33:16//Pro.6:3,5		B	4	-	-	2	-	2	-	-	-	-	-	-	-	-	-	-	-	-	-	-	-	-	-	-	M	-	B
		Jer.7:10//Am.3:12/Mi.4:10//		C	5	-	1	2	2	-	-	-	-	-	-	-	2	2	-	-	-	-	-	-	-	-	-	-	M	-	C
		Isa.20:6/Hab.2:9																													
248	**NQB**	named/be referred	Iq	TOT	6	-	6	-	-	-	2	-	-	-	-	-	-	-	-	-	-	-	-	-	-	-	13	-	-	-	TOT
		Num.1:17/Ezr.8:20/1Chr.12:32/		A	6	-	6	-	-	-	-	-	-	-	-	-	-	-	-	-	-	-	-	-	-	-	7	-	-	-	A
		16:41/2Chr.28:15/31:19																													
				B	-	-	-	-	-	-	-	-	-	-	-	-	-	-	-	-	-	-	-	-	-	-	2	-	-	-	B
				C	-	-	-	-	-	-	2	-	-	-	-	-	-	-	-	-	-	-	-	-	-	-	4	-	-	-	C
249	**NQH**	be innocent/be nullified	Ip	TOT	25	-	11	12	1	1	-	-	-	-	-	-	-	-	-	-	-	-	-	-	-	-	1	17	-	-	TOT
		see 3.3		A	8	-	6	1	-	1	-	-	-	-	-	-	-	-	-	-	-	-	-	-	-	-	-	9	-	-	A
				B	8	-	1	7	-	-	-	-	-	-	-	-	-	-	-	-	-	-	-	-	-	-	-	5	-	-	B
				C	9	-	4	4	1	-	-	-	-	-	-	-	-	-	-	-	-	-	-	-	-	-	1	3	-	-	C
250	**NQM**	avenge oneself/be avenged*	Iq	TOT	12	-	3	4	3	2	-	-	-	-	-	-	3	-	-	3	-	5	2	-	3	-	12	2	-	-	TOT
		Judg.15:7/1Sam.14:24/Ez.25:12		A	8	-	3	3	2	-	-	-	-	-	-	-	3	-	-	3	-	-	-	-	-	-	8	1	-	-	A
		//Ex.21:20*/Judg.16:28/Ez.25:																													
		15//1Sam.18:25/Esth.8:13																													

	ROOT	MEANING	DIV	G	NIPH'AL TOT	PT	PF	IMPF	INF	IMPV	PQ	PU'AL TOT	PT	PF	IMPF	O	HOPH'AL TOT	PT	PF	IMPF	O	HITPA'EL TOT	PT	PF	IMPF	O	QAL	PI	HI	O	G
				B	-	-	-	-	-	-	-	-	-	-	-	-	-	-	-	-	-	2	2	-	-	-	2	-	-	-	B
		Isa.1:24//Jer.46:10// Jer.15:15/50:15		C	4	-	-	1	1	2	-	-	-	-	-	-	-	-	-	-	-	3	-	-	3	-	2	1	-	-	C
251	**NQP**	cut down	II	TOT	1	-	1	-	-	-	-	-	-	-	-	-	-	-	-	-	-	-	-	-	-	-	-	1	-	-	TOT
		Job19:26		B	1	-	1	-	-	-	-	-	-	-	-	-	-	-	-	-	-	-	-	-	-	-	-	-	-	-	B
				C	-	-	-	-	-	-	-	-	-	-	-	-	-	-	-	-	-	-	-	-	-	-	-	1	-	-	C
252	**NQŠ**	be driven//be snared	Ip	TOT	1	-	-	1	-	-	-	-	-	-	-	-	-	-	-	-	-	1	1	-	-	-	1	2	-	-	TOT
		Deut.12:30		A	1	-	-	1	-	-	-	-	-	-	-	-	-	-	-	-	-	1	1	-	-	-	-	-	-	-	A
				B	-	-	-	-	-	-	-	-	-	-	-	-	-	-	-	-	-	-	-	-	-	-	1	2	-	-	B
253	**NŚA**	be lifted up/carried away	Iq	TOT	32	10	8	9	2	3	8	-	-	-	-	-	-	-	-	-	-	10	2	-	6	2	M	13	2	-	TOT
		see 3.3		A	11	-	6	3	2	-	1	-	-	-	-	-	-	-	-	-	-	6	1	-	4	1	M	9	2	-	A
				B	4	-	-	1	-	3	3	-	-	-	-	-	-	-	-	-	-	4	1	-	2	1	M	1	-	-	B
				C	17	10	2	5	-	-	4	-	-	-	-	-	-	-	-	-	-	-	-	-	-	-	M	3	-	-	C
254	**NŠA**	be deceived	Ih	TOT	1	-	1	-	-	-	-	-	-	-	-	-	-	-	-	-	-	-	-	-	-	-	-	-	15	-	TOT
				A	-	-	-	-	-	-	-	-	-	-	-	-	-	-	-	-	-	-	-	-	-	-	-	-	6	-	A
				B	-	-	-	-	-	-	-	-	-	-	-	-	-	-	-	-	-	-	-	-	-	-	-	-	2	-	B
		Isa.19:13		C	1	-	1	-	-	-	-	-	-	-	-	-	-	-	-	-	-	-	-	-	-	-	-	-	7	-	C
255	**NŠH**	be forgotten	Iq	TOT	1	-	-	1	-	-	-	-	-	-	-	-	-	-	-	-	-	-	-	-	-	-	2	1	2	-	TOT
				A	-	-	-	-	-	-	-	-	-	-	-	-	-	-	-	-	-	-	-	-	-	-	-	1	-	-	A
				B	-	-	-	-	-	-	-	-	-	-	-	-	-	-	-	-	-	-	-	-	-	-	2	-	2	-	B
		Isa.44:21		C	1	-	-	1	-	-	-	-	-	-	-	-	-	-	-	-	-	-	-	-	-	-	-	-	-	-	C
256	**NŚQ**	be kindled	Ih	TOT	1	-	1	-	-	-	-	-	-	-	-	-	-	-	-	-	-	-	-	-	-	-	-	-	2	-	TOT
				A	-	-	-	-	-	-	-	-	-	-	-	-	-	-	-	-	-	-	-	-	-	-	-	-	1	-	A
		Ps.78:21		B	1	-	1	-	-	-	-	-	-	-	-	-	-	-	-	-	-	-	-	-	-	-	-	-	-	-	B
				C	-	-	-	-	-	-	-	-	-	-	-	-	-	-	-	-	-	-	-	-	-	-	-	-	1	-	C
257	**NŠT**	become dry/dry up	I=q	TOT	1	-	1	-	-	-	-	-	-	-	-	-	-	-	-	-	-	-	-	-	-	-	2	-	-	-	TOT
		Isa.19:5		C	1	-	1	-	-	-	-	-	-	-	-	-	-	-	-	-	-	-	-	-	-	-	2	-	-	-	C
258*	**NTK**	be poured out	I=q	TOT	8	1	7	-	-	-	-	-	-	-	-	-	1	-	-	1	-	-	-	-	-	-	7	-	5	-	TOT
		Ex.9:33/2Sam.21:10/Jer.42:18 /Ez.22:21/24:11/2Chr.34:21		A	6	-	6	-	-	-	-	-	-	-	-	-	1	-	-	1	-	-	-	-	-	-	6	-	4	-	A
				B	-	-	-	-	-	-	-	-	-	-	-	-	-	-	-	-	-	-	-	-	-	-	1	-	1	-	B
		Jer.7:20//Nah.1:6		C	2	1	1	-	-	-	-	-	-	-	-	-	-	-	-	-	-	-	-	-	-	-	-	-	-	-	C
259	**NTN**	be given/be placed	Iq	TOT	82	3	48	27	4	-	10	-	-	-	-	-	8	-	-	8	-	-	-	-	-	-	M	-	-	-	TOT
		see 3.3		A	71	2	40	25	4	-	10	-	-	-	-	-	7	-	-	7	-	-	-	-	-	-	M	-	-	-	A
				B	2	-	2	-	-	-	-	-	-	-	-	-	1	-	-	1	-	-	-	-	-	-	M	-	-	-	B
				C	9	1	6	2	-	-	-	-	-	-	-	-	-	-	-	-	-	-	-	-	-	-	M	-	-	-	C
260	**NT'**	be struck out	III	TOT	1	-	1	-	-	-	-	-	-	-	-	-	-	-	-	-	-	-	-	-	-	-	-	-	-	-	TOT
		Job4:10		B	1	-	1	-	-	-	-	-	-	-	-	-	-	-	-	-	-	-	-	-	-	-	-	-	-	-	B
261	**NTṢ**	be destroyed/demolished	Iq	TOT	3	-	3	-	-	-	1	1	-	1	-	-	1	-	-	1	-	-	-	-	-	-	30	6	-	-	TOT
		Ezek.16:39		A	1	-	1	-	-	-	1	1	-	1	-	-	1	-	-	1	-	-	-	-	-	-	24	6	-	-	A
				B	-	-	-	-	-	-	-	-	-	-	-	-	-	-	-	-	-	-	-	-	-	-	3	-	-	-	B
		Jer.4:26/Nah.1:6		C	2		2	-	-	-	-	-	-	-	-	-	-	-	-	-	-	-	-	-	-	-	3	-	-	-	C
262	**NTQ**	be broken/torn loose	Iq	TOT	10	-	5	5	-	-	1	-	-	-	-	-	1	-	1	-	-	-	-	-	-	-	3	11	2	-	TOT
		Josh.4:18//8:10/Judg.16:9/ Eccl.4:12		A	4	-	1	3	-	-	1	-	-	-	-	-	1	-	1	-	-	-	-	-	-	-	2	5	1	-	A

	ROOT	MEANING	DIV	G	NIPH'AL TOT	PT	PF	IMPF	INF	IMPV	PQ	PU'AL TOT	PT	PF	IMPF	O	HOPH'AL TOT	PT	PF	IMPF	O	HITPA'EL TOT	PT	PF	IMPF	O	QAL	PI	HI	O	G
		Job17:11//18:14		B	2	-	1	1	-	-	-	-	-	-	-	-	-	-	-	-	-	-	-	-	-	-	-	2	-	-	B
		Isa.5:27/Jer.6:29/10:20/		C	4	-	3	1	-	-	-	-	-	-	-	-	-	-	-	-	-	-	-	-	-	-	1	4	1	-	C
		Isa. 33:20																													
263	NTŠ	be uprooted/destroyed	Iq	TOT	4	-	-	4	-	-	-	-	-	-	-	-	1	-	-	1	-	-	-	-	-	-	16	-	-	-	TOT
		Jer.31:40/Dan.11:4		A	2	-	-	2	-	-	-	-	-	-	-	-	-	-	-	-	-	-	-	-	-	-	6	-	-	-	A
				B	-	-	-	-	-	-	-	-	-	-	-	-	-	-	-	-	-	-	-	-	-	-	1	-	-	-	B
		Jer.18:14/Am.9:15		C	2	-	-	2	-	-	-	-	-	-	-	-	1	-	-	1	-	-	-	-	-	-	9	-	-	-	C
264	SBB	turn oneself/surround	Ih	TOT	20	-	14	6	-	-	-	-	-	-	-	-	6	5	-	1	-	-	-	-	-	-	89	1	33	11	TOT
		Gen.19:4/Num.34:4,5/Josh.7:9/		A	19	-	13	6	-	-	-	-	-	-	-	-	5	5	-	-	-	-	-	-	-	-	53	1	29	1	A
		15:3,10/16:6/18:14/19:14/Judg.																													
		19:22/Jer.31:39/Ezek.26:2/41:7																													
		//1:9,12,17/10:11(2x),16																													
				B	-	-	-	-	-	-	-	-	-	-	-	-	-	-	-	-	-	-	-	-	-	-	28	-	2	10	B
		Jer.6:12		C	1	-	1	-	-	-	-	-	-	-	-	-	1	-	-	1	-	-	-	-	-	-	8	-	2	-	C
265*	SGR	be closed/lock oneself up	Iq	TOT	8	-	1	6	-	1	12	5	1	4	-	-	-	-	-	-	-	-	-	-	-	-	43	4	30	-	TOT
		1Sam.23:7//Num.12:14,15/Ez.		A	6	-	1	4	-	1	11	2	1	1	-	-	-	-	-	-	-	-	-	-	-	-	34	4	18	-	A
		46:2/Neh.13:19//Ez.3:24																													
				B	-	-	-	-	-	-	1	-	-	-	-	-	-	-	-	-	-	-	-	-	-	-	5	-	8	-	B
		Isa.45:1/60:11		C	2	-	-	2	-	-	-	3	-	3	-	-	-	-	-	-	-	-	-	-	-	-	4	-	4	-	C
266	SWG	turn back	Iq	TOT	14	2	5	6	1	-	-	-	-	-	-	-	-	1	-	-	-	-	-	-	-	-	3	-	7	-	TOT
		Jer.38:22		A	1	-	1	-	-	-	-	-	-	-	-	-	-	-	-	-	-	-	-	-	-	-	-	-	2	-	A
		2Sam.1:22/Ps.44:19//35:4/		B	7	-	2	5	-	-	-	-	-	-	-	-	-	-	-	-	-	-	-	-	-	-	3	-	3	-	B
		40:15/70:3/78:57/129:5																													
		Jer.46:5/Zeph.1:6//Isa.42:		C	6	2	2	1	1	-	-	-	-	-	-	-	-	1	-	-	-	-	-	-	-	-	-	-	2	-	C
		17/50:5//Mi.2:6//Isa.59:13																													
267	SḤP	be cast to earth	II	TOT	1	-	1	-	-	-	-	-	-	-	-	-	-	-	-	-	-	-	-	-	-	-	1	-	-	-	TOT
				B	-	-	-	-	-	-	-	-	-	-	-	-	-	-	-	-	-	-	-	-	-	-	1	-	-	-	B
		Jer.46:15		C	1	-	1	-	-	-	-	-	-	-	-	-	-	-	-	-	-	-	-	-	-	-	-	-	-	-	C
268*	SKL	act foolishly	Ih	TOT	4	-	-	4	-	-	-	-	-	-	-	-	-	-	-	-	-	-	-	-	-	-	-	2	2	-	TOT
		1Sam.13:13/2Sam.24:10/		A	4	-	-	4	-	-	-	-	-	-	-	-	-	-	-	-	-	-	-	-	-	-	-	1	2	-	A
		1Chr.21:8/2Chr.16:9																													
				C	-	-	-	-	-	-	-	-	-	-	-	-	-	-	-	-	-	-	-	-	-	-	-	1	-	-	C
269	SKN	endanger oneself	II	TOT	1	-	-	1	-	-	-	1	1	-	-	-	-	-	-	-	-	-	-	-	-	-	7	-	4	-	TOT
		Eccl.10:9		A	1	-	-	1	-	-	-	-	-	-	-	-	-	-	-	-	-	-	-	-	-	-	2	-	2	-	A
				B	-	-	-	-	-	-	-	-	-	-	-	-	-	-	-	-	-	-	-	-	-	-	4	-	2	-	B
				C	-	-	-	-	-	-	-	1	1	-	-	-	-	-	-	-	-	-	-	-	-	-	1	-	-	-	C
270	SKR	be stopped/be closed	II	TOT	2	-	-	2	-	-	-	-	-	-	-	-	-	-	-	-	-	-	-	-	-	-	-	-	1	-	TOT
		Gen.8:2		A	1	-	-	1	-	-	-	-	-	-	-	-	-	-	-	-	-	-	-	-	-	-	-	-	-	-	A
		Ps.63:12		B	1	-	-	1	-	-	-	-	-	-	-	-	-	-	-	-	-	-	-	-	-	-	-	-	-	-	B
				C	-	-	-	-	-	-	-	-	-	-	-	-	-	-	-	-	-	-	-	-	-	-	-	-	1	-	C
271	SLḤ	be forgiven	Iq	TOT	13	-	13	-	-	-	-	-	-	-	-	-	-	-	-	-	-	-	-	-	-	-	31	-	-	-	TOT
		Lev.4:20,26,31,35/5:10,13,16,		A	13	-	13	-	-	-	-	-	-	-	-	-	-	-	-	-	-	-	-	-	-	-	23	-	-	-	A
		18,26/19:22/Num.15:25,26,28																													
				B	-	-	-	-	-	-	-	-	-	-	-	-	-	-	-	-	-	-	-	-	-	-	3	-	-	-	B
				C	-	-	-	-	-	-	-	-	-	-	-	-	-	-	-	-	-	-	-	-	-	-	5	-	-	-	C

	ROOT	MEANING	DIV	G	NIPH'AL TOT	PT	PF	IMPF	INF	IMPV	PQ	PU'AL TOT	PT	PF	IMPF	O	HOPH'AL TOT	PT	PF	IMPF	O	HITPA'EL TOT	PT	PF	IMPF	O	QAL	PI	HI	O	G
272	**SMK**	lean on	Iq	TOT	6	-	2	4	-	-	3	-	-	-	-	-	-	-	-	-	-	-	-	-	-	-	41	1	-	-	TOT
		Judg.16:29/2Kin.18:21/Isa.		A	4	-	-	4	-	-	-	-	-	-	-	-	-	-	-	-	-	-	-	-	-	-	26	-	-	-	A
		36:6/2Chr.32:8																													
		Ps.71:6		B	1	-	1	-	-	-	2	-	-	-	-	-	-	-	-	-	-	-	-	-	-	-	10	1	-	-	B
		Isa.48:2		C	1	-	1	-	-	-	1	-	-	-	-	-	-	-	-	-	-	-	-	-	-	-	5	-	-	-	C
273	**SMN**	?	III	TOT	1	1	-	-	-	-	-	-	-	-	-	-	-	-	-	-	-	-	-	-	-	-	-	-	-	-	TOT
		Isa.28:25		C	1	1	-	-	-	-	-	-	-	-	-	-	-	-	-	-	-	-	-	-	-	-	-	-	-	-	C
274*	**S'R**	be stirred up	II	TOT	1	-	-	1	-	-	-	2	1	-	1	-	-	-	-	-	-	-	-	-	-	-	3	1	-	-	TOT
		2Kin.6:11		A	1	-	-	1	-	-	-	-	-	-	-	-	-	-	-	-	-	-	-	-	-	-	2	-	-	-	A
				C	-	-	-	-	-	-	-	2	1	-	1	-	-	-	-	-	-	-	-	-	-	-	1	1	-	-	C
275	**SPD**	be lamented	Iq	TOT	2	-	-	2	-	-	-	-	-	-	-	-	-	-	-	-	-	-	-	-	-	-	28	-	-	-	TOT
				A	-	-	-	-	-	-	-	-	-	-	-	-	-	-	-	-	-	-	-	-	-	-	14	-	-	-	A
				B	-	-	-	-	-	-	-	-	-	-	-	-	-	-	-	-	-	-	-	-	-	-	2	-	-	-	B
		Jer.16:4/25:33		C	2	-	-	2	-	-	-	-	-	-	-	-	-	-	-	-	-	-	-	-	-	-	12	-	-	-	C
276	**SPH**	be taken away/snatched away	Iq	TOT	9	3	1	5	-	-	-	-	-	-	-	-	-	-	-	-	-	-	-	-	-	-	11	-	1	-	TOT
		1Chr.21:12//1Sam.26:10//Gen.		A	7	1	1	5	-	-	-	-	-	-	-	-	-	-	-	-	-	-	-	-	-	-	4	-	-	-	A
		19:15,17/Num.16:26/1Sam.12:																													
		25/27:1																													
		Pro.13:23		B	1	1	-	-	-	-	-	-	-	-	-	-	-	-	-	-	-	-	-	-	-	-	1	-	1	-	B
		Isa.13:15		C	1	1	-	-	-	-	-	-	-	-	-	-	-	-	-	-	-	-	-	-	-	-	6	-	-	-	C
277	**SPḤ**	attach oneself	Iq	TOT	1	-	1	-	-	-	-	1	-	1	-	-	-	-	-	-	-	1	-	-	-	1	1	2	-	-	TOT
				A	-	-	-	-	-	-	-	-	-	-	-	-	-	-	-	-	-	1	-	-	-	1	1	-	-	-	A
				B	-	-	-	-	-	-	-	1	-	1	-	-	-	-	-	-	-	-	-	-	-	-	-	-	-	-	B
		Isa.14:1		C	1	-	1	-	-	-	-	-	-	-	-	-	-	-	-	-	-	-	-	-	-	-	-	2	-	-	C
278	**SPR**	be counted	Iq	TOT	8	-	-	8	-	-	-	5	-	1	4	-	-	-	-	-	-	-	-	-	-	-	26	67	-	-	TOT
		Gen.16:10/32:13/1Kin.3:8/8:5/		A	7	-	-	7	-	-	-	-	-	-	-	-	-	-	-	-	-	-	-	-	-	-	17	26	-	-	A
		1Chr.23:3/2Chr.5:6/Jer.33:22																													
				B	-	-	-	-	-	-	-	3	-	-	3	-	-	-	-	-	-	-	-	-	-	-	7	34	-	-	B
		Hos.2:1		C	1	-	-	1	-	-	-	2	-	1	1	-	-	-	-	-	-	-	-	-	-	-	2	7	-	-	C
279	**SQL**	be stoned	Iq	TOT	4	-	-	4	-	-	-	2	-	2	-	-	-	-	-	-	-	-	-	-	-	-	12	4	-	-	TOT
		Ex.19:13/21:28,29,32		A	4	-	-	4	-	-	-	2	-	2	-	-	-	-	-	-	-	-	-	-	-	-	12	2	-	-	A
				C	-	-	-	-	-	-	-	-	-	-	-	-	-	-	-	-	-	-	-	-	-	-	-	2	-	-	C
280	**SRḤ**	be clouded(?)	II	TOT	1	-	1	-	-	-	4	-	-	-	-	-	-	-	-	-	-	-	-	-	-	-	6	-	-	-	TOT
				A	-	-	-	-	-	-	2	-	-	-	-	-	-	-	-	-	-	-	-	-	-	-	4	-	-	-	A
		Jer.49:7		C	1	-	1	-	-	-	2	-	-	-	-	-	-	-	-	-	-	-	-	-	-	-	2	-	-	-	C
281	**STM/**	be forgiven	Iq	TOT	1	-	-	-	1	-	3	-	-	-	-	-	-	-	-	-	-	-	-	-	-	-	11	2	-	-	TOT
	ŚTM	Neh.4:1		A	1	-	-	-	1	-	2	-	-	-	-	-	-	-	-	-	-	-	-	-	-	-	9	2	-	-	A
				B	-	-	-	-	-	-	1	-	-	-	-	-	-	-	-	-	-	-	-	-	-	-	2	-	-	-	B
282	**STR/**	be hidden/hide oneself	Ih	TOT	32	4	13	13	1	1	-	1	1	-	-	-	-	-	-	-	-	5	4	-	1	-	-	1	45	-	TOT
	ŚTR	see 3.3		A	11	2	4	4	-	1	-	-	-	-	-	-	-	-	-	-	-	2	2	-	-	-	-	-	12	-	A
				B	13	2	5	5	1	-	-	1	1	-	-	-	-	-	-	-	-	1	1	-	-	-	-	-	23	-	B
				C	8	-	4	4	-	-	-	-	-	-	-	-	-	-	-	-	-	2	1	-	1	-	-	1	10	-	C
283	**'BD**	be cultivated/subjugate*	Iq	TOT	4	-	2	2	-	-	-	2	-	2	-	-	-	-	-	-	-	-	-	-	-	-	M	-	8	-	TOT
		Eccl.5:8*/Ez.36:9//Deut.		A	4	-	2	2	-	-	-	1	-	1	-	-	-	-	-	-	-	-	-	-	-	-	M	-	5	-	A
		21:4/Ez.36:4																													

	ROOT	MEANING	DIV	G	NIPH'AL TOT	PT	PF	IMPF	INF	IMPV	PQ	PU'AL TOT	PT	PF	IMPF	O	HOPH'AL TOT	PT	PF	IMPF	O	HITPA'EL TOT	PT	PF	IMPF	O	QAL	PI	HI	O	G
				B	-	-	-	-	-	-	-	-	-	-	-	-	-	-	-	-	-	-	-	-	-	-	M	-	-	-	B
				C	-	-	-	-	-	-	-	1	-	1	-	-	-	-	-	-	-	-	-	-	-	-	M	-	3	-	C
284	'BR	be forded	Iq	TOT	1	-	-	1	-	-	-	-	-	-	-	-	-	-	-	-	-	8	3	2	3	-	M	2	78	-	TOT
		Ez.47:5		A	1	-	-	1	-	-	-	-	-	-	-	-	-	-	-	-	-	1	-	-	1	-	M	1	68	-	A
				B	-	-	-	-	-	-	-	-	-	-	-	-	-	-	-	-	-	7	3	2	2	-	M	1	6	-	B
				C	-	-	-	-	-	-	-	-	-	-	-	-	-	-	-	-	-	-	-	-	-	-	M	-	4	-	C
285	'GN	be prevented	III	TOT	1	-	-	1	-	-	-	-	-	-	-	-	-	-	-	-	-	-	-	-	-	-	-	-	-	-	TOT
		Ruth1:13		A	1	-	-	1	-	-	-	-	-	-	-	-	-	-	-	-	-	-	-	-	-	-	-	-	-	-	A
286	'DR	I be missing/lack	II	TOT	6	1	5	-	-	-	-	-	-	-	-	-	-	-	-	-	-	-	-	-	-	-	2	1	-	-	TOT
		1Sam.30:19/2Sam.17:22		A	2	-	2	-	-	-	-	-	-	-	-	-	-	-	-	-	-	-	-	-	-	-	2	1	-	-	A
		Isa.59:15//34:16/40:26/		C	4	1	3	-	-	-	-	-	-	-	-	-	-	-	-	-	-	-	-	-	-	-	-	-	-	-	C
		Zeph.3:5																													
287	'DR	II be hoed	III	TOT	2	-	-	2	-	-	-	-	-	-	-	-	-	-	-	-	-	-	-	-	-	-	-	-	-	-	TOT
		Isa.5:6/7:25		C	2	-	-	2	-	-	-	-	-	-	-	-	-	-	-	-	-	-	-	-	-	-	-	-	-	-	C
288*	'WH	be perverse	II	TOT	4	2	2	-	-	-	-	-	-	-	-	-	-	-	-	-	-	-	-	-	-	-	2	2	9	-	TOT
		1Sam.20:30		A	1	1	-	-	-	-	-	-	-	-	-	-	-	-	-	-	-	-	-	-	-	-	2	-	5	-	A
		Pro.12:8//Ps.38:7		B	2	1	1	-	-	-	-	-	-	-	-	-	-	-	-	-	-	-	-	-	-	-	-	1	2	-	B
		Isa.21:3		C	1	-	1	-	-	-	-	-	-	-	-	-	-	-	-	-	-	-	-	-	-	-	-	1	2	-	C
289	'WR	I be made bare	III	TOT	1	-	-	1	-	-	-	-	-	-	-	-	-	-	-	-	-	-	-	-	-	-	-	-	-	-	TOT
		Hab.3:9		C	1	-	-	1	-	-	-	-	-	-	-	-	-	-	-	-	-	-	-	-	-	-	-	-	-	-	C
290*	'WR	II be aroused/be awakened	Iq	TOT	7	-	1	6	-	-	-	-	-	-	-	-	-	-	-	-	-	4	1	1	1	1	15	-	33	14	TOT
				A	-	-	-	-	-	-	-	-	-	-	-	-	-	-	-	-	-	-	-	-	-	-	-	-	8	3	A
		Job14:12		B	1	-	-	1	-	-	-	-	-	-	-	-	-	-	-	-	-	2	-	1	1	-	10	-	10	7	B
		Zech.2:17//Jer.6:22/25:32/		C	6	-	1	5	-	-	-	-	-	-	-	-	-	-	-	-	-	2	1	-	-	1	5	-	15	4	C
		50:41/Jo.4:12/Zech.4:1																													
291	'ZB	be(come) deserted	Iq	TOT	9	3	2	4	-	-	12	2	-	2	-	-	-	-	-	-	-	-	-	-	-	-	M	-	-	-	TOT
		Ez.36:4//Neh.13:11//Lev.26:43		A	3	1	1	1	-	-	4	-	-	-	-	-	-	-	-	-	-	-	-	-	-	-	M	-	-	-	A
		Ps.37:25//Job18:4		B	2	1	-	1	-	-	1	-	-	-	-	-	-	-	-	-	-	-	-	-	-	-	M	-	-	-	B
		Isa.27:10//62:12//7:16/18:6		C	4	1	1	2	-	-	7	2	-	2	-	-	-	-	-	-	-	-	-	-	-	-	M	-	-	-	C
292	'ZR	be helped	Iq	TOT	4	-	1	2	1	-	1	-	-	-	-	-	-	-	-	-	-	-	-	-	-	-	76	-	2	-	TOT
		Dan.11:34/1Chr.5:20//		A	3	-	-	2	1	-	-	-	-	-	-	-	-	-	-	-	-	-	-	-	-	-	39	-	2	-	A
		2Chr.26:15																													
		Ps.28:7		B	1	-	1	-	-	-	-	-	-	-	-	-	-	-	-	-	-	-	-	-	-	-	23	-	-	-	B
				C	-	-	-	-	-	-	1	-	-	-	-	-	-	-	-	-	-	-	-	-	-	-	14	-	-	-	C
293	'ṬP	languish	II	TOT	1	-	-	-	1	-	2	-	-	-	-	-	-	-	-	-	-	6	-	-	3	3	5	-	1	-	TOT
		Eccl.2:11		A	1	-	-	-	1	-	1	-	-	-	-	-	-	-	-	-	-	-	-	-	-	-	1	-	1	-	A
				B	-	-	-	-	-	-	1	-	-	-	-	-	-	-	-	-	-	6	-	-	3	3	3	-	-	-	B
				C	-	-	-	-	-	-	-	-	-	-	-	-	-	-	-	-	-	-	-	-	-	-	1	-	-	-	C
294*	'KR	be stirred	Iq	TOT	2	2	-	-	-	-	-	-	-	-	-	-	-	-	-	-	-	-	-	-	-	-	12	-	-	-	TOT
				A	-	-	-	-	-	-	-	-	-	-	-	-	-	-	-	-	-	-	-	-	-	-	9	-	-	-	A
		Ps.39:3/Pro.15:6		B	2	2	-	-	-	-	-	-	-	-	-	-	-	-	-	-	-	-	-	-	-	-	3	-	-	-	B
295*	'LH	rise up/be taken away	Iq	TOT	16	-	6	4	5	1	-	-	-	-	-	-	4	-	4	-	-	1	-	-	1	-	M	-	M	-	TOT
		see 3.3		A	14	-	4	4	5	1	-	-	-	-	-	-	2	-	2	-	-	-	-	-	-	-	M	-	M	-	A
				B	2	-	2	-	-	-	-	-	-	-	-	-	-	-	-	-	-	-	-	-	-	-	M	-	M	-	B
				C	-	-	-	-	-	-	-	-	-	-	-	-	2	-	2	-	-	1	-	-	1	-	M	-	M	-	C

	ROOT	MEANING	DIV	G	NIPH'AL TOT	PT	PF	IMPF	INF	IMPV	PQ	PU'AL TOT	PT	PF	IMPF	O	HOPH'AL TOT	PT	PF	IMPF	O	HITPA'EL TOT	PT	PF	IMPF	O	QAL	PI	HI	O	G
296	**'LM**	be hidden/hide oneself	Ih	TOT	11	4	7	-	-	-	1	-	-	-	-	-	-	-	-	-	-	6	-	2	3	1	1	-	10	-	TOT
		1Kin.10:3/Eccl.12:14//Lev.4: 13/5:2,3,4/Num.5:13/2Chr.9:2		A	8	2	6	-	-	-	-	-	-	-	-	-	-	-	-	-	-	3	-	2	-	1	-	-	4	-	A
		Ps.26:4//Job28:21		B	2	1	1	-	-	-	1	-	-	-	-	-	-	-	-	-	-	2	-	-	2	-	1	-	4	-	B
		Nah.3:11		C	1	1	-	-	-	-	-	-	-	-	-	-	-	-	-	-	-	1	-	-	1	-	-	-	2	-	C
297	**'LS**	flap	I=q?	TOT	1	-	1	-	-	-	-	-	-	-	-	-	-	-	-	-	-	1	-	-	1	-	1	-	-	-	TOT
		Job39:13		B	1	-	1	-	-	-	-	-	-	-	-	-	-	-	-	-	-	1	-	-	1	-	1	-	-	-	B
298	**'NH**	I be answered	Iq	TOT	5	1	1	3	-	-	-	-	-	-	-	-	-	-	-	-	-	-	-	-	-	-	M	-	1	-	TOT
		Ez.14:7//14:4		A	2	1	1	-	-	-	-	-	-	-	-	-	-	-	-	-	-	-	-	-	-	-	M	-	-	-	A
		Job11:2/19:7/Pro.21:13		B	3	-	-	3	-	-	-	-	-	-	-	-	-	-	-	-	-	-	-	-	-	-	M	-	1	-	B
				C	-	-	-	-	-	-	-	-	-	-	-	-	-	-	-	-	-	-	-	-	-	-	M	-	-	-	C
299	**'NH**	II be oppressed/bow down	Ip	TOT	4	2	1	-	1	-	-	4	1	1	1	1	-	-	-	-	-	6	-	2	1	3	4	56	2	-	TOT
		oneself Ex.10:3		A	1	-	-	-	1	-	-	1	1	-	1	-	-	-	-	-	-	5	-	2	-	3	-	38	2	-	A
		Ps.119:107		B	1	-	1	-	-	-	-	2	-	1	-	1	-	-	-	-	-	1	-	-	1	-	2	12	-	-	B
		Isa.53:7/58:10		C	2	2	-	-	-	-	-	1	1	-	-	-	-	-	-	-	-	-	-	-	-	-	2	6	-	-	C
300	**'NŠ**	be fined	Iq	TOT	3	-	2	1	-	-	1	-	-	-	-	-	-	-	-	-	-	-	-	-	-	6	-	-	-	-	TOT
		Ex.21:22		A	1	-	-	1	-	-	-	-	-	-	-	-	-	-	-	-	-	-	-	-	-	3	-	-	-	-	A
		Pro.22:3/27:12		B	2	-	2	-	-	-	-	-	-	-	-	-	-	-	-	-	-	-	-	-	-	2	-	-	-	-	B
				C	-	-	-	-	-	-	1	-	-	-	-	-	-	-	-	-	-	-	-	-	-	1	-	-	-	-	C
301	**'ṢB**	be grieved/be hurt*	Iq	TOT	7	-	2	5	-	-	1	-	-	-	-	-	-	-	-	-	-	2	-	-	2	-	3	2	1	-	TOT
		1Sam.20:34/2Sam.19:3//Gen. 45:5/1Sam.20:3/Neh.8:10,11/ Eccl.10:9*		A	7	-	2	5	-	-	-	-	-	-	-	-	-	-	-	-	-	2	-	-	2	-	2	-	-	-	A
				B	-	-	-	-	-	-	-	-	-	-	-	-	-	-	-	-	-	-	-	-	-	-	-	1	1	-	B
				C	-	-	-	-	-	-	1	-	-	-	-	-	-	-	-	-	-	-	-	-	-	-	1	1	-	-	C
302	**'ṢL**	be slow/delay	III	TOT	1	-	-	1	-	-	-	-	-	-	-	-	-	-	-	-	-	-	-	-	-	-	-	-	-	-	TOT
		Judg.18:9		A	1	-	-	1	-	-	-	-	-	-	-	-	-	-	-	-	-	-	-	-	-	-	-	-	-	-	A
303	**'ṢR**	be kept (away)	Iq	TOT	10	1	1	6	2	-	-	-	-	-	-	-	-	-	-	-	-	-	-	-	-	36	-	-	-	-	TOT
		1Sam.21:8//Num.17:15//17:13/ /25:8/2Sam.24:21,25/1Chr.21: 22//1Kin.8:35/2Chr.6:26		A	9	1	1	5	2	-	-	-	-	-	-	-	-	-	-	-	-	-	-	-	-	30	-	-	-	-	A
		Ps.106:30		B	1	-	-	1	-	-	-	-	-	-	-	-	-	-	-	-	-	-	-	-	-	4	-	-	-	-	B
				C	-	-	-	-	-	-	-	-	-	-	-	-	-	-	-	-	-	-	-	-	-	2	-	-	-	-	C
304	**'QR**	be uprooted	Iq	TOT	1	-	-	1	-	-	-	-	-	-	-	-	-	-	-	-	-	-	-	-	-	1	5	-	-	-	TOT
				A	-	-	-	-	-	-	-	-	-	-	-	-	-	-	-	-	-	-	-	-	-	-	4	-	-	-	A
				B	-	-	-	-	-	-	-	-	-	-	-	-	-	-	-	-	-	-	-	-	-	1	1	-	-	-	B
		Zeph.2:4		C	1	-	-	1	-	-	-	-	-	-	-	-	-	-	-	-	-	-	-	-	-	-	-	-	-	-	C
305	**'QŠ**	twist/go crooked ways	Ip?	TOT	1	1	-	-	-	-	-	-	-	-	-	-	-	-	-	-	-	-	-	-	-	-	3	1	-	-	TOT
		Pro.28:18		B	1	1	-	-	-	-	-	-	-	-	-	-	-	-	-	-	-	-	-	-	-	-	1	1	-	-	B
				C	-	-	-	-	-	-	-	-	-	-	-	-	-	-	-	-	-	-	-	-	-	-	2	-	-	-	C
306	**'RH**	be poured out	Ip	TOT	1	-	-	1	-	-	-	-	-	-	-	-	-	-	-	-	-	2	1	-	1	-	8	3	-	-	TOT
				A	-	-	-	-	-	-	-	-	-	-	-	-	-	-	-	-	-	-	-	-	-	-	2	2	-	-	A
				B	-	-	-	-	-	-	-	-	-	-	-	-	-	-	-	-	-	2	1	-	1	-	2	-	-	-	B
		Isa.32:15		C	1	-	-	1	-	-	-	-	-	-	-	-	-	-	-	-	-	-	-	-	-	-	4	1	-	-	C
307	**'RL**	be uncovered	Iq	TOT	1	-	-	-	-	1	-	-	-	-	-	-	-	-	-	-	-	-	-	-	-	-	1	-	-	-	TOT

	ROOT	MEANING	DIV	G	NIPH'AL TOT	PT	PF	IMPF	INF	IMPV	PQ	PU'AL TOT	PT	PF	IMPF	O	HOPH'AL TOT	PT	PF	IMPF	O	HITPA'EL TOT	PT	PF	IMPF	O	QAL	PI	HI	O	G
				A	-	-	-	-	-	-	-	-	-	-	-	-	-	-	-	-	-	-	-	-	-	-	1	-	-	-	A
		Hab.2:16		C	1	-	-	-	-	1	-	-	-	-	-	-	-	-	-	-	-	-	-	-	-	-	-	-	-	-	C
308	'RM	be heaped up/piled up	III	TOT	1	-	1	-	-	-	-	-	-	-	-	-	-	-	-	-	-	-	-	-	-	-	-	-	-	-	TOT
		Ex.15:8		B	1	-	1	-	-	-	-	-	-	-	-	-	-	-	-	-	-	-	-	-	-	-	-	-	-	-	B
309	'RṢ	terrible/awesome	Iq	TOT	1	1	-	-	-	-	-	-	-	-	-	-	-	-	-	-	-	-	-	-	-	-	11	-	3	-	TOT
				A	-	-	-	-	-	-	-	-	-	-	-	-	-	-	-	-	-	-	-	-	-	-	5	-	-	-	A
		Ps.89:9		B	1	1	-	-	-	-	-	-	-	-	-	-	-	-	-	-	-	-	-	-	-	-	3	-	-	-	B
				C	-	-	-	-	-	-	-	-	-	-	-	-	-	-	-	-	-	-	-	-	-	-	3	-	3	-	C
310	'ŚH	be done/be made	Iq	TOT	96	4	35	54	3	-	16	1	-	1	-	-	-	-	-	-	-	-	-	-	-	-	M	2	-	-	TOT
		See 3.3		A	89	4	32	50	3	-	14	-	-	-	-	-	-	-	-	-	-	-	-	-	-	-	M	2	-	-	A
				B	1	-	1	-	-	-	2	1	-	1	-	-	-	-	-	-	-	-	-	-	-	-	M	-	-	-	B
				C	6	-	2	4	-	-	-	-	-	-	-	-	-	-	-	-	-	-	-	-	-	-	M	-	-	-	C
311	'TM	be burned	III	TOT	1	-	1	-	-	-	-	-	-	-	-	-	-	-	-	-	-	-	-	-	-	-	-	-	-	-	TOT
		Isa.9:18		C	1	-	1	-	-	-	-	-	-	-	-	-	-	-	-	-	-	-	-	-	-	-	-	-	-	-	C
312*	'TR	allow oneself to be persuaded by prayer	Iq/II*	TOT	9	1	1	5	2	-	-	-	-	-	-	-	-	-	-	-	-	-	-	-	-	-	5	-	8	-	TOT
		Gen.25:21/2Sam.21:14/24:25/ Ezra8:23/2Chr.33:13//1Chr.5: 20/2Chr.33:19		A	7	-	-	5	2	-	-	-	-	-	-	-	-	-	-	-	-	-	-	-	-	-	4	-	7	-	A
		Pro.27:6*		B	1	1	-	-	-	-	-	-	-	-	-	-	-	-	-	-	-	-	-	-	-	-	1	-	1	-	B
		Isa.19:22		C	1	-	1	-	-	-	-	-	-	-	-	-	-	-	-	-	-	-	-	-	-	-	-	-	-	-	C
313	PGŠ	meet each other	Iq	TOT	3	-	3	-	-	-	-	-	-	-	-	-	-	-	-	-	-	-	-	-	-	-	10	1	-	-	TOT
				A	-	-	-	-	-	-	-	-	-	-	-	-	-	-	-	-	-	-	-	-	-	-	7	-	-	-	A
		Ps.85:11/Pro.22:2/29:13		B	3	-	3	-	-	-	-	-	-	-	-	-	-	-	-	-	-	-	-	-	-	-	1	1	-	-	B
				C	-	-	-	-	-	-	-	-	-	-	-	-	-	-	-	-	-	-	-	-	-	-	2	-	-	-	C
314	PDH	be redeemed/be delivered	Iq	TOT	3	-	1	2	-	-	3	-	-	-	-	-	1	-	-	-	1	-	-	-	-	-	50	1	-	-	TOT
		Lev.19:20//27:29		A	2	-	1	1	-	-	1	-	-	-	-	-	1	-	-	-	1	-	-	-	-	-	25	1	-	-	A
				B	-	-	-	-	-	-	-	-	-	-	-	-	-	-	-	-	-	-	-	-	-	-	17	-	-	-	B
		Isa.1:27		C	1	-	-	1	-	-	2	-	-	-	-	-	-	-	-	-	-	-	-	-	-	-	8	-	-	-	C
315*	PWG	become cold/weak	Iq	TOT	1	-	1	-	-	-	-	-	-	-	-	-	-	-	-	-	-	-	-	-	-	-	-	-	3	-	TOT
				A	-	-	-	-	-	-	-	-	-	-	-	-	-	-	-	-	-	-	-	-	-	-	-	-	1	-	A
		Ps.38:9		B	1	-	1	-	-	-	-	-	-	-	-	-	-	-	-	-	-	-	-	-	-	-	-	-	1	-	B
				C	-	-	-	-	-	-	-	-	-	-	-	-	-	-	-	-	-	-	-	-	-	-	-	-	1	-	C
316*	PWṢ	be scattered	Iq	TOT	16	4	12	-	-	-	1	-	-	-	-	-	-	-	-	-	-	-	-	-	-	-	12	-	36	-	TOT
		2Sam.18:8/1Kin.22:17/2Chr. 18:16//Gen.10:18/2Kin.25:5/ Ez.11:17/20:34,41/28:25/29: 13/34:6,12		A	12	3	9	-	-	-	-	-	-	-	-	-	-	-	-	-	-	-	-	-	-	-	7	-	20	-	A
				B	-	-	-	-	-	-	-	-	-	-	-	-	-	-	-	-	-	-	-	-	-	-	2	-	7	-	B
		Isa.11:12//Jer.10:21/40: 15/52:8		C	4	1	3	-	-	-	1	-	-	-	-	-	-	-	-	-	-	-	-	-	-	-	3	-	9	-	C
317	PWŠ	be scattered	III	TOT	1	-	1	-	-	-	-	-	-	-	-	-	-	-	-	-	-	-	-	-	-	-	-	-	-	-	TOT
		Nah.3:18		C	1	-	1	-	-	-	-	-	-	-	-	-	-	-	-	-	-	-	-	-	-	-	-	-	-	-	C
318	PZR	be scattered	Ip	TOT	1	-	1	-	-	-	1	1	1	-	-	-	-	-	-	-	-	-	-	-	-	-	-	7	-	-	TOT
				A	-	-	-	-	-	-	-	1	1	-	-	-	-	-	-	-	-	-	-	-	-	-	-	-	-	-	A

	ROOT	MEANING	DIV	G	NIPH'AL TOT	PT	PF	IMPF	INF	IMPV	PQ	PU'AL TOT	PT	PF	IMPF	O	HOPH'AL TOT	PT	PF	IMPF	O	HITPA'EL TOT	PT	PF	IMPF	O	QAL	PI	HI	O	G
		Ps.141:7		B	1	-	1	-	-	-	-	-	-	-	-	-	-	-	-	-	-	-	-	-	-	-	-	5	-	-	B
				C	-	-	-	-	-	-	1	-	-	-	-	-	-	-	-	-	-	-	-	-	-	-	-	2	-	-	C
319	**PLA**	be miraculous/extraordinary	Ih	TOT	55	46	3	6	-	-	-	-	-	-	-	-	-	-	-	-	-	-	1	-	-	1	-	3	11	-	TOT
		see 3.3		A	13	8	-	5	-	-	-	-	-	-	-	-	-	-	-	-	-	-	-	-	-	-	-	3	6	-	A
				B	39	36	3	-	-	-	-	-	-	-	-	-	-	-	-	-	-	-	1	-	-	1	-	-	1	-	B
				C	3	2	-	1	-	-	-	-	-	-	-	-	-	-	-	-	-	-	-	-	-	-	-	-	4	-	C
320	**PLG**	be divided	Iq	TOT	2	-	2	-	-	-	-	-	-	-	-	-	-	-	-	-	-	-	-	-	-	-	-	2	-	-	TOT
		Gen.10:25/1Chr.1:19		A	2	-	2	-	-	-	-	-	-	-	-	-	-	-	-	-	-	-	-	-	-	-	-	-	-	-	A
				B	-	-	-	-	-	-	-	-	-	-	-	-	-	-	-	-	-	-	-	-	-	-	-	2	-	-	B
321	**PLH**	be distinguished	Ih	TOT	1	-	1	-	-	-	-	-	-	-	-	-	-	-	-	-	-	-	-	-	-	-	-	-	5	-	TOT
		Ex.33:16		A	1	-	1	-	-	-	-	-	-	-	-	-	-	-	-	-	-	-	-	-	-	-	-	-	3	-	A
				B	-	-	-	-	-	-	-	-	-	-	-	-	-	-	-	-	-	-	-	-	-	-	-	-	2	-	B
322	**PSḤ**	lame/become lame	Iq	TOT	1	-	-	1	-	-	-	-	-	-	-	-	-	-	-	-	-	-	-	-	-	-	5	1	-	-	TOT
		2Sam.4:4		A	1	-	-	1	-	-	-	-	-	-	-	-	-	-	-	-	-	-	-	-	-	-	4	1	-	-	A
				C	-	-	-	-	-	-	-	-	-	-	-	-	-	-	-	-	-	-	-	-	-	-	1	-	-	-	C
323	**P'M**	be troubled/be confused	Iq	TOT	3	-	1	2	-	-	-	-	-	-	-	-	-	-	-	-	-	1	-	-	1	-	1	-	-	-	TOT
		Gen.41:8/Dan.2:3		A	2	-	-	2	-	-	-	-	-	-	-	-	-	-	-	-	-	1	-	-	1	-	1	-	-	-	A
		Ps.77:5		B	1	-	1	-	-	-	-	-	-	-	-	-	-	-	-	-	-	-	-	-	-	-	-	-	-	-	B
324	**PQD**	be visited/be missed/lack	Iq	TOT	20	-	4	14	2	-	78	2	-	2	-	-	8	6	2	-	-	4	-	2	2	-	M	1	28	4	TOT
		see 3.3		A	16	-	4	10	2	-	78	1	-	1	-	-	7	6	1	-	-	4	-	2	2	-	M	-	23	4	A
				B	1	-	-	1	-	-	-	-	-	-	-	-	-	-	-	-	-	-	-	-	-	-	M	-	2	-	B
				C	3	-	-	3	-	-	-	1	-	1	-	-	1	-	1	-	-	-	-	-	-	-	M	1	3	-	C
325	**PQḤ**	be opened (of eyes)	Iq	TOT	3	-	1	2	-	-	1	-	-	-	-	-	-	-	-	-	-	-	-	-	-	-	17	-	-	-	TOT
		Gen.3:5//3:7		A	2	-	1	1	-	-	1	-	-	-	-	-	-	-	-	-	-	-	-	-	-	-	10	-	-	-	A
				B	-	-	-	-	-	-	-	-	-	-	-	-	-	-	-	-	-	-	-	-	-	-	4	-	-	-	B
		Isa.35:5		C	1	-	-	1	-	-	-	-	-	-	-	-	-	-	-	-	-	-	-	-	-	-	3	-	-	-	C
326*	**PRD**	be separated	Ih	TOT	12	3	3	4	1	1	1	1	1	-	-	-	-	-	-	-	-	4	-	1	3	-	-	1	7	-	TOT
		Judg.4:11/Neh.4:13//Gen. 10:5,32//2:10/13:11/25: 23//13:14//13:9		A	9	2	2	3	1	1	1	1	1	-	-	-	-	-	-	-	-	-	-	-	-	-	-	-	3	-	A
		Pro.18:1//2Sam.1:23//Pro.19:4		B	3	1	1	1	-	-	-	-	-	-	-	-	-	-	-	-	-	4	-	1	3	-	-	-	4	-	B
				C	-	-	-	-	-	-	-	-	-	-	-	-	-	-	-	-	-	-	-	-	-	-	-	1	-	-	C
327	**PR'**	be set free	Iq	TOT	1	-	-	1	-	-	2	-	-	-	-	-	-	-	-	-	-	-	-	-	-	-	13	-	2	-	TOT
				A	-	-	-	-	-	-	2	-	-	-	-	-	-	-	-	-	-	-	-	-	-	-	8	-	2	-	A
		Pro.29:18		B	1	-	-	1	-	-	-	-	-	-	-	-	-	-	-	-	-	-	-	-	-	-	5	-	-	-	B
328	**PRṢ**	be spread	Iq	TOT	2	1	1	-	-	-	4	2	2	-	-	-	-	-	-	-	-	1	1	-	-	-	46	-	-	-	TOT
		1Sam.3:1//1Chr.13:2		A	2	1	1	-	-	-	3	2	2	-	-	-	-	-	-	-	-	1	1	-	-	-	29	-	-	-	A
				B	-	-	-	-	-	-	1	-	-	-	-	-	-	-	-	-	-	-	-	-	-	-	11	-	-	-	B
				C	-	-	-	-	-	-	-	-	-	-	-	-	-	-	-	-	-	-	-	-	-	-	6	-	-	-	C
329	**PRŚ**	be scattered	II	TOT	1	-	-	1	-	-	3	-	-	-	-	-	-	-	-	-	-	-	-	-	-	-	56	9	-	-	TOT
		Ezek.17:21		A	1	-	-	1	-	-	1	-	-	-	-	-	-	-	-	-	-	-	-	-	-	-	34	-	-	-	A
				B	-	-	-	-	-	-	-	-	-	-	-	-	-	-	-	-	-	-	-	-	-	-	13	3	-	-	B
				C	-	-	-	-	-	-	2	-	-	-	-	-	-	-	-	-	-	-	-	-	-	-	9	6	-	-	C
330	**PRŠ**	be scattered	II	TOT	1	1	-	-	-	-	-	2	1	1	-	-	-	-	-	-	-	-	-	-	-	-	1	-	1	-	TOT
		Ezek.34:12		A	1	1	-	-	-	-	-	2	1	1	-	-	-	-	-	-	-	-	-	-	-	-	1	-	-	-	A

	ROOT	MEANING	DIV	G	NIPH'AL TOT	NIPH'AL PT	NIPH'AL PF	NIPH'AL IMPF	INF	IMPV	PQ	PU'AL TOT	PU'AL PT	PU'AL PF	PU'AL IMPF	PU'AL O	HOPH'AL TOT	HOPH'AL PT	HOPH'AL PF	HOPH'AL IMPF	HOPH'AL O	HITPA'EL TOT	HITPA'EL PT	HITPA'EL PF	HITPA'EL IMPF	HITPA'EL O	QAL	PI	HI	O	G
				B	-	-	-	-	-	-	-	-	-	-	-	-	-	-	-	-	-	-	-	-	-	-	-	-	1	-	B
331	**PS'**	offended	II	TOT	1	1	-	-	-	-	-	-	-	-	-	-	-	-	-	-	-	-	-	-	-	-	40	-	-	-	TOT
				A	-	-	-	-	-	-	-	-	-	-	-	-	-	-	-	-	-	-	-	-	-	-	18	-	-	-	A
		Pro.18:19		B	1	1	-	-	-	-	-	-	-	-	-	-	-	-	-	-	-	-	-	-	-	-	4	-	-	-	B
				C	-	-	-	-	-	-	-	-	-	-	-	-	-	-	-	-	-	-	-	-	-	-	18	-	-	-	C
332	**PTH**	be seduced/convinced	Ip	TOT	2	-	1	1	-	-	-	3	-	-	3	-	-	-	-	-	-	-	-	-	-	-	5	16	2	-	TOT
				A	-	-	-	-	-	-	-	1	-	-	1	-	-	-	-	-	-	-	-	-	-	-	1	11	1	-	A
		Job31:9		B	1	-	1	-	-	-	-	1	-	-	1	-	-	-	-	-	-	-	-	-	-	-	3	3	1	-	B
		Jer.20:7		C	1	-	-	1	-	-	-	1	-	-	1	-	-	-	-	-	-	-	-	-	-	-	1	2	-	-	C
333*	**PTḤ**	be opened	Iq/p*	TOT	17	1	6	9	1	-	13	-	-	-	-	-	-	-	-	-	-	1	-	-	1	-	96	27	-	-	TOT
		Gen.7:11/Ezek.1:1//24:27/ 33:22/44:2/46:1/Neh.7:13.		A	7	-	2	5	-	-	10	-	-	-	-	-	-	-	-	-	-	-	-	-	-	-	52	9	-	-	A
		Job12:14*/32:19*		B	2	-	-	2	-	-	2	-	-	-	-	-	-	-	-	-	-	-	-	-	-	-	27	10	-	-	B
		Zech.13:1//Isa.5:27/24:18/Neh. 2:7/3:13//Isa.35:5/Jer.1:14// Isa.51:14*		C	8	1	4	2	1	-	1	-	-	-	-	-	-	-	-	-	-	1	-	-	1	-	17	8	-	-	C
334	**PTL**	wrestle, pt: twisted	III	TOT	3	2	1	-	-	-	-	-	-	-	-	-	-	-	-	-	-	2	-	-	2	-	-	-	-	-	TOT
		Gen.30:8		A	1	1	-	-	-	-	-	-	-	-	-	-	-	-	-	-	-	-	-	-	-	-	-	-	-	-	A
		Pro.8:8//Job5:13		B	2	1	1	-	-	-	-	-	-	-	-	-	-	-	-	-	-	2	-	-	2	-	-	-	-	-	B
335	**ŞDH**	be destroyed	III	TOT	1	-	1	-	-	-	-	-	-	-	-	-	-	-	-	-	-	-	-	-	-	-	-	-	-	-	TOT
		Zeph.3:6		C	1	-	1	-	-	-	-	-	-	-	-	-	-	-	-	-	-	-	-	-	-	-	-	-	-	-	C
336	**ŞDQ**	be reconsecrated	Ih	TOT	1	-	1	-	-	-	-	-	-	-	-	-	-	-	-	-	-	1	-	-	1	-	22	5	12	-	TOT
		Dan.8:14		A	1	-	1	1	-	-	-	-	-	-	-	-	-	-	-	-	-	1	-	-	1	-	2	2	6	-	A
				B	-	-	-	-	-	-	-	-	-	-	-	-	-	-	-	-	-	-	-	-	-	-	17	2	3	-	B
				C	-	-	-	-	-	-	-	-	-	-	-	-	-	-	-	-	-	-	-	-	-	-	3	1	3	-	C
337	**ŞMD**	join	Ih	TOT	3	1	-	2	-	-	-	1	1	-	-	-	-	-	-	-	-	-	-	-	-	-	-	-	1	-	TOT
		Num.25:5//3		A	2	1	-	1	-	-	-	1	1	-	-	-	-	-	-	-	-	-	-	-	-	-	-	-	-	-	A
		Ps.106:28		B	1	-	-	1	-	-	-	-	-	-	-	-	-	-	-	-	-	-	-	-	-	-	-	-	1	-	B
338	**ŞMT**	cease/be destroyed	Ih	TOT	2	-	2	-	-	-	-	-	-	-	-	-	-	-	-	-	-	-	-	-	-	-	-	2	9	-	TOT
		Job6:17/23:17		B	2	-	2	-	-	-	-	-	-	-	-	-	-	-	-	-	-	-	-	-	-	-	-	2	9	-	B
339*	**Ş'Q**	be called up/be called upon	Iq	TOT	6	-	-	6	-	-	-	-	-	-	-	-	-	-	-	-	-	-	-	-	-	-	46	1	1	-	TOT
		Judg.7:23,24/10:17/12:1/ 1Sam.13:4/1Kin.3:21		A	6	-	-	6	-	-	-	-	-	-	-	-	-	-	-	-	-	-	-	-	-	-	31	1	1	-	A
				B	-	-	-	-	-	-	-	-	-	-	-	-	-	-	-	-	-	-	-	-	-	-	8	-	-	-	B
				C	-	-	-	-	-	-	-	-	-	-	-	-	-	-	-	-	-	-	-	-	-	-	7	-	-	-	C
340	**ŞPN**	be hidden	Iq	TOT	3	-	3	-	-	-	6	-	-	-	-	-	-	-	-	-	-	-	-	-	-	-	27	-	3	-	TOT
				A	-	-	-	-	-	-	1	-	-	-	-	-	-	-	-	-	-	-	-	-	-	-	3	-	1	-	A
		Job15:20/24:1		B	2	-	2	-	-	-	4	-	-	-	-	-	-	-	-	-	-	-	-	-	-	-	23	-	2	-	B
		Jer.16:17		C	1	-	1	-	-	-	1	-	-	-	-	-	-	-	-	-	-	-	-	-	-	-	1	-	-	-	C
341	**ŞRB**	be scorched	III	TOT	1	-	1	-	-	-	-	-	-	-	-	-	-	-	-	-	-	-	-	-	-	-	-	-	-	-	TOT
		Ezek.21:3		A	1	-	1	-	-	-	-	-	-	-	-	-	-	-	-	-	-	-	-	-	-	-	-	-	-	-	A
342	**ŞRP**	be purified	Iq	TOT	1	-	-	1	-	-	5	-	-	-	-	-	-	-	-	-	-	-	-	-	-	-	30	2	-	-	TOT
		Dan.12:10		A	1	-	-	1	-	-	-	-	-	-	-	-	-	-	-	-	-	-	-	-	-	-	5	-	-	-	A
				B	-	-	-	-	-	-	5	-	-	-	-	-	-	-	-	-	-	-	-	-	-	-	11	-	-	-	B
				C	-	-	-	-	-	-	-	-	-	-	-	-	-	-	-	-	-	-	-	-	-	-	14	2	-	-	C

	ROOT	MEANING	DIV	G	NIPH'AL TOT	PT	PF	IMPF	INF	IMPV	PQ	PU'AL TOT	PT	PF	IMPF	O	HOPH'AL TOT	PT	PF	IMPF	O	HITPA'EL TOT	PT	PF	IMPF	O	QAL	PI	HI	O	G
343	QBṢ	assemble oneself/be gathered	Iq	TOT	31	2	8	13	4	4	1	1	1	-	-	-	-	-	-	-	-	8	-	2	5	1	37	49	-	-	TOT
		see 3.3		A	19	1	2	12	3	1	1	1	1	-	-	-	-	-	-	-	-	6	-	2	4	-	31	19	-	-	A
				B	2	-	-	-	1	1	-	-	-	-	-	-	-	-	-	-	-	-	-	-	-	-	3	12	-	-	B
				C	10	1	6	1	-	2	-	-	-	-	-	-	-	-	-	-	-	2	-	-	1	1	3	18	-	-	C
344	QBR	be buried	Iq	TOT	39	-	-	39	-	-	2	1	-	1	-	-	-	-	-	-	-	-	-	-	-	-	86	6	-	-	TOT
		see 3.3		A	33	-	-	33	-	-	2	1	-	1	-	-	-	-	-	-	-	-	-	-	-	-	83	4	-	-	A
				B	1	-	-	1	-	-	-	-	-	-	-	-	-	-	-	-	-	-	-	-	-	-	2	-	-	-	B
				C	5	-	-	5	-	-	-	-	-	-	-	-	-	-	-	-	-	-	-	-	-	-	1	2	-	-	C
345	QDŠ	be sanctified	Ip	TOT	11	-	7	2	2	-	-	5	5	-	-	-	-	-	-	-	-	24	2	7	7	8	11	74	44	-	TOT
		Ex.29:43/Lev.22:32/Ez.20:41/ /28:22,25/39: 27//Lev.10:3/ Num.20:13//Ez.36:23/38:16		A	10	-	6	2	2	-	-	4	4	-	-	-	-	-	-	-	-	22	1	6	7	8	9	60	38	-	A
				B	-	-	-	-	-	-	-	-	-	-	-	-	-	-	-	-	-	-	-	-	-	-	-	2	-	-	B
		Isa.5:16		C	1	-	1	-	-	-	-	1	1	-	-	-	-	-	-	-	-	2	1	1	-	-	2	12	6	-	C
346	QHL	gather oneself/assemble	Ih	TOT	19	1	4	12	2	-	-	-	-	-	-	-	-	-	-	-	-	-	-	-	-	-	-	-	20	-	TOT
		see 3.3		A	19	1	4	12	2	-	-	-	-	-	-	-	-	-	-	-	-	-	-	-	-	-	-	-	19	-	A
				B	-	-	-	-	-	-	-	-	-	-	-	-	-	-	-	-	-	-	-	-	-	-	-	-	1	-	B
347	QWH	assemble oneself	II	TOT	2	-	1	1	-	-	-	-	-	-	-	-	-	-	-	-	-	-	-	-	-	-	6	40	-	-	TOT
		Gen.1:9		A	1	-	-	1	-	-	-	-	-	-	-	-	-	-	-	-	-	-	-	-	-	-	-	-	-	-	A
				B	-	-	-	-	-	-	-	-	-	-	-	-	-	-	-	-	-	-	-	-	-	-	4	22	-	-	B
		Jer.3:17		C	1	-	1	-	-	-	-	-	-	-	-	-	-	-	-	-	-	-	-	-	-	-	2	18	-	-	C
348*	QṬṬ /QWṬ	loathe	I=q	TOT	4	-	4	-	-	-	-	-	-	-	-	-	-	-	-	-	-	2	-	-	2	-	2	-	-	-	TOT
		Ezek.6:9/20:43/36:31		A	3	-	3	-	-	-	-	-	-	-	-	-	-	-	-	-	-	-	-	-	-	-	-	-	-	-	A
		Job10:1		B	1	-	1	-	-	-	-	-	-	-	-	-	-	-	-	-	-	2	-	-	2	-	2	-	-	-	B
349	QṬP	be cut off	Iq	TOT	1	-	-	1	-	-	-	-	-	-	-	-	-	-	-	-	-	-	-	-	-	-	4	-	-	-	TOT
				A	-	-	-	-	-	-	-	-	-	-	-	-	-	-	-	-	-	-	-	-	-	-	3	-	-	-	A
		Job8:12		B	1	-	-	1	-	-	-	-	-	-	-	-	-	-	-	-	-	-	-	-	-	-	1	-	-	-	B
350	QLH	I burning/lit	II	TOT	1	1	-	-	-	-	2	-	-	-	-	-	-	-	-	-	-	-	-	-	-	-	3	-	-	-	TOT
				A	-	-	-	-	-	-	2	-	-	-	-	-	-	-	-	-	-	-	-	-	-	-	3	-	-	-	A
		Ps.38:8		B	1	1	-	-	-	-	-	-	-	-	-	-	-	-	-	-	-	-	-	-	-	-	-	-	-	-	B
351	QLH	II be despicable/be of little value	Ih	TOT	5	3	2	-	-	-	-	-	-	-	-	-	-	-	-	-	-	-	-	-	-	-	-	-	1	-	TOT
		1Sam.18:23//Deut.25:3		A	2	1	1	-	-	-	-	-	-	-	-	-	-	-	-	-	-	-	-	-	-	-	-	-	1	-	A
		Pro.12:9		B	1	-	1	-	-	-	-	-	-	-	-	-	-	-	-	-	-	-	-	-	-	-	-	-	-	-	B
		Isa.3:5/16:4		C	2	2	-	-	-	-	-	-	-	-	-	-	-	-	-	-	-	-	-	-	-	-	-	-	-	-	C
352*	QLL	be easy/fast/small	I=q	TOT	11	7	3	1	-	-	-	3	1	-	2	-	-	-	-	-	-	1	-	1	-	-	12	39	13	2	TOT
		1Sam.18:23/1Kin.16:31/2Kin. 20:10/Ezek.8:17//2Sam.6:22/ 2Kin.3:18		A	6	4	2	-	-	-	-	-	-	-	-	-	-	-	-	-	-	-	-	-	-	-	5	28	11	1	A
		Pro.14:6		B	1	-	1	-	-	-	-	2	1	-	1	-	-	-	-	-	-	-	-	-	-	-	4	9	-	1	B
		Isa.49:6/Jer.6:14/8:11// Isa.30:1		C	4	3	-	1	-	-	-	1	-	-	1	-	-	-	-	-	-	1	-	1	-	-	3	2	2	-	C
353	QNH	be bought	Iq	TOT	2	-	1	1	-	-	-	-	-	-	-	-	-	-	-	-	-	-	-	-	-	-	79	-	1	-	TOT
		Jer.32:43//32:15		A	2	-	1	1	-	-	-	-	-	-	-	-	-	-	-	-	-	-	-	-	-	-	50	-	-	-	A
				B	-	-	-	-	-	-	-	-	-	-	-	-	-	-	-	-	-	-	-	-	-	-	18	-	-	-	B

	ROOT	MEANING	DIV	G	NIPH'AL TOT	PT	PF	IMPF	INF	IMPV	PQ	PU'AL TOT	PT	PF	IMPF	O	HOPH'AL TOT	PT	PF	IMPF	O	HITPA'EL TOT	PT	PF	IMPF	O	QAL	PI	HI	O	G
				C	-	-	-	-	-	-	-	-	-	-	-	-	-	-	-	-	-	-	-	-	-	-	11	-	1	-	C
354	QPṢ	draw oneself together	Iq	TOT	1	-	-	1	-	-	-	-	-	-	-	-	-	-	-	-	-	-	-	-	-	-	5	1	-	-	TOT
				A	-	-	-	-	-	-	-	-	-	-	-	-	-	-	-	-	-	-	-	-	-	-	1	-	-	-	A
		Job24:24		B	1	-	-	1	-	-	-	-	-	-	-	-	-	-	-	-	-	-	-	-	-	-	3	1	-	-	B
				C	-	-	-	-	-	-	-	-	-	-	-	-	-	-	-	-	-	-	-	-	-	-	1	-	-	-	C
355	QRA	I be proclaimed	Iq	TOT	63	4	29	30	-	-	11	7	1	6	-	-	-	-	-	-	-	-	-	-	-	-	M	-	-	-	TOT
		see 3.3		A	37	2	17	18	-	-	9	1	-	1	-	-	-	-	-	-	-	-	-	-	-	-	M	-	-	-	A
				B	1	-	-	1	-	-	1	-	-	-	-	-	-	-	-	-	-	-	-	-	-	-	M	-	-	-	B
				C	25	2	12	11	-	-	1	6	1	5	-	-	-	-	-	-	-	-	-	-	-	-	M	-	-	-	C
356*	QRA	II be found	Iq	TOT	5	-	2	2	1	-	-	-	-	-	-	-	-	-	-	-	-	-	-	-	-	-	M	-	1	-	TOT
		Ex.5:3/2Sam.20:1//Deut.22:6/ 2Sam.18:9//1:6		A	5	-	2	2	1	-	-	-	-	-	-	-	-	-	-	-	-	-	-	-	-	-	M	-	1	-	A
				B	-	-	-	-	-	-	-	-	-	-	-	-	-	-	-	-	-	-	-	-	-	-	6	-	-	-	B
				C	-	-	-	-	-	-	-	-	-	-	-	-	-	-	-	-	-	-	-	-	-	-	8	-	-	-	C
357	QRB	approach/be brought	Iq	TOT	2	-	2	-	-	-	-	-	-	-	-	-	-	-	-	-	-	-	-	-	-	-	M	8	M	-	TOT
		Ex.22:7/Josh.7:4		A	2	-	2	-	-	-	-	-	-	-	-	-	-	-	-	-	-	-	-	-	-	-	M	3	M	-	A
				B	-	-	-	-	-	-	-	-	-	-	-	-	-	-	-	-	-	-	-	-	-	-	M	2	1	-	B
				C	-	-	-	-	-	-	-	-	-	-	-	-	-	-	-	-	-	-	-	-	-	-	M	3	4	-	C
358	QRH	come to meet/meet	Iq	TOT	6	-	2	4	-	-	-	-	-	-	-	-	-	-	-	-	-	-	-	-	-	-	12	5	3	-	TOT
		Ex.3:18/2Sam.1:6//		A	6	-	2	4	-	-	-	-	-	-	-	-	-	-	-	-	-	-	-	-	-	-	9	4	3	-	A
		Num.23:3,4,15,1 6		B	-	-	-	-	-	-	-	-	-	-	-	-	-	-	-	-	-	-	-	-	-	-	3	1	-	-	B
359	QRḤ	shave/make oneself bald	Iq	TOT	1	-	-	1	-	-	-	-	-	-	-	-	1	1	-	-	-	-	-	-	-	-	2	1	-	-	TOT
				A	-	-	-	-	-	-	-	-	-	-	-	-	1	1	-	-	-	-	-	-	-	-	1	-	-	-	A
		Jer.16:6		C	1	-	-	1	-	-	-	-	-	-	-	-	-	-	-	-	-	-	-	-	-	-	1	1	-	-	C
360	QR'	be torn	Iq	TOT	5	-	2	3	-	-	7	-	-	-	-	-	-	-	-	-	-	-	-	-	-	-	59	-	-	-	TOT
		1Kin.13:3,5//Ex.28:32/ 39:23/1Sam.15:27		A	5	-	2	3	-	-	7	-	-	-	-	-	-	-	-	-	-	-	-	-	-	-	50	-	-	-	A
				B	-	-	-	-	-	-	-	-	-	-	-	-	-	-	-	-	-	-	-	-	-	-	4	-	-	-	B
				C	-	-	-	-	-	-	-	-	-	-	-	-	-	-	-	-	-	-	-	-	-	-	5	-	-	-	C
361	QŠH	distressed	Iq	TOT	1	1	-	-	-	-	-	-	-	-	-	-	-	-	-	-	-	-	-	-	-	-	5	1	20	-	TOT
				A	-	-	-	-	-	-	-	-	-	-	-	-	-	-	-	-	-	-	-	-	-	-	4	1	15	-	A
		Isa.8:21		B	-	-	-	-	-	-	-	-	-	-	-	-	-	-	-	-	-	-	-	-	-	-	1	-	3	-	B
				C	1	1	-	-	-	-	-	-	-	-	-	-	-	-	-	-	-	-	-	-	-	-	-	-	2	-	C
362	QŠR	be bound/be joined together	Iq	TOT	2	-	1	1	-	-	3	1	1	-	-	-	-	-	-	-	-	3	1	1	1	-	36	2	-	-	TOT
		1Sam.18:1//Neh.3:38		A	2	-	1	1	-	-	2	1	1	-	-	-	-	-	-	-	-	3	1	1	1	-	28	-	-	-	A
				B	-	-	-	-	-	-	1	-	-	-	-	-	-	-	-	-	-	-	-	-	-	-	6	2	-	-	B
				C	-	-	-	-	-	-	-	-	-	-	-	-	-	-	-	-	-	-	-	-	-	-	2	-	-	-	C
363*	RAH	be seen/appear	Iq/h?	TOT	99	3	34	50	11	1	1	1	-	1	-	-	4	1	3	-	-	5	-	-	5	-	M	-	62	-	TOT
		see 3.3		A	84	3	29	42	9	1	1	-	-	-	-	-	4	1	3	-	-	5	-	-	5	-	M	-	39	-	A
				B	7	-	3	4	-	-	-	1	-	1	-	-	-	-	-	-	-	-	-	-	-	-	M	-	9	-	B
				C	8	-	2	4	2	-	-	-	-	-	-	-	-	-	-	-	-	-	-	-	-	-	M	-	14	-	C
364	RGN	murmur/slander	I=q	TOT	6	4	-	2	-	-	-	-	-	-	-	-	-	-	-	-	-	-	-	-	-	-	1	-	-	-	TOT
		Deut.1:27		A	1	-	-	1	-	-	-	-	-	-	-	-	-	-	-	-	-	-	-	-	-	-	-	-	-	-	A
		Pro.16:28/18:8/26:20,22// Ps.106:25		B	5	4	-	1	-	-	-	-	-	-	-	-	-	-	-	-	-	-	-	-	-	-	-	-	-	-	B

	ROOT	MEANING	DIV	G	NIPH'AL TOT	PT	PF	IMPF	INF	IMPV	PQ	PU'AL TOT	PT	PF	IMPF	O	HOPH'AL TOT	PT	PF	IMPF	O	HITPA'EL TOT	PT	PF	IMPF	O	QAL	PI	HI	O	G
				C	-	-	-	-	-	-	-	-	-	-	-	-	-	-	-	-	-	-	-	-	-	-	1	-	-	-	C
365	RG'	be quiet	Ih	TOT	1	-	-	-	-	1	-	-	-	-	-	-	-	-	-	-	-	-	-	-	-	-	5	-	5	-	TOT
				A	-	-	-	-	-	-	-	-	-	-	-	-	-	-	-	-	-	-	-	-	-	-	1	-	2	-	A
				B	-	-	-	-	-	-	-	-	-	-	-	-	-	-	-	-	-	-	-	-	-	-	3	-	-	-	B
		Jer.47:6		C	1	-	-	-	-	1	-	-	-	-	-	-	-	-	-	-	-	-	-	-	-	-	1	-	3	-	C
366	RDM	fall into deep sleep	III	TOT	7	4	2	1	-	-	-	-	-	-	-	-	-	-	-	-	-	-	-	-	-	-	-	-	-	-	TOT
		Jon.1:6/Dan.10:9//8:18/		A	5	2	2	1	-	-	-	-	-	-	-	-	-	-	-	-	-	-	-	-	-	-	-	-	-	-	A
		Judg.4:21//Jon.1:5																													
		Ps.76:7/Pro.10:5		B	2	2	-	-	-	-	-	-	-	-	-	-	-	-	-	-	-	-	-	-	-	-	-	-	-	-	B
367	RDP	be persecuted	Iq	TOT	2	1	1	-	-	-	-	1	-	1	-	-	-	-	-	-	-	-	-	-	-	-	127	8	1	-	TOT
		Eccl.3:15		A	1	1	-	-	-	-	-	-	-	-	-	-	-	-	-	-	-	-	-	-	-	-	83	-	-	-	A
		Lam.5:5		B	1	-	1	-	-	-	-	-	-	-	-	-	-	-	-	-	-	-	-	-	-	-	32	6	-	-	B
				C	-	-	-	-	-	-	-	1	-	1	-	-	-	-	-	-	-	-	-	-	-	-	12	2	1	-	C
368	RZH	become lean	Iq	TOT	1	-	-	1	-	-	-	-	-	-	-	-	-	-	-	-	-	-	-	-	-	-	1	-	-	-	TOT
		Isa.17:4		C	1	-	-	1	-	-	-	-	-	-	-	-	-	-	-	-	-	-	-	-	-	-	1	-	-	-	C
369	RḤB	extended	Iq	TOT	1	1	-	-	-	-	-	-	-	-	-	-	-	-	-	-	-	-	-	-	-	-	3	-	21	-	TOT
				A	-	-	-	-	-	-	-	-	-	-	-	-	-	-	-	-	-	-	-	-	-	-	1	-	4	-	A
				B	-	-	-	-	-	-	-	-	-	-	-	-	-	-	-	-	-	-	-	-	-	-	1	-	9	-	B
		Isa.30:23		C	1	1	-	-	-	-	-	-	-	-	-	-	-	-	-	-	-	-	-	-	-	-	1	-	8	-	C
370*	RMM	rise upwards	Iq	TOT	4	-	-	3	-	1	-	-	-	-	-	-	-	-	-	-	-	-	-	-	-	-	2	-	-	-	TOT
		Ezek.10:15,17,19//Num.17:10		A	4	-	-	3	-	1	-	-	-	-	-	-	-	-	-	-	-	-	-	-	-	-	-	-	-	-	A
				B	-	-	-	-	-	-	-	-	-	-	-	-	-	-	-	-	-	-	-	-	-	-	2	-	-	-	B
371	RMS	be trodden down	Iq	TOT	1	-	-	1	-	-	-	-	-	-	-	-	-	-	-	-	-	-	-	-	-	-	18	-	-	-	TOT
				A	-	-	-	-	-	-	-	-	-	-	-	-	-	-	-	-	-	-	-	-	-	-	9	-	-	-	A
				B	-	-	-	-	-	-	-	-	-	-	-	-	-	-	-	-	-	-	-	-	-	-	2	-	-	-	B
		Isa.28:3		C	1	-	-	1	-	-	-	-	-	-	-	-	-	-	-	-	-	-	-	-	-	-	7	-	-	-	C
372	R''	be treated poorly	Iq/h*	TOT	2	-	-	2	-	-	-	-	-	-	-	-	-	-	-	-	-	-	-	-	-	-	29	-	68	-	TOT
				A	-	-	-	-	-	-	-	-	-	-	-	-	-	-	-	-	-	-	-	-	-	-	24	-	28	-	A
		Pro.11:15/13:20*		B	2	-	-	2	-	-	-	-	-	-	-	-	-	-	-	-	-	-	-	-	-	-	3	-	19	-	B
				C	-	-	-	-	-	-	-	-	-	-	-	-	-	-	-	-	-	-	-	-	-	-	2	-	21	-	C
373	R'Ś	be made to quiver	I=q	TOT	1	-	1	-	-	-	-	-	-	-	-	-	-	-	-	-	-	-	-	-	-	-	22	-	7	-	TOT
				A	-	-	-	-	-	-	-	-	-	-	-	-	-	-	-	-	-	-	-	-	-	-	4	-	1	-	A
				B	-	-	-	-	-	-	-	-	-	-	-	-	-	-	-	-	-	-	-	-	-	-	6	-	2	-	B
		Jer.50:46		C	1	-	1	-	-	-	-	-	-	-	-	-	-	-	-	-	-	-	-	-	-	-	12	-	4	-	C
374	RPA	healthy/be healed	Iq	TOT	17	-	7	6	4	-	-	-	-	-	-	-	-	-	-	-	-	3	-	-	-	3	37	9	-	-	TOT
		Lev.13:18,37/14:3,48//1Sam.		A	12	-	5	4	3	-	-	-	-	-	-	-	-	-	-	-	-	3	-	-	-	3	11	5	-	-	A
		6:3/2Kin.2:22/Ezek.47:9,11//																													
		Deut.28:27,35//Jer.19:11																													
				B	-	-	-	-	-	-	-	-	-	-	-	-	-	-	-	-	-	-	-	-	-	-	12	-	-	-	B
		Isa.53:5/Jer.51:9//17:14/		C	5	-	2	2	1	-	-	-	-	-	-	-	-	-	-	-	-	-	-	-	-	-	14	4	-	-	C
		51:8//15:18																													
375	RPH	weak/lazy	Iq	TOT	2	2	-	-	-	-	-	-	-	-	-	-	-	-	-	-	-	3	2	1	-	-	14	5	21	-	TOT
		Ex.5:8,17		A	2	2	-	-	-	-	-	-	-	-	-	-	-	-	-	-	-	1	1	-	-	-	8	4	14	-	A
				B	-	-	-	-	-	-	-	-	-	-	-	-	-	-	-	-	-	2	1	1	-	-	-	1	7	-	B

	ROOT	MEANING	DIV	G	NIPH'AL						PQ	PU'AL					HOPH'AL					HITPA'EL					QAL	PI	HI	O	G
					TOT	PT	PF	IMPF	INF	IMPV		TOT	PT	PF	IMPF	O	TOT	PT	PF	IMPF	O	TOT	PT	PF	IMPF	O					
				C	-	-	-	-	-	-	-	-	-	-	-	-	-	-	-	-	-	-	-	-	-	-	6	-	-	-	C
376	RPŚ/	muddied/polluted	Iq	TOT	1	1	-	-	-	-	-	-	-	-	-	-	-	-	-	-	-	2	1	-	-	1	2	-	-	-	TOT
	RPS			A	-	-	-	-	-	-	-	-	-	-	-	-	-	-	-	-	-	-	-	-	-	-	1	-	-	-	A
		Pro.25:26		B	1	1	-	-	-	-	-	-	-	-	-	-	-	-	-	-	-	2	1	-	-	1	-	-	-	-	B
				C	-	-	-	-	-	-	-	-	-	-	-	-	-	-	-	-	-	-	-	-	-	-	1	-	-	-	C
377	RṢH	be(come) accepted	Iq	TOT	7	-	2	5	-	-	2	-	-	-	-	-	-	-	-	-	-	1	-	-	1	-	46	1	1	-	TOT
		Lev.1:4//7:18/19:7/ 22:23,25,27		A	6	-	1	5	-	-	1	-	-	-	-	-	-	-	-	-	-	1	-	-	1	-	15	-	1	-	A
				B	-	-	-	-	-	-	1	-	-	-	-	-	-	-	-	-	-	-	-	-	-	-	21	1	-	-	B
		Isa.40:2		C	1	-	1	-	-	-	-	-	-	-	-	-	-	-	-	-	-	-	-	-	-	-	10	-	-	-	C
378	RṢH	be killed/murdered	Iq	TOT	2	1	-	1	-	-	-	-	-	-	-	-	-	-	-	-	-	-	-	-	-	-	40	5	-	-	TOT
		Judg.20:4		A	1	1	-	-	-	-	-	-	-	-	-	-	-	-	-	-	-	-	-	-	-	-	37	1	-	-	A
		Pro.22:13		B	1	-	-	1	-	-	-	-	-	-	-	-	-	-	-	-	-	-	-	-	-	-	1	2	-	-	B
				C	-	-	-	-	-	-	-	-	-	-	-	-	-	-	-	-	-	-	-	-	-	-	2	2	-	-	C
379	RṢṢ	be broken	Iq	TOT	2	-	1	1	-	-	7	-	-	-	-	-	-	-	-	-	-	1	-	-	1	-	11	3	1	1	TOT
		Eccl.12:6//Ezek.29:7		A	2	-	1	1	-	-	3	-	-	-	-	-	-	-	-	-	-	1	-	-	1	-	4	1	1	1	A
				B	-	-	-	-	-	-	-	-	-	-	-	-	-	-	-	-	-	-	-	-	-	-	1	2	-	-	B
				C	-	-	-	-	-	-	4	-	-	-	-	-	-	-	-	-	-	-	-	-	-	-	6	-	-	-	C
380	RTQ	be broken	III	TOT	1	-	-	1	-	-	-	1	-	1	-	-	-	-	-	-	-	-	-	-	-	-	-	-	-	-	TOT
		Eccl.12:6		A	1	-	-	1	-	-	-	-	-	-	-	-	-	-	-	-	-	-	-	-	-	-	-	-	-	-	A
				C	-	-	-	-	-	-	-	1	-	1	-	-	-	-	-	-	-	-	-	-	-	-	-	-	-	-	C
381*	ŚGB	high/be inaccessible	II	TOT	10	6	4	-	-	-	-	1	-	-	1	-	-	-	-	-	-	-	-	-	-	-	2	6	1	-	TOT
				A	-	-	-	-	-	-	-	-	-	-	-	-	-	-	-	-	-	-	-	-	-	-	1	-	-	-	A
		Ps.148:13/Pro.18:11//Ps.139: 6/Pro.18:10		B	4	2	2	-	-	-	-	1	-	-	1	-	-	-	-	-	-	-	-	-	-	-	1	5	1	-	B
		Isa.12:4/26:5/30:13/33:5// 2:11,17		C	6	4	2	-	-	-	-	-	-	-	-	-	-	-	-	-	-	-	-	-	-	-	-	1	-	-	C
382	ŚWG	turn back (variant of 266)	II	TOT	1	-	1	-	-	-	-	-	-	-	-	-	-	-	-	-	-	-	-	-	-	-	-	-	1	-	TOT
		2Sam.1:22		B	1	-	1	-	-	-	-	-	-	-	-	-	-	-	-	-	-	-	-	-	-	-	-	-	1	-	B
383	ŚKR	hire oneself out	Iq	TOT	1	-	1	-	-	-	1	-	-	-	-	-	-	-	-	-	-	2	2	-	-	-	17	-	-	-	TOT
				A	-	-	-	-	-	-	1	-	-	-	-	-	-	-	-	-	-	-	-	-	-	-	15	-	-	-	A
		1Sam.2:5		B	1	-	1	-	-	-	-	-	-	-	-	-	-	-	-	-	-	-	-	-	-	-	1	-	-	-	B
				C	-	-	-	-	-	-	-	-	-	-	-	-	-	-	-	-	-	2	2	-	-	-	1	-	-	-	C
384	ŚNA	be hated	Iq	TOT	2	-	-	2	-	-	9	-	-	-	-	-	-	-	-	-	-	-	-	-	-	-	M	15	-	-	TOT
				A	-	-	-	-	-	-	7	-	-	-	-	-	-	-	-	-	-	-	-	-	-	-	M	1	-	-	A
		Pro.14:17,20		B	2	-	-	2	-	-	1	-	-	-	-	-	-	-	-	-	-	-	-	-	-	-	M	14	-	-	B
				C	-	-	-	-	-	-	1	-	-	-	-	-	-	-	-	-	-	-	-	-	-	-	M	-	-	-	C
385	Ś'R	storm, cf. 274	Iq?	TOT	1	-	1	-	-	-	-	-	-	-	-	-	-	-	-	-	-	1	-	-	1	-	5	1	-	-	TOT
				A	-	-	-	-	-	-	-	-	-	-	-	-	-	-	-	-	-	1	-	-	1	-	2	-	-	-	A
		Ps.50:3		B	1	-	1	-	-	-	-	-	-	-	-	-	-	-	-	-	-	-	-	-	-	-	2	1	-	-	B
				C	-	-	-	-	-	-	-	-	-	-	-	-	-	-	-	-	-	-	-	-	-	-	1	-	-	-	C
386	ŚQD	?	III	TOT	1	-	1	-	-	-	-	-	-	-	-	-	-	-	-	-	-	-	-	-	-	-	-	-	-	-	TOT
		Lam.1:14		B	1	-	1	-	-	-	-	-	-	-	-	-	-	-	-	-	-	-	-	-	-	-	-	-	-	-	B
387	ŚRṬ	injure oneself/make cuts	Iq	TOT	1	-	-	1	-	-	-	-	-	-	-	-	-	-	-	-	-	-	-	-	-	-	2	-	-	-	TOT
				A	-	-	-	-	-	-	-	-	-	-	-	-	-	-	-	-	-	-	-	-	-	-	1	-	-	-	A

	ROOT	MEANING	DIV	G	NIPH'AL TOT	PT	PF	IMPF	INF	IMPV	PQ	PU'AL TOT	PT	PF	IMPF	O	HOPH'AL TOT	PT	PF	IMPF	O	HITPA'EL TOT	PT	PF	IMPF	O	QAL	PI	HI	O	G
		Zech.12:3		C	1	-	-	1	-	-	-	-	-	-	-	-	-	-	-	-	-	-	-	-	-	-	1	-	-	-	C
388	ŚRP	be burnt	Iq	TOT	14	-	-	14	-	-	5	1	-	1	-	-	-	-	-	-	-	-	-	-	-	-	M	-	-	-	TOT
		Gen.38:24/Lev.4:12/7:17,19/		A	11	-	-	11	-	-	3	1	-	1	-	-	-	-	-	-	-	-	-	-	-	-	M	-	-	-	A
		6:23/13:52/19:6/21:9/Josh.																													
		7:15/Jer.38:17/1Chr.14:12																													
		2Sam.23:7/Pro.6:27		B	2	-	-	2	-	-	1	-	-	-	-	-	-	-	-	-	-	-	-	-	-	-	3	-	-	-	B
		Mi.1:7		C	1	-	-	1	-	-	1	-	-	-	-	-	-	-	-	-	-	-	-	-	-	-	8	-	-	-	C
389	ŚTR	break out (?)	III	TOT	1	-	-	1	-	-	-	-	-	-	-	-	-	-	-	-	-	-	-	-	-	-	-	-	-	-	TOT
		1Sam.5:9		A	1	-	-	1	-	-	-	-	-	-	-	-	-	-	-	-	-	-	-	-	-	-	-	-	-	-	A
390*	ŠAH	rage/be destroyed*	II/Iq*	TOT	3	-	-	3	-	-	-	-	-	-	-	-	-	-	-	-	-	1	1	-	-	-	1	-	2	-	TOT
				A	-	-	-	-	-	-	-	-	-	-	-	-	-	-	-	-	-	1	1	-	-	-	-	-	1	-	A
				B	-	-	-	-	-	-	-	-	-	-	-	-	-	-	-	-	-	-	-	-	-	-	-	-	1	-	B
		Isa.6:11*/17:12,13		C	3	-	-	3	-	-	-	-	-	-	-	-	-	-	-	-	-	-	-	-	-	-	1	-	-	-	C
391	ŠAL	ask for oneself	Iq	TOT	5	-	3	-	2	-	2	-	-	-	-	-	-	-	-	-	-	-	-	-	-	-	M	2	2	-	TOT
		1Sam.20:6,28/Neh.13:6//		A	5	-	3	-	2	-	2	-	-	-	-	-	-	-	-	-	-	-	-	-	-	-	M	1	2	-	A
		1Sam.20:6,28																													
				B	-	-	-	-	-	-	-	-	-	-	-	-	-	-	-	-	-	-	-	-	-	-	M	1	-	-	B
				C	-	-	-	-	-	-	-	-	-	-	-	-	-	-	-	-	-	-	-	-	-	-	M	-	-	-	C
392	ŠAR	be left over/remain	Ih	TOT	91	40	41	10	-	-	-	-	-	-	-	-	-	-	-	-	-	-	-	-	-	-	1	38	-	-	TOT
		see 3.3		A	76	33	35	8	-	-	-	-	-	-	-	-	-	-	-	-	-	-	-	-	-	-	1	31	-	-	A
				B	1	-	1	-	-	-	-	-	-	-	-	-	-	-	-	-	-	-	-	-	-	-	-	-	-	-	B
				C	14	7	5	2	-	-	-	-	-	-	-	-	-	-	-	-	-	-	-	-	-	-	-	7	-	-	C
393	ŠBH	be taken prisoner (of war)	Iq	TOT	8	-	8	-	-	-	2	-	-	-	-	-	-	-	-	-	-	-	-	-	-	-	39	-	-	-	TOT
		Gen.14:14/Ex.22:9/1Sam.30:3,5		A	7	-	7	-	-	-	1	-	-	-	-	-	-	-	-	-	-	-	-	-	-	-	31	-	-	-	A
		/1Kin.8:47/Ezek.6:9/2Chr.6:37																													
				B	-	-	-	-	-	-	-	-	-	-	-	-	-	-	-	-	-	-	-	-	-	-	3	-	-	-	B
		Jer.13:17		C	1	-	1	-	-	-	1	-	-	-	-	-	-	-	-	-	-	-	-	-	-	-	5	-	-	-	C
394	ŠB'	swear	Ih	TOT	152	11	92	39	3	7	1	-	-	-	-	-	-	-	-	-	-	-	-	-	-	-	1	-	31	-	TOT
		see 3.3		A	110	1	68	33	1	7	1	-	-	-	-	-	-	-	-	-	-	-	-	-	-	-	1	-	26	-	A
				B	12	1	11	-	-	-	-	-	-	-	-	-	-	-	-	-	-	-	-	-	-	-	-	-	5	-	B
				C	30	9	13	6	2	-	-	-	-	-	-	-	-	-	-	-	-	-	-	-	-	-	-	-	-	-	C
395	ŠBR	be broken	Iq	TOT	58	11	24	22	1	-	2	-	-	-	-	-	1	-	1	-	-	-	-	-	-	-	53	36	1	-	TOT
		see 3.3		A	29	5	11	12	1	-	1	-	-	-	-	-	-	-	-	-	-	-	-	-	-	-	31	22	-	-	A
				B	12	3	2	7	-	-	1	-	-	-	-	-	-	-	-	-	-	-	-	-	-	-	9	11	-	-	B
				C	17	3	11	3	-	-	-	-	-	-	-	-	1	-	1	-	-	-	-	-	-	-	13	3	1	-	C
396*	ŠBT	cease/be stopped	Iq	TOT	4	-	4	-	-	-	-	-	-	-	-	-	-	-	-	-	-	-	-	-	-	-	26	-	40	-	TOT
		Ezek.6:6/30:18/33:28		A	3	-	3	-	-	-	-	-	-	-	-	-	-	-	-	-	-	-	-	-	-	-	16	-	24	-	A
				B	-	-	-	-	-	-	-	-	-	-	-	-	-	-	-	-	-	-	-	-	-	-	4	-	6	-	B
		Isa.17:3		C	1	-	1	-	-	-	-	-	-	-	-	-	-	-	-	-	-	-	-	-	-	-	6	-	10	-	C
397	ŠGL	be raped	Iq	TOT	2	-	-	2	-	-	-	1	-	1	-	-	-	-	-	-	-	-	-	-	-	-	1	-	-	-	TOT
				A	-	-	-	-	-	-	-	-	-	-	-	-	-	-	-	-	-	-	-	-	-	-	1	-	-	-	A
		Isa.13:16/Zech.14:2		C	2	-	-	2	-	-	-	1	-	1	-	-	-	-	-	-	-	-	-	-	-	-	-	-	-	-	C
398	ŠDD	be destroyed	Iq	TOT	1	-	1	-	-	-	4	18	-	18	-	-	2	-	-	2	-	-	-	-	-	-	11	2	-	1	TOT
				B	-	-	-	-	-	-	2	-	-	-	-	-	-	-	-	-	-	-	-	-	-	-	7	2	-	-	B
		Mi.2:4		C	1	-	1	-	-	-	2	18	-	18	-	-	2	-	-	2	-	-	-	-	-	-	4	-	-	1	C

	ROOT	MEANING	DIV	G	NIPH'AL TOT	PT	PF	IMPF	INF	IMPV	PQ	PU'AL TOT	PT	PF	IMPF	O	HOPH'AL TOT	PT	PF	IMPF	O	HITPA'EL TOT	PT	PF	IMPF	O	QAL	PI	HI	O	G
399	ŠḤḤ	be humiliated	Iq	TOT	4	-	-	4	-	-	-	-	-	-	-	-	-	-	-	-	-	-	-	-	-	-	11	-	2	-	TOT
		Eccl.12:4		A	1	-	-	1	-	-	-	-	-	-	-	-	-	-	-	-	-	-	-	-	-	-	7	-	-	-	A
		Isa.2:9/5:15/29:4		C	3	-	-	3	-	-	-	-	-	-	-	-	-	-	-	-	-	-	-	-	-	-	4	-	2	-	C
400	ŠḤṬ	be slaughtered	Iq	TOT	3	-	-	3	-	-	7	-	-	-	-	-	-	-	-	-	-	-	-	-	-	-	79	-	-	-	TOT
		Lev.6:18(2x)/Num.11:22		A	3	-	-	3	-	-	6	-	-	-	-	-	-	-	-	-	-	-	-	-	-	-	73	-	-	-	A
				C	-	-	-	-	-	-	1	-	-	-	-	-	-	-	-	-	-	-	-	-	-	-	6	-	-	-	C
401	ŠḤT	be spoiled/be destroyed	Ih/p*	TOT	6	1	3	2	-	-	-	-	-	-	-	-	2	2	-	-	-	-	-	-	-	-	39	M	-	-	TOT
		Ezek.20:44//Gen.6:12//		A	4	1	1	2	-	-	-	-	-	-	-	-	-	-	-	-	-	-	-	-	-	-	26	M	-	-	A
		6:11/Ex.8:20*		B	-	-	-	-	-	-	-	-	-	-	-	-	1	1	-	-	-	-	-	-	-	-	3	M	-	-	B
		Jer.13:7/18:4		C	2	-	2	-	-	-	-	-	-	-	-	-	1	1	-	-	-	-	-	-	-	-	10	M	-	-	C
402	ŠṬP	be washed off/away	Iq	TOT	2	-	-	2	-	-	-	1	-	1	-	-	-	-	-	-	-	-	-	-	-	-	28	-	-	-	TOT
		Lev.15:11/Dan.11:22		A	2	-	-	2	-	-	-	1	-	1	-	-	-	-	-	-	-	-	-	-	-	-	10	-	-	-	A
				B	-	-	-	-	-	-	-	-	-	-	-	-	-	-	-	-	-	-	-	-	-	-	6	-	-	-	B
				C	-	-	-	-	-	-	-	-	-	-	-	-	-	-	-	-	-	-	-	-	-	-	12	-	-	-	C
403	ŠKB	be slept on	Iq	TOT	2	-	-	2	-	-	-	1	-	1	-	-	3	1	1	-	1	-	-	-	-	-	M	-	8	-	TOT
				A	-	-	-	-	-	-	-	-	-	-	-	-	3	1	1	-	1	-	-	-	-	-	M	-	6	-	A
				B	-	-	-	-	-	-	-	-	-	-	-	-	-	-	-	-	-	-	-	-	-	-	M	-	1	-	B
		Isa.13:16/Zech.14:2		C	2	-	-	2	-	-	-	1	-	1	-	-	-	-	-	-	-	-	-	-	-	-	M	-	1	-	C
404	ŠKḤ	be forgotten	Iq	TOT	13	3	5	5	-	-	-	-	-	-	-	-	-	-	-	-	-	1	-	-	1	-	86	1	1	-	TOT
		Gen.41:30/Eccl.2:16/9:5// Deut.31:21		A	4	-	3	1	-	-	-	-	-	-	-	-	-	-	-	-	-	-	-	-	-	-	22	-	-	-	A
		Job28:4//Ps.31:13//9:19		B	3	1	1	1	-	-	-	-	-	-	-	-	-	-	-	-	-	1	-	-	1	-	44	1	-	-	B
		Isa.23:15,16//65:16//Jer. 20:11/23:40/50:5		C	6	2	1	3	-	-	-	-	-	-	-	-	-	-	-	-	-	-	-	-	-	-	20	-	1	-	C
405	ŠLH	remain quiet	Iq	TOT	1	-	-	1	-	-	-	-	-	-	-	-	-	-	-	-	-	-	-	-	-	-	6	-	1	-	TOT
		2Chr.29:11		A	1	-	-	1	-	-	-	-	-	-	-	-	-	-	-	-	-	-	-	-	-	-	-	-	1	-	A
				B	-	-	-	-	-	-	-	-	-	-	-	-	-	-	-	-	-	-	-	-	-	-	5	-	-	-	B
				C	-	-	-	-	-	-	-	-	-	-	-	-	-	-	-	-	-	-	-	-	-	-	1	-	-	-	C
406	ŠLḤ	be sent	Iq	TOT	1	-	-	-	1	-	7	10	3	6	1	-	-	-	-	-	-	-	-	-	-	-	M	M	5	-	TOT
		Esth.3:13		A	1	-	-	-	1	-	5	3	-	3	-	-	-	-	-	-	-	-	-	-	-	-	M	M	4	-	A
				B	-	-	-	-	-	-	1	3	1	1	1	-	-	-	-	-	-	-	-	-	-	-	M	M	-	-	B
				C	-	-	-	-	-	-	1	4	2	2	-	-	-	-	-	-	-	-	-	-	-	-	M	M	1	-	C
407	ŠMD	be destroyed/exterminated	Ih	TOT	21	-	9	3	9	-	-	-	-	-	-	-	-	-	-	-	-	-	-	-	-	-	-	-	69	-	TOT
		Gen.34:30/Judg.21:16/2Sam. 21:5//Deut.4:26//4:26/7:23/ 12:30/28:20,24,45,51,61		A	12	-	3	1	8	-	-	-	-	-	-	-	-	-	-	-	-	-	-	-	-	-	-	-	51	-	A
		Ps.37:38/83:11//Pro.14:11// Ps.92:8		B	4	-	2	1	1	-	-	-	-	-	-	-	-	-	-	-	-	-	-	-	-	-	-	-	5	-	B
		Jer.48:8,42/Ezek.32:12/ Hos.10:8//Isa.48:19		C	5	-	4	1	-	-	-	-	-	-	-	-	-	-	-	-	-	-	-	-	-	-	-	-	13	-	C
408	ŠMṬ	be thrown down	Iq	TOT	1	-	1	-	-	-	-	-	-	-	-	-	-	-	-	-	-	-	-	-	-	-	7	-	1	-	TOT
				A	-	-	-	-	-	-	-	-	-	-	-	-	-	-	-	-	-	-	-	-	-	-	6	-	1	-	A
		Ps.141:6		B	1	-	1	-	-	-	-	-	-	-	-	-	-	-	-	-	-	-	-	-	-	-	-	-	-	-	B
				C	-	-	-	-	-	-	-	-	-	-	-	-	-	-	-	-	-	-	-	-	-	-	1	-	-	-	C
409	ŠMM	be destroyed/be frightened	Iq	TOT	25	11	14	-	-	-	-	-	-	-	-	-	5	-	-	-	5	5	-	-	5	-	39	-	15	4	TOT

	ROOT	MEANING	DIV	G	NIPH'AL TOT	PT	PF	IMPF	INF	IMPV	PQ	PU'AL TOT	PT	PF	IMPF	O	HOPH'AL TOT	PT	PF	IMPF	O	HITPA'EL TOT	PT	PF	IMPF	O	QAL	PI	HI	O	G
		see 3.3		A	12	7	5	-	-	-	-	-	-	-	-	-	4	-	-	-	4	1	-	-	1	-	23	-	9	4	A
				B	3	1	2	-	-	-	-	-	-	-	-	-	1	-	-	-	1	2	-	-	2	-	12	-	1	-	B
				C	10	3	7	-	-	-	-	-	-	-	-	-	-	-	-	-	-	2	-	-	2	-	4	-	5	-	C
410	ŠM'	be heard	Iq	TOT	44	6	20	17	1	-	-	-	-	-	-	-	-	-	-	-	-	-	-	-	-	-	M	2	61	-	TOT
		see 3.3		A	27	3	13	10	1	-	-	-	-	-	-	-	-	-	-	-	-	-	-	-	-	-	M	2	21	-	A
				B	5	1	2	2	-	-	-	-	-	-	-	-	-	-	-	-	-	-	-	-	-	-	M	-	8	-	B
				C	12	2	5	5	-	-	-	-	-	-	-	-	-	-	-	-	-	-	-	-	-	-	M	-	32	-	C
411	ŠMR	keep oneself for/be guarded	Iq	TOT	37	-	11	2	-	24	3	-	-	-	-	-	-	-	-	-	-	3	-	-	3	-	M	1	-	-	TOT
		see 3.3		A	29	-	7	2	-	20	2	-	-	-	-	-	-	-	-	-	-	-	-	-	-	-	M	-	-	-	A
				B	2	-	1	-	-	1	1	-	-	-	-	-	-	-	-	-	-	2	-	-	2	-	M	-	-	-	B
				C	6	-	3	-	-	3	-	-	-	-	-	-	-	-	-	-	-	1	-	-	1	-	M	1	-	-	C
412	ŠNA/	be repeated	Iq	TOT	1	-	-	-	1	-	-	1	-	-	1	-	-	-	-	-	-	1	-	1	-	-	14	9	-	-	TOT
	SNH	Gen.41:32		A	1	-	-	-	1	-	-	-	-	-	-	-	-	-	-	-	-	1	-	1	-	-	7	3	-	-	A
				B	-	-	-	-	-	-	-	1	-	-	1	-	-	-	-	-	-	-	-	-	-	-	6	4	-	-	B
				C	-	-	-	-	-	-	-	-	-	-	-	-	-	-	-	-	-	-	-	-	-	-	1	2	-	-	C
413	ŠSS	be plundered	Iq	TOT	2	-	-	1	1	-	-	-	-	-	-	-	-	-	-	-	-	-	-	-	-	-	3	-	-	-	TOT
				A	-	-	-	-	-	-	-	-	-	-	-	-	-	-	-	-	-	-	-	-	-	-	2	-	-	-	A
				B	-	-	-	-	-	-	-	-	-	-	-	-	-	-	-	-	-	-	-	-	-	-	1	-	-	-	B
		Zech.14:2//Isa.13:6		C	2	-	-	1	1	-	-	-	-	-	-	-	-	-	-	-	-	-	-	-	-	-	-	-	-	-	C
414	Š'N	lean on/trust in	III	TOT	22	4	5	8	4	1	-	-	-	-	-	-	-	-	-	-	-	-	-	-	-	-	-	-	-	-	TOT
		see 3.3		A	13	4	4	1	3	1	-	-	-	-	-	-	-	-	-	-	-	-	-	-	-	-	-	-	-	-	A
				B	3	-	-	3	-	-	-	-	-	-	-	-	-	-	-	-	-	-	-	-	-	-	-	-	-	-	B
				C	6	-	1	4	1	-	-	-	-	-	-	-	-	-	-	-	-	-	-	-	-	-	-	-	-	-	C
415	ŠPH	naked/wiped clean	III	TOT	1	1	-	-	-	-	-	1	-	-	1	-	-	-	-	-	-	-	-	-	-	-	-	-	-	-	TOT
				B	-	-	-	-	-	-	-	1	-	-	1	-	-	-	-	-	-	-	-	-	-	-	-	-	-	-	B
		Isa.13:2		C	1	1	-	-	-	-	-	-	-	-	-	-	-	-	-	-	-	-	-	-	-	-	-	-	-	-	C
416	ŠPṬ	be judged	Iq	TOT	17	5	5	4	3	-	-	-	-	-	-	-	-	-	-	-	-	-	-	-	-	-	M	-	-	1	TOT
		Ez.17:20/20:35,36/38:22//20:36/1Sam.12:7//2Chr.22:8		A	7	-	4	2	1	-	-	-	-	-	-	-	-	-	-	-	-	-	-	-	-	-	M	-	-	-	A
		Pro.29:9//Ps.9:20//37:33/109:7		B	4	1	-	1	2	-	-	-	-	-	-	-	-	-	-	-	-	-	-	-	-	-	M	-	-	1	B
		Isa.59:4/66:16/Jer.2:35/25:31//Jo.4:2//Isa.43:26		C	6	4	1	1	-	-	-	-	-	-	-	-	-	-	-	-	-	-	-	-	-	-	M	-	-	-	C
417	ŠPK	be poured out	Iq	TOT	8	-	3	4	1	-	3	3	-	3	-	-	-	-	-	-	-	3	-	-	2	1	98	-	-	-	TOT
		1Kin.13:3//Gen.9:6/Deut.12:27/19:10/1Kin.13:5//Ez.16:36		A	6	-	1	4	1	-	2	1	-	1	-	-	-	-	-	-	-	-	-	-	-	-	62	-	-	-	A
		Ps.22:5/Lam.2:11		B	2	-	2	-	-	-	1	1	-	1	-	-	-	-	-	-	-	3	-	-	2	1	18	-	-	-	B
				C	-	-	-	-	-	-	-	1	-	1	-	-	-	-	-	-	-	-	-	-	-	-	18	-	-	-	C
418	ŠQL	be weighed	Iq	TOT	3	-	1	2	-	-	-	-	-	-	-	-	-	-	-	-	-	-	-	-	-	-	19	-	-	-	TOT
		Ezra8:33		A	1	-	1	-	-	-	-	-	-	-	-	-	-	-	-	-	-	-	-	-	-	-	12	-	-	-	A
		Job6:22/28:15		B	2	-	-	2	-	-	-	-	-	-	-	-	-	-	-	-	-	-	-	-	-	-	2	-	-	-	B
				C	-	-	-	-	-	-	-	-	-	-	-	-	-	-	-	-	-	-	-	-	-	-	5	-	-	-	C
419	ŠQ'	sink	I=q	TOT	1	-	1	-	-	-	-	-	-	-	-	-	-	-	-	-	-	-	-	-	-	-	3	-	2	-	TOT
				A	-	-	-	-	-	-	-	-	-	-	-	-	-	-	-	-	-	-	-	-	-	-	1	-	-	-	A
				B	-	-	-	-	-	-	-	-	-	-	-	-	-	-	-	-	-	-	-	-	-	-	-	-	1	-	B

	ROOT	MEANING	DIV	G	NIPH'AL TOT	PT	PF	IMPF	INF	IMPV	PQ	PU'AL TOT	PT	PF	IMPF	O	HOPH'AL TOT	PT	PF	IMPF	O	HITPA'EL TOT	PT	PF	IMPF	O	QAL	PI	HI	O	G
		Am.8:8		C	1	-	1	-	-	-	-	-	-	-	-	-	-	-	-	-	-	-	-	-	-	-	2	-	1	-	C
420	**ŠQP**	look down/ascend*	I=h/II*	TOT	10	3	7	-	-	-	-	-	-	-	-	-	-	-	-	-	-	-	-	-	-	-	-	-	12	-	TOT
		Num.23:28/1Sam.13:18//Num.21: 20/2Sam.6:16/1Chr.15:29		A	5	2	3	-	-	-	-	-	-	-	-	-	-	-	-	-	-	-	-	-	-	-	-	-	8	-	A
		Song6:10*//Judg.5:28/Ps.85: 12/Pro.7:6		B	4	1	3	-	-	-	-	-	-	-	-	-	-	-	-	-	-	-	-	-	-	-	-	-	4	-	B
		Jer.6:1		C	1	-	1	-	-	-	-	-	-	-	-	-	-	-	-	-	-	-	-	-	-	-	-	-	-	-	C
421	**ŠTH**	be drunk (said of a liquid)	Iq	TOT	1	-	-	1	-	-	-	-	-	-	-	-	-	-	-	-	-	-	-	-	-	-	M	-	-	-	TOT
		Lev.11:34		A	1	-	-	1	-	-	-	-	-	-	-	-	-	-	-	-	-	-	-	-	-	-	M	-	-	-	A
				B	-	-	-	-	-	-	-	-	-	-	-	-	-	-	-	-	-	-	-	-	-	-	M	-	-	-	B
				C	-	-	-	-	-	-	-	-	-	-	-	-	-	-	-	-	-	-	-	-	-	-	M	-	-	-	C
422*	**TKN**	be judged*/be just/right	Iq*/II	TOT	10	-	1	9	-	-	-	1	1	-	-	-	-	-	-	-	-	-	-	-	-	-	3	4	-	-	TOT
		Ezek.18:25(3x),29(3x)/ 33:17(2x),20		A	9	-	-	9	-	-	-	1	1	-	-	-	-	-	-	-	-	-	-	-	-	-	-	-	-	-	A
		1Sam.2:3		B	1	-	1	-	-	-	-	-	-	-	-	-	-	-	-	-	-	-	-	-	-	-	3	2	-	-	B
				C	-	-	-	-	-	-	-	-	-	-	-	-	-	-	-	-	-	-	-	-	-	-	-	2	-	-	C
423	**TLA/ TLH**	be hung	Iq	TOT	2	-	1	1	-	-	6	-	-	-	-	-	-	-	-	-	-	-	-	-	-	-	26	2	-	-	TOT
		Esth.2:23		A	1	-	1	-	-	-	4	-	-	-	-	-	-	-	-	-	-	-	-	-	-	-	21	2	-	-	A
		Lam.5:12		B	1	-	-	1	-	-	1	-	-	-	-	-	-	-	-	-	-	-	-	-	-	-	3	-	-	-	B
				C	-	-	-	-	-	-	1	-	-	-	-	-	-	-	-	-	-	-	-	-	-	-	2	-	-	-	C
424	**TMK**	be held	Iq	TOT	1	-	-	1	-	-	-	-	-	-	-	-	-	-	-	-	-	-	-	-	-	-	20	-	-	-	TOT
				A	-	-	-	-	-	-	-	-	-	-	-	-	-	-	-	-	-	-	-	-	-	-	2	-	-	-	A
		Pro.5:22		B	1	-	-	1	-	-	-	-	-	-	-	-	-	-	-	-	-	-	-	-	-	-	13	-	-	-	B
				C	-	-	-	-	-	-	-	-	-	-	-	-	-	-	-	-	-	-	-	-	-	-	5	-	-	-	C
425	**T'B**	be abhorred/become an abomination	Ip	TOT	3	2	1	-	-	-	-	-	-	-	-	-	-	-	-	-	-	-	-	-	-	-	-	14	4	-	TOT
		1Chr.21:6		A	1	-	1	-	-	-	-	-	-	-	-	-	-	-	-	-	-	-	-	-	-	-	-	4	2	-	A
		Job15:16		B	1	1	-	-	-	-	-	-	-	-	-	-	-	-	-	-	-	-	-	-	-	-	-	7	2	-	B
		Isa.14:19		C	1	1	-	-	-	-	-	-	-	-	-	-	-	-	-	-	-	-	-	-	-	-	-	3	-	-	C
426	**T'H**	be deceived	Ih*/q	TOT	2	-	1	-	1	-	-	-	-	-	-	-	-	-	-	-	-	-	-	-	-	-	25	-	21	-	TOT
				A	-	-	-	-	-	-	-	-	-	-	-	-	-	-	-	-	-	-	-	-	-	-	9	-	4	-	A
		Job15:31*		B	1	-	1	-	-	-	-	-	-	-	-	-	-	-	-	-	-	-	-	-	-	-	9	-	6	-	B
		Isa.19:14		C	1	-	-	-	1	-	-	-	-	-	-	-	-	-	-	-	-	-	-	-	-	-	7	-	11	-	C
427	**TPŠ**	be caught/be apprehended	Iq	TOT	15	-	9	5	1	-	1	-	-	-	-	-	-	-	-	-	-	-	-	-	-	-	47	1	-	-	TOT
		Num.5:13/Ez.12:13/17:20//21: 29/Jer.34:3/38:23//Ez.21:28		A	7	-	3	3	1	-	-	-	-	-	-	-	-	-	-	-	-	-	-	-	-	-	37	-	-	-	A
		Ps.10:2		B	1	-	-	1	-	-	-	-	-	-	-	-	-	-	-	-	-	-	-	-	-	-	2	1	-	-	B
		Ezek.19:4,8/Jer.48:41/50:24, 46/51:32//51:41		C	7	-	6	1	-	-	1	-	-	-	-	-	-	-	-	-	-	-	-	-	-	-	8	-	-	-	C
428	**TQ'**	be blown/be beaten	Iq	TOT	3	-	-	3	-	-	1	-	-	-	-	-	-	-	-	-	-	-	-	-	-	-	64	-	-	-	TOT
				A	-	-	-	-	-	-	-	-	-	-	-	-	-	-	-	-	-	-	-	-	-	-	47	-	-	-	A
		Job17:3		B	1	-	-	1	-	-	-	-	-	-	-	-	-	-	-	-	-	-	-	-	-	-	6	-	-	-	B
		Isa.27:13/Am.3:6		C	2	-	-	2	-	-	1	-	-	-	-	-	-	-	-	-	-	-	-	-	-	-	11	-	-	-	C

13 **AMN** A PT: Num. 12:7/ Deut. 7:9/ 28:59(2x)/ 1Sam. 2:35(2x)/ 3:20/ 22:14/ 25:28/ 1Kin. 11:38/ Neh. 9:8/ 13:13/ Jer. 42:5 PF: 2Sam. 7:16 IMPF: Gen. 42:20/ 1Kin. 8:26/ 1 Chr. 17:23, 24/ 2Chr. 1:9/ 6:17/ 20:20

B PT: Ps. 19:8/ 89:29, 38/ 101:6/ 111:7/ Pro. 11:3/ 25:13 / 27:6/ Job 12:20 PF: Ps. 78:8, 37/ 93:5

C PT: Isa. 1:21, 26/ 8:22/ 22:23, 25/ 33:16/ 49:7/ 55:3/ Hos. 5:9/ 12:1 PF: Jer. 15:18 IMPF: Isa. 7:9

14 **AMR** A PF: Dan. 8:26 IMPF: Gen. 10:9/ 22:14/ 32:29/ Num. 21:14/ Josh. 2:2/ Ez. 13:12

B IMPF: Num. 23:23/ Ps. 87:5

C IMPF: Isa. 4:3/ 19:18/ 32:5/ 61:6/ 62:4(2x)/ Jer. 4: 11/ 7:32/ 16:4/ Hos. 2:1(2x)/ Zeph. 3:16

18 **ASP** A PT: Gen. 49:29/ 1Sam. 13:11 PF: Gen. 29:3/ 34:30/ Lev. 26:25/ Num. 27:13(2x)/ Judg. 2:10/ 6:33/ 16:23/ 1Sam. 13:5/ 17:2/ 23:9/ 2Kin. 22:20/ 1Chr. 11:13/ 19:7/ 2 Chr. 12:5/ 30:3/ 34:28/ Neh. 8:13/ 9:1/ IMPF: Gen. 25: 8, 17/ 29:8/ 35:29/ 49:33/ Ex. 9:19/ 32:26/ Num. 11: 22, 30/ 12:14/ 20:24, 26/ 31:2/ Deut. 32: 50/ Judg. 9:6/ 10:17/ 20: 11, 14/ Josh. 10:5/ 1Sam. 17:1(2x)/ 2 Sam. 10:15/ 14:14/ 17:11, 13/ 23:11/ Ez. 29:5/ Ezra 3: 1/ 9:4/ Neh. 8:1/ 12:28/ 2Chr. 30:13 INF: Gen. 29:7/ Num. 12:15/ 2Sam. 17:11 IMPV: Deut. 32:50/ Ez. 39:17

B PF: Ps. 35:15(2x)/ 47:10/ Pro. 27:25 IMPF: Ps. 104: 22/ Job 27:19 IMPV: Gen. 49:1

C PT: Isa. 13:4/ 57:1 PF: Isa. 16:10/ 57:1/ Jer. 48: 33/ Mi. 4:11/ Zech. 12:3 IMPF: Isa. 43:9/ 49:5/ 60: 20/ Jer. 8:2/ 25:33/ Hos. 4:3 IMPV: Jer. 4:5/ 8:14/ 47:6/ Am. 3:9

27 **BHL** A PF: Gen. 45:3/ 1Sam. 28:21/ 2Sam. 4:1/ Ez. 26:18 IMPF: Judg. 20:41/ Ez. 7:27/ Eccl. 8:3

B PT: Ps. 30:8/ Pro. 28:22 PF: Ex. 15:15/ Ps. 6:3, 4/ 48:6/ 90:7/ Job 21:6 IMPF: Ps. 6:11/ 83:18/ 104:29/ Job 4:5/ 23:15

C PT: Zeph. 1:18 PF: Isa. 13:8/ 21:3/ Jer. 51:32

33 **BJN** A PT: Gen. 41:33, 39/ Deut. 1:13/ 4:6/ 1Sam. 16:18/ 1 Kin. 3:12/ Eccl. 9:11

B PT: Pro. 1:5/ 10:13/ 14:6, 33/ 15:4/ 16:21/ 17:28/ 18: 15/ 19:25

C PT: Isa. 3:3/ 5:21/ 29:14/ Jer. 4:22/ Hos. 14:10 PF: Isa. 10:13

35 **BNH** A PT: 1Chr. 22:19 PF: Num. 13:22/ 1Kin. 3:2/ 6:7/ Neh. 7:1/ Jer. 30: 18/ 31:4, 38/ Ez. 36:33/ Dan. 9:25 IMPF: Gen. 16:2/ 30:3/ Deut. 13: 17/ Ez. 26:14/ 36:10 INF: 1 Kin. 6:7(2x)

B IMPF: Num 21:27/ Ps. 89:3/ Pro. 24:3/ Job 12:14/ 22:23

C PF: Jer. 12:16/ Mal. 3:15 IMPF: Isa. 25:2/ 44:26, 28/ Zech. 1:16 INF: Hag. 1:2/ Zech. 8:9

52 **GLH** A PT: Deut. 29:28/ 1Sam. 2:27 PF: Gen. 35:7/ 1Sam. 2:27/ 3:21/ 14:8/ 2Sam. 6:20/ Ez. 13:14/ Dan. 10:1 IMPF: Ex. 20:26/ 1Sam. 3:7/ 14: 11/ Ez. 16:36, 57 INF: 1Sam. 2: 27/ 2Sam. 6:20(2x)/ Ez. 21:29

B PF: Job 38:17 IMPF: 2Sam. 22:16/ Ps. 18:16/ Pro. 26:26

C PF: Isa. 22:14/ 23:1/ 38:12/ 40:5/ 53:1/ Jer. 13:22/
Hos. 7:1 IMPF: Isa 47:3 INF: Isa. 56:1 IMPV: Isa. 49:9

77 **HJH** A PF: Ex. 11:6/ Deut. 4:32/ 27:9/ Judg. 19:30/ 20:3, 12/
1Kin. 1:27/ 12: 24/ Ez. 21:12/ 39:8/ Dan. 2:1/ 8:27/
12:1/ Neh. 6:8/ 2Chr. 11:4
B PT: Pro. 13:19
C PF: Jer. 5:30/ 48:19/ Jo. 2:2/ Mi. 2:4/ Zech. 8:10

80 **HPK** A PT: Jon. 3:4 PF: Ex. 7:15,17/ Lev. 13:16,17,25/ Josh.
8:20/ 1Sam. 4:19/ 10:6/ Jer. 30:6/ Esth. 9:22/ Dan.
10:8, 16 IMPF: Ex. 7:20/ 14:5/ Ez. 4:8 INF: Esth. 9:1
B PT: Pro. 17:20 PF: Ps. 32:4/ 78:57/ Job 19:19/ 20: 14/
28:5/ 41:20/ Lam. 1:20/ 5:2, 15 IMPF: Job 30:21
C PF: Isa. 34:9/ Jer. 2:21/ Hos. 11:8 IMPF: Isa. 60:5/
63:10/ Jo. 3:4

94 **ḤBA** A PT: Josh. 10:17/ 1Sam. 10:22/ 2Sam. 17:9 PF: Gen. 31:
27/ Josh. 2: 16/ 10:27/ Judg. 7:5/ 1Sam. 19:2 IMPF:
Gen. 3:10/ Josh. 10:16 INF: 1Kin. 22:15/ 2Kin. 7:12/
Dan. 10:7/ 2Chr. 18:24
B PF: Job 29:8, 10 IMPF: Job 5:21
C IMPF: Am. 9:3 INF: Jer. 49:10

120 **ḤŠB** A PT: 1Kin. 10:2/ 2Chr. 9:20 PF: Gen. 31:15/ Num. 18:
27, 30/ Neh. 13:13 IMPF: Lev. 7:4, 18/ 25:31/ Deut. 2:
11, 20/ Josh. 13:3/ 2Sam. 4:4/ 2Kin. 22:7
B PF: Ps. 44:23/ 88:5/ Job 18:3/ 41:21/ Lam. 4:2 IMPF:
Ps. 106:31/ Pro. 17:28/ 27:14
C PT: Isa. 2:22 PF: Isa. 5:28/ 40:15, 17/ Hos. 5:7
IMPF: Isa. 29: 16, 17/ 32:15

125 **ḤTT** A IMPF: Deut. 1:21/ 31:8/ Josh. 1:9/ 8:1/ 10:25/ 1Sam.
17:11/ Jer. 30: 13/ Ez. 2:6/ 3:9/ 1Chr. 22:13/ 28: 20/
2Chr. 20:15, 17/ 32:7
B IMPF: 1Sam. 2:10/ Job 21:13/ 39:22
C PF: Mal. 2:5 IMPF: Isa. 7:8*/ 30:31/ 31:4/ 51:6*, 7/
Jer. 1:17/ 10:2(2x)/ 17:18(2x)/ 23:4/ 46:27

135 **JD'** A PT: Eccl. 6:10 PF: Gen. 41:21/ Ex. 2:14/ 6:3/ 21:36/
Lev. 4:14/ Deut. 21:1/ Judg. 16:9/ 1Sam. 6:3/ 22:6/ 2
Sam. 17:9/ Ez. 20:9/ 35:11/ 38:23/ Neh. 4:9 IMPF: Gen.
41:31/ Ex. 33:16/ 1Kin. 18:36/ Jer. 28:9/ Ez. 20:5/
36:32/ Ruth 3:3, 14/ Esth. 2:22 INF: Jer. 31:19
B PT: Ps. 76:2/ Pro. 31:23 PF: Ps. 9:17/ 48:4/ 77:20
IMPF: Ps. 74:5/ 79:10/ 88:13/ Pro. 10:9/ 12:16/ 14:33
C PF: Isa. 19:21/ 61:9/66:14/ Nah. 3:17 IMPF: Zech. 14:7

138 **JLD** A PT: Gen. 21:3/ 48:5/ 1Kin. 13:2/ 1Chr. 7:21/ 22:9/
Ezra 10:3 PF: Eccl. 4:14/ 1Chr. 2:3, 9/ 3:1, 4, 5/
20:6, 8/ 26:6/ IMPF: Gen. 4: 18/ 10:1/ 17:17/ 46:40/
Lev. 22:27/ Num. 26:60/ Deut. 15:19/ 23:9/ 2Sam. 3:2/
5:13/ 14:27 INF: Gen. 21:5/ Eccl. 7:1
B PT: Ps. 22:32 IMPF: Ps. 78:6/ Pro. 17:17/ Job 1:2/ 3:
2/ 11:12/ 15:7/ 38:21
C IMPF: Isa. 66:8 INF: Hos. 2:5

148 **JRA** A PT: Gen. 28:17/ Ex. 34:10/ Deut. 1:19/ 7:21/ 8:15/ 10:
17, 21/ 28:25/ Judg. 13:6/ 2Sam. 7:23/ Ez. 1:22/ Dan.
9:4/ Neh. 1:5/ 4:8/ 9:23/ 1Chr. 17:21
B PT: Ex. 15:11/ Ps. 45:5/ 47:3/ 65:5/ 66:3, 5/ 68:36/

76:8, 13/ 89:8/ 96:4/ 99:3/ 106:22/ 111:9/ 139:14/ 145:6/ Job 37:22/ 1Chr. 16:25 IMPF: Ps. 130:4

C PT: Isa. 18:2, 7/ 21:1/ 64:2/ Jo. 2:11/ 3:4/ Hab. 1:7/ Zeph. 2:11/ Mal. 1:14/ 3:23

154 **JTR** A PT: Gen. 30:36/ Ex. 12:10/ 28:10/ 29:34/ Lev. 2:3, 10/ 6:9/ 7:16, 17/ 8:32/ 10:12(2x), 16/ 14:18, 29/ 19:6/ 27:18/ Josh. 17:2, 6/ 21:5, 20, 26, 34, 38/ Judg. 8: 10/ 21:7, 16/ 1Sam. 2:36/ 30:9/ 1Kin. 9:20/ 15:18/ 20: 30/ 2Kin. 4:7/ Jer. 27:18, 19, 21/ 34:7/ Ez. 34:18/ 39:14/ 48:15, 18, 21/ 1Chr. 6:46, 55, 62/ 24:20/ 2Chr. 8:7/ 31:10 PF: Ex. 10:15/ Num. 26:65/ Josh. 11:11, 22/ 1Sam. 25:34/ 2Sam. 9:1/ 13:30/ 17: 12/ 1Kin. 9:21/ 17:17/ 18:22/ Ez. 14:22/ Dan. 10:13/ Neh. 6:1/ 2Chr. 8:8 IMPF: Gen32:25/ 44:20/ Ex. 29: 34/ Judg. 9:5/ Josh. 18:2/ 1Kin. 19:10, 14/ 2Kin. 20: 17

B PF: Ps. 106:11 IMPF: Pro. 2:21

C PT: Isa. 4:3/ 7:22/ Zech. 14:16 PF: Isa. 1:8/ 30:7 IMPF: Isa. 39:6/ Am. 6:9/ Zech. 13:8

156 **KBD** A PT: Gen. 34:19/ Num. 22:15/ Deut. 28:58/ 1Sam. 9:6/ 22:14/ 2Sam. 23:19, 23/ 1Chr. 4:9/ 11:21, 25 PF: 2Sam. 6:20/ Ez. 28:22 IMPF: Ex. 14:4, 17/ Lev. 10:3/ 2Sam. 6:22 INF: Ex. 14:18/ Ez. 39:13 IMPV: 2Kin. 14:10

B PT: Ps. 87:3/ 148:9/ Pro. 8:24

C PT: Isa. 3:5/ 23:8, 9/ Nah. 3:10 PF: Isa. 26:15/ 43: 4 IMPF: Isa. 49:5/ Hag. 1:8(2x)

159 **KWN** A PT: Gen. 41:32/ Ex. 8:22/ 19:11, 15/ 34:2/ Deut. 13: 15/ 17:4/ Judg. 16:26, 29/ Josh. 8:4/ 1Sam. 23:23/ 26: 4/ 2Sam. 7:16, 26/ 1Kin. 2:45/ Neh. 8:10/ 1Chr. 17:14, 24 PF: 1Kin. 2:46/ Ez. 16:17 IMPF: 1Sam. 20:31/ 1Kin. 2:12/ Jer. 30:20/ 2Chr. 8:16/ 29:35/ 35:10, 16 IMPV: Ez. 38:7/ 2Chr. 35:4(K)

B PT: Ps. 5:10/ 38:18/ 51:12/ 57:8(2x)/ 78:37/ 93:2/ 108: 2/ 112:7/ Pro. 4:18/ Job 12:5/ 15:23/ 18:12/ 21:8/ 42:7, 8 PF: Pro. 19:29 IMPF: Ps. 89:22, 38/ 93:1/ 96: 10/ 101:7/ 102:29/ 119:5/ 140:12/ 141:2/ Pro. 12:3,19/ 4:26/ 16:3,12/ 20:18/ 22:18/ 25:5/ 29:14

C PT: Isa. 2:2/ Hos. 6:3/ Mi. 4:1 IMPV: Am. 4:12

164 **KLM** A PT: 2Sam. 10:5/ 19:4/ Ez. 16:27/ 1Chr. 19:5 PF: Jer. 31:19/ Ez. 16:54, 61/ 43:11/ Ezra 9:6/ 2Chr. 30:15 IMPF: Num. 12:14/ Ez. 43: 10 IMPV: Ez. 36:32

B PT: Ps. 74:21 IMPF: Ps. 35:4/ 40:15/ 69:7/ 70:3

C PF: Isa. 45:16/ 50:7/ Jer. 22:22 IMPF: Isa. 41:11/ 45: 17/ 54:4/ INF: Jer. 3:3/ 8:12

166 **KN'** A PF: 1Kin. 21:29(2x)/ 2Chr. 12:7(2x)/ 30:11/ 33:23/ 36: 12 IMPF: Lev. 26:41/ Judg. 3:30/ 8:28/ 11:33/ 1Sam. 7: 13/ 2Kin. 22:19/ 1Chr. 20:4/ 2Chr. 7:14/ 12:6/ 13: 18/ 32:26/ 33:12/ 34:27(2x) INF: 2Chr 12:12/ 33:19, 23

B IMPF: Ps. 106:42

173 **KRT** A PF: Gen. 17:14/ Ex. 12:15, 19/ 30:33, 38/ 31:14/ Lev. 7:20, 21, 25, 27/ 17:4, 9/ 19:8/ 18:29/ 20:17, 18/ 22: 3/ 23:29/ Num. 9:13/ 15:30/ 19: 13, 20/ Josh. 3:16/ 4: 7 IMPF: Gen. 9:11/ 41:36/ Lev. 17:14/ Num. 11: 33/ 15: 3/ Josh. 3:13/ 9:23/ 2Sam. 3:29/ 1Kin. 2: 4/ 8:25/ 9:

5/ Jer. 33: 17, 18/ 35:19/ Ruth 4:10/ Dan. 9:26/ 2Chr. 6:16/ 7:18 INF: Num. 15: 31

B PF: Ps. 37:28, 38 IMPF: Ps. 37:9, 22/ Pro. 2:22/ 10: 31/ 23:18/ 24: 14/ Job 14:7 INF: Ps. 37:34

C PF: Isa. 22:25/ 29:20/ Jer. 7:28/ Jo. 1:5, 16/ Ob. 10/ Nah. 2:1/ Zeph. 1:11/ Zech. 9:10 IMPF: Isa. 11: 13/ 48:19/ 55:13/ 56:5/ Hos. 8:4/ Ob. 9/ Mi. 5:8/ Zeph. 3: 7/ Zech. 13:8/ 14:2

183 **LḤM** A PT: Ex. 14:25/ Deut. 3:22/ Josh. 10:14, 25, 42/ 23:3/ Judg. 9:45/ 1Sam. 17:19/ 23:1/ 25:28/ 28:15/ 31:1/ 2 Kin. 6:18/ 19:8/ Isa. 37:8/ Jer. 34:1, 7/ 32:24, 29/ 37:10 PF: Ex. 1:10/ Num. 21:26/ Deut. 1:41/ Judg. 9: 17/ 11:5, 8, 25/ 1Sam. 4:9/ 8:20/ 15:18/ 17: 32/ 29:8/ 2 Sam. 8:10/ 12: 27/ 1Kin. 14:19/ 22:46/ 2Kin. 13:12/ 14:15, 28/ Jer. 34:22/ 37:8/ Dan. 11: 11/ 1Chr. 10:1/ 18:10/ 2Chr. 17:10/ 20:29/ 27:5 IMPF: Ex. 14:14/ 17:8/ Num. 21:1, 23/ Deut. 1:30, 42/ Josh. 10:5, 29, 31, 34, 36, 38/ 19:17/ 24:8, 9, 11/ Judg. 1:3, 5, 8/ 9:35, 52/ 11:4, 6, 20/ 12:4/ 1Sam. 4:10/ 12:9/ 17:10/ 14:47/ 19: 8/ 23:5/ 2Sam. 10:17/ 11:17/ 12:26, 29/ 21:15/ 1Kin. 12:24/ 20:1, 23, 25/ 22:31/ 2Kin. 12:18/ Jer. 32:5/ Neh. 4:14/ 1Chr. 19:17/ 2Chr. 11:4/ 13:12/ 18:30/ 26:6 INF: Ex. 17:10/ Num. 22:11/ Deut. 20:4, 10, 19/ Josh. 9:2/ 11:5/ Judg. 1:1, 9/ 8:1/ 10:9, 18/ 11:9, 12, 25, 27, 32/ 12:1, 3/ 1Sam. 13:5/ 17:9, 33/ 28:1/ 2Sam. 2: 28/ 11:20/ 1Kin. 12:21/ 22:32/ 2Kin. 3:21/ 8:29/ 9:15/ 16:5/ 19:9/ Isa. 37:9/ Jer. 33:5/ 41:12/ Dan. 10:20/ Neh. 4:2/ 2Chr. 11:1/ 18: 31/ 20:17/ 22:6/ 35:20, 22 (2x)/ 32:8 IMPV: Ex. 17:9/ Judg. 9:38/ 1Sam. 18:17/ 2 Kin. 10:3/ Neh. 4:8

B PF: Judg. 5:19, 20 IMPF: Ps. 109:3

C PT: Jer. 21:2, 4 PF: Isa. 19:2/ 30:32/ 63:10/ Jer. 1: 19/ 15:20/ 21:5/ Zech. 10:5/ 14:3 IMPF: Isa. 20:1/ Zech. 14:14 INF: Isa. 7: 1/ Jer. 51:30/ Zech. 14:3

185 **LKD** A PT: Josh. 1:15 PF: 1Kin. 16:8/ 2Kin. 18:10/ Jer. 38: 28 IMPF: Josh. 7:16, 17, 18/ 1Sam. 10:20, 21(2x)/ 14: 41, 42/ Eccl. 7:26

B PF: Ps. 9:16/ Pro. 6:2/ Lam. 4:20 IMPF: Ps. 59:13/ Pro. 11:6/ Job 36:8

C PF: Isa. 8:15/ 28:13/ Jer. 48:1, 41/ 50:2, 24/ 51: 31, 41, 56/ Zech. 14:2 IMPF: Isa. 24:18/ Jer. 6:11/ 8:9/ 48:7, 44/ 50:9

201 **MLA** A IMPF: Gen. 6:11/ Ex. 1:7/ 7:25/ Num. 14:21/ 1Kin. 7: 14/ 2Kin. 3:17, 20/ 10:21/ Ez. 9:9/ 10:4/ 23:33/ 26:2/ Esth. 3:5/ 5:9/ Eccl. 1:8/ 6:7/ 11:3

B PT: Song 5:2 IMPF: 2Sam. 23:7/ Ps. 71:8/ 72:19/ 126: 2/ Pro. 3:10/ 20:17/ 24:4/ Job 15:32

C IMPF: Isa. 2:7, 8/ 6:4/ Jer. 13:12(2x)/ Ez. 27:25/ 32: 6/ Hab. 2:14/ Zech. 8:5

203 **MLṬ** A PT: 1Kin. 19:17(2x) PF: Judg. 3:26, 29/ 1Sam. 23:13/ 27:1/ 30:17/ 2Sam. 1:3/ 4:6/ 2Kin. 19:37/ Isa. 37: 38/ Jer. 41:15/ Ez. 17:15/ 2Chr. 16:17 IMPF: Gen. 19:20/ Judg. 3:26/ 1Sam. 19:10, 12, 17, 18/ 20: 29/ 22:1, 20/

27:1/ 1Kin. 18:40/ 20:20/ 2Kin. 10:24/ Jer. 32:4/ 34: 3/ 38:18, 23/ Ez. 17:15, 18/ Dan. 11: 41/ 12:1/ Eccl. 7:26/ INF: Gen. 19:19/ 1Sam. 27:1/ Esth. 4:13 IMPV: Gen. 19:17, 22

B PF: Ps. 22:6/ 124:7(2x)/ Job 22:30/ Pro. 11:21 IMPF: Job 1:15, 16, 17, 18/ Pro. 19:5/ 28:26

C PT: Jer. 48:19 IMPF: Isa. 20:6/ 49:24, 25/ Jer. 46: 6/ 48:8/ Jo. 3: 5/ Am. 9:1/ Mal. 3:15 IMPV: Zech. 2:11

211 **MṢA** A PT: Gen. 19:15/ 47:14/ Deut. 20:11/ Judg. 20:48(2x)/ 1 Sam. 13:15, 16/ 21:4/ 2Kin. 12:11, 19/ 14:4/ 16:8/ 18: 15/ 19:14/ 22:9, 13/ 23:2/ 25:19/ Isa. 37:4/ Jer. 52: 25/ Esth. 1:5/ 4:16/ Ezra 8:25/ Dan. 12:1/ 1Chr. 29:8/ 2Chr. 5:11/ 21:17/ 25:24/ 29:29/ 30:21/ 31:1/ 34:17, 30, 32, 33/ 35:7, 17, 18/ 36:8 PF: Gen. 41: 38/ 44:16, 17/ Ex. 21:16/ 35:23, 24/ Deut. 22:20, 28/ Josh. 10: 17/ 1Sam. 9:8, 20/ 10:2, 16, 21/ 13:22/ 2Sam. 17: 12, 13/ 1Kin. 14:13/ 2Kin. 20:13/ 25:19/ Isa. 39:2/ Jer. 29:14/ Dan. 1:9/ Ezra 2:62/ Neh. 7: 64/ 13:1/ 1Chr. 4: 41/ 29:17/ 2Chr. 19:3/ 34:21 IMPF: Gen. 18:29, 30, 31, 32/ 44:9, 10, 12/ Ex. 9:19/ 12: 19/ 22: 1, 3, 6, 7/ Deut. 17:2/ 18:10/ 21:1, 17/ 22: 22/ 24:7/ Josh. 17: 16/ 1Sam. 13:19, 22/ 25:28/ 1Kin. 1:52/ 2Kin. 12:6/ Ez. 26:21/ Esth. 2:23/ 6: 2/ Ezra 10:18/ 1Chr. 24:4/ 26:31/ 28:9/ 2Chr. 2:16/ 15:2, 4, 15/ Dan. 11:19 INF: Ex. 22:3

B PF: Ps. 37:36/ 46:2/ Pro. 6:31/ Job 19:28/ 42:15 IMPF: Pro. 10:13/ 16:31/ Job 28:12, 13

C PT: Isa. 13:15/ 22:3 PF: Isa. 65:1/ Jer. 2:34/ 5:26/ 11:9/ 15:16/ 41:3, 8/ 48:27/ 50:24/ 52:25/ Ez. 28:15/ Hos. 14:9/ Mi. 1:13/ Mal. 2: 6 IMPF: Isa. 30:14/ 35:9/ 51:3/ 65:8/ Jer. 2:26/ 50:22/ Zeph. 3:13/Zech. 10:10 INF: Isa. 55:6

219 **NBA** A PT: 1Sam. 19:20/ 1Kin. 22:12/ Jer. 27:10, 14, 15 (2x), 16(2x)/ 29:9, 21/ 32:3/ Ez. 13:2, 16/ 38:17/ 1Chr. 25: 1/ 2Chr. 18:11 PF: 1Sam. 10: 11/ Jer. 20:1, 6/ 26:9, 11, 18/ 29:31/ 28:6/ 37:19/ Ez. 4:7/ 12:27/ 37: 7/ 1 Chr. 25:2, 3 IMPF: Jer. 26:20/ 29:8, 9 INF: Jer. 19: 14/ 26:12/ Ez. 11:13/ 37:7 IMPV: Ez. 6:2/ 11:4/ 13:2, 17/ 21:2, 7, 14, 19, 33/ 25: 2/ 28:21/ 29:2/ 30:2/ 34: 2/ 35:2/ 36:1, 3, 6/ 37:4, 9, 12/ 38: 2, 14/ 39:1

C PT: Jer. 14:14, 15, 16/ 23:16, 25, 26, 32 PF: Jer. 2: 8/ 5:31/ 23:21/ 25:13/ Jo. 3:1 IMPF: Jer. 11:21/ 25: 30/ Am. 2:12/ 3:8/ 7:12, 16/ Zech. 13:13 INF: Am. 7: 13/ Zech. 13:3, 4 IMPV: Am. 7:15

221 **NGP** A PT: Deut. 28:7, 25/ Judg. 20:39(2x) PF: Lev. 26:17/ Judg. 20:36/ 2Sam. 10:15, 19/ 1Chr. 19:16, 19 IMPF: Num. 14:42/ Deut. 1:42/ 1Sam. 4:2, 10/ 7:10/ 2Sam. 2: 17/ 18:7/ 2Kin. 14:2/ 2Chr. 6:24/ 20:22/ 25:22 INF: Judg. 20:39/ 1Kin. 8:33

225 **NDḤ** A PT: Deut. 22:1/ 30:4/ 2Sam. 14:13, 14/ Jer. 30:17/ Ez. 34:4, 16/ Neh. 1:9 PF: Deut. 4:19/ 19:5/ 30:17/ Jer. 40:12/ 43:5

B PT: Ps. 147:2 PF: Job 6:13

C PT: Isa. 11:12/ 16:3, 4/ 27:13/ 56:8/ Jer. 49:36/ Mi. 4:16/ Zeph. 3: 19 PF: Jer. 49:5

231 **NḤM** A PT: Jon. 4:2 PF: Gen. 6:7/ Judg. 21:15/ 1Sam. 15:11, 35/ 2Sam. 13: 6:6/ 24:67/ 38:12/ Ex. 13:17/ 32:14/ Judg. 2:18/ 21:6/ 1Sam. 15:29/ 2Sam. 24:16/ Jer. 26: 13, 19/ Ez. 24:14/ 31:16/ Jon. 3:10/ 1Chr. 21: 15 INF: 1Sam. 15:29/ Jer. 31:15 IMPV: Ex. 32:12

B PF: Job 42:6 IMPF: Ps. 106:45/ 110:4 INF:Ps. 77:3 IMPV: Ps. 90 :13

C PT: Jer. 8:6/ Jo. 2:13 PF: Jer. 4:28/ 18:8, 10/ 20: 16/ Jo. 2:14/ Am. 7:3, 6/ Zech. 8:14 IMPF: Isa. 1: 24/ 57:6 INF: Jer. 15:6

244 **NṢB** A PT: Gen. 18:2/ 24:13, 43/ 28:13/ 45:1/ Ex. 5:20/ 17: 9/ 18:14/ Num. 16: 27/ 22:23, 31, 34/ 23:6, 17/ Deut. 29:9/ Judg. 18:16, 17/ 1Sam. 1:26/ 4: 20/ 19: 20/ 22: 6, 7, 9, 17/ 2Sam. 13:31/ 1Kin. 4:5, 7/ 5:7, 30/ 9:23/ 22: 48/ Ruth 2:5, 6/ 2Chr. 8:10 PF: Gen. 37:7/ Ex. 7: 15/ 15:8/ 33:8, 21/ 34:2

B PT: Ps. 39:6/ 82:1/ 119:89/ Lam. 2:4 PF: Ps. 45:10/ Pro. 8:2

C PT: Isa. 3:13/ 21:8/ Am. 7:7/ 9:1/ Zech. 11:16

249 **NQH** A PF: Gen. 24:8/ Ex. 21:19/ Num. 5:28, 31/ Judg. 15:3/ 1Sam. 26:9 IMPF: Gen. 24:41 IMPV: Num. 5:19

B PF: Ps. 19:14 IMPF: Pro. 6:29/ 11:21/ 16:5/ 17:5/ 19: 5, 9/ 18:20

C PF: Isa. 3:26/ Jer. 2:35/ Zech. 5:3(2x) IMPF: Jer. 25: 29(2x)/ 49:12(2x) INF: Jer. 25:29

253 **NŚA** A PF: Ex. 25:28/ 2Sam. 19:43/ 2Kin. 20:17/ Isa. 39:6/ Dan. 11:20/ 1Chr. 14:2 IMPF: Ez. 1:19, 20, 21 INF: Ez. 1:19, 21

B IMPF: Pro. 30:13 IMPV: Ps. 7:7/ 24:7/ 94:2

C PT: Isa. 2:2, 12, 13, 14/ 6:1/ 30:25/ 57:7, 15/ Mi. 4: 1/ Zech. 5:7 PF: Isa. 52:13/ Jer. 51:9 IMPF: Isa. 33: 10/ 40:4/ 49:22/ 66:12/ Jer. 10:15

259 **NTN** A PT: Ex. 5:16/ 2Kin. 22:7 PF: Gen. 9:2/ 38:14/ Lev. 10: 14/ 19:20/ 26:25/ Num. 26:62/ Josh. 24:33/ 1Sam. 18: 19/ 25:27/ 2Kin. 25:30/ Jer. 32:24, 25, 36, 43/ 38:18/ 52:34/ Ez. 11:15/ 15:4/ 16:34/ 31:14/ 32:20, 23, 25, 29/ 33:24/ 35:12/ 47:1/ Eccl. 10:16/ 12:11/ Esth. 3: 15/ 4:8/ 6:8/ 8:14/ Dan. 11:11/ Ezra 9:7/ Neh. 10:30/ 13:1/ 1Chr. 5:1/ 2Chr. 28:5/ 34:16/ IMPF: Ex. 5:18/ Lev. 24:20/ 2Sam. 21:6/ 2Kin. 18:30/ 19:10/ Isa. 36: 15/ 37:10/ Jer. 32:4/ 34:3/ 37:19/ 38:3/ 39:17/ Esth. 2:13/ 5:3, 6/ 7:2, 3/ 9:12, 13, 14/ Dan. 8:12/ 11:6/ 1 Chr. 5:20/ 2Chr. 2:13/ 18:14 INF: Jer. 32:4/ 38:3/ Esth. 3:14/ 8:13

B PF: Job 9:24/ 15:19

C PT: Isa. 33:16 PF: Isa. 9:5/ 29:12/ 35:2/ Jer. 13:20/ 46:24/ 51:55 IMPF: Isa. 51:12/ Jer. 21:10

282 **STR** A PT: Deut. 7:20/ 29:28 PF: Num. 5:13/ 1Sam. 20:5, 19/ 1 Kin. 17:3 IMPF: Gen. 4:14/ 31:49/ 1Sam. 5:9/ 20:24 IMPV: Jer. 36:19

B PT: Ps. 19:7, 13 PF: Ps. 38:10/ Pro. 22:3/ 27:12/ Job

3:23/ 28:21 IMPF: Ps. 55:13/ 89:47/ Pro. 22:3/ 28:28/ Job 13:20 INF: Job 34:22

C PF: Isa. 28:15/ 40:27/ 65:16/ Jer. 16:17 IMPF: Jer. 23:24/ Hos. 13:14/ Am. 9:3/ Zeph. 2:3

295 **'LH** A PF: Num. 9:21/ 10:11/ 2Sam. 2:27/ Ez. 9:3 IMPF: Ex. 40:37/ Num. 16:27/ Jer. 37:5/ Ez. 36:3 INF: Ex. 40:36 /Num. 9:17,22/ Jer. 37:11/ Ezra 1:11 IMPV: Num. 16:24

B PF: Ps. 47:10/ 97:9.

310 **'ŚH** A PT: Ez. 9:4/ Neh. 5:18/ Eccl. 4:1/ Esth. 9:28 PF: Lev. 7:9/ 18:30/ Num. 15:24/ Deut. 13:15/ 17:4/ Judg. 16: 11/ 2Sam. 17:23/ 1Kin. 10:20/ 2Kin. 23:22, 23/ Ez. 15: 5/ Eccl. 1:9, 13, 14/ 2:17/ 4:13/ 8:9, 11, 14, 16, 17/ 9:3, 6/ Esth. 4:1/ 6:3/ Dan. 9:12/ 11:36/ Neh. 5:18/ 6:16/ 2Chr. 9:19/ 35:18, 19 IMPF: Gen. 20:9/ 29:26/ 34:7/ Ex. 2:4/ 12:16/ 21:31/ 25: 31/ 31:15/ 35:2/ Lev. 2:7, 8, 11/ 4:2, 13, 22, 27/ 5:17/ 6:14/ 7:24/ 11:32/ 13:51/ 23:3/ 24:19/ Num. 4:26/ 6:4/ 15:11, 34/ 28:15, 24/ Deut. 25:9/ Judg. 11:37/ 1Sam. 11:7/ 17:26, 27/ 2 Sam. 13:12/ 2Kin. 12:14/ Ez. 12:11, 25, 28/ 15:5/ 44: 14/ Eccl. 1:9/ Esth. 2:11/ 5:6/ 6:9, 11/ 7:2/ 9:12/ Ezra 10:3/ Neh. 6:9 INF: Ez. 43:18/ Esth. 9:1, 14

B PF: Ps. 33:6

C PF: Isa. 46:10/ Mal. 2:11 IMPF: Isa. 3:11/ Jer. 3: 16/ 5:13/ Ob. 15

319 **PLA** A PT: Ex. 3:20/ 34:10/ Deut. 30:11/ Josh. 3:5/ Judg. 6: 13/ Neh. 9:17/ Dan. 8:24/ 11:36 IMPF: Gen. 18:14/ Deut. 17:8/ 2Sam. 13:12/ Jer. 32:17, 27

B PT: Ps. 9:2/ 26:7/ 40:6/ 71:17/ 72:18/ 75:2/ 78:4, 11, 32/ 86:10/ 96:3/ 98:1/ 105:2, 5/ 106:7, 22/ 107:8, 15, 21, 24, 31/ 111:4/ 119:18, 27/ 131: 1/ 136:4/ 139:14/ 145:5/ Job 5:9/ 9:10/ 37:5, 14/ 42:3/ 1Chr. 16:9, 12, 24 PF: 2Sam. 1:26/ Ps. 118:23/ Pro. 30:18

C PT: Jer. 21:2/ Mi. 7:15 IMPF: Zech. 8:6

324 **PQD** A PF: Num. 31:49/ 1Sam. 20:18/ 25:7, 21 IMPF: Num. 16: 29/ 1Sam. 20:18, 25, 27/ 2Sam. 2:30/ 1Kin. 20:39/ 2 Kin. 10:19/ Ez. 38:8/ Neh. 7:1/ 12:44 INF: Judg. 21: 3/ 1Kin. 20:39

B IMPF: Pro. 19:23

C IMPF: Isa. 24:22/ 29:6/ Jer. 23:4

343 **QBṢ** A PT: Jer. 40:15 PF: Josh. 10:6/ Ezra 10:1 IMPF: 1Sam. 7:6/ 25:1/ 28:4/ Ez. 29:5/ Ezra 10:9/ Neh. 4:14/ 1Chr. 11:1/ 13:2/ 2Chr. 13:7/ 15:10/ 20:4/ 32:4 INF: Esth. 2:8, 19/ Ezra 10:7 IMPV: Ez. 39:17

B INF: Ps. 102:23 IMPV: Gen. 49:2

C PT: Isa. 56:8 PF: Isa. 34:15/ 43:9/ 49:18/ 60:4/ Hos. 2:2/ Jo. 4:11 IMPF: Isa. 60:7 IMPV: Isa. 45:20/ 48:14

344 **QBR** A IMPF: Gen. 15:15/ 35:8, 19/ Num. 20:1/ Deut. 10:6/ Judg. 8:32/ 10:2, 5/ 12:7, 10, 12, 15/ 2Sam. 17:23/ 1 Kin. 2:10, 34/ 14:31/ 11:43/ 15:24/ 16:6, 28/ 22: 51/ 2Kin. 8:24/ 13:13/ 14:16, 20/ 15:38/ 16:20/ 21: 18/ 2 Chr. 12:16/ 21:1/ 35:24/ Ruth 1:17/ Jer. 20:16

B IMPF: Job 27:15

C IMPF: Jer. 8:2/ 16:4, 6/ 22:19/ 25:33

346 **QHL** A PT: Ez. 38:7 PF: Esth. 9:2, 16, 18/ 2Chr. 20:26 IMPF: Ex. 32:1/ Lev. 8:4/ Num. 16:3/ 20:2/ Josh. 18:1/ 22:2/ Judg. 20:1/ 2Sam. 20:14/ 1Kin. 8:2/ Jer. 26:9/ Esth.9: 15/ 2Chr. 5:3 INF: Num. 17:7/ Esth. 8:11

355 **QRA** A PT: Jer. 44:26/ Esth. 6:1 PF: Deut. 25:10/ 28:10/ 2 Sam. 6:2/ 12: 28/ 1Kin. 8:43/ Jer. 32:34/ 34:15/ Esth. 2:14/ 4:11/ Eccl. 6:10/ Dan. 9:18, 19/ 10:1/ Neh. 13: 1/ 1Chr. 13:6/ 2Chr. 6:33/ 7:14 IMPF: Gen. 2: 23/ 17: 5/ 21:12/ 35:10/ 48:6, 16/ Deut. 3:13/ 1Sam. 9: 9/ 2 Sam. 18:18/ Jer. 19:6/ Ez. 20:29/ Ruth 4:14/ Esth. 3: 12/ 4:11/ 8:9/ Ezra 2:61/ Neh. 7:63/ 1Chr. 23:14

B IMPF: Pro. 16:21

C PT: Isa. 43:7/ 48:1 PF: Isa. 48:2/ 63:19/ Jer. 4:20/ 7:10, 11, 14, 30/ 14:19/ 15:16/ 25:29/ Am. 9:12/ Zech. 8:3 IMPF: Isa. 1:26/ 4:1/ 14:20/ 31:4/ 32:5/ 35:8/ 54: 5/ 56:7/ 61:6/ 62:4, 12

363 **RAH** A PT: Gen. 12:7/ 35:1/ 1Kin. 6:8 PF: Gen. 8:5/ 9:14/ 48: 3/ Ex. 3:16/ 4:1, 5/ 16:10/ Lev. 9:4/ 13:7, 19/ 14:35/ Num. 14:10, 14/ Judg. 13:10/ 19:30/ 1Sam. 1:22/ 1Kin. 3:5/ 9:2/ 10:12/ 11:9/ 2Kin. 23:24/ Jer. 31:3/ Ez. 10: 1/ Dan. 1:15/ 8:1(2x)/ 2Chr. 1:7/ 3:1/ 9:11 IMPF: Gen. 1:9/ 12:7/ 17:1/ 18:1/ 22:14/ 26:2, 24/ 35:9/ 46:29/ Ex. 3:2/ 6:3/ 13:7/ 23:15, 17/ 33:23/ 34:3, 20, 23/ Lev. 9:6, 23/ 13:57/ 16:2/ Num. 16:9/ 17:7/ 20:6/ Deut. 16:4, 16/ 31:15/ Judg. 5:8/ 6:12/ 13:3/ 2Sam. 22: 11, 16/ 1Kin. 8:8(2x)/ 9:2/ 18:15/ Ez. 10:8/ Dan. 1:13/ 2Chr. 5:9 (2x)/ 7:12 INF: Ex. 34:24/ Lev. 13:7, 14/ Deut. 31:11/ Judg. 13:21/ 1Sam. 3:21/ 2Sam. 17:17/ 1Kin. 18:2/ Ez. 21:29 IMPV: 1Kin. 18:1

B PF: Ps. 102:17/ Pro. 27:25/ Song 2:12 IMPF: Ps. 18:16/ 42:3/ 84:8/ 90:16

C PF: Isa. 16:12/ Jer. 13:26 IMPF: Isa. 47:3/ 60:2/ Ez. 19:11/ Zech. 9:14 INF: Isa. 1:12/ Mal. 3:2

392 **ŠAR** A PT: Gen. 14:10/ 32:9/ Ex. 10:5/ Lev. 5:9/ 26:36, 39/ Deut. 7:20/ 19: 20/ Josh. 13:2/ 23:4, 7, 12/ 1Sam. 9: 24/ 11:11/ 2Kin. 7:13/ 10:11, 17/ 19:30/ 25:11, 22/ Isa. 37:21/ Jer. 38:4/ 39:9/ 40:6/ 41:10/ 52:15/ Ez. 6:12/ 17:21/ Ezra 1:4/ Neh. 1:3/ 1Chr. 13:2/ 2Chr. 30: 6/ 34:21 PF: Gen. 42:38/ 47:18/ Ex. 8:27/ 10:19/14:28/ Lev. 25:52/ Deut. 3:11/4:27/ 28:62/ Josh. 8:7/ 11:22/ 13:1, 12/ Judg. 4:16/ 7:3/ 1Sam. 5:4/ 11:11/ 2Sam. 14: 7/ 1Kin. 22:47/ 2Kin. 7:13/ 10:21/ 17:18/ 24:14/ Jer. 34:7/ 37:10/ 38:22/ 42:2/ Ez. 9:8/ Dan. 10:8(2x), 17/ Ezra 9:15/ Neh. 1:2, 3/ 2Chr. 21:7 IMPF: Gen. 7: 23/ Ex. 8:5, 7/ 10:26/ Num. 11:26/ Ez. 36:36/ Ruth 1:3, 5

B PF: Job 21:34

C PT: Isa. 4:3/ Jer. 8:3/ 21:7/ 24:8/ Hag. 2:3/ Zech. 11:9/ 12:14 PF: Isa. 17:6/ 24:6, 12/ 49:21/ Zech. 9:7 IMPF: Isa. 11:11, 16

394 **ŠB'** A PT: Eccl. 9:2 PF: Gen. 21:31/ 22:16/ 24:7/ 26:31/ 50: 24/ Ex. 13:5, 11/ 32:13/ 33:1/ Lev. 5:22/ Num. 11:12/ 14:23/ 32:11/ Deut. 1:8, 35/ 2:14/ 4:31/ 6: 10, 18, 23/ 7:8, 12, 13/ 8:1, 11, 18/ 9:5, 21/ 10:1, 11/ 13:8/

19:8/ 26:3, 15/ 28:9, 11/ 29:12/ 30:20/ 31:7, 20, 21, 22, 23/ 34:4/ Josh. 1:6/ 5:6/ 6:22/ 9: 18, 19, 20/ 21: 41, 42/ Judg. 2:1/ 21:1, 7, 18/ 1Sam. 3: 14/ 20:42/ 2Sam. 3:9/ 19:8/ 21:2, 17/ 1Kin. 1:13, 17, 30/ Jer. 32:22/ 44:26/ 2Chr. 15:15 IMPF: Gen. 21:24/ 24:9/ 25: 33/ 26:31/ 31:53/ 47: 31/ Lev. 5:4, 24/ 19:12/ Num. 32:10/ Deut. 1:34/ 4:21/ 6:13/ 10: 20/ Josh. 14:9/ 9: 15/ 1Sam. 19:6/ 20:3/ 24: 23/ 28: 10/ 2Sam. 3:35/ 19: 24/ 1Kin. 1:29, 51/ 2:8, 23/ 2Kin. 25:24/ Jer. 38:16/ 40:9/ Ez. 16:8/ Ezra 10:5/ Dan. 12:7/ 2Chr. 15:14 INF: Num. 30:3 IMPV: Gen. 21: 23/ 25:33/ 47:31/ Josh. 2:12/ Judg. 15:12/ 1Sam. 24:22/ 30:15

B PT: Ps. 63:12 PF: Ps. 15:4/ 24:4/ 89:4, 20, 36/ 95: 11/ 102:9/ 110:4/ 119:106/ 132:2, 11

C PT: Isa. 19:18/ 48:1/ 65:16/ Am. 8:14/ Zeph. 1:5 (2x)/ Zech. 5:3, 4/ Mal. 3:5 PF: Isa. 14:24/ 45:23/ 54:23/ 62:8/ Jer. 4:2/ 11:5/ 22:5/ 49:13/ 51:14/ Am. 4:2/ 6: 8/ 8:7/ Mi. 7:20 IMPF: Isa. 45:23/ 65:16/ Jer. 5:2, 7/ Hos. 4:1, 5 INF: Jer. 7:9/ 12:16

395 **ŠBR** A PT: Ez. 27:34/ 30:22/ 34:4, 16/ Dan. 8:22 PF: Ex. 22: 9, 13/ 1Kin. 22:49(2x)/ Ez. 6:4, 6, 9/ 26:2/ 30: 8/ Dan. 8:8/ 2Chr. 14:12 IMPF: Lev. 6:21/ 15:12/ 1Sam. 4: 18/ Ez. 29:7/ 31:12/ 32:28/ Eccl. 12:6/ Dan. 8:25/ 11: 4, 20, 22/ 2Chr. 20:37 INF: Jon. 1:4

B PT: Ps. 34:19/ 51:19(2x) PF: Ps. 34:21/ 124:7 IMPF: Ps. 37:15, 17/ Pro. 6:15/ 29:1/ Job 24:20/ 31:22/ 38:15

C PT: Isa. 61:1/ Jer. 2:13/ Zech. 11:16 PF: Isa. 8:15/ 14:29/ 24: 10/ 28:13/ Jer. 14:17/ 23:9/ 22:20/ 48:4, 17, 25/ 51:30 IMPF: Isa. 27:11/ Jer. 50:23/ 51:8

409 **ŠMM** A PT: Ez. 29:12/ 30:7/ 36:34, 35(2x), 36/ Jer. 33:10 PF: Lev. 26:22/ Ez. 4:17/ 6:4/ 25:3/ 30:7

B PT: Ps. 69:22 PF: Job 18:20/ Lam. 4:5

C PT: Isa. 54:3/ Ez. 32:15/ Am. 9:4 PF: Isa. 33:8/ Jer. 4:19/ 12:11/ Jo. 1:17/ Am. 7:9/ Zeph. 3:6/ Zech. 7:14

410 **ŠM'** A PT: Jer. 31:15/ Eccl. 9:16, 17 PF: Gen. 45:16/ Ex. 28: 35/ Deut. 4: 32/ 1 Kin. 6:7/ Jer. 38:27/ Ez. 10:5/ Eccl. 12:13/ Ezra 3:13/ Neh. 6:1, 6/ 13:27/ Dan. 10: 12/ Esth. 1:20 IMPF: Ex. 23:13/ 1Sam. 1:13/ 17: 31/ 2 Sam. 22:45/ Jer. 33:10/ Ez. 19:9/ 26:13/ Neh. 6:7/ 12: 43/ 2Chr. 30:27 INF: Esth. 2:8

B PT: Ps. 19:4 PF: Job 26:14/ Song 2:12 IMPF: Ps. 18: 45/ Job 37:4

C PT: Jer. 3:21/ 51:46 PF: Isa. 15:4/ Jer. 8:16/ 9:18/ 38:27/ 49:21 IMPF: Isa. 60:18/ 65:19/ Jer. 6:7/ 18: 22/ Nah. 2:14

414 **Š'N** A PT: 2Sam. 1:6/ 2Kin. 5:18/ 7:2, 17 PF: Num. 21:15/ 2 Chr. 13:18/ 14:10/ 16:7 IMPF: Judg. 16:26 INF: Ez. 29: 7/ 2Chr. 16:7, 8 IMPV: Gen. 18:4

B IMPF: Job 8:15/ 24:24/ Pro. 3:5

C PF: Isa. 10:20 IMPF: Isa. 30:12/ 31:1/ 50:10/ Mi. 3: 11 INF: Isa. 10:20

3.4 Notes to the roots

These notes represent remarks on the choice and justification of the translation of ni.-forms and on the semantic relationship of these to one of the active verbal stems. In a number of instances my classification differs from that of LAMBERT 1900, 196-204 (referred to below as 'LAMBERT'). These cases will be discussed if necessary. The instances where Lambert is mistaken due to lack of care are not included (e.g. on p. 209 he treats the ni. of **P'M** as a pi. passive which does not occur in the OT). Due to the extent of our work we decided not to give a detailed account of each included form. A discussion of the applied general principles may be found in Appendix B. The roots discussed below are marked in the tables by means of an asterisk after the root number.

4 **AWH**: According to LAMBERT, 209 a pass. of the pi. ('wish'). This cannot be established beyond doubt.

5 **AWR**: DHORME 1967, 506 regards the ni. in Job 33:30 as a pass. of the hi. because the qal expresses intransitive meaning and therefore does not allow receiving a passive. He refers to GESENIUS-KAUTZSCH 1909, &51 h. LAMBERT does not mention this root; see also 2.2.4; the translation is uncertain. Dhorme's argument does not apply since ni.-forms may be related to intransitive qal-stems, compare JENNI 1969, 63ff.

6 **AWT**: GESENIUS-KAUTZSCH 1909, &72h and BERGSTRäSSER 1918, &28b want to read the ni.-forms of this root as qal since 'reliable forms of the qal are lacking'. The argument is not extremely convincing. For, apart from the above-mentioned forms, absolutely no other forms of the root occur in the OT. So, on the basis of Masoretic vocalization I opt for the ni. For the qal one would expect **JāAūT**.

16 **ANQ**: So also LAMBERT, 210. There may, at the most, be a difference in nuance between qal and ni. The ni. expresses crying for mourning, the qal expresses crying for bodily pain (Ezek. 26:15; Jer. 51:52).

24 **AŠM**: Many commentators (RUDOLPH 1971, 41; WOLFF 1969, 22; KELLERMAN, 469) suggest a textual change in Jo. 1:18: **NāŠaMMu** (of the root **ŠMM** 'destroy'); LAMBERT, 210 agrees (sic. read 'Joel' instead of 'Job'). Arguments used in support of the suggested change are unconvincing. It is argued that the root **AŠM** never occurs in relation to animals. This may also be said of the root **ŠMM.** See for this KAPELRUD 1948, 66ff. and KNIERIM 1971, 256 who translates it as: *Schuldpflicht, Schuldverhaftung erleiden*

33 **BJN**: The relation between ni. (primarily participle) and qal, respectively hi. is not clear to me. According to LAMBERT, 211 the ni. is synonymous to the hi. (Isa. 10:13).

36 **B'H**: This may be a case of two homonymous roots.

41 **BQ'**: LAMBERT takes some ni.-forms to be reflexives of the qal (Ex. 14:21, etc.), others as reflexives of the pi. (Isa.

59:5, etc.; cf. pi. in 5a), or as pass. of the hi. (2 Kin. 25:4; Jer. 52:7 and Ez. 30:16). The last three forms may just as well be regarded as passives of the qal (1 Chron. 21:17; 32:1).

45 **BRR:** According to LAMBERT, 198 it is a reflexive of the pi.; it occurs, however, only once (Dan. 11:35, inf.; see also JENNI 1968, 210). The ni.-forms may possibly be related to the qal as well.

47 **GAL** II: See 2.2.5. It is remarkable that forms of this root occur in late texts (pi. Mal. 1:7; pu. Mal. 1:7, 12; Ezra 2:62; Neh. 7:64; hi.: Isa. 63:6 and hitp.: Dan. 1:8(2x). The similar form **G'L**, with the same meaning in David's lament, 2 Sam. 1:21, is fairly early. Perhaps **GAL** is a later variant of **G'L**.

52 **GLH:** According to LAMBERT it is a reflexive of the pi. (Gen. 35:7, etc.) or it may be synonymous to the qal (Isa. 38: 12). The latter form might also be regarded as a pass. of the qal. (Cf. 12a: ni. of **NSA**). To my mind, it is impossible to ascertain whether the ni. occurs in relation to the qal or in relation to the pi.

56 **G'L:** See under 47 (contra LAMBERT, 207, pass. of the qal.).

61 **DGL:** See for another translation GORDIS 1969.

70 **DMH:** LAMBERT, 212 classifies this root and the root **DMM** (71) among those of which ni. and qal are complementary forms of a pattern (**DMH**: qal-imperf. vs. ni.-perf.; **DMM**: qal-imperf. vs. ni.-perf). They may also be regarded as passives of the qal.

71 **DMM:** See at 70.

72 **D'K:** According to LAMBERT, 210 synonymous to the qal.

77 **HJH:** According to LAMBERT, 210 it is synonymous to the qal, yet JENNI 1969, 64 translates: '*sich begeben, sich zutragen, sich ereignen*' with reference to Ex. 11:6; Deut. 4:32; Dan. 12:1. See p. 22ff.

86 **ZKR:** LAMBERT, 199 defines the ni. in Num. 10:9 and Ez. 21:9 as reflexive of the hi. These forms, however, may just as well be regarded as passives with respect to the qal.

89 **Z'K:** Possibly a variant of the root **D'K**, see DHORME 1967, 242.

97 **ḪLH:** According to LAMBERT, 210 it is synonymous to the qal, yet JENNI 1969, 66 distinguishes between qal ('*krank, schwach sein*') and ni. ('*von Krankheit befallen werden, sich als krank erweisen*'). This does not apply for Jer. 12:13.

107 **ḪPH:** LAMBERT, 207 classifies Ps. 68:14 as a qal pass.; pi. pass. would be more appropriate ('overlay with gold').

118 **ḪRR:** According to LAMBERT, 211 **HRR** is synonymous to the qal. It would be more appropriate to regard it as a pass. qal.

128 **ṬMA:** According to LAMBERT, 213 the ni.-participle and perfect and the hitp. imperfect are the complementary forms of a pattern, see also 4.5.2.

129 **ṬMH:** See 2.2.3; GORDIS 1978, 190 describes the ni. in Job 18:13 as belonging to the root **ṬMM** ('considered stupid').

133 **JAŠ:** According to LAMBERT, 198 it is a refl. of the pi. (once in Eccl. 2:20). Since no forms of other verbal stems of

the root occur in the OT, apart from the ni.-forms and a single pi.-form, it is difficult to draw any conclusion about nature of the relationship between ni. and pi.

135 **JD'**: According to LAMBERT, 199, 209 the following ni.-forms may occur in relationship to the hi. Ex. 6:3; Isa. 19:21; 56:16; Jer. 31:19; Ez. 20:5; 21:9; 25:11; 36:32; 38:23; Ps. 9:17; 48:4; 74:5 (?); 76:2; 84:10; Ruth 3:3; Pro. 10:9. These forms might also be regarded as pass. qals.

136 **JḤL**: The semantic relationship of the ni.-forms is unclear: there is no difference between ni., pi., and hi.

142 **J'D**: According to LAMBERT 197 it is a recipr. of the qal; this is debatable according to my view.

146 **JṢT/ṢWT**: According to LAMBERT, 212 the ni.-perf. and qal-imperf. are complementary forms of a pattern.

147 **JQŠ/QWŠ**: The ho.-forms of the root may be read as pu. forms, see e.g. GESENIUS 1915.

177 **LAH**: According to LAMBERT, 212 the qal-imperf. and ni.-perf. are complementary forms of a pattern.

181 **LWZ**: According to LAMBERT, 211 the root is synonymous to the qal. It cannot be maintained with absolute certainty.

201 **MLA**: The cases which LAMBERT, 198 quotes as refl. of the pi. may just as well be regarded as pass. of the qal.

209 **MSS**: According to LAMBERT, 199 the root is a refl. of the hi. Yet the available textual data for this root is too scarce to draw any conclusion.

211 **MṢA**: LAMBERT, 199 describes Isa. 55:6; 65:1; Jer. 19:14 and 1Chron. 28:9 as refl. of the hi.

224 **NGŠ**: According to LAMBERT the qal (imperf., impv. and inf.) and ni. (perf.) are complementary forms of a pattern.

244 **NṢB**: LAMBERT, 213 states that the perf. and participle of the ni. and the imperf. of the hitp. of **JṢB** (which he apparently regards as belonging to the same root) are complementary forms of a pattern. If his assumption is correct, this would be extremely peculiar since the ni. may be related to the hi.

245 **NṢH**: According to LAMBERT, 211 ni. and hi. are synonymous to each other.

258 **NTK**: According to LAMBERT, 212 qal-imperf. and ni.-perf. function as complementary forms of a pattern.

265 **SGR**: According to LAMBERT, 199 Num. 12: 14,15; 1 Sam. 23:7 and Ez. 3:24 are refl. of the hi., but these forms may just as well be regarded as refl./pass. of the qal.

268 **SKL**: According to LAMBERT, 211 the ni. and hi. are synonymous to each other.

274 **S'R**: LAMBERT's view that the ni. and the qal are synonymous here is incorrect.

288 **'WH**: According to LAMBERT, 198 refl. of the pi. The alleged relationship between ni. vs. pi. or hi. is unclear to me.

290 **'WR**: LAMBERT, 212 describes the ni.-perf. and -impf. and qal-impv. and participle as complementary forms of a pattern.

294 **'KR**: Some take Prov. 15:6 as a subst. or want to change the text; according to LAMBERT this form and a form from Ps. 39:3 are synonymous to the qal.

295 **'LH:** According to LAMBERT, 212 this root is identical to the qal. This is incorrect.

312 **'TR:** It is possible that we are dealing here with two homonymous roots.

315 **PWG:** According to LAMBERT, 212 the ni.-perf. and qal-imperf. are two complementary forms of a pattern.

316 **PWṢ:** According to LAMBERT, 213 the ni.-perf. and -participle, and qal-imperf. and -impv. are two complementary forms of a pattern. The ni. may also be regarded as qal pass.

326 **PRD:** The pi. in Hos. 4:14 is uncertain, see JENNI 1968, 180.

333 **PTḤ:** According to LAMBERT, 198 the ni.-form in Isa. 51:14 is a refl. of the pi. If Jenni's view on the function of this root is correct (JENNI 1968, 202: "the loosing of something that is bound"), the ni.-forms in Job 12:14; 32:19 and Isa. 51:14 should be seen as pass. off the pi.

339 **Ṣ'Q:** According to LAMBERT, 199 it is a refl. of the hi. Because there is only one hi.-form in the OT (1 Sam. 10:17) it is hard to determine the exact relationship.

348 **QṬṬ/: QWṬ** According to LAMBERT, 211 the ni.-perf. and qal-imperf. are two complementary forms of a pattern.

352 **QLL:** According to LAMBERT, 199 the ni. in 2 Sam. 6:22 is a refl. of the hi.; the form may just as likely be regarded as a pass./refl. of the qal.

356 **QRA** II: According to LAMBERT, 199 it is a refl. of the hi.; the hi. occurs yet only once (Jer. 32:32); these forms may also be seen as pass. of the qal.

363 **RAH:** According to LAMBERT, 199 certain ni.-forms may also occur as refl. of the hi. He notices that it is often difficult to distinguish between *se montrer* (hi.) and *être vu* (ni.). The forms may just as well be treated as pass. of the qal.

370 **RMM:** According to LAMBERT, 211 the qal and ni. are synonymous to each other.

381 **ŚGB:** According to LAMBERT, 211 the qal and ni. are synonymous to each other. This is incorrect in my view.

390 **ŚAH:** According to LAMBERT, 213 the qal-perf. and ni.-imperf. are two complementary forms of a pattern

396 **ŠBT:** According to LAMBERT, 211 the qal and ni. are synonymous to each other.

422 **TKN:** LAMBERT, 198 prefers to treat these forms as refl. of the pi. since only participles of the qal occur. In my view the ni. should preferably be related to the qal., on the basis of its semantic values.

IV The relationship between the niph'al and other passive-reflexive verbal stems

4.1 Introduction and statistic research

4.1.1 The niph'al in the OT

4.1.1.1 The distribution of ni-forms over the various books. According to my calculations there are 4143 niph'al forms in total in the OT.[225] First of all, I will present a general overview of the number of ni.-forms per Bible book, distributed over the various tenses, irrespective of genre. The percentages of the various tenses per book are given between parentheses. Whenever a book contains less than 40 ni.-forms, these percentages are not mentioned, for such calculations are of limited value when they are applied to a very small number of ni.-forms.

	Total	Participle	Perfect	Imperfect	Infinitive	Imperative
Gen	211(100%)	26(12.3%)	50(23.7%)	104(49.3%)	17(8.1%)	14(6.6%)
Ex	177(100%)	26(14.7%)	58(32.8%)	79(44.6%)	8(4.5%)	6(3.4%)
Lev	184(100%)	23(12.5%)	59(32.1%)	93(50.5%)	9(4.9%)	-
Num	150(100%)	13(8.7%)	56(37.3%)	66(44 %)	10(6.7%)	5(3.3%)
Deut	159(100%)	28(17.6%)	59(37.1%)	47(29.6%)	14(8.8%)	11(6.9%)
Pent	881(100%)	116(13.2%)	282(32 %)	389(44.2%)	58(6.6%)	36(4.1%)
Josh	98(100%)	19(19.4%)	37(37.8%)	37(37.8%)	3(3.1%)	2(2 %)
Judg	122(100%)	16(13.1%)	36(29.5%)	52(42.6%)	15(12.3%)	3(2.5%)
1 Sam	193(100%)	43(22.3%)	65(33.7%)	67(34.7%)	14(7.3%)	4(2.1%)
2 Sam	122(100%)	18(14.7%)	45(36.9%)	51(41.8%)	8(6.6%)	-
1 Kin	116(100%)	27(16.3%)	33(28.4%)	46(39.7%)	9(7.8%)	1(0.9%)
2 Kin	92(100%)	25(27.2%)	23(25 %)	34(37 %)	7(7.6%)	3(3.3%)
Josh-Kin	743(100%)	148(19.9%)	239(32.2%)	287(38.6%)	56(7.5%)	13(1.8%)
Isa	394(100%)	98(24.9%)	135(34.3%)	141(35.8%)	12(3 %)	8(2 %)
Jer	404(100%)	68(16.8%)	174(43.1%)	131(32.4%)	20(5 %)	11(2.7%)
Ez	325(100%)	46(14.2%)	118(36.3%)	106(32.6%)	23(7.1%)	32(9.8%)
Hos	35	5	14	14	2	-
Jo	19	3	13	3	-	-
Am	37	4	15	14	1	3
Ob	6	-	4	2	-	-
Jon	8	3	2	2	1	-

	Total	Participle	Perfect	Imperfect	Infinitive	Imperative
Mi	19	6	6	7	-	-
Na	18	4	9	5	-	-
Hab	6	2	-	2	1	1
Zeph	21	9	5	7	-	-
Hag	4	1	-	2	1	-
Zech	56(100%)	13(23.2%)	16(28.6%)	21(37.5%)	6(10.7%)	-
Mal	18	7	8	2	1	-
Total	1370(100%)	269(19.6%)	519(37.9%)	459(33.5%)	68(5 %)	55(4 %)
(Hos-Mal)	247(100%)	57(23.1%)	92(37.2%)	81(32.8%)	13(5.3%)	4(1.6%)
Ps	313(100%)	98(31.3%)	111(35.5%)	89(28.4%)	10(3.2%)	5(1.6%)
Job	132(100%)	22(16.7%)	46(34.8%)	61(46.2%)	2(1.5%)	1(0.8%)
Pro	154(100%)	48(31.2%)	35(22.7%)	68(44.2%)	1(0.6%)	2(1.3%)
Total	599(100%)	168(28 %)	192(32.1%)	218(36.4%)	13(2.2%)	8(1.3%)
Ruth	12	2	-	10	-	-
Song	9	4	5	-	-	-
Eccl	49(100%)	7(14.3%)	23(46.9%)	14(28.6%)	4(8.2%)	1(2 %)
Lam	22	5	15	2	-	-
Esth	74(100%)	7(9.5%)	23(31.1%)	31(41.9%)	13(17.6%)	-
Dan	70(100%)	10(14.3%)	37(52.9%)	20(28.6%)	3(4.3%)	-
Ezra	28	4	10	11	2	1
Neh	62(100%)	14(22.6%)	24(38.7%)	21(33.8%)	2(3.2%)	1(1.6%)
1Chron	78(100%)	22(28.2%)	33(42.3%)	22(28.2%)	1(1.3%)	-
2Chron	146(100%)	25(17.1%)	42(28.8%)	60(41.1%)	16(11 %)	3(2 %)
Total	550(100%)	100(18.2%)	212(38.5%)	191(34.7%)	41(7.5%)	6(1.1%)
OT	4143(100%)	801(19.3%)	1444(34.9%)	1544(37.3%)	236(5.7%)	118(2.8%)

In each book of the OT ni.-forms are found. The forms are distributed evenly over the various books, so that both in the relatively early books (e.g. Gen., Ex., Josh), as well as in the relatively late books (e.g. Dan., Ezra, Neh.), ni.-forms may be found. It is remarkable that certain books contain a great amount of ni.-forms (e.g. In the book of Esther we found 74 forms distributed over ten chapters and in the book of Zephaniah 21 distributed over three chapters. Compare this to e.g. 211 forms occurring in 50 chapters of the book of Genesis and 150 forms in 36 chapters of the book of Numbers).

When percentages for the various verbal forms of the whole OT are compared to those of the individual books, the following comes to light: the book of Numbers as well as the book of Esther have a relatively low percentage in participle forms (8.7 and 9.5 % respectively, vs. the OT 19.3 %). Contrary to that, the percentage of participle forms in Psalms and Proverbs is relatively high (31.3 and 31.2 % vs. the OT 19.3 %). The percentages per book may differ considerably for other tenses as well. Cf. for the perfect: Gen. 23.7 % and Dan. 52.9 % (OT 34.9 %) and for the imperfect: Ps. 28.4 % and Lev. 50.5 % (OT 37.3 %). Concerning the infinitive the book of Esther is remarkable with a score of 17.6 % (OT 5.7 %). The book of Ezekiel numbers relatively many imperative forms: 9.8 vs.

OT 2.8 %. The 32 imperative forms make up for about one quarter of the total number of ni.-imperatives in the OT.

The figures here and in the rest of this paragraph do not lead to any definitive conclusions. Various causes may account for the fact that a certain book contains relatively many forms of a certain tense. Apart from linguistic reasons, other factors such as content, genre, and the presence of direct or indirect speech may play a role in this. Moreover, it is not always possible for us to determine to what extent Masoretic vocalization has affected the outcome. The above-mentioned figures and percentages have limited value. The figures gain in significance only when the ni. is studied in relation to one of the other verbal stems.

4.1.1.2 The distribution of ni.-forms over the various genres

4.1.1.2.1 Prose. The totals of ni. occurring in OT prose are the following:

Total	Part.	Perf.	Imperf.	Inf.	Impv.
2584	431	861	1018	118	86
100%	16.7%	33.3	39.4%	7.3%	3.3%

4.1.1.2.2 Poetry.

a) Poetry fragments in the Pentateuch show the following scores of ni.-forms:

	Total	Part.	Perf.	Imperf.	Inf.	Impv.
Gen. 49	2	-	-	-	-	2
Ex. 15	6	3	3	-	-	-
Num. 23,24	2	-	-	2	-	-
Deut. 33	2	-	1	1	-	-
Total	12	3	4	3	-	2

These 12 forms comprise a negligible quantity compared to that of the whole Pentateuch (881 occurrences).

b) The poetry fragments of Joshua through to Kings:

	Total	Part.	Perf.	Imperf.	Inf.	Impv.
Judg. 5	4	-	4	-	-	-
1 Sam. 2	5	1	2	2	-	-
2 Sam. 1	6	1	5	-	-	-
2 Sam. 22	3	1	-	2	-	-
2 Sam. 23	2	-	-	2	-	-
Judg-Sam	20	3	11	6	-	-

These 20 forms comprise a negligible amount on the total of forms from Josh. through to Kin. (743 occurrences)

c) The poetic books.

	Total	Part.	Perf.	Imperf.	Inf.	Impv.
Ps	313	98	111	89	10	5
Prov	154	48	35	68	1	2
Job	124	20	45	56	2	1
Song	9	4	5	-	-	-
Lam	22	5	15	2	-	-
Total	622	175	211	215	13	8

(It should be noticed that in the prose fragments of Job chs. 1, 2 and 42:7-17 there are 8 ni.: 2 part.; 1 perf. and 5 imperf.).

d) Other poetic fragments:

	Total	Part.	Perf.	Imperf.	Inf.	Impv.
1Chron.16	5	4	-	1	-	-

The total number of ni.-forms in the poetic texts of the O.T. may be divided as follows:

	Total	Part.	Perf.	Imperf.	Inf.	Impv.
OT	659(100%)	185(28.1%)	226(34.3%)	225(34.1%)	13(2%)	10(1.5%)

4.1.1.2.3 Prophecy

	Total	Part.	Perf.	Imperf.	Inf.	Impv.
Isa	381(100%)	94(24.7%)	131(34.4%)	137(36 %)	11(2.9%)	8(2.7%)
Jer	268(100%)	36(13.4%)	130(48.5%)	82(30.6%)	10(3.7%)	10(3.7%)
Ez	11	1	5	3	2	-

For the prose parts of these books the following findings apply:

	Total	Part.	Perf.	Imperf.	Inf.	Impv.
Isa	13	4	4	4	1	-
Jer	136(100%)	31(22.8%)	45(33.1%)	49(36 %)	10(7.4%)	1(0.7%)
Ez	314(100%)	45(14.3%)	113(36 %)	103(32.8%)	21(6.7%)	32(10.2%)

The next tabulation represents our findings for the prophecy sections in the minor prophets minus prose in Jonah:

	Total	Part.	Perf.	Imperf.	Inf.	Impv.
	239	54	90	79	12	4
Jonah	2	1	-	1	-	-
Total	240	54	91	79	12	4

The total number of niph'als occurring in prophetic texts may be represented as follows:

Total	Part.	Perf.	Imperf.	Inf.	Impv.
900(100%)	185(20.6%)	357(39.7%)	301(33.4%)	35(3.9%)	22(2.4%)

Finally, these percentages reflect the occurrence of niph'als for the various genres:

	Total	Part.	Perf.	Imperf.	Inf.	Impv.
OT	100%	19.3%	34.9%	37.3%	5.7%	2.8%
Prose	100%	16.7%	33.3%	39.4%	7.3%	3.3%
Poetry	100%	28.1%	34.3%	34.1%	2 %	1.5%
Prophecy	100%	20.6%	39.7%	33.3%	3.9%	2.4%

As noted above, the figures presented here have a limited value.

4.1.1.3 Statistics of the classification of verb forms.

In chapter 3 a total of 428 roots, of which ni.-forms occur in the OT, are summed up in the tables. Terminology used below in relation to this is explained in ch. 3. The roots concerned may be divided into three groups:

I. Roots which occur in an oppositional/semantic relationship

- to the qal: 265 roots (61.9 %). 21 of these roots (4.9 %) may also occur in relation to other active verbal stems (Iq/II: 8x; Iq/p: 7x; and Iq/h: 6x).

- to the pi'el: 40 roots (9.3%). 10 of these roots (2.3 %) allow for ni.-forms which may occur in a relationship to other active verbal stems (Iq/p: 7x en Ip/h: 3x).

- to the hiph'il: 48 roots (11.2%). 10 of these roots allow for ni.-forms which may occur in a relationship to other active verbal stems (Iq/h: 6x; Ip/h: 3x en Ih/II: 1x).

II. Roots which normally do not allow for an oppositional/semantic relationship between the ni. and one of the active verbal stems: 53 roots (12.4 %) 9 roots of which (2.1 %) have certain ni.-forms which may occur in relationship to one of the active verbal stems (Iq/II: 8x and Ih/II: 1x).

III. Roots which normally do not allow for forms of the active verbal stems: 49 roots (11.4 %).

In conclusion, we may assert that ni.-forms are related to the qal for more than 60 % of the total number of roots. Ni.-forms are related to the hiph'il for more than 10 % of the roots and of almost 10 % of the roots ni.-forms are related to the pi'el.

4.1.2 The pu'al in the OT

4.1.2.1 The distribution of pu'al forms over OT Bible books. According to our calculations based on the Mandelkern concordance and checked in the various editions of the HAL lexicon, there are 180 verb roots of which pu.-forms occur in the Masoretic text of the OT. The total number of these roots is 457. Jenni in THAT, p. 542 arrives at almost the same total: 190 roots with a total of 460 pu.-forms (rounded up).[226] These roots make up about 12 % of the total number of verb roots which occur in the Hebrew OT.

First, I will present a general overview of the number of pu.-forms per book of the Bible, distributed over the various tenses, irrespective of genre. Where it may prove useful the percentages of the various tenses per book or part of the OT are mentioned between parentheses. The percentages of the ni. are also included in order to provide data for comparison.

	Total	Part.	Perf.	Imperf.	Inf.	Impv.
Gen	27	3	20	4	1	-
Ex	29	19	9	1	-	-
Lev	12	1	9	2	-	-
Num	10	3	6	1	-	-
Deut	8	5	3	-	-	-
Pent	86	31	47	8	1	-
	(100%)	(36 %)	(54.7%)	(9.3%)	(0.1%)	(0 %)
cf. Ni.	(100%)	(13.2%)	(32 %)	(44.2%)	(6.6%)	(4.1%)
Josh	5	5	-	-	-	-
Judg	12	2	9	1	-	-
1Sam	2	2	-	-	-	-
2Sam	8	3	3	2	-	-
1Kin	9	6	3	-	-	-
2Kin	10	10	-	-	-	-
Josh-	46	28	15	3	-	-
Kings	(100%)	(60.8%)	(33.6%)	(6.6%)	(0 %)	(0 %)
cf. Ni.	(100%)	(19.9%)	(32.2%)	(38.6%)	(7.5%)	(1.8%)
Isa	71	28	36	7	-	-
	(100%)	(39.4%)	(59.7%)	(9.9%)	(0 %)	(0 %)
cf. Ni.	(100%)	(24.9%)	(34.3%)	(35.8%)	(3 %)	(2 %)
Jer	31	7	21	3	-	-
Ez	31	14	15	2	-	-
Hos	10	2	4	4	-	-
Jo	1	-	1	-	-	-
Amos	1	-	-	1	-	-
Ob	1	-	-	1	-	-
Jon	-	-	-	-	-	-
Mic	-	-	-	-	-	-
Nahum	7	3	3	1	-	-
Hab	3	1	1	1	-	-
Zeph	1	-	1	-	-	-
Hag	1	-	1	-	-	-
Zech	6	-	6	-	-	-
Mal	3	2	1	-	-	-

	Total	Part.	Perf.	Imperf.	Inf.	Impv.
Hos-Mal	167	57	90	20	-	-
prophecy	(100%)	(34.1%)	(53.9%)	(12 %)	(0 %)	(0 %)
cf.Ni.	(100%)	(19.6%)	(37.9%)	(33.5%)	(5 %)	(4 %)
Hos-Mal	34	8	18	8	-	-
Ps	47	22	17	7	1	-
Job	33	3	12	18	-	-
Prov	30	11	2	17	-	-
Total	110	36	31	42	1	-
	(100%)	(32.7%)	(28.2%)	(38.2%)	(0.9%)	(0 %)
cf. Ni.	(100%)	(28 %)	(32.1%)	(36.4%)	(2.2%)	(1.3%)
Ruth	2	1	1	-	-	-
Song	5	4	-	1	-	-
Eccl	4	1	1	2	-	-
Lam	1	1	-	-	-	-
Esth	4	3	-	1	-	-
Dan	1	-	1	-	-	-
Ezra	5	5	-	-	-	-
Neh	7	5	2	-	-	-
1 Chron	9	8	1	-	-	-
2 Chron	10	9	1	-	-	-
Total	48	37	7	4	-	-
	(100%)	(77.1%)	(14.6%)	(8.3%)	(0 %)	(0 %)
cf. Ni.	(100%)	(18.2%)	(38.5%)	(34.7%)	(7.5%)	(1.1%)
Total OT	457(100%)	188(41.1%)	191(41.8%)	76(16.6%)	2(0.4%)	0(0 %)
cf. Ni.	(100%)	(19.3%)	(34.9%)	(37.3%)	(5.7%)	(2.8%)

Pu.-forms are found in almost every book of the OT, except in Jonah and Micah. The book of Isaiah stands out with 71 pu. Yet Daniel and Lamentations contain only 1 pu.-form whereas 1 Samuel contains 2. With respect to the distribution over the tenses it is evident that pu. participles are relatively numerous whereas pu.-imperfects occur much less frequent than comparable ni. forms. Pu. imperatives are lacking entirely. The figures and percentages above are of limited value since they apply only for the total number of occurrences of the pu. and the ni. while genre and distinctions among the roots have not been taken into consideration.

4.1.2.2 The distribution of pu'al-forms over the different genres
4.1.2.2.1 Prose. The prose parts of the OT contain the following occurrences of pu.-forms: (see 4.1.2.3 for a list of these roots and locations):

	Total	Part.	Perf.	Imperf.	Inf.	Impv.
	205	105	85	14	1	
	(100%)	(51.2%)	(41.5%)	(6.8%)	(0.5%)	(0 %)
cf. Ni.	(100%)	(16.7%)	(33.3%)	(39.4%)	(7.3%)	(3.3%)

4.1.2.2.2 Poetry The poetic parts of the OT contain the following occurrences of pu.-forms; (4.1.2.3 lists pu.-roots and locations):

	Total	Part.	Perf.	Imperf.	Inf.	Impv.
Ps	47	22	17	7	1	-
Prov	30	11	2	17	-	-
Job	33	3	12	18	-	-
Lam	1	1	-	-	-	-
Song	5	4	-	1	-	-
Ex 15	1	1	-	-	-	-
Deut 32,33	2	1	1	-	-	-
Judg 5	2	-	1	1	-	-
2Sam 22	1	1	-	-	-	-
1Chron 16	1	1	-	-	-	-
Total	123	44	34	44	1	-
	(100%)	(35.7%)	(27.6%)	(35.7%)	(0.8%)	(0 %)
cf. Ni.	(100%)	(28.1%)	(34.3%)	(34.1%)	(2 %)	(1.5%)

4.1.2.2.3 Prophecy The prophetic parts of the OT contain the following scores of pu.-forms (for a complete list of these roots and their locations see 4.1.2.3):

	Total	Part.	Perf.	Imperf.	Inf.	Impv.
Isa	71	27	36	7	-	-
Jer	25	4	18	3	-	-
Hos - Mal	34	8	18	8	-	-
Total	129	39	72	18	-	-
	(100%)	(30.2%)	(55.8%)	(14 %)	(0 %)	(0 %)
cf. Ni.	(100%)	(20.6%)	(39.7%)	(33.3%)	(3.9%)	(2.4%)

Note that the prophetic parts of Ezek. do not contain any pu. Yet the prose parts of Isa. 1 contain 1 pu. pt., and that of Jer. 3 pu.-pt. and 3 pu.-pf. Finally, below the percentages for the different genres are listed:

	Total	Part.	Perf.	Imperf.	Inf.	Impv.
O.T.	100%	41.1%	41.8%	16.6%	0.4%	-
Prose	100%	51.2%	41.5%	6.8%	0.5%	-
Poetry	100%	35.7%	27.6%	35.7%	0.8%	-
Prophecy	100%	30.2%	55.8%	14 %	-	-

The high percentage of imperfect-forms in poetry is remarkable in comparison to that for prose and prophecy. However, prose contains a relatively great amount of pu.-participles.

4.1.2.3 Pu.-forms in the Masoretic text of the Old Testament. Note that in the following list an underlined root indicates that it only occurs in pu.-forms and that it is not found as a form of another verbal stem. An asterisk (*) indicates that there are also ni.-forms of that particular root in the respective genre.

	ROOT	LOCATION(S)	G	TOT	PT	PU'AL PF	IMPF	INF	IMPV
1	**ADM**	Ex.25:5/26:14/35:7,23/36:19/39:34	A	6	6	–	–	–	–
		Nah.2:14	C	1	1	–	–	–	–
2	**AZL**	Ez.27:19	A	1	1	–	–	–	–
3	**AKL***	Ex.3:2//Neh.2:3,13	A	3	1	2	–	–	–
	*	Nah.1:10//Isa.1:20	C	2	–	1	1	–	–
4	**ANH** II	Ps.91:10/Pro.12:21	B	2	–	–	2	–	–
5	**ASP***	Ez.38:12	A	1	1	–	–	–	–
	*	Isa.24:22/33:4/Hos.10:10/ Zech.14:14	C	4	–	4	–	–	–
6	**ASR**	Isa.22:3	C	1	–	1	–	–	–
7	**ARŚ**	Dt.22:23,25,27//Ex.22:15/Dt.22:28	A	5	3	2	–	–	–
8	**AŠR**	Ps.41:3//Pro.3:18	B	2	1	–	1	–	–
		Isa.9:15	C	1	1	–	–	–	–
9	**BHL***	Esth.8:14	A	1	1	–	–	–	–
	*	Pro.20:21Q	B	1	1	–	–	–	–
10	**BḤL**	Pro.20:21K	B	1	1	–	–	–	–
11	**BZZ***	Jer.50:37	C	1	–	1	–	–	–
12	**BḤN***	Ez.21:18	A	1	–	1	–	–	–
		Isa.28:16	C	1	1	–	–	–	–
13	**BL'**	2Sam.17:16	A	1	–	–	1	–	–
		Job37:20	B	1	–	–	1	–	–
	*	Isa.9:15	C	1	1	–	–	–	–
14	**BLQ**	Nah.2:11	C	1	1	–	–	–	–
15	**B'R** II	Jer.36:22	A	1	1	–	–	–	–
16	**BQ'***	Josh.9:4/Ez.26:10	A	2	2	–	–	–	–
	*	Hos.14:1	C	1	–	–	1	–	–
17	**BQŠ**	Ez.26:21/Esth.2:23	A	2	–	–	2	–	–
		Jer.50:20	C	1	–	–	1	–	–
18	**BŠL**	Ex.12:9/1Sam.2:15//Lev.6:21// 6:21	A	4	2	1	1	–	–
19	**BRK***	Num.22:6/1Chr.17:27//2Sam.7:29	A	3	2	–	1	–	–
		Dt.33:13/Job1:21/Ps.37:22/113:2 //112:2/128:4/Judg.5:24/ Pro.20:21/22:9	B	9	4	–	5	–	–
20	**GAL***	Mal.1:7,12	C	2	2	–	–	–	–
21	**GDL**	Ps.144:12	B	1	1	–	–	–	–
22	**GD'**	Isa.9:9	C	1	–	1	–	–	–
23	**GLH**	Jer.41:5/Judg.16:17,22	A	3	1	2	–	–	–
	*	Pro.27:5	B	1	1	–	–	–	–
	*	Nah.2:8	C	1	–	1	–	–	–
24	**GNB***	Gen.40:15/Ex.22:6//Gen.40:15	A	3	–	2	–	1	–
		Job4:12	B	1	–	–	1	–	–
25	**G'Š**	Job34:20	B	1	–	–	1	–	–
26	**GRŠ**	Ex.12:39	A	1	–	1	–	–	–
		Job30:5	B	1	–	–	1	–	–
27	**GŠM**	Ez.22:24	A	1	–	1	–	–	–
28	**DBQ**	Job38:38/41:9	B	2	–	–	2	–	–
29	**DBR***	Ps.87:3//Song8:8	B	2	1	–	1	–	–

	ROOT	LOCATION(S)	G	TOT	PT	PU'AL PF	IMPF	INF	IMPV
30	**DḤH***	Ps.36:16	B	1	-	1	-	-	-
31	**DKA**	Jer.44:10	A	1	-	1	-	-	-
		Job22:9	B	1	-	-	1	-	-
	*	Isa.53:5/19:10	C	2	2	-	-	-	-
32	**D'K***	Ps.118:12	B	1	-	1	-	-	-
33	**DQR**	Isa.37:10	A	1	1	-	-	-	-
		Lam.4:9	B	1	1	-	-	-	-
	*	Jer.51:4	C	1	1	-	-	-	-
34	**DŠN**	Pro.11:25/13:4/28:25	B	3	-	-	3	-	-
		Isa.34:6	C	1	-	-	1	-	-
35	**HLL**	2Sam.22:4/Ps18:4/48:2/96:4/113:14 /145:3/1Chr.16:25//Ps.78:63// Pro.12:8	B	9	7	1	1	-	-
36	**HRG***	Ps.44:23	B	1	-	1	-	-	-
		Isa.27:7	C	1	-	1	-	-	-
37	**HRH**	Job3:3	B	1	-	1	-	-	-
38	**ZMN**	Ezra10:14/Neh.10:35/13:31	A	3	3	-	-	-	-
39	**ZNH**	Ez.16:34	A	1	-	1	-	-	-
40	**ZQQ**	1Chr.28:18/29:4	A	2	2	-	-	-	-
		Ps.12:7	B	1	1	-	-	-	-
		Isa.25:6	C	1	1	-	-	-	-
41	**ZRB**	Job6:17	B	1	-	-	1	-	-
42	**ZRH**	Pro.1:17//Ps.58:4//Job18:15	B	3	1	1	1	-	-
		Isa.1:6/30:4	C	2	-	2	-	-	-
43	**ZR'***	Isa.40:24	C	1	-	1	-	-	-
44	**ZRQ**	Num.19:13,20	A	2	-	2	-	-	-
45	**ḤBA***	Job24:4	B	1	-	1	-	-	-
46	**ḤBR**	Ex.28:7/39:4//Eccl.9:4(Q)	A	3	-	2	1	-	-
		Ps.122:3	B	1	-	1	-	-	-
47	**ḤBŠ**	Ez.30:21	A	1	-	1	-	-	-
		Isa.1:6	C	1	-	1	-	-	-
48	**ḤṬB**	Ps.144:12	B	1	1	-	-	-	-
49	**ḤKM**	Ps.58:6/Pro.30:24	B	2	2	-	-	-	-
50	**ḤLH***	Isa.40:10	C	1	-	1	-	-	-
51	**ḤLL***	Ez.36:23	A	1	1	-	-	-	-
52	**ḤLQ**	Isa.33:23/Zech.14:1//Am.7:7	C	3	-	2	1	-	-
53	**ḤPŠ**	Lev.19:20	A	1	-	1	-	-	-
		Ps.64:7//Pro.28:12	B	2	1	-	1	-	-
54	**ḤṢB**	Isa.51:1	C	1	-	1	-	-	-
55	**ḤṢṢ**	Job21:21	B	1	-	1	-	-	-
56	**ḤQQ**	Pro.31:5	B	1	1	-	-	-	-
57	**ḤQH**	1Kin.6:35/Ez.8:10/23:14	A	3	3	-	-	-	-
58	**ḤRB**	Judg.16:7,8	A	2	-	2	-	-	-
59	**ḤSQ**	Ex.27:17/38:17	A	2	2	-	-	-	-
60	**ḤTL**	Ez.16:4	A	1	-	1	-	-	-
61	**ṬB'**	Ex.15:4	B	1	-	1	-	-	-
62	**ṬHR**	Ez.22:24	A	1	1	-	-	-	-
63	**ṬLA**	Josh.9:5	A	1	1	-	-	-	-

	ROOT	LOCATION(S)	G	TOT	PT	PU'AL PF	IMPF	INF	IMPV
64	ṬMA*	Ez.4:14	A	1	1	-	-	-	-
65	Ṭ'N	Isa.14:9	C	1	1	-	-	-	-
66	ṬRP*	Gen.37:33/44:28	A	2	-	2	-	-	-
67	JD'*	2Kin.10:11/Ruth2:1	A	2	2	-	-	-	-
	*	Ps.31:12/55:14/88:19/89:9/Job19:4	B	5	5	-	-	-	-
	*	Isa.12:5	C	1	1	-	-	-	-
68	JLD*	Judg.13:8//Gen.4:26/6:1/10:21,25/ 24:15/35:26/36:5/41:50/46:22,27/ 50:23/Judg.18:29/2Sam.3:5/21:20, 21/Ruth4:17/1Chr.1:19	A	18	1	17	-	-	-
	*	Ps.87:4,5,6/90:2/Job5:7	B	5	-	5	-	-	-
	*	Isa.9:5/Jer.20:15,40/22:16	C	4	-	4	-	-	-
69	JSD*	Ezra3:6/1Kin.6:37//7:10/Ez.41:8	A	4	2	2	-	-	-
	*	Song5:15	B	1	1	-	-	-	-
	*	Hag.2:18/Zech.8:9	C	2	-	2	-	-	-
70	JṢR	Ps.139:16	B	1	-	1	-	-	-
71	JŠR	1Kin.6:35	A	1	1	-	-	-	-
72	KBD*	Pro.13:18/27:18	B	2	-	-	2	-	-
	*	Isa.58:12	C	1	1	-	-	-	-
73	KBS	Lev.13:58/15:17	A	2	-	2	-	-	-
74	KLH	Gen.2:1	A	1	-	-	1	-	-
		Ps.72:20	B	1	-	1	-	-	-
75	KSH*	Ez.41:16/1Chr.21:16//Gen.7:19,20/ Eccl.6:4	A	5	2	-	3	-	-
		Ps.80:11/Pro.24:31	B	2	-	2	-	-	-
76	KPR	Ex.29:33//Num.35:33	A	2	-	1	1	-	-
77	<u>KRBL</u>	1Chr.15:27	A	1	1	-	-	-	-
78	KRT*	Judg.6:28/Ez.16:4	A	2	-	2	-	-	-
79	KTT	2Chr.15:6	A	1	-	1	-	-	-
80	LBŠ	1Kin.22:10/Ezra3:10/2Chr.5:12/ 18:9	A	4	4	-	-	-	-
81	LṬŠ	Ps.52:4	B	1	1	-	-	-	-
82	LMD	1Chr.25:7//Jer.31:18	A	2	1	1	-	-	-
		Song3:8	B	1	1	-	-	-	-
		Isa.29:13/Hos.10:11	C	2	2	-	-	-	-
83	LQḤ*	2Kin.2:10//Gen.2:23/3:19,23/ Judg.17:2/Jer.29:22	A	6	1	5	-	-	-
		Isa.52:6/53:8/Jer.48:46	C	3	-	3	-	-	-
84	LQṬ	Isa.27:12	C	1	-	-	1	-	-
85	MḤH	Isa.25:6	C	1	1	-	-	-	-
86	MLA*	Song5:14	B	1	1	-	-	-	-
87	MLḤ	Ex.30:35	A	1	1	-	-	-	-
88	MNH*	1Chr.9:29	A	1	1	-	-	-	-
89	M'D	Pro.25:19	B	1	1	-	-	-	-
90	M'K	Ez.23:3	A	1	-	1	-	-	-
91	MRṬ*	1Kin.7:45/Ez.21:15,16	A	3	1	2	-	-	-
		Isa.18:2,7	C	2	2	-	-	-	-
92	MRQ	Lev.6:21	A	1	-	1	-	-	-

	ROOT	LOCATION(S)	G	PU'AL TOT	PT	PF	IMPF	INF	IMPV
93	**MŠK**	Pro.13:2	B	1	1	-	-	-	-
	*	Isa.18:2,7	C	2	2	-	-	-	-
94	**NDḤ***	Isa.8:22	C	1	1	-	-	-	-
95	**NG'**	Ps.73:5	B	1	-	-	1	-	-
96	**NḤM***	Isa.54:11//Isa.66:13	C	2	-	1	1	-	-
97	**NṬŠ***	Isa.32:14	C	1	-	1	-	-	-
98	**NKH***	Ex.9:31,32	A	2	-	2	-	-	-
99	**NPḤ**	Job20:26	B	1	-	1	-	-	-
100	**NPṢ**	Isa.27:9	C	1	1	-	-	-	-
101	**NQR**	Isa.51:1	C	1	-	1	-	-	-
102	**NTṢ***	Judg.6:28	A	1	-	1	-	-	-
103	**SBK**	Job8:17	B	1	-	-	1	-	-
104	**SBL**	Ps.144:14	B	1	1	-	-	-	-
105	**SGR***	Josh.6:1//Eccl.12:4	A	2	1	1	-	-	-
	*	Isa.24:10,22/Jer.13:19	C	3	-	3	-	-	-
106	**SKN**	Isa.40:20	C	1	1	-	-	-	-
107	**SLH**	Job28:16,19	B	2	-	-	2	-	-
108	**S'R**	Isa.54:11//Hos.13:3	C	2	1	-	1	-	-
109	**SPḤ**	Job30:7	B	1	-	1	-	-	-
110	**SPR**	Ps.22:31/88:12/Job37:20	B	3	-	-	3	-	-
	*	Isa.52:15//Hab.1:5	C	-	-	1	1	-	-
111	**SQL***	1Kin.21:14,15	A	2	-	2	-	-	-
112	**STR***	Pro.27:5	B	1	1	-	-	-	-
113	**'BD***	Deut.21:3	A	1	-	1	-	-	-
		Isa.14:3	C	1	-	1	-	-	-
114	**'ZB***	Isa.32:14/49:25	C	2	2	-	-	-	-
115	**'LP**	Song5:14	B	1	1	-	-	-	-
		Isa.51:20	C	1	-	1	-	-	-
116	**'NG**	Jer.6:2	C	1	1	-	-	-	-
117	**'NH** II*	Lev.23:29	A	1	-	-	1	-	-
		*Ps.119:71//132:1	B	2	-	1	-	1	-
		*Isa.53:4	C	1	1	-	-	-	-
118	**'PL**	Hab.2:4	C	1	-	1	-	-	-
119	**'QL**	Hab.1:14	C	1	1	-	-	-	-
120	**'ŚH***	Ps.139:15	B	1	-	1	-	-	-
121	**'ŠQ**	Isa.23:12	C	1	1	-	-	-	-
122	**PZR**	Esth.3:8	A	1	1	-	-	-	-
123	**PQD***	Ex.38:21	A	1	-	1	-	-	-
	*	Isa.38:10	C	1	-	1	-	-	-
124	**PRD***	Esth.3:8	A	1	1	-	-	-	-
125	**PRṢ***	Neh.1:3/2:13	A	2	2	-	-	-	-
126	**PRS***	Neh.8:8//Num.15:34	A	2	1	1	-	-	-
127	**PTH**	Ez.14:9	A	1	-	-	1	-	-
	*	Pro.25:15	B	1	-	-	1	-	-
	*	Jer.20:10	C	1	-	-	1	-	-
128	**ṢWH**	Gen.45:19/Lev.8:35/10:13/Num.3:16 /36:2/Ez.12:7/24:18/37:3//Ex34:34	A	9	-	8	1	-	-
129	**ṢMD***	2Sam.20:8	A	1	1	-	-	-	-

	ROOT	LOCATION(S)	G	PU'AL TOT	PT	PF	IMPF	INF	IMPV
130	ṢPH	Ex.26:32	A	1	1	-	-	-	-
		Pro.26:33	B	1	1	-	-	-	-
131	ṢR'	Ex.4:6/Lev.14:2/Num.12:10(2x)/ 2Sam.3:29/2Kin.5:1,11,27/7:3, 8/15:5/2Chr.26:20,21(2x),23	A	15	15	-	-	-	-
132	ṢRR	Josh.9:4	A	1	1	-	-	-	-
133	QBṢ*	Ez.38:8	A	1	1	-	-	-	-
134	QBR*	Gen.25:1	A	1	-	1	-	-	-
135	QDŠ*	Ez.48:11/Ezra3:5/2Chr.26:18/31:6	A	4	4	-	-	-	-
	*	Isa.13:3	C	1	1	-	-	-	-
136	QLL*	Ps.37:22/Job24:18	B	2	2	-	-	-	-
	*	Isa.65:20	C	1	-	-	1	-	-
137	QMṬ	Job22:16	B	1	-	1	-	-	-
138	QṢ'	Ex.26:23/36:28	A	2	2	-	-	-	-
139	QṢṢ	Judg.1:7	A	1	1	-	-	-	-
140	QRA I*	Ez.10:13	A	1	-	1	-	-	-
		Isa.48:8,12/58:12/61:3/62:2/65:1	C	6	-	6	-	-	-
141	QRṢ	Job33:6	B	1	-	1	-	-	-
142	QŠR*	Gen.30:41	A	1	1	-	-	-	-
143	RAH*	Job33:21	B	1	-	1	-	-	-
144	RBB	Ps.144:13	B	1	1	-	-	-	-
145	RB'	1Kin.7:31/Ez.40:47/45:2	A	3	3	-	-	-	-
146	RDP	Isa.17:13	C	1	-	1	-	-	-
147	RWḤ	Jer.22:14	C	1	1	-	-	-	-
148	RṬŠ	Hos.10:14//Isa.13:16/Hos.14:1/ Nah.3:10	C	4	-	1	3	-	-
149	RḤM	Pro.28:13	B	1	-	-	1	-	-
		Hos.2:13,25//14:4	C	3	-	2	1	-	-
150	RḤṢ	Ez.16:4	A	1	-	1	-	-	-
		Pro.30:12	B	1	-	1	-	-	-
151	RKK	Isa.1:6	C	1	-	1	-	-	-
152	RNN	Isa.16:10	C	1	-	-	1	-	-
153	RQḤ	2Chr.16:14	A	1	1	-	-	-	-
154	RQM	Ps.139:15	B	1	-	1	-	-	-
155	RQ'	Jer.10:9	C	1	1	-	-	-	-
156	RŠŠ	Mal.1:4	C	1	-	1	-	-	-
157	RTḤ	Job30:27	B	1	-	1	-	-	-
158	ŚGB*	Pro.29:25/Job36:22	B	2	-	-	2	-	-
159	ŚRG	Job40:17	B	1	-	-	1	-	-
160	ŚRP*	Lev.10:16	A	1	-	1	-	-	-
161	ŠBṢ	Ex.28:20	A	1	1	-	-	-	-
162	ŠGL*	Jer.3:2	C	1	-	1	-	-	-
163	ŠG'	Deut.28:34/1Sam.21:16/	A	4	4	-	-	-	-
		2Kin.9:11/Jer.29:26/Hos.9:7	C	1	1	-	-	-	-
164	ŠDD	Isa.15:1/23:1,14/Jer.4:13,20(2x) 9:18/10:20/48:1,15,20/49:3,10/Jo. 1:10/Nah.3:7/Zech.11:3(2x),10	C	18	-	18	-	-	-
165	ŠWH	Job30:22K	B	1	-	-	1	-	-

	ROOT	LOCATION(S)	G	PU'AL TOT	PT	PF	IMPF	INF	IMPV
166	ŠṬP*	Lev.6:21	A	1	-	1	-	-	-
167	ŠKB	Jer.3:2	C	1	-	1	-	-	-
168	ŠLB	Ex.26:17/36:22	A	2	2	-	-	-	-
169	ŠLḤ*	Gen.44:3/Dan.10:11	A	2	-	2	-	-	-
		Pro.29:15//Judg.5:15/Job18:8// Pro.17:11	B	4	1	2	1	-	-
		Isa.16:2/27:10//50:1/Ob.1	C	4	2	2	-	-	-
170	ŠLM	Ps.65:2/Pro.11:31/13:3	B	3	-	-	3	-	-
		Isa.42:9//Jer.18:20	C	1	-	-	1	-	-
171	ŠLŠ	Gen.15:9(2x)/Ez.42:6/Eccl.4:12	A	4	4	-	-	-	-
172	ŠPH	Job33:21	B	1	-	1	-	-	-
173	ŠPK*	Num.35:33	A	1	-	1	-	-	-
	*	Ps.73:2	B	1	-	1	-	-	-
		Zeph.1:17	C	1	-	1	-	-	-
174	ŠQH	Job21:24	B	1	-	-	1	-	-
175	ŠRŠ	Job31:8	B	1	-	-	1	-	-
176	TAR	Josh.19:13	A	1	1	-	-	-	-
177	TKH	Deut.33:3	B	1	-	1	-	-	-
178	TKN*	2Kin.12:12	A	1	1	-	-	-	-
179	TL'	Nah.2:4	C	1	1	-	-	-	-
180	TRGM	Ezra 4:7	A	1	1	-	-	-	-

In prose 92 roots and 205 forms are found (105 participles; 85 perfects, 14 imperfects and one infinitive construct). For poetry the scores are: 76 roots and 123 forms (44 participles, 34 perfects, 44 imperfects and 1 infinitive construct) and for prophecy 69 roots and 129 forms (39 participles, 72 perfects, and 18 imperfects).

4.1.2.4 The niph'al-pu'al relationship: some statistical data. The figures presented above allow for a different approach in that they permit the calculation of the respective share of each verb tense in the totals of ni. and pu. For the whole OT this results in the following tabulation:

	Total	Part.	Perf.	Imperf.	Inf.	Impv.
OT	4600	989	1635	1620	238	118
Niph'al	4143	801	1444	1544	236	118
	(90%)	(81%)	(88.3%)	(95.3%)	(99.2%)	(100%)
Pu'al	457	188	191	76	2	-
	(10%)	(19%)	(11.7%)	(4.7%)	(0.8%)	(0%)

These statistics, though interesting in some respects, are of limited value. The material contains all occurrences of the ni. and pu. It includes roots which occur as ni.-forms but which do not occur in the pu. and vice versa.

Next, we present a tabulation of figures for the various genres, followed by similar calculations for the Pentateuch and Joshua through Kings which do not result in an essentially different outcome.

	Total	Part.	Perf.	Imperf.	Inf.	Impv.
Prose	2789	536	946	1032	189	86
Niph'al	2584	431	861	1018	188	86
	(92.6%)	(80.4%)	(91%)	(98.6%)	(99.5%)	(100%)
Pu'al	205	105	85	14	1	-
	(7.4%)	(19.6%)	(9%)	(1.4%)	(0.5%)	(0%)
Poetry	782	229	260	269	14	10
Niph'al	659	185	226	225	13	10
	(84.3%)	(80.8%)	(86.9%)	(83.6%)	(92.9%)	(100%)
Pu'al	123	44	34	44	1	-
	(15.7%)	(19.2%)	(13.1%)	(16.4%)	(7.1%)	(0%)

Among the poetry sections the book of Psalms provides a different picture with respect to the imperf.: of the total of 96 imperf.-forms there are 89 ni.-imperfects (92.7%) and 7 pu.-imperfects (7.3%). These figures should be compared to the total number of forms in poetry: ni. 86.9% and pu. 13.1%.

	Total	Part.	Perf.	Imperf.	Inf.	Impv.
Prophecy	1029	224	429	319	35	22
Niph'al	900	185	357	301	35	22
	(87.5%)	(82.6%)	(83.2%)	(94.3%)	(100%)	(100%)
Pu'al	129	39	72	18	-	-
	(12.5%)	(17.4%)	(16.8%)	(5.7%)	(0%)	(0%)

The share of pu.-forms in the total of pu. and ni. is the smallest for prose (7.4 %), yet for poetry it is the greatest. For poetry we note the relatively high amount of pu.-imperf. forms. We will make use of such calculations in our discussion of the roots of which ni.- as well as pu.- forms occur.

4.1.3 The hoph'al in the Old Testament

4.1.3.1 The distribution of hoph'al forms over the various Bible books. According to my calculations, based on the Mandelkern concordance, and checked by means of the different editions of the HAL dictionary, there are 105 verb roots of which ho.-forms occur in the Masoretic text of the OT. In total, it concerns 415 forms. Jenni in THAT, p. 542 arrives at an almost equal number: 100 roots, with a total of 400 ho. (rounded down). These roots form about 6.4 % of the total number of verb roots in the Hebrew OT.

First of all, in the following tabulation I present a general overview of the number of ho. per Bible book, distributed over the various tenses, irrespective of genre. Where necessary, the percentages of various tenses per book or per part of the OT are listed between parentheses.

In the Pentateuch more than a third of the total number of ho.-forms may be found. The book of Exodus in particular contains numerous ho.-forms. Among these are 22 participle forms of the root **ŠZR** and 10 imperf.-forms of the root **MWT**. 13 imperf. forms of the last-mentioned root appear in the book of Leviticus.

	Total	Part.	Perf.	Imperf.	Inf.	Impv.
Gen	22	4	5	12	1	-
Ex	53(100%)	27(50.9%)	7(13.2%)	19(35.9%)	-	-
Lev	42(100%)	2(4.8%)	10(23.8%)	26(61.9%)	4(9.5%)	-
Num	20	5	2	13	-	-
Deut	6	-	3	3	-	-
Pentateuch	143	38	27	73	5	-
	(100%)	(26.6%)	(18.9%)	(51 %)	(3.5%)	(0 %)
cf. Ni.	(100%)	(13.2%)	(32 %)	(44.2%)	(6.6%)	(4.1%)
cf. Pu.	(100%)	(36 %)	(54.7%)	(9.3%)	(0.1%)	(0 %)
Josh	4	-	1	2	1	-
Judg	7	1	2	4	-	-
1Sam	13	2	4	7	-	-
2Sam	13	3	2	8	-	-
1Kin	18	8	3	7	-	-
2Kin	18	8	1	8	1	-
Josh-	73	22	13	36	2	-
Kin	(100%)	(30.1%)	(17.8%)	(49.3%)	(2.7%)	(0 %)
cf. Ni.	(100%)	(19.9%)	(32.2%)	(38.6%)	(7.5%)	(1.8%)
cf. Pu.	(100%)	(60.8%)	(33.6%)	(6.6%)	(0 %)	(0 %)

The percentages of the frequency of occurrences of the ho. agree with those found in the Pentateuch.

	Total	Part.	Perf.	Imperf.	Inf.	Impv.
Isa	39	7	10	22	-	-
Jer	29	9	12	8	-	-
Ez	37	15	12	5	4	1
Hos	4	-	1	3	-	-
Jo	1	-	1	-	-	-
Amos	1	1	-	-	-	-
Ob	-	-	-	-	-	-
Jonah	-	-	-	-	-	-
Michah	2	1	-	1	-	-
Nahum	4	-	4	-	-	-
Hab	1	-	1	-	-	-
Zeph	-	-	-	-	-	-
Hag	-	-	-	-	-	-
Zech	6	1	4	1	-	-
Mal	2	2	-	-	-	-
Total	126	36	45	40	4	1
Prophecy	(100%)	(28.6%)	(35.7%)	(31.7%)	(3.2%)	(0.8%)
cf. Ni.	(100%)	(19.6%)	(37.9%)	(33.5%)	(5 %)	(4 %)
cf. Pu.	(100%)	(34.1%)	(53.9%)	(12 %)	(0 %)	(0 %)
Hos-Mal.	21	5	11	5	-	-
Ps	9	3	3	3	-	-
Job	19	2	6	10	-	1

	Total	Part.	Perf.	Imperf.	Inf.	Impv.
Pro	8	2	1	5	-	-
Total	36	7	10	18	-	1
	(100%)	(19.4%)	(27.8%)	(50 %)	(0 %)	(2.8
cf. Ni.	(100%)	(28 %)	(32.1%)	(36.4%)	(2.2%)	(1.3
cf. Pu.	(100%)	(32.7%)	(28.2%)	(38.2%)	(0.9%)	(0
Ruth	2	-	1	-	1	-
Song	1	-	-	1	-	-
Eccl	1	1	-	-	-	-
Lam	2	-	1	1	-	-
Esth	3	-	2	1	-	-
Dan	5	1	4	-	-	-
Ezra	3	1	1	1	-	-
Neh	-	-	-	-	-	-
1Chron	3	1	1	1	-	-
2Chron	17	8	5	3	1	-
Total	37	12	15	8	2	-
	(100%)	(32.4%)	(40.5%)	(21.6%)	(5.4%)	(0
cf. Ni.	(100%)	(18.2%)	(38.5%)	(34.7%)	(7.5%)	(1.1
cf. Pu.	(100%)	(77.1%)	(14.6%)	(8.3%)	(0 %)	(0

The tabulation of distribution of the ho.in the OT is as follows:

	Total	Part.	Perf.	Imperf.	Inf.	Impv.
Total OT	415(100%)	155(27.2%)	110(26.5%)	175(42.2%)	13(3.1%)	(0.5%)
cf. Ni.	(100%)	(19.3%)	(34.9%)	(37.3%)	(5.7%)	(2.8%)
cf. Pu.	(100%)	(41.1%)	(41.8%)	(16.6%)	(0.4%)	(0 %)

Ho. forms do not occur in the books Ob., Jonah, Zeph., Hag., and Neh. A relatively great amount of ho.-forms is found in the books Isa., Jer. and Ez. It is also evident that the distribution over the various tenses of the ho. agrees more with that of the ni. than with that of the pu. The pu. differs especially with respect to the percentage of participles and imperfects that occur. For the ho. there are relatively frequent occurrences of imperfects and relatively few occurrences of perf.-forms.

4.1.3.2 The distribution of ho.-forms over the various genres.
4.1.3.2.1 Prose. The next tabulation represents the figures for the occurrence of ho. in prose fragments of the OT: (see 4.1.3.3 for a list of these roots and their locations).

	Total	Part.	Perf.	Imperf.	Inf.	Impv.
	293	89	68	122	13	1
	(100%)	(30.4%)	(23.2%)	(41.6%)	(4.5%)	(0.3%)
cf. Ni.	(100%)	(16.7%)	(33.3%)	(39.4%)	(7.3%)	(3.3%)
cf. Pu.	(100%)	(51.2%)	(41.5%)	(6.8%)	(0.5%)	(0 %)

These percentages are hardly different from those for the whole OT.

4.1.3.2.2 Poetry. The poetic fragments of the OT contain the following percentages of occurrences of ho.-forms: (see 4.1.3.3 for a list of ho.-stems and their locations).

	Total	Part.	Perf.	Imperf.	Inf.	Impv.
Ps	9	3	3	3	-	-
Pro	19	2	6	10	-	1
Job	8	2	1	5	-	-
Lam	2	-	1	1	-	-
Song	1	-	-	1	-	-
2Sam 3	1	-	1	-	-	-
2Sam 23	1	1	-	-	-	-
Total	41	8	12	20	-	1
	(100%)	(19.5%)	(29.3%)	(48.8%)	(0 %)	(2.4%)
cf. Ni.	(100%)	(28.1%)	(34.3%)	(34.1%)	(2 %)	(1.5%)
cf. Pu.	(100%)	(35.7%)	(27.6%)	(35.7%)	(0.8%)	(0 %)

The relatively small number of participial forms is remarkable.

4.1.3.2.3 Prophecy

	Total	Part.	Perf.	Imperf.	Inf.	Impv.
Isa	39	7	10	22	-	-
Jer	19	6	8	5	-	-
Ez	2	-	1	1	-	-
Hos-Mal	21	5	11	5	-	-
Total	81	18	30	33	-	-
	(100%)	(22.2%)	(37 %)	(40.7%)	(0 %)	(0 %)
cf. Ni.	(100%)	(20.6%)	(39.7%)	(33.3%)	(3.9%)	(2.4%)
cf. Pu.	(100%)	(30.2%)	(55.8%)	(14 %)	(0 %)	(0 %)

Below, I list the percentages for the various genres:

	Total	Part.	Perf.	Imperf.	Inf.	Impv.
O.T.	100%	27.2%	26.5%	42.2%	3.1%	0.5%
Prose	100%	30.4%	23.2%	41.6%	4.5%	0.3%
Poetry	100%	19.5%	29.3%	48.8%	-	2.4%
Prophecy	100%	22.2%	37 %	40.7%	-	-

The low percentage of participial forms in poetry is quite remarkable in comparison to the percentages for prose and prophecy. It should be acknowledged that only 41 ho.-forms occur in poetry.

4.1.3.3 Ho.-forms in the Masoretic text of the Old Testament. Note that roots have been underlined of which only ho.-forms occur at the exception of forms of other verbal stems. An asterisk (*) indicates that ni. of the same root occur in the respective genre.

	ROOT	LOCATION(S)	G	HOPH'AL TOT	PT	PF	IMPF	INF	IMPV
1	**AḤZ***	2Chr.9:18	A	1	1	-	-	-	-
2	**ARR**	Num.22:6	A	1	-	-	1	-	-
3	**BWA**	Gen.43:18/2Kin.12:10,14/22:4/ 2Chr.34:9,14/Ez.23:42/30:11// Gen.33:11/43:18/Ex.27:7/Lev.10:18/ 13:2,9/14:2/16:27/Ez.40:4//Lev. 6:23/11:32/2Kin.12:5,7/Jer.27:22	A	22	8	9	5	-	-
		Ps.45:15	B	1	1	-	-	-	-
		Jer.10:9	C	1	-	-	1	-	-
4	**BQ'***	Jer.39:2	A	1	-	1	-	-	-
5	**GLH***	Jer.40:1//40:7/Esth.2:6(2x)/ 1Chr.9:1	A	5	1	4	-	-	-
	*	Jer.13:19	C	1	-	1	-	-	-
6	**DBQ**	Ps.22:16	B	1	1	-	-	-	-
7	**DWŠ**	Isa.28:27	C	1	-	-	1	-	-
8	**DQQ**	Isa.28:28	C	1	-	-	1	-	-
9	**HDD**	Ez.21:14,15,16	A	3	-	3	-	-	-
10	**HPK***	Job30:15	B	1	-	1	-	-	-
11	**ZWN**	Jer.5:8	C	1	1	-	-	-	-
12	**ZWR**	Ps.69:9	B	1	1	-	-	-	-
13	**ḤBA***	Isa.42:22	C	1	-	1	-	-	-
14	**ḤWL**	Isa.66:8	C	1	-	-	1	-	-
15	**ḤLH***	1Kin.22:34/2Chr.18:33/35:23	A	3	-	3	-	-	-
16	**ḤLL***	Gen.4:26	A	1	-	1	-	-	-
17	**ḤNN**	Pro.21:10	B	1	-	-	1	-	-
	*	Isa.26:10	C	1	-	-	1	-	-
18	**ḤQQ**	Job19:23	B	1	-	-	1	-	-
19	**ḤRB***	Ez.29:12//26:2//2Kin.3:23	A	3	1	1	-	1	-
20	**ḤRM**	Ex.22:19/Lev.27:29/Ezra10:8	A	3	-	-	3	-	-
21	**ḤTL**	Ez.16:4	A	1	-	-	-	1	-
22	**ṬB'**	Jer.38:22	A	1	-	1	-	-	-
		Pro.8:25/Job38:6	B	2	-	2	-	-	-
23	**ṬWL**	Ps.37:24/Pro.16:33/Job41:1	B	3	-	-	3	-	-
		Jer.22:28	C	1	-	1	-	-	-
24	**JBL**	Job10:19/21:30,32/Ps.45:15,16	B	5	-	-	5	-	-
		Isa.18:7/53:7/55:12/Jer.11:19/ Hos.10:6/12:2	C	6	-	-	6	-	-
25	**JD'***	Lev.4:23,28	A	2	-	2	-	-	-
	*	Isa.12:5	C	1	1	-	-	-	-
26	**JKH***	Job33:19	B	1	-	1	-	-	-
27	**JLD***	Gen.40:20/Ez.16:4,5	A	3	-	-	-	3	-
28	**JSD***	Ezra3:1/2Chr.3:3	A	2	-	2	-	-	-
	*	Isa.28:16	C	1	1	-	-	-	-
29	**J'D***	Ez.21:21	A	1	1	-	-	-	-
	*	Jer.24:1	C	1	1	-	-	-	-
30	**J'P**	Dan.9:21	A	1	1	-	-	-	-
		Isa.8:23	C	1	1	-	-	-	-
31	**JṢA**	Gen.38:25/Ez.14:22/47:8/Jer.38: 22//Ez.38:8	A	5	4	1	-	-	-

	ROOT	LOCATION(S)	G	HOPH'AL TOT	PT	PF	IMPF	INF	IMPV
32	JṢ'	Esth.4:3	A	1	-	-	1	-	-
		Isa.14:11	C	1	-	-	1	-	-
33	JṢQ	1Kin.7:16,23,33/2Chr.4:2//	A	5	4	-	1	-	-
		Lev.21:10							
		Job11:15/37:18//Ps.45:3//Job22:16	B	4	2	1	1	-	-
34	JṢR*	Isa.54:17	C	1	-	-	1	-	-
35	JQD	Lev.6:2,5,6	A	3	-	-	3	-	-
		Jer.15:14/17:4	C	2	-	-	2	-	-
36	JQ'	2Sam.21:13	A	1	1	-	-	-	-
37	JQŠ	Eccl.9:12	A	1	1	-	-	-	-
38	JRD	Gen.39:1/Num.10:7/Ez.31:18	A	3	-	3	-	-	-
		Isa.14:11/Zech.10:11//Isa.14:15	C	3	-	2	1	-	-
39	JRH?	Pro.11:25	B	1	-	-	1	-	-
40	JSB̌	Isa.5:8//44:26	C	2	-	1	1	-	-
41	KWN*	Ez.40:43	A	1	1	-	-	-	-
	*	Pro.21:31	B	1	1	-	-	-	-
	*	Isa.16:5/30:33/Nah.2:6/Zech.5:11	C	4	-	4	-	-	-
42	KLM*	1Sam.25:15	A	1	-	1	-	-	-
	*	Jer.14:3	C	1	-	1	-	-	-
43	KRT*	Jo.1:9	C	1	-	1	-	-	-
44	KSL̆	Jer.18:23	C	1	1	-	-	-	-
45	KTT	Job4:20	B	1	-	-	1	-	-
		Isa.24:12/Jer.46:5/Mi.1:7	C	3	-	-	3	-	-
46	LQḤ	Isa.49:24,25	C	2	-	-	2	-	-
47	MWT	see below	A	63	3	3	57	-	-
		Pro.19:16	B	1	-	-	1	-	-
48	MKK	Job24:24	B	1	-	1	-	-	-
49	MLḤ	Ez.16:4//16:4	A	2	-	1	-	1	-
50	MLK	Dan.9:1	A	1	-	1	-	-	-
51	NGD	see below	A	32	-	7	23	2	-
		Isa.21:2/40:21//7:2	C	3	-	2	1	-	-
52	NGR	Mi.1:14	C	1	1	-	-	-	-
53	NGŠ	2Sam.3:34	B	1	-	1	-	-	-
	*	Mal.1:11	C	1	1	-	-	-	-
54	NDD	2Sam.23:6//Job20:8	B	2	1	-	1	-	-
55	NDḤ*	Isa.13:14	C	1	1	-	-	-	-
56	NWḤ	Ez.41:9,11(2x)	A	3	3	-	-	-	-
		Lam.5:5	B	1	-	1	-	-	-
		Zech.5:11	C	1	-	1	-	-	-
57	NWP	Ex.29:27	A	1	-	1	-	-	-
58	NḤL	Job7:3	B	1	-	1	-	-	-
59	NTH*	Ez.9:9	A	1	1	-	-	-	-
	*	Isa.8:8	C	1	1	-	-	-	-
60	NKH*	Ex.5:16/Num.25:14,15,18//25:14/	A	10	4	5	1	-	-
		Ex.22:1/1Sam.5:12/Ez.22:1/							
		33:21// Ex.5:14							
		Ps.102:5	B	1	-	1	-	-	-
		Isa.53:4/Jer.18:21//Hos.9:16/	C	5	2	2	1	-	-
		Zech.13:6//Isa.1:5							

						HOPH'AL			
	ROOT	LOCATION(S)	G	TOT	PT	PF	IMPF	INF	IMPV
61	**NSK**	Ex.25:29/37:16	A	2	-	-	2	-	-
62	**NṢB***	Gen.28:12/Judg.9:6	A	2	2	-	-	-	-
	*****	Nah.2:8	C	1	-	1	-	-	-
63	**NṢL***	Am.4:11/Zech.3:2	C	2	2	-	-	-	-
64	**NQM***	Gen.4:15,24/Ex.21:21	A	3	-	-	3	-	-
65	**NTK***	Ez.22:22	A	1	-	-	1	-	-
66	**NTN***	Lev.11:38/Num.26:54/32:5/2Sam. 18:9/21:6/1Kin.2:21/2Kin.5:17	A	7	-	-	7	-	-
		Job28:15	B	1	-	-	1	-	-
67	**NTṢ**	Lev.11:35	A	1	-	-	1	-	-
68	**NTQ***	Judg.20:31	A	1	-	1	-	-	-
69	**NTŠ**	Ez.19:12	C	1	-	-	1	-	-
70	**SBB***	Ex.28:11/39:6,13/Num.32:38/ Ez.41:24	A	5	5	-	-	-	-
	*****	Isa.28:27	C	1	-	-	1	-	-
71	**SWG***	Isa.59:14	C	1	-	1	-	-	-
72	**SWK**	Ex.30:32	A	1	-	-	1	-	-
73	**SWR**	1Sam.21:7//Lev.4:31/Dan.12:11// Lev.4:35	A	4	1	2	1	-	-
		Isa.17:1	C	1	1	-	-	-	-
74	**'WD**	Ex.21:29	A	1	-	1	-	-	-
75	**'LH***	Judg.6:28/2Chr.20:34	A	2	-	2	-	-	-
		Nah.2:8/Hab.1:15	C	2	-	2	-	-	-
76	**'MD**	1Kin.22:35//Lev.16:10	A	2	1	-	1	-	-
77	**'MM**	Lam.4:1	B	1	-	-	1	-	-
78	**PDH***	Lev.19:20	A	1	-	-	-	1	-
79	**PZZ**	1Kin.10:18	A	1	1	-	-	-	-
80	**PNH**	Ez.9:2	A	1	1	-	-	-	-
		Jer.49:8	C	1	-	1	-	-	-
81	**PQD***	2Kin.12:12/22:5,9/2Chr.34:10,12, 17//Lev.5:23	A	7	6	1	-	-	-
	*****	Jer.6:6	C	1	-	1	-	-	-
82	**PRR**	Jer.33:21	A	1	-	-	1	-	-
		Isa.8:10/Zech.11:11	C	2	-	-	2	-	-
83	**ṢHB**	Ezra8:24	A	1	1	-	-	-	-
84	**QWM**	Ex.40:17/2Sam.23:1/Jer.35:14	A	3	-	3	-	-	-
85	**QṢ'**	Ez.46:22	A	1	1	-	-	-	-
86	**QRH**	Ez.29:18	A	1	1	-	-	-	-
87	**RAH***	Ex.25:40//26:30/Lev.13:49/ Deut.4:35	A	4	1	3	-	-	-
88	**RBK**	Lev.6:14/7:12/1Chr.23:29	A	3	3	-	-	-	-
89	**RWH**	Pro.11:25	B	1	-	-	1	-	-
90	**RWM**	Ex.29:27/Dan.8:11//Lev.4:10	A	3	-	2	1	-	-
91	**RJQ**	Song1:3	B	1	-	-	1	-	-
		Jer.48:11	C	1	-	1	-	-	-
92	**R'L**	Nah.2:4	C	1	-	1	-	-	-
93	**ŠJM**	Gen.24:33/50:26	A	2	-	-	2	-	-
94	**ŠBR***	Jer.8:21	C	1	-	1	-	-	-
95	**ŠDD***	Isa.33:1/Hos.10:14	C	2	-	-	2	-	-

	ROOT	LOCATION(S)	G	TOT	HOPH'AL PT	PF	IMPF	INF	IMPV
96	**ŠWB**	Gen.43:12/Num.5:8/Jer.27:16// Gen.42:28//Ex.10:8	A	5	3	1	1	-	-
		Isa.44:26	C	1	-	-	1	-	-
97	**ŠZR**	Ex.26:1,31,36/27:6,9,16,18,28/ 28:8,15/36:8,35,37/38:9,16,18/ 39:2,5,8,24,28,29	A	22	22	-	-	-	-
98	**ŠḤT**	Pro.25:26	B	1	1	-	-	-	-
		*Mal.1:4	C	1	1	-	-	-	-
99	**ŠJR**	Isa.26:1	C	1	-	-	1	-	-
100	**ŠJT**	Ex.21:30	A	1	-	-	1	-	-
101	**ŠKB**	2Kin.4:32//Ez.32:32//32:19	A	3	1	1	-	-	1
102	**ŠLK**	2Sam.20:21/1Kin.13:24,25,28// Dan.8:11//Ez.16:15	A	6	4	1	1	-	-
		Ps.22:11	B	1	-	1	-	-	-
		Jer.14:16/36:30//Isa.14:19/Jer. 22:28/Ez.19:12//Isa.34:3	C	6	2	3	1	-	-
103	**ŠLM**	Job5:23	B	1	-	1	-	-	-
104	**ŠMM***	Lev.26:34,35,43/2Chr.36:21	A	4	-	-	-	4	-
	*	Job21:5	B	1	-	-	-	-	1
105	**TLL**	Isa.44:20	C	1	-	1	-	-	-

The following ho.-forms of the root **MWT** occur in prose:
PT 3x : 1Sam. 19:11/ 2Kin. 11:12/ 2Chr. 22:11
PF 3x : Deut. 21:22/ 2Sam. 21:9/ 2Kin. 11:2
IMPF 57x: Gen. 26:11/ Ex. 19:12/ 21:12, 15, 16, 17, 2// 22:1// 131: 14, 15/ 35:2/ Lev. 19:20/ 20:2, 9, 10, 11, 12, 13, 15, 16, 27/ 24: 16, 17, 21/ 27:29/ Num. 1:51/ 3:10, 38/ 15: 35/ 18:7/ 35:16, 17, 18, 21, 31/ Deut. 13:6/ 17:6/ 24:16/ Josh. 1:18/ Judg. 6:31/ 21:5/ 1Sam. 11:13/ 19:6/ 20:32/ 2Sam. 19:22, 23/ 1Kin. 2:24/ 2Kin. 11:8, 15, 16/ 14:6, 16/ Jer. 38:4/ Ez. 18:13/ 2Chr. 15:13/ 23:7, 14.
The following ho.-forms of the root **NGD** occur in prose:
PF 7x : Deut. 17:4/ Josh. 9:24/ 1Sam. 23:13/ 1Kin. 10:17/ 18:13/ Ruth 2:11/ 2Chr. 9:6
IMPF 23x: Gen. 22:20/ 27:42/ 31:22/ 38:13, 24/ Ex. 14:5/ Josh. 10: 17/ Judg. 9:25, 47/ 1Sam. 15:12/ 19:19/ 23:7/27:4/ 2Sam. 6:12/ 10: 17/ 19:2/ 21:11/ 1Kin. 1:51/ 2:29, 41/ 6:13/ 8: 7/ 1Chr. 19:17
INF 2x : Josh. 9:24/ Ruth 2:11.
In prose 66 roots occur in 293 forms (89 participles; 68 perf.; 122 imperf., 13 inf.cs. and 1 impv.). For poetry the following figures apply: 30 roots in 41 forms (8 participles.; 12 perf.; 20 imperf. and 1 impv.) and for prophecy: 51 roots in 81 forms (18 participles; 30 perf. and 33 imperf).

4.1.3.4 The relationship between niph'al, pu'al, and hoph'al: Some statistical data. In 4.1.2.4 we calculated the magnitude of the share of a certain verb tense within the framework of the ni. and pu. occurrences in the OT. In the same way we will calculate below the figures for the totals of the ni., pu. and ho. As stated earlier, these calculations have limited value, although they are interesting in some respects. We are dealing here with all material of the ni., pu and ho. Included are roots of which ni.-forms occur but which do not appear as pu.- or ho.-forms and vice versa. For the OT our calculations have resulted in the following outcome:

	Total	Part.	Perf.	Imperf.	Inf.	Impv.
OT	5015	1104	1745	1795	251	118
Niph'al	4143	801	1444	1544	236	118
	(82.6%)	(72.6%)	(82.8%)	(86%)	(94 %)	(98.3%)
Hoph'al	415	115	110	175	13	2
	(8.3%)	(10.4%)	(6.2%)	(9.7%)	(5.2%)	(1.7%)
Pu'al	457	188	191	76	2	0
	(9.1%)	(17 %)	(11 %)	(4.3%)	(0.8%)	(0 %)

Next, we present the statistics as applicable per individual genre:

	Total	Part.	Perf.	Imperf.	Inf.	Impv.
Prose	3082	625	1014	1154	202	87
Niph'al	2584	431	861	1018	188	86
	(83.8%)	(69.0%)	(84.9%)	(88.2%)	(93.1%)	(98.9%)
Hoph'al	293	89	68	122	13	1
	(9.5%)	(14.2%)	(6.7%)	(10.6%)	(6.4%)	(1.1%)
Pu'al	205	105	85	14	1	0
	(6.7%)	(16.8%)	(8.4%)	(1.2%)	(0.5%)	(0 %)

The prose fragments of Ezekiel contain a relatively great amount of ho.-forms as well as pu.-forms. Addition of the ni.-, pu.- and ho.- forms in this book results in the following outcome. The percentages of the respective tenses have been included as well.

	Total	Part.	Perf.	Imperf.	Inf.	Impv.
Ezekiel	380	74	139	109	25	33
Niph'al	314	45	113	103	21	32
	(82.6%)	(60.8%)	(81.3%)	(94.5%)	(84%)	(97%)
Hoph'al	35	15	11	4	4	1
	(9.2%)	(20.3%)	(7.9%)	(3.7%)	(16%)	(3%)
Pu'al	31	14	15	2	0	0
	(9.2%)	(18.9%)	(10.8%)	(1.8%)	(0%)	(0%)

When these percentages are compared to those for prose, it is evident that there is a relatively high amount of participles and a relatively small amount of imperfects in Ezekiel.

	Total	Part.	Perf.	Imperf.	Inf.	Impv.
Poetry	823	237	260	269	14	10
Niph'al	659	185	226	225	13	10
	(80 %)	(78 %)	(83.1%)	(77.8%)	(92.9%)	(90.9%)

Hoph'al	41	8	12	20	0	1
	(5 %)	(3.4%)	(4.4%)	(6.9%)	(0 %)	(9.1%)
Pu'al	123	44	34	44	1	0
	(15 %)	(18.6%)	(12.5%)	(15.2%)	(7.4%)	(0 %)
Prophecy	1110	242	459	352	35	22
Niph'al	900	185	357	301	35	22
	(81.1%)	(76.5%)	(77.8%)	(85.5%)	(100 %)	(100 %)
Hoph'al	81	18	30	33	0	0
	(7.3%)	(7.4%)	(6.5%)	(9.4%)	(0 %)	(0 %)
Pu'al	129	39	72	18	0	0
	(11.6%)	(16.1%)	(15.7%)	(5.1%)	(0 %)	(0 %)

4.1.4 The passive qal-participle in the Old Testament

4.1.4.1 Introduction. According to grammarians the qal has two forms of the participle; that of the active **QōTēL** and that of the passive **QāṬūL**. The latter form is regarded as a remainder of the lost passive stem of the qal.[227] There have been several attempts to identify participle forms of the **QūṬṬaL** type in the OT text. The passive of the **QāṬūL** type is generally regarded as the most original form.[228] The precise identification of passive qal-forms of the **QāṬūL** type results in problems. The Gesenius-Kautzsch grammar asserts that not all forms of the type **QāṬūL** are pass. qal-participles. It states about this: [229] "Mit der Form **Pa'uL** als Part. pass. ist nicht zu verwechseln die gleichlautende Form, die, von intransit. Verbis gebildet, inhärierende Eigenschaften und Zustände bezeichnet." It mentions the following examples such as: **AāMūN** 'trustworthy', **BāṬūaḤ** 'trusted' en **ŠāKūR** 'drunk'. Bergsträsser's grammar classifies these forms as passive qal-participles, even if they allow for an 'active' translation.[230]

According to my calculations there are more than 190 verb roots in the OT of which forms of the passive qal-participle occur. 119 of these roots, of which ni.-forms occur, are included in the lists in 3.2 and following. This group consists in total of 784 forms. I have attempted to include as many forms of the **QāṬūL** type as possible in my collection even if they have an active and non-passive meaning.

We have avoided the inclusion of a complete list of all pass. qal-pt. in the OT. Dictionaries and grammars differ as to which forms belong to this category and which do not. In certain instances it is difficult to make a justifiable decision in this respect. (E.g. is the word **NeAūM** in the expression 'Thus says the Lord' a pass. qal?). Moreover these forms are only important for our study in as far as they may be related to other passive forms. Therefore, I refer to the lists in 3.2 and following for roots of which ni.- as well as pass. qal pt.-forms occur. Below I merely present a list of the roots of which participles occur of pu., ho. or hitp. in as far as they have not been included in my collection above. It concerns a total of 13 roots:

ḤṬB: pass.participle 1x Pro. 7:16 - pu.-participle 1x Ps. 144:12

ḤQQ: pass.participle 1x Ez. 23:14	-	pu.-participle 1x Pro. 31:5
JṢQ: pass.participle 9x Ps. 41:9; Job 28:2, 29:6, 41:15,16(2x), 1Kin. 7:24,30; 2Chron. 4:3,	-	ho.-participle 6x 1Kin. 7:23,33,16, Job 11:15, 37:18; 2Chron. 4:2
LBŠ: pass.participle 16x 1Sam. 17:5; Ez. 9:2,3,11, 10:2,6,7; 23:6, 12, 38:4; Zech. 3:3; Pro. 31:21 Dan. 10:5, 12:6,7; Isa. 14:19	-	pu.-participle 4x 1Kin. 22:10, Ez. 3:10, 2Chron. 5:12, 18:9
NPṢ: pass.participle 2x Jer. 22:28; Isa. 11:12	-	pu.-participle 1x Isa. 27:9
SLL: pass.participle 2x Jer. 18:15; Pro. 15:19	-	hitpol.-participle 1x Ex. 9:17
'ŠQ: pass.participle 8x Deut. 28: 29,33; Hos. 5:11; Pro. 28: 17; Jer. 50:33; Ps. 103:6, 146:7; Eccl. 146:7	-	pu.-participle 1x Isa. 23:12
ṢPH: qal-participle 1x Job 15:22	-	pu.-participle 2x Pro. 26:23, Ex. 26:32
ṢR': qal-participle 5x Lev. 13:44, 45, 14:3, 22:4, Num. 5:2	-	pu.-participle 13x 2Kin. 5:1,11,27, 7:3,8, 15:5; 2Chron. 26:20,21,23; 2Sam. 3:29; Lev. 14:2; Ex. 4:6; Num. 12:10
ṢRR: qal-participle 4x Hos. 13:12; Ex. 12:34; 1Sam. 20:3, 25:29	-	pu.-participle 1x Josh. 9:4
RB': qal-participle 9x Ex. 27:1, 28: 16, 30:2, 37:25, 38:1, 39:9; 1Kin. 7:5, Ez. 41:21, 43:16	-	pu.-participle 3x 1Kin. 7:31, Ez.40: 47, 45:2
ŠWB: qal-participle 1x Micah 2:8 Num.5:8, Jer. 27:16	-	pass. polal-participle 1x Ez. 38:8 ho.-participle 3x Gen. 43:12,
ŠLM: qal-participle 1x 2Sam 20:19	-	pu.-participle 1x Isa. 42:19

Moreover, 12 roots, of which forms of other passive/reflexive verbal stems exist, do not occur in participial form:

for the pu. : **ḤBR**, **ḤBŠ**, **KTT**, **M'K**, **MRQ**, **NPḤ**, **SBK**;
for the ho. : **KTT**, **ŚJM** and **ŠJT**;
for the hitp.: **BLL** and **ŠNN**.

Another interesting group of nineteen roots consists of verbs of which only the pass. qal-pt. occurs and no other forms of the qal or other verbal stems. The group consists of the following roots: **ABS**, **ḤMŠ**, **ḤRM** II, **ḤRT**, **KMS**, **KSḤ**, **MHL**, **NGB**, **NḤṢ**, **NSK** II, **NŠQ**, **SWG** II, **QṬR**, **QLṬ**, **RṢP**, **RŠM**, **ŠPN**, **ŠDP** and **ŠTM**.

4.1.4.2 The distribution of the pass. qal-participle over the various books. The OT contains 784 forms of the pass. qal-pt. of the roots of which ni.-forms occur according to my calculations. Below I will first present a general overview of the number of forms per book of the Bible, irrespective of their genre. Aside from that, the numbers of participles of the ni., pu., ho., and hitp. will be presented. It must be understood that the numbers of pu., ho. and hitp. include all forms of these verbal stems in the OT, whereas the numbers of the pass. qal participles refer only to those roots of which ni.-forms occur.

	Pass.qal pt.	Ni.-pt.	Pu.-pt.	Ho.-pt.	Hitp.-pt.
Gen	39	26	3	4	4
Ex	19	26	19	27	2
Lev	13	23	1	2	12
Num	88	13	3	5	4
Deut	69	28	5	-	2
Pent	228	116	31	38	24

It should be acknowledged that the numbers presented above include the pass. participle of the root **PQD** (occurring 59 times in Num.) and of the root **ARR** (which occurs 18 times in Deut.).

	Pass.qal pt.	Ni.-pt.	Pu.-pt.	Ho.-pt.	Hitp.-pt.
Josh	18	19	5	-	1
Judg	9	16	2	1	3
1 Sam	20	43	2	2	10
2 Sam	18	18	3	3	8
1 Kin	41	27	6	8	7
2 Kin	41	25	10	8	3
Josh-Kin	147	148	28	22	32

Note that 14 pass. qal pt. of **KTB** occur in 1 Kin. and 27 in 2 Kin.

	Pass.qal pt.	Ni.-pt.	Pu.-pt.	Ho.-pt.	Hitp.-pt.
Isa	71	98	28	7	9
Jer	47	68	7	9	10
Ez	36	46	14	15	7
Hos	7	5	2	-	-
Jo	1	3	-	-	-
Am	6	1	-	1	1
Ob	1	-	-	-	-
Jon	-	3	-	-	-
Mi	3	6	-	1	-
Nah	-	4	3	-	-
Hab	1	2	1	-	-
Zeph	5	9	-	-	-
Hag	1	1	-	-	2
Zech	2	13	-	1	2
Mal	2	7	2	2	-
Total	183	269	57	36	31
Hos-Mal	29	57	8	5	5

Ps	56	98	22	3	10
Job	17	22	3	2	6
Pro	12	48	11	2	13
Total	85	168	36	7	29

Note that 17 pass. qal.-pt. of **BRK** occur in the book of Psalms.

	Pass.qal pt.	Ni.-pt.	Pu.-pt.	Ho.-pt.	Hitp.-pt.
Ruth	4	2	1	-	1
Song	6	4	4	-	1
Eccl	8	7	1	1	-
Lam	4	5	1	-	-
Esth	14	7	3	-	2
Dan	5	10	-	1	4
Ezra	4	4	5	1	4
Neh	27	14	5	-	7
1Chron	18	22	8	1	4
2Chron	51	25	9	8	10
Total	141	100	37	12	33

Moreover, the pass. qal pt. of **KTB** occurs 24 times in 2 Chron. Our calculations reveal the following totals for the OT:

	Pass.qal pt.	Ni.-pt.	Pu.-pt.	Ho.-pt.	Hitp.-pt.
Total	784	801	188	155	149

It would be premature to draw conclusions from statistics presented here and in the rest of this paragraph. A certain book may contain relatively frequent occurrences of a certain participle due to a variety of causes; apart from linguistic reasons, factors such as content, genre, and the presence of direct or indirect speech affect the results. Moreover, it should be taken into consideration that out of 782 forms 71 are derived from the root **BRK**, 40 from **ARR**, 112 from **KTB**, 30 from **NṬH**, and 78 from **PQD**. It is not useful, in my opinion, to calculate the various percentages here, as was done in the case of the ni., pu., and ho. above, because the material under discussion is far too diverse in character.

4.1.4.3 Distribution of the pass. qal-participle over the various genres

4.1.4.3.1 Prose. The total number of forms occurring in prose is the following:

Pass.qal pt.	Ni.-pt.	Pu.-pt.	Ho.-pt.	Hitp.-pt.
544	431	105	89	104

4.1.4.3.2 Poetry.

a) Poetry in the Pentateuch shows these amounts of ni.:

	Pass.qal pt.	Ni.-pt.	Pu.-pt.	Ho.-pt.	Hitp.-pt.
Gen.49	1	-	-	-	-
Ex.15	-	3	1	-	-
Num.23,24	3	-	-	-	-
Deut.33	7	-	1	-	-
Total	11	3	2	-	-

b) The poetry parts of Joshua - Kings:

	Pass.qal pt.	Ni.-pt.	Pu.-pt.	Ho.-pt.	Hitp.-pt.
Judg.5	1	-	-	-	-
1Sam.2	-	1	-	-	-
2Sam	3	2	1	2	-
Total	4	3	1	2	-

c) The poetical books:

	Pass.qal pt.	Ni.-pt.	Pu.-pt.	Ho.-pt.	Hitp.-pt.
Ps	56	98	22	3	10
Pro	12	48	11	2	13
Job	17	20	3	2	4
Song	6	4	1	-	1
Lam	4	5	4	-	-
Total	95	175	41	7	28

(We note that there are no pass. qal-participles to be found in the prose parts of Job chs.1, 2 and 42:7-17.

d) Other poetry:

1Chron.16	2	4	1	-	1

Poetry texts in the OT as a whole show the following distribution:

	Pass.qal pt.	Ni.-pt.	Pu.-pt.	Ho.-pt.	Hitp.-pt.
OT Total	112	185	44	8	29

4.1.4.3.3 Prophecy

	Pass.qal pt.	Ni.-pt.	Pu.-pt.	Ho.-pt.	Hitp.-pt.
Isa	67	94	27	7	8
Jer	32	36	4	6	3
Ez	-	1	-	-	-

For prose, these books reveal these results:

	Pass.qal pt.	Ni.-pt.	Pu.-pt.	Ho.-pt.	Hitp.-pt.
Isa	4	4	1	-	1
Jer	15	31	3	3	-
Ez	36	45	14	15	-

The following tabulation represents findings for the twelve minor prophets except for the book of Jonah:

	Pass.qal pt.	Ni.-pt.	Pu.-pt.	Ho.-pt.	Hitp.-pt.
	29	54	8	5	5
Jonah 2	-	-	-	-	-
Total	29	54	8	5	5

The total number of occurrences in the prophetic genre amounts to the following:

Pass.qal pt.	Ni.-pt.	Pu.-pt.	Ho.-pt.	Hitp.-pt.
128	185	39	18	16

Below I list the totals of the various genres including the percentages per verbal stem according to the respective genres:

	Pass.qal pt.	Ni.-pt.	Pu.-pt.	Ho.-pt.	Hitp.-pt.
TOT OT	784 (100 %)	801 (100 %)	188 (100%)	115 (100 %)	149 (100 %)
Prose	544 (69.4%)	431 (53.8%)	105 (55.9%)	89 (77.4%)	104 (69.8%)
Poetry	112 (14.3%)	185 (23.1%)	44 (23.4%)	8 (7 %)	29 (19.5%)
Prophecy	128 (16.3%)	185 (23.1%)	39 (20.7%)	18 (15.6%)	16 (10.7%)

As observed above, the figures and percentages have limited value.

4.1.5 The hitpa'el in the OT

4.1.5.1 Introduction. In comparison with other passive/reflexive verbal stems much has been published on the hitp.[231] A list of all forms and roots may be found in Stein, *Der Stamm des Hithpa'el im Hebräischen,* Leipzig, 1893. According to this calculation there are 225 roots with a total of 1151 hitp.- and other constructed forms with the prefix **HiT-**. However, Bean reports a smaller number of hitp. forms in his dissertation on the hitp. of 1976. He does not mention the number of roots concerned. The reason why Bean reports a smaller number of forms than Stein's is that he includes in his research only those forms that are conjugated according to the normal paradigm of the hitp. He excludes forms of a different paradigm from his discussion, such as hitpo'lel, hitpalpel, hitpalpal, hitpa'lel and nitpa'el.

Bean enumerates all hitp.-forms included in his research in a list in an appendix on p. 188-194. Unfortunately, the list is not ordered according to the respective roots, such as Stein's list, but according to the respective books of the Bible. His enumeration shows that hitp. forms may be found in each book of the OT with exception of Jo. Ob. and Mal.

Jenni in THAT, 542 reports an even smaller total: 830 forms distributed over 175 roots, each of which amounting to 11.2 % of the total number of roots. According to my own calculations, based on Mandelkern and the various editions of the lexicon of HAL, there are 181 roots of which hitp.-forms occur in the OT. The differences between the various calculations are probably due to the fact that grammarians have different opinions on which forms should be regarded as hitp. In view of the purpose of this study, the description of the ni., it seemed inappropriate to make a statement about this. I have adopted Bean's list and refrain from providing statistics for hitp. divided according to prose, poetry, and prophecy as was done in 4.1.2.3 and 4.1.3.3 for the pu. and ho.

Below I present first of all an overview of the hitp.-forms, ordered according to the respective book of the Bible, based on Bean's list. Since Bean does not distinguish between the various tenses I have added these distinctions. The numbers between parenthesis refer to the numbers Stein mentions for the separate books.

4.1.5.2 The distribution of hitpa'el forms over the various books of the Old Testament

	Total	Part.	Perf.	Imperf.	Inf.	Impv.
Gen	41 (66)	4	9	19	3	6
Ex	17 (29)	2	3	7	-	5
Lev	28 (31)	12	8	8	-	-
Num	45 (50)	4	10	26	2	3
Deut[232]	34 (44)	2	11	18	2	1
Pentateuch	165(220)	24	41	78	7	15
	(100%)	(14.5%)	(24.8%)	(47.3%)	(4.2%)	(9.1%)
cf. Ni.	(100%)	(13.2%)	(32 %)	(44.2%)	(6.6%)	(4.1%)
cf. Pu.	(100%)	(36 %)	(54.7%)	(9.3%)	(0.1%)	(0 %)
cf. Ho.	(100%)	(26.6%)	(18.9%)	(51 %)	(3.5%)	(0 %)

We observe that there is a remarkably high number of imperatives among hitp. forms. However, the percentage of pt.-forms is fairly low in comparison to percentages of pu. and ho. respectively.

	Total	Part.	Perf.	Imperf.	Inf.	Impv.
Isa	74 (91)	9	13	34	8	10
Jer	58 (70)	10	8	28	-	12
Ez	28 (33)	7	6	13	1	1
Hos	5 (5)	-	-	5	-	-
Jo	-	-	-	-	-	-
Amos	3 (3)	1	-	2	-	-
Ob	-	-	-	-	-	-
Jon	6 (6)	-	-	5	1	-
Micah[233]	5 (6)	-	-	4	-	1
Nahum	4 (5)	-	1	1	-	2
Hab	4 (5)	-	-	3	-	1
Zeph	1 (4)	-	-	-	-	1
Hag	2 (2)	2	-	-	-	-
Zech	8 (10)	2	1	2	2	1
Mal	-	-	-	-	-	-
Total	198 (240)	31	29	97	12	29

	Total	Part.	Perf.	Imperf.	Inf.	Impv.
Prophecy	(100%)	(15.6%)	(14.7%)	(49 %)	(6.1%)	(14.6%)
cf. Ni.	(100%)	(19.6%)	(37.9%)	(33.5%)	(5 %)	(4 %)
cf. Pu.	(100%)	(34.1%)	(53.9%)	(12 %)	(0 %)	(0 %)
cf. Ho.	(100%)	(28.6%)	(35.7%)	(31.7%)	(3.2%)	(0.8%)
Hos-Mal	38	5	2	22	3	6
Ps	105 (123)	10	10	75	8	2
Job	58 (69)	6	2	40	5	5
Pro	42 (45)	13	2	21	5	1
Total	205 (237)	29	14	136	18	8
	(100%)	(14.1%)	(6.8%)	(66.3%)	(8.8%)	(3.9%)
cf. Ni.	(100%)	(28 %)	(32.1%)	(36.4%)	(2.2%)	(1.3%)
cf. Pu.	(100%)	(32.7%)	(28.2%)	(38.2%)	(0.9%)	(0 %)
cf. Ho.	(100%)	(19.4%)	(27.8%)	(50 %)	(0 %)	(2.8%)

Here, the high percentage of imperfects and the low percentage of perfects of the hitp. is remarkable.

	Total	Part.	Perf.	Imperf.	Inf.	Impv.
Ruth	1 (2)	1	-	-	-	-
Song	1 (1)	1	-	-	-	-
Eccl	6 (6)	-	1	5	-	-
Lam	6 (6)	-	-	4	2	-
Esth	5 (9)	2	-	2	1	-
Dan	25 (28)	4	1	18	2	-
Ezra	15 (15)	4	4	-	7	-
Neh	15 (18)	7	-	7	1	-
1Chron	34 (37)	4	7	8	13	2
2Chron	73 (85)	10	20	28	12	3
Total	181 (207)	33	33	72	38	5
	(100%)	(18.2%)	(18.2%)	(39.8%)	(21 %)	(2.8%)
cf. Ni.	(100%)	(18.2%)	(38.5%)	(34.7%)	(7.5%)	(1.1%)
cf. Pu.	(100%)	(77.1%)	(14.6%)	(8.3%)	(0 %)	(0 %)
cf. Ho.	(100%)	(32.4%)	(40.5%)	(21.6%)	(5.4%)	(0 %)
Total OT	946 (1151)	149	156	475	93	73
	(100%)	(15.8%)	(16.5%)	(50.2%)	(9.8%)	(7.7%)
cf. Ni.	(100%)	(19.3%)	(34.9%)	(37.3%)	(5.7%)	(2.8%)
cf. Pu.	(100%)	(41.1%)	(41.8%)	(16.6%)	(0.4%)	(0 %)
cf. Ho.	(100%)	(27.2%)	(26.5%)	(42.2%)	(3.1%)	(0.5%)

The respective percentages of hitp.-imperfects, infinitives, and imperatives is relatively high, the respective percentages of hitp.- participles and perfects is relatively low.

4.1.5.3 The distribution of hitp.-forms over the various genres

4.1.5.3.1 Prose. OT prose contains the following amounts of hitp.-forms:

	Total	Part.	Perf.	Imperf.	Inf.	Impv.
	575	104	120	246	64	41
	(100%)	(18.1%)	(20.9%)	(42.8%)	(11.1%)	(7.1%)
cf. Ni.	(100%)	(16.7%)	(33.3%)	(39.4%)	(7.3%)	(3.3%)
cf. Pu.	(100%)	(51.2%)	(41.5%)	(6.8%)	(0.5%)	(0 %)
cf. Ho.	(100%)	(30.4%)	(23.2%)	(41.6%)	(4.5%)	(0.3%)

In this case there is also a remarkably frequent occurrence of hitp. infinitives and imperatives.

4.1.5.3.2 Poetry

The poetic parts of the OT contain the amounts of hitp.-forms listed below. Note that in the prose parts of Job there are 7 hitp. forms to be found: 2 participles and 5 infinitives. The relatively small amount of hitp.-participles is quite remarkable.

	Total	Part.	Perf.	Imperf.	Inf.	Impv.
Ps	105	10	10	75	8	2
Pro	42	13	2	21	5	1
Job	51	4	2	40	-	5
Lam	6	-	-	4	2	-
Song	1	1	-	-	-	-
Num.23,24	4	-	-	4	-	-
Deut.31,32	2	-	-	1	1	-
2Sam.22	8	-	-	8	-	-
2Kin.19	2	-	-	-	2	-
1Chron.16	2	-	-	1	-	1
1Chron.29	4	1	1	-	2	-
Total	227	29	15	154	20	9
	(100%)	(12.8%)	(6.6%)	(67.8%)	(8.8%)	(4 %)
cf. Ni.	(100%)	(28.1%)	(34.3%)	(34.1%)	(2 %)	(1.5 %)
cf. Pu.	(100%)	(35.7%)	(27.6%)	(35.7%)	(0.8%)	(0 %)
cf. Ho.	(100%)	(19.5%)	(29.3%)	(48.8%)	(0 %)	(2.4 %)

4.1.5.3.3 Prophecy. The prophetic parts of the OT contain the following numbers of hitp.-forms:

	Total	Part.	Perf.	Imperf.	Inf.	Impv.
Isa	65	8	11	31	6	9
Jer	42	3	6	25	-	8
Ez	3	-	2	1	-	-
Hos-Mal	34	5	2	18	3	6
Total	144	16	21	75	9	23
Prophecy	(100%)	(11.1%)	(14.6%)	(52.1%)	(6.2%)	(16 %)
cf. Ni.	(100%)	(20.6%)	(39.7%)	(33.3%)	(3.9%)	(2.4%)
cf. Pu.	(100%)	(30.2%)	(55.8%)	(14 %)	(0 %)	(0 %)
cf. Ho.	(100%)	(22.2%)	(37 %)	(40.7%)	(0 %)	(0 %)

Below the percentages are listed for the different genres:

	Total	Part.	Perf.	Imperf.	Inf.	Impv.
OT	100%	15.8%	16.5%	50.2%	9.8%	7.7%
Prose	100%	18.1%	20.9%	42.8%	11.1%	7.1%
Poetry	100%	12.8%	6.6%	67.8%	8.8%	4 %
Prophecy	100%	11.1%	14.6%	52.1%	6.2%	16 %

The following observations can be made in view of the comparison of the frequency of hitp. verbal forms in the various genres: In prose hitp.-participles occur relatively frequently (18.1% vs. poetry 12.8% and prophecy 11.1%). It is possible that this correlates with the respective genre in which the forms occur. For participles occur relatively frequently in pu. (51.2% vs. resp. 35.7% and 30.2%) and ho. as well: (30.4% vs. 19.5% and 22.2%). The ni. seems to be the exception to the rule. Ni.-participles occur less frequently in prose than in poetry and prophecy (16.7% vs. resp. 28.1% and 20.6%).

For poetry, we note the low percentage of hitp.-perfects (6.6%) and the high percentage of hitp.-imperfects (67.8%). There might be a possible correlation between these figures and the genre in which the forms occur.

4.1.5.4 Conclusion. Finally, I present the percentages of ni., pu., and hitp. for the whole OT:

	Total	Part.	Perf.	Imperf.	Inf.	Impv.
Ni.	100%	19.3%	34.3%	37.3%	5.7%	2.8%
Pu.	100%	41.1%	41.8%	16.6%	0.4%	-
Ho.	100%	27.2%	26.5%	42.2%	3.1%	0.5%
Hitp.	100%	15.8%	16.5%	50.2%	9.8%	7.7%

The hitp. occurs relatively often as an imperative. In my view this relates to the fact that the forms of this verbal stem often express active meaning contrary to the pu., ho., and to a lesser extent the ni. (see 4.4.1).

4.2 The niph'al-pu'al relationship

4.2.1 Introduction and methodology

4.2.1.1 Passive qal and pu'al. Before we will discuss the relationship between the pu. and the ni. in the OT, we will deal with the question as to what extent certain pu.-forms are remainders of a lost passive-qal. The fact that there are no corresponding pi.- or hi.-forms for a great number of pu.- and ho.-forms has led certain grammarians to the supposition that certain pu.- and ho.-forms in reality belong to the qal-passive.[234]

The most recent article on the passive qal-stem in classical Hebrew is that published by R.J. Williams: "The passive qal theme in Hebrew". In it, Williams presents an overview of older literature on the subject and a list of the roots which, according to his opinion, should be regarded as old passive qal forms. He lists a total of 52 verb roots.[235]

According to Williams' theory and that of his predecessors, originally, a passive of the qal stem existed in West-Semitic languages with the forms **QuṬiLa/YuQṬaL(u)**, which corresponded to the active forms of the qal- perf. and imperf. The forms also existed in Hebrew. Yet ni.-stem, which was the original reflexive of the qal, in usage more and more became the qal passive and, therefore, usage of the original passive of the qal was abandoned. The process, according to Williams, was completed in the days of Biblical Hebrew.[236] However, many remainders can be found in the Masoretic text. Among his examples Williams includes a.o. forms of the root **AKL** (Neh. 2:3, 13; Nahum 1:10 **AūKKeLū**); **ṬRP** (Gen.37:33; 44:28 **ṬōRāP**); **ŠPK** (Zeph.1:17; Num.35:33 **ŠūPPaK**).

The Masoretes interpreted these as pu.- or ho.-forms. Williams is of the opinion that, in fact, many forms of the ni.-imperfect of these roots are passive qals, which were not recognized by the Masoretes as such, for they have been punctuated as ni.[237]

In my view it is quite probable that Hebrew, just like other West-Semitic languages, has had a passive of the qal. Indeed, OT Hebrew contains many occurrences of the participle of the passive qal **QāTūL**. This might explain the existence of a number of pu.- and ho.- forms for which corresponding pi. and hi. are lacking.

In this respect we wish to point at the existence of passive forms of the basic root of the type **YuQṬaL(u)** in the texts of El-Amarna, especially in the letters of Rib-Addi. These Canaanitic forms occur mainly for the stems *lequ* and *nadanu* (cf. **LQḤ** and **NTN**). Therefore, it is not improbable that the pu.-forms of these roots are pass. qals in Hebrew.[238]

Yet I would like to voice certain critical remarks with respect to the theory that certain pu.- and ho.- forms are remainders of the lost passive of the qal.

1) The theory is based on the assumption that, originally, the ni. conveyed reflexive meaning and that only in a later stage it gained a passive meaning. However, as we observed above in chapter 1.3 the assumption cannot be proven so in actual fact its truth value is questionable.

2) Indirectly the theory is based on the assumption that the verbal stems originally formed a closed system within which each verbal stem had its own fixed place. Many grammarians have decided to regard certain pu.-forms as remainders of the passive qal. They have based their decision on the fact that there are indeed pu.-forms, which cannot be related to the pi. since forms of these verbal stems are lacking, but which may be related to the qal.

We observed above that this assumption cannot be proven either. Moreover, it is evident that Masoretic Hebrew does not appear to have a closed system. Ni.-forms may occur in a semantic relationship to the pi. or hi.; similarly, pu.-forms may occur in a semantic relationship to the qal.

3) Irrespective of the accuracy or inaccuracy of the theory mentioned under 2), many questions remain to be answered:

a) Which criteria should we apply to distinguish 'hidden' passive-qal forms from 'genuine' pu.- or ho.-forms?[239]

b) How can it be explained that forms, which Williams

regards as remainders of the passive qal, occur not only in relatively old texts (e.g. Pentateuch) but also in quite young texts? (Compare e.g. **AuKKeLū** in Neh. 2:3, 13; Nahum 1:10; comparatively many forms occur in Isa; Ez; Zeph; etc.)

c) In what way can it be explained that two participle forms of the passive qal may occur side by side (e.g. **JLD**: Judg. 13:8 (**JūLaD**) vs. 1Kin. 3:26, 27 (**JāLūD**).

d) In this respect, how should we regard the relationship pu.-ho.? Why were the passive qal forms of two verbal stems used? (Usu. pu.-perf. and ho.-imperf.)

e) When did the passive qal end up in disuse? Did it still exist at the time of writing of the earliest OT texts? Williams maintains that it had become obsolete before that time. Below we will examine if, and to what extent, our research into the relationship between ni. and pu. can shed new light on the theory of the passive qal.

4.2.1.2 Method of research. We noted that there are 193 verb roots of which pu.-forms occur in the OT. Moreover, pu.- and ni.-forms co-occur of 89 of the 193 roots, which equals about 46 %. In total there are about 1179 in.-forms and 226 pu.-forms. I adopted the following approach for my research:

1) The roots and forms are first categorized according to their respective genre (prose, poetry and prophecy). In the prose texts 39 verb roots are accounted for of which pu.- as well as ni.-forms occur. It concerns 22 and 32 verb roots respectively for poetry and prophecy.

2) Subsequently, the roots are subdivided per genre into four groups according to the following criteria:

I Roots of which the niph'al occurs in a pass./refl. semantic relationship to the qal:

a) Roots of which no pi.-forms occur:
Which semantic and/or functional relationship exists between the ni. and pu. of these roots? May the pu. be regarded as a passive of a hypothetical pi.-stem, or, is there a different explanation that may account for this? What is the mutual relationship between ni.-pt., pu.-pt, and pass. qal-pt.?

b) Roots of which pi.-forms occur:
For this group it is interesting to answer the question about the nature of the relationship between pi. and pu. Is the pu. the pi.-passive? If not, what is its relationship to the ni.?

II Roots of which the niph'al occurs in a pass./refl. semantic relationship to the pi'el:
Which relationship exists here between ni. and pu? Is there an overlap or supplementation? If so, how can it be explained?

III Roots of which the niph'al occurs in a pass./refl. semantic relationship to the hiph'il:
Which relationship exists here between ni. and ho. (in as far as these forms occur) on the one hand and pu. on the other?

IV Roots of which the semantic relationship of the niph'al to the qal, pi'el or hiph'il is unclear:
Here we are dealing with roots of which forms of the active verbal stems are lacking or, of which the semantic value of the ni. is unrelated to one of the active verbal stems in as far as can be observed. What is the semantic relationship between the ni. and pu. of these roots?

3) Next we will study the relationship between ni. and pu. against the background of all the assembled material. There are 15 roots of which ni.- and pu.- forms do not co-occur in a single genre. Therefore, these roots were not discussed before. To what extent do the conclusions, which were made for the individual genres, apply for all the material concerned?

4) In the final conclusion we will examine if and to what extent our conclusions support the theory of the passive qal.

4.2.2 The niph'al-pu'al relationship in the various genres

4.2.2.1 The niph'al-pu'al relationship in prose. In the prose texts of the OT 39 verb roots may be found forms of which occur both in ni.- as well as in pu. The ni., which occurs in 431 forms, appears in formal opposition to the pu. which occurs in 87 forms. The following classification of these roots can be made (starting with the greatest group):

I Roots of which the ni. occurs in semantic relationship to the qal: 27.
a) Roots of which no pi.-forms occur in prose: 15.
b) Roots of which pi.-forms occur in prose: 12.

II Roots of which the ni. occurs in semantic relationship to the pi.: 8.
a) Roots of which no qal-forms occur in prose: 4.
b) Roots of which qal-forms do occur in prose: 4.

III Roots of which the ni. occurs in semantic relationship to the hi.: 3.

IV Roots of which the semantic relationship to the qal, pi. or hi. is unclear: 2.

Below I will discuss these roots per group.

Ia Roots of which the ni. occurs in semantic relationship to the qal and of which no pi.-forms occur in prose: 15.
I will restrict my discussion to two questions:
1) Which relationship exists between the pu. and ni. of these roots?
2) What kind of relationship obtains between the ni.-pt., pu.-pt., and the pass. qal-pt.?

First, we present a survey of the distribution of ni.- and pu.-verb forms over the various tenses. Moreover, we will show the number of forms of the qal, pass. qal-pt. and hitp. of these roots which occur in prose:[240]

Root	Ni. Tot	Pt	Perf	Impf	Rest	Pu. Tot	Pt	Perf	Impf	Rest	Qal	P.Q.pt.	Hitp.
AKL	38	1	1	34	2	3	1	2	–	–	M	–	–
BḤN	2	–	–	2	–	1	–	1	–	–	–	–	–
ṬRP	1	–	–	2	–	2	–	2	–	–	5	–	–
JD'	24	–	14	9	1	2	2	–	–	–	M	1	2
KRT	43	–	24	18	1	2	–	2	–	–	M	2	–
LQḤ	10	–	4	3	3	6	1	5	–	–	M	–	2
MRṬ	2	–	–	2	–	3	1	2	–	–	6	3	–
'BD	3	–	2	2	–	1	–	1	–	–	M	–	–
PQD	16	–	4	10	2	1	–	1	–	–	M	78	4
PRṢ	2	1	1	–	–	2	2	–	–	–	29	3	1
QRA	36	2	16	18	–	1	–	1	–	–	M	9	–
QŠR	2	–	1	1	–	1	1	–	–	–	28	2	3
ŚRP	11	–	–	11	–	1	–	1	–	–	M	3	–
ŠṬP	2	–	–	2	–	1	–	1	–	–	10	–	–
ŠPK	6	–	1	4	1	1	–	1	–	–	62	2	–

Forms of qal, pi., or hitp. of a number of these roots do not occur in prose, yet they may be found in poetry or prophecy. For the sake of completeness they are listed below:

BḤN	:	Qal: 15 in poetry, 10 in prophecy
JD'	:	Pi.: 1 in poetry (Job 38:12)
LQḤ	:	Pass. qal-partic.: 1 in poetry (Pro. 24:11)
PQD	:	Pi.: 1 in prophecy (Isa. 13:4)
ŠPK	:	Hitp.: 3 in poetry (Lam. 2:12; 4:1 and Job 30:16)

It is remarkable that two-thirds of the number of roots is represented as a pass. qal-pt. Especially the root **PQD** occurs in significant numbers with a total of 78 forms. The hitp., on the contrary, occurs at a much lower frequency (5 times). This may not be used as an argument as to whether or not the pi. occurred among these roots. In absolute numbers the hitp. occurs less often in Biblical Hebrew anyhow. There are eight roots, among those of which pi.-forms occur in prose (group Ib: 12), of which hitp.-forms are lacking.

Calculation of the share of the individual verb tenses within the total of the ni. and pu. of this group results in the following outcome. Numbers between parentheses refer to the total in prose.

	Total	Participle	Perfect	Imperfect	Rest
Niph'al	200 (2584)	4 (431)	68 (861)	118 (1018)	10 (277)
	87.7%(92.6%)	33.3%(80.4%)	77.3%(91%)	100%(98.6%)	100%(99.6%)
Pu'al	31 (205)	8 (105)	20 (85)	– (14)	– (1)
	12.3%(7.4%)	66.7%(19.6%)	22.7%(9%)	0%(1.4%)	0%(0.4%)
Total	228 (2789)	12 (536)	88 (946)	118 (1032)	10 (277)

These results compel us to make the following comments:

a) The imperfect does not occur for the pu. The number of forms of the ni.-imperf., on the contrary, is relatively great. This agrees with the general tendency of the ni. and pu. in prose (see above); we note a low percentage of pu.-imperfects and a high percentage of ni.-imperfects.

For 13 out of 15 roots it is difficult to determine a clear distinction in semantic content of the forms of the ni. and those of the pu. Moreover, the pu. in these cases may just as well, or perhaps even much more, be regarded as the passive of the qal:

AKL means in the ni. 'be eaten' and twice 'be burned, be consumed', (Ex. 22:5; Ez. 23: 25), the pu. also expresses the meaning of 'be burned, be consumed' (Neh. 2:3, 13; Ex. 3:2; Isa. 1:20).

ṬRP both in the ni. (Ex. 22:12) as well as in the pu. (Gen. 37:33; 44:28) means to be 'torn apart' (by a wild animal). NB. both forms are made with a qal inf. abs.!

KRT pu. (Ez. 16: 4; Judg. 6:28) has the meaning of 'be cut off, be cut down', cf. qal 2 Kin. 18:4.

LQḤ occurs both in the ni. (10 times, cf. 2 Kin. 2:9) as well as in the pu. (9 occurrences, cf. 2 Kin. 2:10). Of this root ho. and hitp. occur apart from the qal, ni. and pu.

MRṬ Here slight differences in meaning can be detected. The ni. (Lev. 13:40, 41 'be(come) bold') may be regarded as a passive of a qal 'make bare', Ez. 29:18, or of 'pull out hair', Ezra 9:3; Neh. 13:25. The pu. may be regarded (Ez. 21:15, 16 'be sharpened') as a passive of a qal 'sharpen', Ez. 21:14, 33.

'BD in the ni. (4 occurrences, Eccl. 5:8; Ez. 36:9, 34 and Deut. 21:4) has the meaning of 'be tilled' (E.g. that of Eccl. 5:8 is somewhat divergent), the pu. (once, in Deut. 21:3) is the passive of a qal 'be worked' with a heifer.

PQD in the pu. has (once Ex. 38:21 the meaning of 'be counted', cf. the qal Num. 1:3, 19, 44, 49, etc. and also pass. qal participle Ex. 38:21 'cost'.

PRṢ Here the meaning of the ni. (1 Sam. 3:1 and 1 Chron. 13: 2) is not clear. The pu. (Neh. 1:3) can be linked to the qal (Neh. 4:1; 2 Kin. 14:3; 2 Chron. 25:23).

QŠR occurs in the pu. once (pt. Gen. 30:41), cf. pass. qal pt. Gen. 30:24, said of small live stock 'strong'.

QRA Here pu. occurs once (Ez. 10:13) meaning 'be called' (+ **Le**), cf. ni. Jer. 19:6; 2 Sam. 18:18 'be called' (+ **Le**) and qal Jer. 30:17; 33:16, etc.

ŚRP has both in the ni. (cf. Lev. 6:23) as well as in the pu. (Lev. 10:6) the meaning of 'be burnt' by fire.

ŠṬP has, both in the ni. (cf. Lev. 15:12) as well as in the pu. (Lev. 6:21), the meaning of 'be rinsed' with water.

ŠPK in the pu. (Num. 35:33) has the meaning of 'be poured out' of blood, cf. ni. Deut. 19:10 and qal Gen. 37:22.

Only for the roots of **BḤN** and **JD'** it is impossible to establish a clear relationship between the pu. and qal.

BḤN the meaning of the pu. in Ez. 21:18 is uncertain. It is probable that this is not a perfect but a noun. Since it is the only pu.-form of the root, it is hard to draw any conclusion from it.

JD' The pu. pt. is used independently with the meaning of 'family member', Ruth. 2:1; 2 Kin. 10:11.

The Masoretic text appears to show preference for usage of the perfect for the pu. and the imperfect for the ni. among the above-mentioned group of 13 roots. For a number of roots (**ṬRP**, **MRṬ**, **ŚRP** and **ŠṬP**) two complementary forms of one pattern occur: ni.-imperf. and pu.-perf. Other roots indicate a tendency towards this kind of complementary relationship: (**AKL**, **PQD**, **QRA**, and **ŠPK**).

Especially the book of Ezekiel shows a remarkable preference for pu.-perf. and ni.-imperf.: cf. **QRA** ni.-imperf. (Ez. 20:29) vs. pu.-perf. (Ez. 10:13). Compare also **AKL** ni.-imperf. (Ez. 23:25; 45:21) vs. pu. (no perf.), and compare **KRT** and **MRṬ**.[241]

For 10 out of 14 roots (**AKL**, **ṬRP**, **KRT**, **LQḤ**, **MRṬ**, **'BD**, **QRA**, **ŚRP**, **ŠṬP** and **ŠPK**) the pu.-forms may be regarded as remains of the pass. qal. according to Williams.[242] Lambert, for the remaining 5 roots (**BḤN**, **JD'**, **PQD**, **QŠR** and **PRṢ**), treats the pu.-perf. of **PQD** as a remains of the pass. qal.[243]

b) Mutual comparison of the participial-forms of ni., pu. and pass. qal results in an important picture, especially with respect to the overlaps. Below, we present the different figures per root:

Root	Ni.-participle	Pu.-participle	Pass. Qal-participle
AKL	1 (Lev. 11:47)	1 (Ex. 3:2)	-
JD'	-	2 (Ruth 2:11; 2 Kin. 10:11)	2 (Deut. 1:13, 15)
KRT	-	-	3
LQḤ	-	1	-
MRṬ	-	1 (1 Kin. 7:45)	3 (Ez. 21: 14, 33; 29:18
PQD	-	-	78
PRṢ	1 (1 Sam. 3:1)	2 (Neh. 1:3; 2:13K)	3 (Neh. 2:13Q, 4:1; 2 Chron. 32:5)
QRA I	2 (Jer. 44:26; Esther 6:1)	-	9 (Num. 1:16Q; 26:19; 1 Sam. 9:13, 22; 2 Sam. 15:11; 1 Kin. 1:41, 49 Ez. 23:19; Esther 5:12)
QŠR	-	1 (Gen. 30: 41)	2 (Gen. 30: 24; 44:30)
ŚRP	-	-	3
ŠPK	-	-	2

Textual references have been supplied only for those roots of which participial forms of various verbal stems occur. The majority of passive participles consists of the 78 forms of the root **PQD**. The following outcome results if these figures are added up:
total 117: ni. 4 (3.4%), pu. 8 (6.8%), pass. qal-partic. 105 (89.8%) (excluding **PQD** 39: ni. 4(10.3%), pu. 8(20.5%), pass. qal-partic. 27 (69.2%)).

For a number of roots the participles overlap:

ni.-pu. :	**AKL**	(a difference in nuance: Lev. 11:47 'being eaten' vs. Ex. 3:2 'being consumed'
:	**PRŞ**	(difference in meaning: 1 Sam. 3:1 'distributed'(?) vs. pu. 'broken off'.
ni.-pass. qal-pt.:	**QRA**	(differences between ni. 'being read out' and pu. (substantive) 'invited one', 'be summoned' Num 1:16; 16:29).
:	**PRŞ**	(difference in meaning)
pu.-pass. qal-pt.:	**JD'**	(difference between pu. 'related' and pass. qal participle 'skilful'.
:	**MRŢ**	(no clear difference between pass. qal-participle 'sharpened' of a sword Ez. 21:14, 33 vs. pu. 1 Kin. 7:45 'polished', 'whetted' of copper).
:	**PRŞ**	(no difference in opinion between pass. qal participle and pu. It is remarkable that the Masoretes vocalized the pu.-form in Neh. 2:13K as a pass. qal, cf. 1:3, due to the difference in gender of the nominal and the participial form.
:	**QŠR**	(no difference between pass. qal-participle in Gen. 30:42 and pu.-participle in Gen. 30:41; nevertheless Gen. 44:30 'bound to', cf. ni. 1 Sam. 18:1!).

The ni. pt. and the pass. qal-pt. occur side by side for two roots (**PRŞ** and **QRA**). Four roots (**JD'**, **MRŢ**, **PRŞ**, and **QRA**) show co-occurrence of pu.-pt. and pass. qal-pt. These overlaps do not fit easily into the pass. qal theory. For five roots (**JD'**, **LQḤ**, **PQD**, **PRŞ** and **QŠR**) forms of the hitp. occur. Except for the root **PQD**, the forms have a meaning which may clearly be distinguished from that of the pu. and ni.[244]

Ib Roots of which the ni. occurs in semantic relationship to the qal and of which pi.-forms occur in prose: 12
In accordance with our treatment under 1a we will restrict ourselves to discussing two questions:
1) Which relationship exists between the pu. and ni. of these roots?
2) What is the mutual relationship between the ni.-pt., pu.-pt. and the pass. qal-pt.?

First, we present an overview of the distribution of verbal forms over the various tenses. Moreover, we mention how many forms of the qal, pi. and pass. qal-pt. of these roots occur in prose:

Root	Ni.					Pu.					Qal	P.Q.pt.	Pi.
	Total	Pt	Perf	Impf	Rest	Total	Pt	Perf	Impf	Rest			
ASP	58	2	19	32	5	1	1	-	-	-	M	1	5
BQ'	8	-	2	5	1	2	2	-	-	-	8	-	7

GNB	1	-	-	1	-	3	-	2	-	1	21	3	1
JLD	28	6	9	11	2	18	1	17	-	-	M	3	10
JSD	1	-	-	-	1	4	2	2	-	-	2	-	6
MNH	5	-	-	4	1	1	1	-	-	-	8	-	7
NTṢ	1	-	1	-	-	1	-	1	-	-	24	1	6
SGR	6	-	1	4	1	2	1	1	-	-	34	11	4
SQL	4	-	-	4	-	2	-	2	-	-	12	-	4
QBṢ	19	1	2	12	4	1	1	-	-	-	31	1	19
QBR	33	-	-	33	-	1	-	1	-	-	83	1	4
ŠLḤ	1	-	-	-	1	3	-	3	-	-	M	5	M
Total	165	9	34	106	16	399	29	-	1	26			

In prose, the hitp. of four roots occurs (**BQ'** 1; **GNB** 2; **JLD** 1; and **QBṢ** 6). Note that **ASP** occurs once as a inf. hitp. in poetry. The root **BQ'** is mentioned twice in this study. It is mentioned both here as well as under group IIb because it cannot be ascertained whether the ni.-forms occur in a relationship to the qal or to the pi. A calculation of the share of verb tenses among the totals of ni. and pu. of the group results in the following outcome. Parenthetical figures refer to respective totals in prose.

	Total	Participle	Perfect	Imperfect	Rest
Niph'al	165 (2584)	9 (431)	34 (861)	106 (1018)	16 (277)
	80.9%(92.6%)	50%(80.4%)	54%(91%)	100%(98.6%)	94.1%(99.6%)
Pu'al	39 (205)	9 (105)	29 (85)	- (14)	1 (1)
	19.1%(7.4%)	50%(19.6%)	46%(9%)	0%(1.4%)	5.9%(0.4%)
Total	204 (2789)	18 (536)	63 (946)	106 (1032)	17 (277)

Compare this outcome with the percentages applicable for group Ia:

	Total	Participle	Perfect	Imperfect	Rest
Niph'al	200	4	68	118	10
	87.7%	33.3%	77.3%	100%	100%
Pu'al	31	8	20	-	-
	12.3%	66.7%	22.7%	0%	0%
Total	231	12	88	118	10

Based on these figures the following remarks can be made:

a) The imperfect of the pu. of these roots does not occur. Yet the percentage of pu.-perfects is relatively high. This percentage is twice as high as for group Ia (22.7 % vs 46 %, cf. the total of pu.-perfects for prose being 9 %!).

Since pi. forms occur in this group of roots, one might expect that the pu. functions here as a passive of the pi. Yet, for a number of roots this is not the case. The pi. has a specific meaning, different from the qal, whereas the pu. functions as the pass. of the qal.

JLD pu. 'be born', cf. pi.-pt. 'midwife' (Ex. 1:15, 17 etc., 'help to deliver' (Ex. 1:16).

SGR pu. 'be closed' (Josh. 6:1; Eccl. 12:4), the pi. has the meaning of 'deliver someone' (1 Sam. 17:46; 18:18), cf. JENNI 1968, 199.

SQL pu. 'be stoned' of a man; yet the pi. has the meaning of 'throw stones' (2 Sam. 16:6, 13), cf. JENNI 1968, 209; the qal means: 'stone' (1 Kin. 21:13).

QBR pu. 'be buried' (Gen. 25:10); the pi. has the meaning of 'bury many' cf. JENNI 1968, 150ff.

Possibly, the same argument applies for the following roots:

ASP (?) pu. (Ez. 38:12) cf. pass. qal-partic. (Ez. 34:29).

GNB (?) pu. 'be abducted, stolen' (resp. Gen. 40:15; Ex. 22:6); cf. ni. 'be stolen' (Ex. 22:11) and pi. 'steal the heart', i.e. 'deceive' (2 Sam. 15:16), cf. JENNI 1968, 190ff.

NTṢ (?) pu. (Judg. 6:28) vs. qal (Judg. 6:30ff).

It is not easy to determine the pu.-qal or pu.-pi. relationship for the other roots (**BQ'**, **JSD**, **MNH**, **QBṢ** and **ŠLḤ**), since forms of the perf. and imperf. are lacking. Williams lists the forms of **JLD**, **NTṢ** and **QBR** as remains of the pass. qal-stem. We note a remarkable feature of the roots the pu.-forms of which grammarians do not regard as remains of the passive qal. For a number of them the pu. may occur in a relationship to the qal whilst, generally speaking, the pu. shows preference for usage of the perfect whilst the ni. shows preference for usage of the imperfect.

b) Mutual comparison of the participial forms of the ni., pu. and pass. qal results in an important finding, especially with respect to the overlaps. Below we record the different figures per individual root:

Root	Ni.-participle	Pu.-participle	Pass. Qal-participle
ASP	2 (Gen. 49:29; 1 Sam. 13:11)	1 (Ez. 38:12)	1 (Ez. 34:29)
BQ'	-	2	-
GNB	-	-	3
JLD	6 (Gen. 21:3; 48:5; 1 Kin. 13:2; 1 Chron. 7:21; 22:9; Ezra 10:3)	1 (Judg. 13:8)	3 (1 Kin. 3:26, 27 1 Chron. 14:14)
JSD	-	2	-
MNH	-	1	-
NTṢ	-	-	1
SGR	-	1 (Josh. 6:1)	11 (see below)
QBṢ	1 (Jer. 40:15)	1 (Ez. 38:8)	1 (Neh. 5:16)
QBR	-	-	1
ŠLḤ	-	-	5
	9	9	26

Textual references have been supplied only for the roots of which participial forms occur in various verbal stems.

The 11 forms of the pass. qal-participle of **SGR** are: in the expression **ZaHaB SăGŪR**: 1 Kin. 6:20, 21; 7:49, 50; 10:21; 2 Chron. 4:20, 22; 9:20; 'closed' of a gate: Ez. 44:1, 2; 46:1. Addition of these figures results in the following outcome: total 44; ni. 9 (20.5%), pu. 9 (20.5%), pass. qal-pt. 26 (59%)

Overlaps occur for the roots **ASP, JLD, SGR** and **QBṢ.** A difference in meaning between the pass. qal-participle (substantival use 'baby') and the forms of ni. and pu. is evident only in the case of the verb **JLD.** It should be noted that the participle-form of the pu. in Judg. 13:8 has been constructed without **Me-**! There is no evidence for a difference in meaning between the participle forms of ni., pu. and pass. qal. of the other roots.

In conclusion, we may state that both the pu.-pt. as well as the pass. qal-pt. occur for many of the above-mentioned roots. Yet the ni.-pt. occurs for only three of them. The significance of these particular findings remains to be questioned, since the absolute number of occurrences is fairly small.

II Roots of which the niph'al occurs in semantic relationship to the pi'el: 8

We will discuss IIa and IIb here together because only eight roots are involved. First, we present an overview of how the verbal forms of the ni. and the pu. are distributed over the various tenses. Moreover, we include information on how many forms of the qal, pi. and pass. qal-pt. of these roots occur in prose:

IIa Roots of which no qal-forms occur in prose: 4

Root	Ni.					Pu.					Pi.	Hitp.
	Tot	Pt	Perf	Impf	Rest	Tot	Pt	Perf	Impf	Rest		
BHL	7	-	4	3	-	1	1	-	-	-	5	-
ḤLL	9	-	3	2	4	1	1	-	-	-	50	-
KSH	1	-	-	-	1	5	2	-	3	-	M	3
'NH II	1	-	-	-	1	1	-	-	1	-	38	5

IIb Roots of which qal-forms occur in prose: 4

Root	Ni.					Pu.					Qal	Pi.	Hitp.
	Tot	Pt	Perf	Impf	Rest	Tot	Pt	Perf	Impf	Rest			
BQ'	8	-	2	5	1	1	1	-	-	-	8	7	1
BRK	3	-	3	-	-	3	2	-	1	-	44	M	3
ṬMA	15	2	13	-	-	1	1	-	-	-	71	45	14
QDŠ	10	-	6	2	2	4	4	-	-	-	9	60	22
Total	54	9	31	12	9	17	12	-	5	-			

Forms of the qal and hitp. of a few roots, which do not occur in prose, do occur in poetry:

KSH: qal: 3 occurrences in poetry (Pro. 12: 16, 23 participle, and Ps. 32:1 pass. participle.)

'NH: qal: 2 occurrences in poetry (Ps. 116:10; 119:67) and 2 in prophecy (Isa. 31:2; Zech. 10:2). According to GESENIUS 1915 the form **Jā'āNeH** in Isa. 25:5 is also a qal-form. Most commentators, however, read a hi.-form here. Vocalization does allow for this.

ṬMA: hotp. 1 occurrence in poetry (Deut. 24:4).

We have calculated the share of each verb tense within the total of the ni. and pu. for this group. The results are presented below. Figures between parentheses refer to the respective totals in prose.

	Total	Participle	Perfect	Imperfect	Rest
Niph'al	54 (2584)	2 (431)	31 (861)	12 (1018)	9 (277)
	76.1%(92.6%)	14.3%(80.4%)	100%(91%)	70.6%(98.6%)	100%(99.6%)
Pu'al	17 (205)	12 (105)	- (85)	5 (14)	- (1)
	23.9%(7.4%)	85.7%(19.6%)	0%(9 %)	29.4%(1.4%)	0%(0.4%)
Total	71 (2789)	14 (536)	31 (946)	17 (1032)	9 (277)

On the basis of these figures the following remarks can be made:

a) It is remarkable for this group that the pu.-perfects are lacking. This is contrary to our findings in groups Ia and Ib where especially the perfects of the pu. are found. We do note that there are 5 imperfects of the pu. in this group. There are no overlaps between ni. and pu. for the four roots of which qal-forms occur in prose. Nor do we record any overlaps for the two roots of group IIb (**BQ'** and **QDŠ**). The pu.-forms of these eight roots may be regarded as pure passives of the pi.

b) The relatively small number of participles of the ni. is quite remarkable (2x **ṬMA** Ez. 20:30, 31). The percentage of pu.-participles, however, is relatively high (12 out of 17 forms). For these roots it is impossible to make a clear distinction in meaning between pu. and ni. Forms of the pass. qal-participle occur only for the root **BRK** (42x). For six of these eight roots there are no overlaps between the various participles. Overlap does occur for **BRK** (pu. pt., 2x Num. 22:6; 1 Chron. 17:22) and pass. qal-pt. (Num. 22:12 etc.) and **ṬMA** (pu.-pt. Ez. 4:14 vs. ni.-pt. Ez. 20:30, 31).

III Roots of which the ni. occurs in semantic relationship to the hiph'il: 3

This group consists of only three roots. The distribution over the various tenses is as follows:

Root	Ni. Tot	Pt	Perf	Impf	Rest	Pu. Tot	Pt	Perf	Impf	Rest	Ho	Qal	Pi.	Hi.
NKH	1	-	1	-	-	2	-	2	-	-	10	-	-	M
PRD	9	2	2	3	2	1	1	-	-	-	-	-	1	7
ṢMD	2	1	-	1	-	1	1	-	-	-	-	-	-	1

The pi. of the root **PRD** occurs once in prophecy (Hos. 4:14) and its hitp. occurs four times in poetry.

Ho. forms occur only of the root **NKH** (10x: partic. 4x; perf. 5x and imperf. 1x) We will deal later with the ni.-ho. relationship.245 We note that there are clear semantic differences between the pu. and the ni. of these roots:

PRD: The pu.-participle of **PRD** 'set apart' (Esther 3:8) serves as a passive of the pi. (cf. Hos. 4:14). The participle of the ni. (e.g. Judg. 4:11; Neh. 4:13) has the meaning of 'having separated oneself', cf. JENNI 1968, 180.
NKH: pu. 'be smitten, destroyed' by hail (Ex. 9:31, 32) vs. ni. 'be hit' (2 Sam. 11:5).
ṢMD: pu. 'tied' (2 Sam. 20:8) vs. ni. 'join oneself to' (Num. 25:3, 5). No pi.-forms of **NKH** and **ṢMD** occur.

IV Roots of which the semantic relationship to qal, pi. or hi. is unclear: 2

Root	Niph'al	Pu'al	Qal	Pi'el	Hiph'il
PRŠ	1	2	1	-	-
TKN	9	1	-	-	-

The pi. of the root **PRŠ** occurs three times in poetry and six times in prophecy; the hi. occurs once in poetry (Pro. 23:32). The qal of the root **TKN** occurs three times in poetry (Pro. 16:2; 21:2; 24: 12); the pi. occurs twice in poetry (Job 28:25; Ps. 75:4) and twice in prophecy (Isa. 40:12, 13).

Little is to be said about these two roots:

PRŠ : Not a single semantic relationship between the ni. and the pu. appears to exist. According to certain commentators, the ni.-participle (Ez. 34:12) **NiPRăŠōT** should be read as **NiPRăŠōT** 'being dispersed'. The pu. (Num. 15: 34, perf. and Neh. 8:8, participle) has the following meanings, respectively. 'be established' and 'explained'(?). Perhaps these forms should be regarded as qal passives (1x Lev. 24:12).

TKN : In this case the semantic relationship is hard to define between ni. (9x in Ez.) 'be right' and pu. (2 Kin. 12:12, participle) 'counted' of money. Nor is the relationship to pi. evident. The only ni.-form in poetry (1 Sam. 2:3) should probably be regarded as a passive of the qal (only in poetry: 'test').

Preliminary conclusions

The pu. may often be regarded as a passive of the qal for the roots of groups Ia and Ib for which the ni. occurs in semantic relationship to the qal. (Grammarians have noticed this phenomenon before and they have determined that some of these forms are the remains of a lost passive qal). This observation does not only apply for the roots which grammarians have designated as remains of the passive qal, but it applies as well for the great majority of roots discussed under Ia and Ib. It does not matter in this respect whether or not the pi. occurs. In general the ni. shows preference for usage of the imperf., the pu. for usage of the perf. For certain roots two complementary forms of a single pattern can be observed (e.g. **GNB**, **ṬRP**, **MRṬ**, **SKL**, **ŚRP**, **ŠṬP** and **QBR**). For other roots this preference is less prominent although there is a tendency towards this kind of complementary relationship (e.g. **AKL**, **JLD**, **SGR**, and **ŚPK**).

The case is quite different for the roots of group II of which the ni. occurs in a semantic relationship to the pi. In this group it is striking to note the relatively great amount of pu.-participles against a relatively small number of ni.-participles.- Pu. perf. forms do not occur in this group.

The material of groups III and IV is too insignificant to draw any conclusions from.

4.2.2.2 The niph'al-pu'al relationship in poetry. Twenty-one verb roots may be found in the poetic texts of the OT of which ni.- as well as pu.- forms occur. In this context the ni., with 87 forms, occurs in formal opposition to the pu. of which 32 forms may be listed. In agreement with 4.2.2.1 I have made the following classification (starting with the largest group):246

I Roots of which the ni. occurs in semantic relationship to the qal: 11.
- a) Roots of which no pi.-forms occur in poetry: 7.
- b) Roots of which pi.-forms occur in poetry: 4.

II Roots of which the ni. occurs in semantic relationship to the pi.: 6.
- a) Roots of which no qal-forms occur in poetry: 1.
- b) Roots of which qal-forms do occur in poetry: 5.

III Roots of which the ni. occurs in semantic relationship to the hi.: 3.

IV Roots of which the semantic relationship to the qal, pi. or hi. is unclear: 2.

Below I will discuss these roots per group.

Ia Roots of which the ni. occurs in semantic relationship to the qal and of which no pi.-forms occur in poetry: 7.
As in 4.2.2.1 we will restrict ourselves to the discussion of two questions:
1) Which relationship exists between the pu. and ni. of these stems?
2) What is the mutual relationship between the ni.-participle, pu.-participle and the pass. qal-participle?

First of all we will present an overview of the distribution of the verbal forms of the ni. and pu. over the various tenses. Aside from this we also include the number of occurrences of the qal, pass. qal-participle and the hitp. of these roots in prose:

Root	Ni. Tot	Pt	Perf	Impf	Rest	Pu. Tot	Pt	Perf	Impf	Rest	Qal	P.Q.pt.	Hitp.
DḤH	1	-	-	1	-	1	-	1	-	-	5	1	-
D'K	1	-	1	-	-	1	-	1	-	-	6	-	-
HRG	1	-	-	1	-	1	-	1	-	-	M	1	-
JLD	8	1	-	7	-	5	-	5	-	-	M	3	-
'SH	1	-	1	-	-	1	-	1	-	-	M	-	-
RAH	7	-	3	4	-	1	-	1	-	-	M	-	-
ŠPK	2	-	2	-	-	1	-	1	-	-	18	1	3
Total	21	1	7	13	-	11	-	11	-	-			

One hitp. form of the root **JLD** occurs in prose (Num. 1:18).

A calculation of the share of each verb tense within the totals for the ni. and pu. of this group results in the following outcome. Parenthetical figures indicate the totals of occurrences in poetry.

	Total	Participle	Perfect	Imperfect	Rest
Ni.	21 (659)	1 (185)	7 (226)	13 (225)	-(23)
	65.6%(84.3%)	100%(80.8%)	38.9%(86.9%)	100%(83.6%)	-(95.8%)
Pu.	11 (123)	- (44)	11 (34)	- (44)	-(1)
	34.4%(15.7%)	0%(19.2%)	61.1%(13.1%)	0%(16.4%)	-(4.2%)
Total	32 (782)	1 (229)	18 (260)	13 (269)	-(24)

By means of these figures the following observations can be made:

a) In this group it is remarkable that the pu. occurs only in perfect forms. The group deviates from the general impression of the pu. in poetry in which the perf.-forms comprise only 13.1 % (34 out of 260) of the total. Williams regards all these forms (except for those of the root **D'K**) as old qal-passives.247

It is impossible to distinguish between the meanings of the ni. and pu. respectively for a number of these roots:

DḤH : ni. (Pro. 14:32) as well as pu. (Ps. 36:13) mean 'be cast down'

HRG : ni. (Lam. 2:20) as well as pu. (Ps. 44:23) have the meaning of 'be killed'; the pu. in this verse parallels the ni. of **HSB**!

JLD : the ni (cf. Job 15:7) as well as the pu. (Job 5:7 have the meaning of 'be born'.

'SH : the ni. (Ps. 33:6) and the pu. (Ps. 139:15) convey the meaning of 'be made'

RAH : the ni. (7x cf. Ps. 102:17) as well as the pu. (Job 33:21) have the meaning of 'be seen'

ŠPK : ni. (Ps. 22:15) 'be poured out' as water; pu. (Ps. 73:2) 'be poured out', i.e. 'slip' of footsteps.

For the above-mentioned roots the pu. as well as the ni. function as the pass. of the qal. This applies as well for the root **D'K.**

However, here it is possible to detect a distinctive nuance between the ni. and pu.

D'K : the ni. (Job 6:17) has the meaning of 'dry up', 'dried up' of water; the pu. (Ps. 118:12) 'be extinguished' of fire, cf. the qal 'go out', 'extinguish', of light (Job 18:5, 6 etc.)

The ni. shows a strong preference for the imperfect and in case of the roots **DḤH**, **HRG**, and **JLD** it appears that two complementary forms of a pattern are involved. Since only a few forms occur it is difficult to determine how significant this observation may be. The roots **'SH** and **ŠPK** do not comply with this trend.

b) As far as the participles are concerned, we note that there is only one ni.-participle, of the root **JLD** (Ps. 22:32). Although there is an overlap with the pass. qal-participle (Job 14:1; 15:14 and 25:4), one can distinguish between the meaning of the ni. and pass. qal-participle. The last-mentioned form is used substantivally in the expression **JeLūD AIŠŠā** ('baby').

Ib Roots of which the ni. occurs in semantic relationship to the qal and of which pi.-forms occur in poetry: 4

Root	Ni. Tot	Pt	Perf	Impf	Rest	Pu. Tot	Pt	Perf	Impf	Rest	Qal	P.Q.pt.	Pi.
GLH	4	-	1	3	-	1	1	-	-	-	7	2	9
JD'	11	2	3	6	-	5	5	-	-	-	M	-	1
MLA	9	1	-	8	-	1	1	-	-	-	M	-	20
QLL	1	-	1	-	-	2	1	-	1	-	4	-	6
Total	25	3	5	17	-	9	8	-	1	-			

Expressed in percentages, this provides the following results:

	Total	Part.	Perf	Imperf	Rest
Ni.	25 (659)	3 (185)	5 (226)	17 (225)	-(23)
	73.5%(84.3%)	27.3%(80.8%)	100%(86.9%)	94.4%(83.6%)	-(95.8%)
Pu.	9 (123)	8 (44)	- (34)	1 (44)	-(1)
	26.5%(15.7%)	72.7%(19.2%)	0%(13.1%)	5.6%(16.4%)	-(4.2%)
Total	34 (782)	11 (229)	6 (260)	18 (269)	-(24)

The outcome may be used as a basis for the following observations.

a) It is remarkable about this group that, contrary to findings for group Ia, the pu.-perf. forms are lacking completely.
The following may be said concerning these roots:

GLH : here, a clear difference between ni. (Pro. 13:13) 'taken as a pledge' and pu. (Job 17:1) 'be destroyed', passive of pi. (Song 2:15). HAL lists the forms under two verbs.

QLL : the pu.-imperf. (Job. 24:18) is the passive of the pi. 'curse' (cf. Job 3:1).

b) When we compare the participial forms of ni. and pu., and the pass. qal participle we notice the formal overlaps of the roots

GLH, **JD'**, and **MLA**. We note the semantic differences per root:

GLH : it is remarkable that the pass. qal-participle (Num. 24: 4, 16) can be related to the pi. (cf. Num. 22:31; Ps. 119:18) 'be opened', 'open' of eyes. The pu. participle (Pro. 27:5) has a different meaning: 'audience'.

JD' : pu. (Job 19:4) has the meaning of 'relative'; ni. (Ps. 76:2 and Pro. 31:23) that of 'known', see also p. 53.

MLA : the pu.-participle (Song 5:14) means 'studded', 'adorned' with precious stones, cf. pi. (Ex. 28:17; 39:10); the ni.-participle (Song 5:2) 'full'.

II Roots of which the ni. occurs in semantic relationship to the pi.: 6

Here we discuss groups IIa and IIb together.

a) Roots of which no qal-forms occur in poetry: 1

Root	Ni.					Pu.					Pi.	Hitp.
	Tot	Pt	Perf	Impf	Rest	Tot	Pt	Perf	Impf	Rest		
BHL	13	2	6	5	-	1	1	-	-	-	3	-

b) Roots of which qal-forms do occur in poetry: 5

Root	Ni.					Pu.					Qal	P.Q.pt.	Pi.
	Tot	Pt	Perf	Impf	Rest	Tot	Pt	Perf	Impf	Rest			
GLH	4	-	1	3	-	1	1	-	-	-	7	2	9
DBR	1	-	1	-	-	2	1	-	1	-	12	1	M
KBD	3	3	-	-	-	2	-	-	2	-	6	-	12
'NH	1	-	1	-	-	2	-	1	-	1	2	-	12
PTH	1	-	1	-	-	1	-	-	1	-	3	-	3
Total	23	5	10	8	-	9	3	1	4	1			

One hitp.-form of the roots **KBD** and **'NH** occurs in poetry. Four hitp. forms of the root **DBR** occur in prose. The root **GLH** is also mentioned under group Ib. It cannot be determined whether the forms of the ni. relate to the qal or the pi. Expressed in percentages, the outcome is as follows:

	Total	Part.	Perf	Imperf	Rest
Ni.	23 (659)	5 (185)	10 (226)	8(225)	- (23)
	71.9%(84.3%)	62.5%(80.8%)	90.9%(86.9%)	75%(83.6%)	0%(95.8%)
Pu.	9 (123)	3 (44)	1 (34)	4(44)	1 (1)
	28.1%(15.7%)	37.5%(19.2%)	9.1%(13.1%)	25%(16.4%)	100%(4.2%)
Total	32 (782)	8 (229)	11 (260)	12 (269)	1 (24)

We present a few observations even though the material is scarce:

a) One perf. occurs in the pu. of these roots (cf. under prose: 0 pu.-perf). Yet in the ni. there are ten perfects. A study of the individual roots reveals that no formal overlaps occur between pu. and ni. for the perf. and the imperf. An exception to this is **'NH** II. A pu.-perf. (Ps. 119:71) and a ni.-perf. (Ps. 119:

107) of this root occur, and between these two forms no semantic distinction seems to apply ('be oppressed').

b) As far as the participle is concerned, a formal overlap is only found for the root **BHL.** Two ni. participles occur: Ps. 30:8 ('be troubled') and Pro. 28:22 ('hasten after' wealth). The pu.-form (Pro. 20:21), written as **MeBōḤeLeT**, is read by the Masoretes as **MeBōHeLeT** ('hasten after'). This reading fits the context well. In this case there is no difference in meaning between pu. and ni.

III Roots of which the ni. occurs in semantic relationship to the hi.: 3.

Root	Ni.					Pu.					Qal	Pi.	Hi.	Ho.
	Tot	Pt	Perf	Impf	Rest	Tot	Pt	Perf	Impf	Rest				
ḤBA	3	-	2	1	-	1	-	1	-	-	-	-	-	-
STR	13	2	5	5	1	1	1	-	-	-	-	-	23	-
RAH	7	-	3	4	-	1	-	1	-	-	M	-	8	-

Six hi. forms of the root **ḤBA** occur, five of which in prose (Josh. 6:17, 25; 1 Kin. 18:3, 4 and 2 Kin. 6:29) and one in prophecy (Isa. 49:2), moreover, one ho.-form occurs in prophecy (Isa. 42:22). One pi.-form of the root **STR** occurs in prophecy (Isa. 16:3). The root **RAH**, also mentioned under group Ia, occurs in four ho.-forms in prose (Lev. 13:49; Deut. 4:35; Ex. 25:40, 26:30). It is difficult to accurately determine a semantic relationship between pu. and ni. because pi. forms of the roots are lacking. For **ḤBA** and **STR** there is no apparent difference between pu. (Job 24:4 'hide oneself' (?) and Pro. 27:5 'hidden') and ni. For **RAH** refer to 4.2.2.1: II.

IV Roots of which the semantic relationship to the qal, pi. or hi. is unclear: 2.

Root	Ni.	Pu.	Qal	Pi.	Hi.
JSD	2	1	9	1	-
ŚGB	4	1	1	5	1

The ni.-forms of **JSD** (Ps. 2:2 and Ps. 31:4) have the meaning of 'conspire', whereas the pu.-form (Song 5:15) may be translated as 'founded'. HAL and GESENIUS 1915 list the ni. and pu. under two different roots.
The pu. of **ŚGB** (Pro. 29:25) serves as a passive of the pi. (cf. Ps. 20:2; 69:30; 91:14, etc.). The semantic relationship of the ni. to the qal or pi. is unclear.

Preliminary Conclusions

The conclusions which were drawn from the prose material appear to apply for the greater part for poetry as well. It should be taken into consideration that the number of poetry forms is only one-fourth of that of prose.

The pu. may be regarded as a passive of the qal for the roots of group Ia of which the ni. occurs in a semantic relationship to the qal and of which no pi.-forms occur in prose. The ni. shows preference for the usage of the imperf. It is possible that ni.-imperf. and pu.-perf. are complementary forms, in as far as could be ascertained by means of the small amount of available material.

For the roots of group II, of which the ni. occurs in a semantic relationship to the pi., the general outcome agrees with that related to prose; we note a relatively small number of pu.-perf. and a relatively large number pu.-imperf. For one root, **'NH** II, it is possible that there are two complementary forms of one pattern with respect to the ni.-perf. and pu.-imperf.

The number of forms in groups III and IV is so small that it is impossible to draw any meaningful conclusions.

4.2.2.3 The niph'al-pu'al relationship in prophecy. The prose texts of the OT contain 27 verbal stems of which both ni.- as well as ho.- forms occur. In this context the ni., with 499 forms, occurs in formal opposition to the ho. with 81 forms. I have made the following division of these roots (beginning at the largest group).

I Roots of which the ni. occurs in semantic relationship to the qal: 24.
   a) Roots of which no pi.-forms occur in prophecy: 14.
   b) Roots of which pi.-forms occur in prophecy: 10

II Roots of which the ni. occurs in semantic relationship to the pi.: 9.
   a) Roots of which no qal-forms occur in prophecy: 3
   b) Roots of which qal-forms do occur in prophecy: 6

III Roots of which the ni. occurs in semantic relationship to the hi.: 1.

Below, we discuss these roots per group.

Ia Roots of which the ni. occurs in semantic relationship to the qal and of which no pi.-forms occur in prophecy: 14.

Root	Ni. Tot	Pt	Perf	Impf	Rest	Pu. Tot	Pt	Perf	Impf	Rest	Qal	P.Q.pt.	Hitp.
AKL	6	-	-	6	-	2	-	1	1	-	M	-	-
BZZ	3	-	1	1	1	1	-	1	-	-	10	1	-
DQR	1	-	-	1	-	1	1	1	-	-	2	-	-
ZR'	1	-	-	1	-	1	-	-	-	-	15	1	-
JD'	5	-	4	1	-	1	1	-	-	-	M	1	-
JLD	2	-	-	1	1	3	-	3	-	-	M	-	-
MŠK	1	-	-	1	-	2	2	1	-	-	5	-	-
NṬŠ	3	-	3	-	-	1	-	1	-	-	9	1	-
SGR	2	-	-	2	-	3	-	3	-	-	4	-	-
'ZB	4	1	1	2	-	2	-	2	-	-	M	7	-
QRA	25	2	12	11	-	6	1	5	-	-	M	1	-
ŠGL	2	-	-	2	-	1	-	1	-	-	-	-	-
ŠDD	1	-	1	-	-	18	-	18	-	-	24	2	2
ŠKB	2	-	-	2	-	1	-	1	-	-	M	-	-
Total	58	3	22	31	2	43	5	37	1	-		14	

The pi. of the root **ZR'** occurs three times in prose.
The **JD'** pi. occurs once in poetry; its hitp. occurs twice in prose.
The pi. of **JLD** occurs ten times in prose, the hitp. once, the pass. qal-partic. occurs three times in prose and three times in poetry.
The pi. of **SGR** occurs four times in prose, the pass. qal-partic. occurs eleven times in prose and once in poetry.
The qal of **ŚGL** occurs once in prose (Deut. 28:30).
The pi. of **ŠDD** occurs twice in poetry (Pro. 19:26; 24:15).

The following results are the outcome of a calculation of the share of each respective verb tense within the total of the ni. and pu. for this group. Figures between parentheses refer to the total in prophecy.

	Total	Part.	Perf	Imperf	Rest
Ni.	58 (900)	3 (185)	22 (357)	31 (301)	2 (57)
	57.4%(87.5%)	37.5%(82.6%)	37.3%(83.2%)	96.9%(94.3%)	100%(100%)
Pu.	43 (129)	5 (39)	37 (72)	1 (18)	- -
	42.6%(12.5%)	62.5%(17.4%)	62.7%(16.8%)	3.1%(5.7%)	- (0%)
Total	101 (1029)	8 (224)	59 (429)	32 (319)	2 (57)

Based on these figures, the following observations can be made:

a) Only one pu. imperf. occurs in this group (**AKL**, Isa. 1:20), yet there are relatively many ni.-imperfects. It is also quite remarkable that there is such a great amount of pu.-perfects (which seems to agree to findings for this group in poetry, see 4.1.5.4).

Williams regards the pu.-forms of a number of these roots as remains of the old passive qal-stem. Indeed, it is striking that for these roots (**AKL**, **BZZ**, **ZR'**, **JLD**, **NṬŠ**, **'ZB**, **QRA**, **ŚGL** and **ŠDD**) there appears to be no distinction in the meanings of their respective ni. and pu. forms nor is it possible to determine a semantic relationship which applies between the pu. and qal:

AKL : See 4.2.2.1: Ia
BZZ : 1 pu. (Jer. 50:37) 'be plundered', also as ni. (Isa. 24:3; Am. 3:11)
ZR' : pu. (Isa. 40:24) 'be sown', cf. qal 'sow', also as ni. (Lev. 11:37, etc.)
JLD : see 4.2.2.1: Ib
NṬŠ : pu. (Isa. 32:14) 'be forsaken', also as ni. (Isa. 7:16; 27:10, etc.)
'ZB : pu. (Isa. 32:14; Jer. 49:25) 'be forsaken', also as ni. (Isa. 7:16; 27:10, etc.)
QRA : see 4.2.2.1; the pu. (Isa. 48:8, 12, etc) has the meaning of 'be called', 'be named', also as ni.
ŚGL : pu. (Jer. 3:2) 'be defiled', compare to this ni. (Isa. 13:16, Zech. 14:2).

However, it is easier to regard the pu.-forms of the other roots (**DQR**, **JD'**, **MŠK** and **SGR**) as passives of the qal than to regard them as passives of a (hypothetical) pi.-stem.:

DQR : pu. (Jer. 51:4) 'pierced', cf. ni. (Isa. 13:15).
JD' : see p. 60, the pu.-participle (Isa. 12:5) is K, note that Q is ho.!

MŠK(?): the pu.-participles (Isa. 18:2, 7) have the meaning of 'long', 'tall', cf. qal 'draw'.
SGR : see 4.2.2.1: Ib.

The distribution of verbal forms over various tenses in the last-mentioned group is not different from that of the other forms. One may speak of two complementary forms of a single pattern for the roots **ZR'**, **JLD**, **SGR**, and **ŚGL**: imperf.-ni. and perf.-pu. For other roots we note a tendency towards this kind of complementary relationship (with the exception of **JD'** and **QRA**).

b) The frequency of occurrence of pu. and ni. participles is much lower: respectively three occurrences of two roots and five occurrences of four roots. Yet there are fourteen forms of the pass. qal-participle of seven roots. Formal overlap occurs for:

JD' : pu.-participle (Isa. 12:5) and pass. qal-participle (Isa. 53:3).
'ZB : ni.-participle (Isa. 27:10) and pass. qal-participle: 7.
QRA : ni.-participle (Isa. 43:7; 48:1), pu.-participle (Isa. 48:12) and pass. qal participle (Zeph. 1:7).

Only for the root **QRA** also a functional difference between the various participles can be ascertained: the pass. qal participle is used substantivally ('invited', 'guest'), as opposed to the pu. and ni. ('call', 'name').

Ib Roots of which the ni. occurs in semantic relationship to the qal and of which pi.-forms occur in prophecy: 10

Root	Ni. Tot	Pt	Perf	Impf	Rest	Pu. Tot	Pt	Perf	Impf	Rest	Qal	P.Q.pt.	Pi.
ASP	17	2	5	6	4	4	-	4	-	-	M	-	3
BL'	2	-	2	-	-	1	1	-	-	-	3	-	6
BQ'	4	-	2	2	-	1	-	-	1	-	4	-	2
GD'	5	-	5	-	-	1	-	1	-	-	3	1	1
GLH	10	-	7	1	2	1	-	1	-	-	17	-	10
ḤLH	6	4	2	-	-	1	-	1	-	-	5	-	4
JSD	1	-	-	1	-	2	-	2	-	-	8	-	3
SPR	1	-	-	1	-	2	-	1	1	-	2	-	7
PQD	3	-	-	3	-	1	-	1	-	-	M	-	1
QLL	4	3	-	1	-	1	-	-	1	-	3	-	2
Total	53	9	23	15	6	15	1	11	3	-		1	

Expressed in percentages, the outcome is as follows:

	Total	Part.	Perf	Imperf	Rest
Ni.	53 (900)	9 (185)	23 (357)	15 (301)	6 (57)
	77.9%(87.5%)	90%(82.6%)	67.6%(83.2%)	83.6%(94.3%)	100%(100%)
Pu.	15 (129)	1 (39)	11 (72)	3 (18)	- -
	22.1%(12.5%)	10%(17.4%)	32.4%(16.8%)	16.7%(5.7%)	0%(0%)
Total	68 (1029)	10 (224)	34 (429)	18 (319)	6 (57)

Pass. qal pts. occur in other genres for the following roots:

ASP : 1 in prose
GLH : 4 in prose, 2 in poetry
PQD : 78 in prose.
These results allow for the following observations:

a) Compared to group Ib in prose and poetry, it is remarkable that there are relatively many pu. perfects. The percentage of pu.-participles, however, is relatively low. There are relatively few occurrences of the ni.-imperfect and there are relatively few pu. participles (only 1 of the root **BL'**). Moreover, the pass. qal participle occurs only once (for the root **GD'**).

b) Only one participial form of the pu. occurs (**BL'**, Isa. 9:15). Here no formal overlaps occur between the pu.-, ni.- and the pass. qal participles.

II Roots of which the ni. occurs in semantic relationship to the pi.: 9.

Again, I will discuss groups IIa and IIb together:

a) Roots of which no qal-forms occur in prophecy: 3

Root	Ni.					Pu.					Pi.	Hitp.
	Tot	Pt	Perf	Impf	Rest	Tot	Pt	Perf	Impf	Rest		
GAL II	2	1	1	-	-	2	2	-	-	-	1	1
DKA	1	1	-	-	-	2	2	-	-	-	2	-
NḪM	13	2	8	2	1	2	-	1	1	-	15	-

b) Roots of which qal-forms do occur in prophecy: 6

Root	Ni.					Pu.					Qal	P.Q.pt.	Pi.
	Tot	Pt	Perf	Impf	Rest	Tot	Pt	Perf	Impf	Rest			
BQ'	4	-	2	2	-	1	-	-	1	-	4	-	2
GLH	10	-	7	1	2	1	-	1	-	-	17	-	10
KBD	9	4	2	3	-	1	1	-	-	-	3	-	7
'NH II	2	2	-	-	-	1	1	-	-	-	2	-	6
PTH	1	-	-	1	-	1	-	-	1	-	1	-	2
QDŠ	1	-	1	-	-	1	1	-	-	-	2	-	12
Total	43	10	21	9	3	12	7	2	3	-			

For the roots **BQ'**, **KBD** and **QDŠ** we note the occurrence of one, two and two hitp.-forms respectively in prophecy. In other genres, we have recorded the occurrence of hitp.-forms of the following roots:
DKA : 2 in poetry;
NḪM : 4 in prose; 3 in poetry;
'NH II: 5 in prose; 1 in poetry.
The roots **BQ'** and **GLH** are also mentioned under group Ia. Expressed in percentages, the outcome is as follows:

	Total	Part.	Perf	Imperf	Rest
Ni.	43 (659)	10 (185)	21 (226)	9 (225)	3 (23)
	78.2%(84.3%)	58.8%(80.8%)	91.3%(86.9%)	75%(83.6%)	100%(95.8%)
Pu.	12 (123)	7 (44)	2 (34)	3 (44)	- (1)
	21.8%(15.7%)	41.2%(19.2%)	8.7%(13.1%)	25%(16.4%)	0%(4.2%)
Total	55 (782)	17 (229)	23 (260)	12 (269)	3 (24)

With help of these figures the following observations can be made:

a) In comparison to the same group in prose and poetry, the pu. in this group shows relatively few occurrences of the perfect (2: **NḤM**, Isa. 54:11 and **GLH**, Nah. 2:8). For these forms there is no difference in meaning to be observed between the ni. and pu. Neither is it possible to distinguish the meanings of the pu.- (3: **NḤM**, Isa. 66:13, **BQ'**, Hos. 14:1 and **PTH**, Jer. 20:12) and ni.- imperfects.

b) There are relatively many pu.-pts. Formal overlap occurs among the roots **GAL**, **DKA**, **KBD** and **'NH** II, but no differences in meaning occur (with the exception of **KBD**, Isa. 58:13, cf. 13b: pi.)

III Roots of which the ni. occurs in semantic relationship to the hi.: 1.

Root	Ni.	Pu.	Ho.	Pi.	Hi.
NDḤ	9	1	1	-	9

Only one root is involved here. We note its occurrence in eight participles and one perfect in prophecy. One pu.- and a ho.- pt. occur in poetry (Isa. 8:22 and 13:14 respectively). There is no difference in meaning to be observed among the pu. and ni. forms ('be banished', 'be thrown out'). It is possible that the ho. differs in meaning from the pu. and ni. ('chased' of a gazelle).

Preliminary conclusions

The conclusions drawn above with respect to prose and poetry appear to apply in most respects for prophecy as well. The number of forms involved in the genre is smaller than that found in prose although it is slightly greater than the number of forms found in poetry.

However, the general picture of group Ib, roots of which the ni. occurs in semantic relationship to the qal and of which pi.-forms occur in prophecy, differs from that of the corresponding Ib groups in prose and poetry. In group Ib in prophecy there are relatively few ni.-imperfects and pu.-participles.

4.2.3 Conclusions

To what extent does this research into the relationship between pu'al and niph'al support the theory of the passive qal? Below (4.2.3.1) we will discuss the arguments in its favor after which we will deal with the arguments against it in (4.2.3.2.2).

4.2.3.1 Arguments in favor of the theory of the passive qal are the following:

a) It is remarkable that in group Ia, (roots of which the ni. occurs in a semantic relationship to the qal and of which pi.-forms in the respective genre are lacking), almost no pu. imperfects occur. In certain cases, where individual forms were in fact old pass. qals that had not been recognized by the Masoretes as such, forms could be vocalized only as pu. perfects on the basis of the written characters. Yet the imperfects of the pass. qal could be vocalized as ni.-imperfects without any problems. This may be an explanation for the non-occurrence of pu.-imperfects of these roots.

We are dealing here with roots the majority of pu.-forms of which are treated by Williams as remains of the passive qal (in prose ten out of fifteen; in poetry six out of seven, and in prophecy nine out of fourteen). There is only one pu.-imperfect (i.e. **AKL**, Isa. 1:20), which Williams also explains as a remains of the pass. qal imperfect. The other roots of group Ia can be divided into two groups:

1) Roots of which only participles occur in the pu. (in prose: 3; in prophecy: 3).
2) Roots of which only perfects occur in the pu. (in prose: 2, **BḤN**[248] and **PQD**; in poetry 1: **D'K** and in prophecy 2: **SGR** and **ŠKB.**[249]

Three roots remain to be discussed since their ni. and pu.-forms do not occur in the same genres, yet they are found in different genres. They fit the general picture as outlined above. Williams assumes that these are remains of the old pass. qal verbal stem. Here, I present the figures for ni. and pu. for he whole OT:

Root.	Niph'al Total	Partic.	Perf.	Imperf.	Rest	Pu'al Total	Partic.	Perf.	Imperf.	Rest
ASR	5	-	-	4	1	2	-	2	-	-
ḤŞB	1	-	-	1	-	1	-	1	-	-
JŞR	1	-	1	-	-	1	-	1	-	-

The pu.-forms of these roots may be regarded as qal-passives. Although we note the occurrence of one ni.-perfect, this may be read as a participle (Isa. 43:10 **LAo NōŞaR**).

b) In this respect it is remarkable that group Ib, roots of which the ni. occurs in semantic relationship to the qal and of which pi.-forms occur in the respective genre, shows much agreement with group Ia. Even here pu.-imperf. forms are almost completely lacking. Four imperfects occur: (2 **QLL** (1 in poetry and 1 in prophecy); **BQŠ** (1 in prophecy); and **SPR** (1 in prophecy)).

The pu.-forms of **SPR** and **QLL** should be regarded as pi.-passives. They are clearly to be distinguished from the ni., the qal pass./ refl. The same observation applies probably for **BQ'**.[250]

Only for a few roots, Williams regards the forms of the pu.-perf. as remains of the pass. qal (in prose: **JLD**, **NTŞ**, and **QBR**). This may not be adduced as an argument against the theory of the passive qal verbal root. Grammarians differ in opinion as to which forms may and which forms may not be regarded as remains of the pass. qal. Williams' list is not normative. Therefore, it need not be exhaustive.[251] For a number of roots in this group the pu. should rather be treated as a qal than a pi. passive.[252] This argues in favor of the theory of the pass. qal.

c) An argument in favor of the theory of the pass. qal is also the fact that for those roots of which the ni. occurs in a semantic relationship to the pi. there are relatively many pu.-imperfects. Above we presented various examples of roots of which the pu. serves as a pi.-passive and where it is clearly distinct from the ni., the pas./refl. of the qal (**SPR, QLL**).

Below I list the roots that have not been discussed before since their ni. and pu. forms occur in different genres. The tabulation includes the respective figures of the ni. and pu. of these roots and the figures of the whole OT.

Root	Niph'al					Pu'al					P.Qal pt
	Total	Part.	Perf.	Imperf.	Rest	Total	Part.	Perf.	Imperf.	Rest	
GRŠ	1	-	1	-	-	2	-	1	1	-	5
HPŚ	1	-	1	-	-	2	1	-	1	-	-
NG'	1	-	-	1	-	1	-	-	1	-	2
SPḤ	1	-	1	-	-	1	-	1	-	-	-
RDP	2	1	1	-	-	1	-	1	-	-	-
ŠNA/H	1	-	-	-	1inf.	1	-	-	1	-	-

The pu.-forms of these roots serve as passives of the pi. and not of the qal. Of the total of eight pu.-forms there are four imperfects.

For roots of which the ni. occurs in a semantic relationship to the pi. we also note a relatively high amount of pu.-imperfects. However, there are relatively few pu.-perfects (cf. in prose: 5 imperf. vs. 0 perf.; poetry: 4 imperf. vs. 1 perf. and prophecy: 3 imperf. vs. 2 perf.; in total 12 imperf. vs. 3 perf.). We will deal with this distribution of root forms later.

4.2.3.2 An argument against the theory of the passive qal is the fact that there is a number of roots for which participle forms of ni., pu. and pass. qal exist side by side. In these cases it is often difficult, if not impossible, to discover a semantic difference between the respective forms.

a) Williams regards the pu.-participle of the following roots (constructed without **Me**) as remains of the old passive qal verbal root: **'KL** (Ex. 3:2); **JLD** (Judg. 13:8); **LQḤ** (2 Kin. 2:10); **MRṬ** (Isa. 18:2, 7). Although this assumption is very well possible in view of the consonantal script, it is still necessary to explain why, apart from this, pass. qal participles (**QāṬūL**) exist (e.g. **JLD** 1 Chron. 14:4, 1 Kin. 3:26, 27,etc.; **LQḤ** Pro. 24:11 and **MRṬ** Ez. 21: 14, 33; 29:18).

A similar question may be asked with respect to the pu.-partic. (constructed with **Me**), which Williams also regards as remains of the old pass. qal verbal root (e.g. **QRA**, Isa. 48:12). If this assumption is correct, then why are there pass. qal participles of the same root as well (e.g. Esther 5:12; 2 Sam. 15:11; Ez. 23:23; etc.)?

b) Pu.-participles (constructed with **Me**) are found for a number of roots of which the pu.-perfects are the possible remains of the old pass. qal verbal root. These participles are not regarded as old pass. qal participles. Thus, there may be two possibilities:

1) They are the remains of the old pass. qal, which is improbable judging by the script. Moreover, a plausible solution ought to be found why, aside from this pass-qal. participles of the **QaṬUL** type occur.

2) They are not the remains of the old pass. qal. In this case it is remarkable that these forms can be related to the qal but not to the pi.

4.2.3.3 The issue of the pass. qal may also be approached in a different manner:

1) Perhaps the consonantal text meant to refer to the pass. qal, yet the Masoretes may have vocalized it as a pu.

2) Perhaps the consonantal text did refer to the pu. This latter possibility in itself does not militate against the pass. qal theory, but it presupposes the disappearance of the pass. qal prior to the time when the respective parts of the OT were committed to writing. These questions cannot be answered easily because of the following reasons:

a) We determined above that the theory of the pass. qal verbal root is based on two assumptions. First, it is assumed that the pu., or, in more precise terms the 'pure' pu., can only occur in a semantic relationship to the pi. and not to the qal or the hi. This does not apply for Masoretic Hebrew. Therefore, it does not have to apply for the *Vorlage* either. In many cases the pu. functions as a passive of the qal. This does not only apply for the perf.-forms, which are regarded as remains of the passive qal, but also for the forms, (especially the participles), which may not be regarded as pass. qals on the basis of the consonantal text.

In general it may be said that the mutual relationships between the verbal stems in Masoretic Hebrew are not as fixed as is assumed by e.g. Jenni. (E.g. the ni. may occur in a semantic relationship to the qal, pi. or hi. in as much as the ho. may occur in a relationship to the qal or hi.).

The second assumption which people adhere to and which, as was shown above, cannot be proven, is that originally the ni. was the reflexive of the qal and only in a later phase of language development it adopted the function of the passive qal. Even if this assumption about the 'then' is correct it is evident that this does not apply for the 'now' of Masoretic Hebrew since the ni. can occur in a relationship to the pi. or the hi.

b) Williams suggests that a number of ni.-imperf. were punctuated incorrectly by the Masoretes and that these must be 'hidden' passive qal-imperfects.[253] He mentions the stems **HRG**, **DḤH**, **ḤṢB**, **ṬRP**, **MRṬ**, **ŚRP**, **ŠṬP** and **ŠGL**. This may be an explanation for the fact that the forms of ni.-imperf. and pu.-perf. supplement one another. It is remarkable that this supplementation occurs for a great number of other stems as well (in prose: **AKL**, **BḤN**, **GNB**, **SQL**, **QBR**, and **ŠPK**; in poetry: **JLD**; in prophecy: **AKL**, **ZR'**, **JLD**, **JSD**, **PQD**, **SGR**, and **ŠKB**).[254]

To illustrate this, I present the percentages of the distribution of the perf. over the ni. and pu. of the various genres:

Prose	tot.Ni.-perf.	91.0 %	Pu.-perf.	9.0 %	
	Ia	77.3 %		22.7 %	
	Ib	54.0 %		46.0 %	(!)
Poetry	tot.Ni.-perf.	86.9 %	Pu.-perf.	13.1 %	
	Ia	38.9 %		61.1 %	(!)
	Ib	83.3 %		16.7 %	
Prophecy	tot.Ni.-perf.	83.2 %	Pu.-perf.	16.8 %	
	Ia	37.3 %		62.7 %	(!)
	Ib	67.6 %		32.4 %	

The high percentages of pu.-perfects for group Ia in poetry and prophecy is quite remarkable.

If Williams' suggestion is correct, then it should be assumed that the Masoretes mistakenly vocalized a greater number of ni.-imperfects than that which he arrives at. Although this may be partly true, I question whether we should accept this notion as a basis ourselves. In this context I would like to point to the fact that the reverse appears to be true for the roots of group II, where the ni. occurs in a semantic relationship to the pi. In this case, the pu. shows a preference for usage of the imperf., the ni. appears to favor usage of the perf. Moreover, for certain roots we note the occurrence of two complementary forms in a single pattern: ni.-perf. and pu.-imperf. (prose: **BRK**; poetry: **DBR** and **PTH**).

Presented below are the percentages of the distribution of the perf. over the ni. and pu. of various genres illustrating the comments just made. The question raises itself as to what might explain the evident preference for the perf. under the ni. and the pu. of various genres:

Prose	tot.Ni.-perf.	91.0 %	Pu.-perf.	9.0 %	
	IIa+b	100.0 %		0.0 %	(!)
Poetry	tot.Ni.-perf.	86.9 %	Pu.-perf.	13.1 %	
	IIa+b	90.9 %		9.1 %	
Prophecy	tot.Ni.-perf.	83.2 %	Pu.-perf.	16.8 %	
	IIa+b	91.3 %		8.7 %	[255]

4.2.3.4 Based on the above, it may be surmised that the distinction pass.-qal vs. pu. became obsolescent before or during the period of classical Hebrew. Eventually, the pu. remained most prominent. Yet since, apart from the old pass. qal-verbal stem, the ni. was used as passive of the qal, the pass. qal was not only replaced by the pu. but also by the ni. This may be an explanation of the fact that the Masoretes vocalized pass. qals as pu.-forms. Since two forms could be used as qal passives (ni.- and passive qal), and because the ni. outnumbered the pu., the ni. gradually replaced the passive qal. The occurrence of such a process can also be explained from the fact that the semantic opposition between the individual verbal stems had weakened at an early stage of language development. (This may have been before the times of Biblical Hebrew, given that the opposition has ever been as fixed as what is assumed now). A merging of pu.-perf. and the pass. qal-perf. (which is quite similar in form) occurred because the pu. functioned in a semantic relationship not only to the pi. but also to the qal, and because the ni. was used as a passive of the qal.

Apart from the above-mentioned tendency towards merging the verbal stems, the following may also be an explanation of the fact that users preferred the ni.-imperf. as the pass. imperf. to the qal and the pu. as a passive perf. to the qal:

a) The passive qal had two participles: one with the form **QaṬūL** and another with the form **QūṬṬaL**. The second form became obsolete much before the time of classical Hebrew and only continued to exist as a remains (cf. **MRṬ**: pu.-participle with **Me**: 1 Kin. 7:45 and without **Me**: Isa. 18:2, 7). Because of the fact that pu.-participles (with **Me**) can also function as passives to the qal, and due to the external similarity these remains dissolved in the pu.

b) In a later stage merging of pass. qal-perf. and pu.-perf. occurred especially because of the agreements in the orthography of these forms. In my view, it is hard to determine to what extent these forms could be distinguished in the times of classical Hebrew. The fact that for the roots of groups Ia and Ib the pu. shows a preference for the perf. appears to indicate that this was the case. For the roots of which both pass. qal, pu. as well as the ni. functioned as passive to the qal, the pu. shows preference for the perf. and the ni. for the imperf. The last-mentioned development may possibly be accounted for in that agreement in orthography was less important. Here we note as it were a merging process of the ni. and pu. verbal stems.

c) The fact that for the pu. the imperfects are often lacking, may just as well be accounted for in that the Masoretes have vocalized these (originally) pass. qal-forms as ni.-imperfects. The merging process of these verbal stems may, therefore, be attributed to Masoretic vocalization. This accounts for the fact that pu.-pts. occur for the root **LQḤ** but not for **NTN**; presumably, these are vocalized as ni.-imperfects. In my view, the Masoretes could vocalize the originally pass. qals as pu. and ho. respectively on the basis of the process described above. The process already included the disappearance of the pass. qal in favor of the other verbal stems. However, a reverse development may be observed for those roots of which the pu.- and the ni.-forms functioned as passive of the pi. Contrary to the development sighted for the roots mentioned under Ia and Ib, the ni. showed preference for usage of the perf. whereas the pu. showed preference for the imperf. However, the material is too scarce to draw meaningful conclusions.

In conclusion we may state that, certainly prior to and possibly during the times of classical Hebrew, the passive qal-pf. functioned as a passive of the qal just as the ni. and pu. It cannot be ascertained to what extent, and whether completely or partly, it merged with the pu. in that time. In our discussion of the niph'al-hoph'al relationship we will return to these conclusions.

4.3 The niph'al-hoph'al relationship

4.3.1 Introduction and methodology

4.3.1.1 Passive qal and hoph'al. We referred to the theory of pass. qal (4.2.1.1) in our discussion of the relationship of the ni. and the pu. Not only certain pu.-forms may be regarded as remains of a lost pass. qal, even certain ho.-forms may be traced back to this pass. qal-stem. Here, we are exclusively concerned with the ho.-imperf. Williams mentions the following sample roots: **ARR** (imperf. **JūAāR**, Num. 22: 6); **DWŠ** (imperf. **JūDāŠ**, Isa. 28:27) and **NTN** (imperf. **JuTTaN**, 1 Kin. 2:21; Lev. 11:38; etc.), cf. El-Amarna). As evidence for the validity of this assumption Williams adduces that for certain roots (e.g. **JṢR**, **LQḤ** and **ŠDD**) the pu.-perf. and ho.-imperf. complement one another.

The critical remarks concerning this theory, which we voiced above under the discussion of the pu.-ni. relationship, also apply for the ho.-forms. Moreover, we must make the following comments:

a) It is not always easy to determine whether certain forms are pu. or ho. For instance, I attribute the imperfects of the root **LQḤ** to the pu. whilst others regard these as ho.-forms. On the basis of the El-Amarna texts one might suppose that these are forms of the old pass. qal verbal stem. Moreover, one may have differing views for the *primae nun* verbs (e.g. **NQM**) whether these are (Masoretic) pu.- or ho.-forms.

b) It may be questioned whether all ho.-forms of which corresponding hi.-forms are lacking may be regarded as remains of the old passive qal-stem. If this is not the case then an explanation must be sought for the fact that the ho. occurs in a semantic relationship to the qal.

c) Williams observes correctly that for a number of roots pu.-perf. and ho.-imperf. supplement one another (**JṢR**, **LQḤ** and **ŠDD**, if the imperf.-forms belong to the ho.). However, this is not the case for a great number of other roots.

d) According to my calculations there are nineteen roots of which both ni., pu. and ho. occur. For only three of these roots ni.-perf. as well as ho.-impf. occur (**JṢR**, **NTṢ**, and **ŠDD** if **LQḤ** is left out of consideration). It could be expected, if these are mistakenly vocalized old pass. qal-forms, that the number of roots with ni.-perf. and ho.-imperf. would be much higher.

Below, we will examine if and to what extent our research into the relationship between ni. and ho. of those roots of which the ho. does not occur in a pass. relationship to the hi. may shed new light on the theory of the pass. qal.

4.3.1.2 Method of research. We determined above that there are 106 verb roots of which ho. forms occur in the OT. Fifty-two of these 106 roots, or 49 %, also appear in ni.-forms. Thus a total of 117 ho.-forms may be studied in opposition to 959 ni.-forms. In my discussion of the ni.-ho. relationship I will restrict myself to the following issues:

1) Are there functional and semantic differences, and, if so, which and where, between ni.-forms of the roots of which the ni. occurs in a pass./refl. relationship to the hi. and ho. forms of

the respective roots? According to grammarians the primary meaning of the ho. is that of the passive of the hi.[256] What is the distribution over the various verbal forms, and what conclusions can be drawn from these percentages? Can we detect overlap and/or supplementation of the ni. and ho.?

2) Hi. forms are lacking for sixteen out of fifty-two roots in the OT. Should the ho. in this case be treated as a passive of a hypothetical hi.-stem, should it be seen as a form of the old passive qal, or are there any other explanations possible? The Gesenius-Kautzsch grammar postulates that a secondary function of the ho. is that it may be used as the passive of the qal.[257]

3) The other roots will be discussed to a limited extent. For a number of roots the ho. may be regarded as a passive of the hi. In such cases, the ni. functions as the passive or reflexive of the qal or pi. For other roots the ni.-ho. relationship is not as evident. These will be dealt with briefly. Especially for the roots of which pu.-forms exist we will deal with the ni.-pu.-ho. relationship and we will assess as to what extent these findings support the theory of the passive qal.

4.3.2 The niph'al-hoph'al relationship in the various genres

4.3.2.1 The niph'al-hoph'al relationship in prose. In the prose texts of the OT 27 verb roots may be found of which ni.- as well as ho.-forms occur. The ni. (449 forms) occurs in formal opposition to the ho. (81 forms). The following classification of these roots can be made, beginning with the largest group:

I Roots of which the ni. occurs in a pass./refl. semantic relationship to the hi.: 6
II Roots of which no hi.-forms occur in prose: 8
III Roots of which hi.-forms occur in prose but of which the relationship between ho. and hi. is unclear: 9

Four roots will be excluded from this overview:
GLH : ho. 5: passive of the hi. (34 x) 'go in exile'
ḤLL : ho. 1: passive of the hi. (2 x) 'begin'
JD' : ho. 2: passive of the hi. (31 x) 'make known'
PQD : ho. 7: passive of the hi. (23 x) 'appoint', 'entrust'
The ho. of these roots serves as a passive for the hi.; the ni. serves as a passive for the qal or pi. and differs, where its meaning is concerned, from the ho. Below, I will discuss these roots per group.

I Roots of which the ni. occurs in a pass./refl. semantic relationship to the hi.: 6

First we will present an overview of the distribution of the verbal forms of ni. and ho. over the various tenses. Moreover, we mention how many forms of the hi., qal, pass. qal-participle and the pu. occur for these roots in prose. In prose, we note a single occurrence of the pass. qal.-pt. of the root **RAH**.

Root	Niph'al					Hoph'al					Hi.	Qal	Pu.
	Tot	Pt	Perf	Impf	Rest	Tot	Pt	Perf	Impf	Rest			
KWN	29	18	2	7	2	6	2	4	-	-	M	-	-
KLM	13	4	6	2	1	1	-	1	-	-	4	-	-
NKH	1	-	1	-	-	10	4	5	1	-	M	-	2perf.
NṢB	40	34	6	-	-	2	2	-	-	-	14	-	-
SBB	19	-	13	6	-	5	5	-	-	-	29	53	-
RAH	84	3	29	42	10	4	1	3	-	-	39	M	-
Total	186	59	57	57	13	28	14	13	1	-			

A calculation of the share of each verb tense within the total of the ni. and ho. for this group results in the following outcome:

	Total	Participle	Perf	Imperf	Rest
Total	214	73	70	58	13
Niph'al	186	59	57	57	13
	86.9%	80.8%	81.4%	98.3%	100%
Hoph'al	28.0	14	13	1	-
	13.1%	19.2%	18.6%	1.7%	0%

With help of these figures the following remarks can be made: Practically no imperfects occur of the ho. of this group. There is only one form of the root **NKH** (Ex. 5:14) 'be beaten'. Moreover, one form of the ni. occurs (2 Sam. 11:15, perf.) meaning 'strike dead' (cf. hi. 2 Sam. 13:30). This form, which the Masoretes vocalized as a ni., might just as well be read as a pu. on the basis of its orthography. It is remarkable that the two pu.-perfects of **NKH** (Ex. 9:31, 32) show no difference in meaning to that of the ho.-forms. The pi. does not exist (see 4.2.2.1: III).

Formal overlap occurs for the roots **KWN** (perf. and partic.), **KLM** (perf.), **NKH** (perf.), **NṢB** (partic.) and **RAH** (partic., perf.). Just as for the root **NKH** it is often possible to distinguish differences in nuance between ni. and ho.:

NṢB : ni. partic. (1 Sam. 22:9) 'be appointed over' of persons vs. ho. (Gen. 28:12; Judg. 9:6) 'be placed' of objects.

KLM : ni. (2 Sam. 10:5) 'be humiliated', cf. hi. 1 Sam. 20:34, vs. ho.-perf. (1 Sam. 25:15) 'be mistreated', cf. hi. 1 Sam. 25:7. Compare to this also in prophecy: **KLM** ni., **BWŠ** (Isa. 45:16) and **KLM** ho. **BWŠ** (Jer. 14:3), (see also 4.3.2.3: I).

The significance of all this is not immediately evident. For the roots **KWN** and **SBB** there appears to exist no clear distinction between ni. and ho.

II Roots of which no hi.-forms occur in prose: 8

First of all, we present an overview of the distribution of ni., ho. and pu. verbal forms over the various tenses. Moreover, we include the number of occurrences of the qal and the pass. qal-participle of these roots in prose:

Root	Niph'al					Hoph'al					Pu'al				
	Tot.	Pt.	Pf.	Imp.	R.	Tot.	Pt.	Pf.	Imp	R.	Tot.	Pt.	Pf.	Imp.	R.
AḤZ	7	1	3	1	2	1	1	-	-	-	-	-	-	-	-
ḤLH	4	3	1	-	-	3	-	3	-	-	-	-	-	-	-
JSD	1	-	-	-	1inf	2	-	-	-	2inf	4	2	2	-	-
J'D	16	5	4	7	-	1	1	-	-	-	-	-	-	-	-
LQḤ	10	-	4	3	3inf	3	-	-	3	-	6	1	5	-	-
NQM	8	-	3	3	2inf	3	-	-	3	-	-	-	-	-	-
NTN	71	2	40	25	4	7	-	-	7	-	-	-	-	-	-
NTṢ	1	-	1	-	-	1	-	-	1	-	1	-	1	-	-
Total	118	11	56	39	12	21	2	3	14	2	11	3	8	-	-

The distribution of the various verbal forms of ho., ni., and pu. may be diagramed as follows:

	Total	Part.	Perf.	Imperf.	Rest
Niph'al	118	11	56	39	12
	(78.7 %)	(68.8 %)	(83.6 %)	(73.6 %)	(85.7 %)
Hoph'al	21	2	3	14	2
	(14.0 %)	(12.4 %)	(4.5 %)	(26.4 %)	(14.3 %)
Pu'al	11	3	8	-	-
	(7.3 %)	(18.8 %)	(11.9 %)	(0 %)	(0 %)
Total	150	16	67	53	14

Compare this with the percentage totals for prose in general:

	Total	Part.	Perf.	Imperf.	Inf.	Imper.
Prose	3082	625	1014	1154	202	87
Niph'al	2584	431	861	1018	188	86
	(83.8%)	(69 %)	(84.9%)	(88.2%)	(93.1%)	(98.9%)
Hoph'al	293	89	68	122	13	1
	(9.5%)	(14.2%)	(6.7%)	(10.6%)	(6.4%)	(1.1%)
Pu'al	205	105	85	14	1	-
	(6.7%)	(16.8%)	(8.4%)	(1.2%)	(0.5%)	(0 %)

If the outcome is compared to that of group I and the general outcome of prose a remarkably high percentage of ho.-imperf. and a relatively low percentage of ho. perfects is found. All ho.-imperf. occur for those roots of which Williams regards the ho.-imperfects as remains of the passive qal (cf. **NTN** 2 Sam. 21:6 reads a ni.). It is also remarkable that the roots concerned are of the *primae nun* type! These forms function as passives of the qal. It is impossible to make a semantic distinction between the forms of the ni. and those of the ho. Pu.-forms of the roots **LQḤ** and **NTṢ** occur as well. Again, it is impossible to make a semantic distinction between pu., ho. and ni. (For the root **NTṢ** see 4.2.2.1: Ib).

When these roots are examined more closely, we discover the following aspects:
AḤZ : for the ni.- and ho.-participles we note a formal over-

lap. The meaning of the ho. (2Chron. 9:18) is not entirely clear; the ni. is related to the qal.

ḤLH : hi.-forms of the root occur in poetry and prophecy. Perhaps, the ho. serves as a pass. to the hi., cf. hi. (Mi. 6:13) 'wound' vs. ho. (1Kin. 22:34; 2Chron. 18:33; 35:23) 'be wounded'. The ni. serves as a pass. to the qal.

JSD : Here we find a formal overlap of the inf. where a semantic distinction may be made. The ho.-inf. used independently as 'foundation' (2Chron. 3:3, Ezra 3:11); see the ni.: Ex. 9:18 (note that Mandelkern reads it as a perf).

J'D : Of this root only the ho. participle can be found (Ez. 21:21). Possibly, there is a relationship to the qal (Jer. 47:7). The relationship to the hi. (in prophecy: Jer. 49:19; 50:44) and in poetry: Job 9:19) is unclear.

III Roots of which hi.-forms occur in prose but of which the relationship between ho. and hi. is unclear: 9

First of all we list an overview of the distribution of the ni. and ho. verbal forms over the various tenses. Apart from this we record the number of occurrences of hi., qal, pass. qal-participle and pu. forms derived from these roots in the prose category:

Root	Niph'al Tot	Pt	Perf	Impf	Rest	Hoph'al Tot	Pt	Perf	Impf	Rest	Hi.	Qal	Pu.
BQ'	8	-	2	5	1	1	-	1	-	-	1	26	2
ḤRB	2	2	-	-	-	3	1	1	-	1	4	5	-
JLD	28	6	9	11	2	3	-	-	-	3	M	M	18
JQŠ	1	-	-	1	-	1	1	-	-	-	9	-	-
NTK	6	-	6	-	-	1	-	-	1	-	4	6	-
NTQ	4	-	1	3	-	1	-	1	-	-	1	2	-
'LH	14	-	4	4	6	2	-	2	-	-	M	M	-
PDH	2	-	1	1	-	1	-	-	-	1	1	25	-
ŠMM	12	7	5	-	-	4	-	-	-	4	9	23	-

In prose, we note the occurrence of respectively 4, 3, and 1 pass. qal-participle for the roots **BQ'**, **JLD** and **NTQ**.

	Total	Part.	Perf.	Imperf.	Inf.	Imper.
Niph'al	77	15	28	25	8	1
	81.9 %	88.2 %	84.8 %	96.2 %	47.1 %	100 %
Hoph'al	17	2	5	1	9	-
	18.1 %	11.8 %	15.2 %	3.8 %	52.9 %	-
Total	94	17	33	26	17	1

We note the remarkably low percentage of ho. imperf.-forms in this group. There is only one occurrence of an imperfect form of the root **NTK** (Ez. 22:22). The meaning of this form cannot be distinguished from that of the ni. (cf. Ez. 20:21).

Ho.-forms are restricted to ho.-inf. of the roots **JLD, PDH** and **ŠMM** (often in a fixed expression with **JŌM**), e.g. **JLD** (Gen. 40:20; Ez. 16:4, 5); **ŠMM** (Lev. 26:34, 35; 2 Chron. 36:21)-- an exception to this is Lev. 26:43-- or related to the ni., **PDH** (Lev. 19:20). Also of the root **JLD** ni.-infinitives occur combined with **JŌM** (Eccl. 7:1 and Hos. 2:5), but these forms relate to the actual day of birth. For these three roots the semantic relationship between qal and ho. is much more evident than that between hi. and ho. An inf. abs. occurs of the root **ḤRB** which is related to the ni. (2 Kin. 3: 21). The following applies for the remaining roots:

BQ' : ho. perf. (Jer. 39:2) may be related to the qal (2 Chron. 21:17; 32:1) as well as to the hi. (Isa. 7:6)

JQŠ : Williams regards the ho.-partic. (constructed without **Me**, Eccl. 9:12), as a remains of the pass. qal

NTQ : The ho.-forms of this root (Judg. 20:31) may be related to qal (Judg. 20:32) as well as to hi. (Josh. 8:6).

Preliminary Conclusions

a) In 4.1.3.2 we calculated that imperfects comprise 41.6 % of the total of ho.-forms in prose. Yet, the ho.-imperfects of the 21 roots studied in the preceding section comprise only 24.2 % (16 out of 66 forms). Besides, we note an percentage of imperfects of 46.7 for the ho.-stems which were not discussed due to a lack of corresponding ni.-forms in the prose genre (106 out of 227 forms).[258]

b) It is remarkable that these ho.-imperfects occur only for the *primae nun* roots (the number of occurrences is supplied between parentheses): in group I **NKH** (1), in group II **LQḤ**(3); **NQM** (3); **NTN** (7) and **NTṢ** (1) and in group III **NTK** (1). In general, the forms of group II are attributed to the remains of the pass. qal.

c) It is possible that the ho.-imperf. and the ni.perf. of the root **NTK** complement one another.

d) In group III we note the occurrence of the ho.-infinitives (**ḤRB**, **JLD**, **PTH** and **ŠMM**), which should be related to the qal rather than to the hiph'il.

4.3.2.2 The niph'al-hoph'al relationship in poetry. Only five roots occur, in the poetic texts of the OT, of which ni.-as well as ho.- forms occur. These roots are the following:

Root	Niph'al					Hoph'al				
	Tot	Pt	Perf	Impf	Rest	Tot	Pt	Perf	Impf	Rest
HPK	11	1	9	1	-	1	-	1	-	-
JKḤ	1	1	-	-	-	1	-	1	-	-
KWN	35	16	1	18	-	4	-	4	-	-
NTN	2	-	2	-	-	1	-	-	1	-
ŠMM	3	1	2	-	-	1	-	-	-	1imper.

In view of the limited number of roots we will not classify them according to groups. When necessary, individual roots will be discussed. The roots **HPK** and **NTN** belong to group II.

HPK : No hi.-forms occur of this root. There does not appear to be any significant difference between the ho.-perf. (Job 30:15) and the nine ni.-perfects (cf. Job 19:19). Both ni. as well as ho. may be related to the qal.

JKḤ : The ho. perfect (Job 33:19) can be regarded as a hi. passive (cf. Job 5:17; 13:10; 22:4). The relationship between the ni. and hi. is unclear (no forms of other active verbal stems exist). Here, the hi. has the meaning of 'rebuke', 'punish', the ni. (Job 23:7) means 'plead', 'enter into discussion'.

KWN : the ho.-participle (Pro. 21:31), 'be prepared', 'be adorned' of a horse, may be regarded as a hi. passive. The ni. occurs in a semantic relationship to the pi.

ŠMM : One ho.-imper. occurs (Job 21:5), according to Mandelkern and Olshaussen. Yet Gesenius-Kautzsch (1909, &67f etc.) regard this form as a hi. Both views are possible. The same expression is found in Job 18:20 (ni.: 'be amazed') and there does not seem to be a difference in meaning between the ni.-form and the ho.- (or hi.-) form.

We refrain from drawing significant conclusions since the amount of available material is too limited.

4.3.2.3 The niph'al-hoph'al relationship in prophecy. In OT texts categorized as prophecy, 25 roots are found of which ni. and ho. forms occur. In this context ni. and ho. occur in formal opposition with 122 and 81 forms respectively. The roots may be classified as follows, starting at the largest group:

I Roots of which the ni. occurs in a semantic relationship to the hi.: 8

II Roots of which no hi.-forms occur in prophecy: 6

III Roots of which hi.-forms occur in prophecy but of which the relationship between ho. and hi. is unclear: 8.

In this overview three roots are not discussed:

GLH : ho. 1 x, Jer. 13:19, passive of the hi., 'be exiled'
KŠL : ho. 1 x, Isa. 12:5, passive of the hi., 'cause to stumble'
NGŠ : ho. 1 x, Mal. 1:11, passive of the hi. 'bring (sacrifices)'

Below I discuss these roots according to their respective groups:

I Roots of which the ni. occurs in a semantic relationship to the hi.: 8

First we present an overview of the distribution of the verbal forms of ni. and ho. over the various tenses. Moreover, we list the number of occurrences in prophecy of the hi., qal, pass. qal-participle and the pu. of these roots:

Root	Niph'al					Hoph'al					Hi.	Qal	Pu.
	Tot	Pt	Perf	Impf	Rest	Tot	Pt	Perf	Impf	Rest			
ḤBA	2	-	-	1	1inf.	1	-	1	-	-	1	1	-
KWN	4	3	-	-	1imp.	4	-	4	-	-	M	-	-
KLM	8	-	3	3	2inf.	1	-	1	-	-	1	-	-
NDḤ	9	8	1	-	-	1	1	-	-	-	9	-	1
NṢB	5	5	-	-	-	1	-	1	-	-	1	-	-
SBB	1	-	1	-	-	1	-	-	1	-	2	8	-
NṢL	5	-	1	2	2inf.	2	2	-	-	-	M	-	-
ŠḤT	2	-	2	-	-	1	1	-	-	-	M	-	10
Total	36	16	8	6	6	12	4	7	1	-			

Note: 1 pu.-form of **ḤBA** occurs in poetry;
1 qal-form of **NDḤ** and **SBB** each occurs in prose.
A calculation of the share of each verb tense within the total of the ni. and ho. for this group results in the following outcome:

	Total	Part.	Perf.	Imperf.	Rest
Niph'al	36	16	8	6	6
	75 %	80 %	53.3 %	58.7 %	100 %
Hoph'al	12	4	7	1	-
	25 %	20 %	46.7 %	14.3 %	0 %
Total	48	20	15	7	6

A remarkable aspect of these figures is that ho. perfects occur relatively often, as opposed to a much more rare occurrence of participles and imperfects. Since we have dealt with a small number of forms these figures must be applied cautiously.

For the roots **KLM** and **NDḤ** formal overlap occurs for the pf. and the pt. respectively. There does not appear to be a significant difference in meaning between the ni. and ho. of the root **KLM** (cf. ni. Isa. 45:17 and ho. Jer. 14:3). For the root **NDḤ** there may be a possible difference in nuance (ho. Isa. 13:14 'a chased gazelle' vs. ni. Isa. 16:4 'outcasts'. With respect to the other roots, we observe that the meaning of the ho. perf. of **NṢB**, Nah. 2:8, and its relationship to the other forms of **NṢB** is unclear. For the roots **ḤBA**, **KWN**, **SBB** and **ŠHT** there is no apparent difference in meaning between ni. and ho. forms. For the root **NŠL** there may be a difference in meaning between ni. and ho.

II Roots of which no hi.-forms occur in prophecy: 6

Root	Niph'al					Hoph'al					Qal	Pu
	Tot	Pt	Perf	Impf	Rest	Tot	Pt	Perf	Impf	Rest		
DWŠ	2	-	1	-	1inf	1	-	-	1	-	8	-
ḤNN	1	-	1	-	-	1	-	-	1	-	7	-
JSD	1	-	-	1	-	1	1	-	-	-	8	-
JṢR	1	-	1	-	-	1	-	-	1	-	40	-
NTŠ	2	-	-	2	-	1	-	-	1	-	9	-
ŠDD	1	-	1	-	-	2	-	-	2	-	-	18

Note that a pu.-perf. of the root **JṢR** occurs in poetry. 18 pu.-pf. forms of the root **ŠDD** occur in prophecy. A calculation of the distribution of the various ho. and ni. verbal forms results in the following tabulation expressed in percentages (see below).

Again, we note the remarkably high number of ho.-imperfects. Yet there is a total absence of ho.-perfects (cf. prose 4.3.2.1). Williams regards all the above-mentioned ho.-forms, except those of **JSD**, as remains of the lost pass. qal imperf. The ho.-forms of these roots occur only in the impf. Apart from the root **NTŠ**, these appear to be two complementary forms (ni.-perf. and ho.-impf.) of a pattern. According to Williams, however, the ho.-impf. and the pu.-perf. of the root **ŠDD** complement one another.

	Total	Part	Perf	Imperf	Rest
Niph'al	8	-	4	3	1
	53.3%	0%	100%	33.3%	100%
Hoph'al	7	1	-	6	-
	46.7%	100%	0%	66.7%	0%
Total	15	1	4	9	1

Ni.- as well as ho.-imperfects occur of the root **NTŠ.** Perhaps, it is possible to make a semantic distinction between ni. and ho. (ni. Amos 9:15, 'be expelled'; metaphorically said of plants 'be pulled up'; Jer. 18:14, this is an unclear meaning, vs. Ez. 19:12 'be pulled out', said of a vine). The participle form of **JSD** is found in the phrase **MūSāD/MūSaD,** a 'fixed' foundation (Isa. 28:16).

III Roots of which hi.-forms occur in prophecy but of which the relationship between ho. and hi. is unclear: 8.

It must be noted that the pass. qal-participle and pu.-forms of the root **KRT** occur in other genres. A qal-participle of the root **PQD** occurs in prose. Qal forms and pass. qal-participles of the root **SWG** occur in poetry. Pass. qal-participles of the root **ŠBR** occur in prose and poetry.

Root	Niph'al					Hoph'al					Hi.	Qal	Pu.
	Tot	Pt	Perf	Impf	Rest	Tot	Pt	Perf	Impf	Rest			
JD'	5	-	4	1	-	1	1	-	-	-	12	M	1
J'D	1	-	1	-	-	1	1	-	-	-	2	2	-
JŠB	3	-	3	-	-	2	-	1	1	-	4	M	-
KRT	19	-	9	10	-	1	-	1	-	-	26	M	-
NṬH	2	-	-	2	-	1	1	-	-	-	18	27	-
PQD	3	-	-	3	-	1	-	1	-	-	3	M	1
SWG	6	2	2	1	1inf	1	-	1	-	-	2	-	-
ŠBR	17	3	11	3	-	1	-	1	-	-	1	13	-

Expressed in percentages, the distribution of the various verbal ho.- and ni.- forms results in the following outcome:

	Total	Part	Perf	Imperf	Rest
Niph'al	65	5	30	20	1
	86.2 %	62.5 %	58.7 %	95.2 %	100 %
Hoph'al	9	3	5	1	-
	13.8 %	37.5 %	14.3 %	4.8 %	0 %
Total	65	8	35	21	1

In this outcome the low percentage of ho.-imperfects stands out (as in prose, 4.3.2.1). Only one imperf.-form occurs (**JŠB,** Isa. 44:26 'be inhabited'). This form cannot be related to the hi. although a relationship with the qal is possible. There is no semantic distinction with the ni. Williams regards this imperfect form as an old passive qal.

Yet the ho.-perf. of **JŠB** (Isa. 5:8) may be regarded as a passive of the hi. (cf. hi. Isa. 54:3). Moreover, the perf. of the ho. of **PQD** (Jer. 6:6) may be regarded rather as a passive of the qal than as a hi. passive ('the city is visited').

The ho.-perf. of **ŠBR** (Jer. 8:21) may also be related to the qal. No semantic distinction with the ni. can be observed (cf. Jer. 23:9). As for the other roots, the following observations can be made:

JD' : see 4.2.2.3 Ia; K. reads pu.-form.

J'D : see 4.3.2.1 II.

KRT : it is impossible to determine whether the ho. (Joel 1:9) must be related to the qal or to the hi.

NṬH : the participle form of Isa. 8:8 is used as a noun ('the spreading out of the wings').

SWG : the ho. (Isa. 59:14) may be related to the qal as well as to the hi.

Preliminary conclusions

In agreement with our findings for the prose category, the percentage of imperf.-forms of the ho. in prophecy for the above-mentioned roots is lower than that for the total amount of forms in prophecy (25.8 % vs. 40.7 %).

These eight imperfects are found of seven roots (**DWŠ**, **ḤNN**, **JṢR**, **JŠB**, **NTŠ**, **SBB**, and **ŠDD**). Williams regards these forms as old passive qal-forms, with the exception of **SBB**. Except for the root **NTŠ** it is impossible to distinguish between the meanings of ni. and ho. Perhaps it is possible to speak of two complementary forms of one pattern (ni.-perf. and pu.-imperf.). A pu.-imperf. and two ni.-imperf. forms of **NTŠ** occur. Between these forms there are semantic differences.

We observe that a number of ho.-forms may rather be related to the qal than to the hi. for the eight roots, of which hi.-forms occur in prophecy and which have an unclear relationship between ho. and hi. (**J'D**, **PQD**, **ŠBR** and possibly **KRT** and **SWG**). The ho. impf. of **JŠB** is related to the qal, yet its perfect relates to the hi.

4.3.3 Conclusions

The question raises itself as to what extent this research into the ho.-ni. relationship supports the theory of the pass. qal. In keeping with my presentation of the conclusions of the research into the ni.-pu. I will first present the arguments in favor of this theory. Later, I will deal with the arguments against it.

4.3.3.1 The following arguments may be used in favor of the theory of the pass. qal:

a) Twelve roots in the OT which may be classified as group II: those of which no hi.-forms occur. The ho. of ten of these roots occurs only in the imperfect. For prose the following roots are involved: **LQḤ**, **NQM**, **NTN** and **NTṢ**; for poetry: **NTN** and for prophecy: **DWŠ**, **ḤNN**, **JṢR**, **NTŠ**, **ŠDD** and **ARR**. The last root has not been dealt with before because ni. and ho. do not occur in the same genre.

The **ARR** ho. occurs only as an imperf.

These hoph'als function as a passive of the qal. Williams regards these as remains of the pass. qal. Yet relatively few imperfects occur for the roots of groups I and III. In prose one impf. of the root **NKH** occurs and one of the root **NTK**. The last-mentioned form might also be regarded as a pass. qal since it functions as a passive of the qal (see 4.3.2.1 III). In poetry, one ho.-impf. of **NTN** occurs (see 4.3.2.2). Therefore, it is possible that the Masoretes did not recognize these forms as pass. qals and thus vocalized them as ho.

b) For some roots (**JṢR**, **LQḤ**, **NTŠ** and **ŠDD**) only perfects occur of the pu. whereas the ho. is restricted to imperfects. Pu. as well as ho. function as passive of the qal. The Masoretes might not have recognized these forms as old pass. qals. Therefore, they vocalized them as pu.-perf. and ho.-imperf.

4.3.3.2 Against the theory of the pass. qal the following arguments may be adduced:

a) It is remarkable that relatively great numbers of ni.-perfects occur for the roots of group II, where the ho.-imperf. were identified as remains of the pass. qal. Below we present an overview of the respective distribution of ni., ho. and, in as far as they occur, pu. as set against the total amount of OT material. In my opinion, the root **NTK** belongs to this group as well (see above).

Root	Niph'al					Hoph'al					Pu'al				
	Tot.	Pt.	Pf.	Ip.	R	Tot.	Pt.	Pf.	Ip.	R	Tot.	Pt.	Pf.	Ip.	R
'RR	1	1	-	-	-	1	-	-	1	-	-	-	-	-	-
DWŠ	2	-	1	-	1inf	1	-	-	1	-	-	-	-	-	-
ḤNN	1	-	1	-	-	2	-	-	2	-	-	-	-	-	-
JṢR	1	-	1	-	-	1	-	-	1	-	1	-	1	-	-
LQḤ	10	-	4	3	3inf	6	-	-	6	-	9	1	8	-	-
NQM	12	-	3	4	5inf	3	-	-	3	-	-	-	-	-	-
NTK	8	1	7	-	-	1	-	-	1	-	-	-	-	-	-
NTN	82	3	48	27	4inf	8	-	-	8	-	-	-	-	-	-
NTṢ	3	-	3	-	-	1	-	-	1	-	1	-	1	-	-
NTŠ	4	-	-	4	-	1	-	-	1	-	-	-	-	-	-
ŠDD	1	-	1	-	-	2	-	-	2	-	18	-	18	-	-

The ni., ho. and pu. of these roots function as passive of the qal whilst ni. perfects appear quite frequently. The ho. occurs only in imperf. forms, the pu. in the perfect. For a number of roots (**DWŠ**, **ḤNN**, **JṢR** (?), **NTK**, **NTṢ** (?) and **ŠDD** (?)) one might consider the possibility that the ho.-imperf. has adopted the place of the ni.-imperf. Since the ni. perfects, due to their orthographic representation, cannot be read as pass. qal perfects, this might be a possible argument against a too one-sided interpretation of the pass. qal (with respect to certain roots).

It remains a striking fact that a number of roots in this group belong to the *primae nun* verbs. Therefore, vocalization could occur in various ways.

b) For a number of roots (**ḤRB**, **JLD**, **PDH** and **ŠMM**) infinitive forms of the ho. occur. In meaning they may be related to the qal but not to the hi. (see 4.3.2.1.III). In as far as can be ascertained no attempts have been made to identify the remains of the pass. qal-inf. These forms can neither be regarded as inf. of the pass. qal (due to the prefix **H**-). However, it may be concluded from this that not all ho.-forms that are related to the qal can be regarded as remains of the pass. qal. Moreover, similarly, perf.-forms of the ho. may be related to the qal.

c) In this context, it is interesting to note that the ni. shows preference for usage of the imperf. and the ho. for usage of the perf. of the roots of group I, of which the ni. occurs in a semantic relationship to the hi. Since the material of the various genres is fairly limited we present the distribution of the niph'al and hoph'al over the various tenses in the OT (see table p. 164).

Ni. imperfects and ho. perfects occur relatively frequently; this might support the fact that there has been a development in which verbal stems merged into one another. On the basis of the above-mentioned arguments it might be assumed that for the ho. a similar development has occurred as for the pu.

Possibly, the semantic relationship between the oppositional verbal stems ho. and hi. had weakened in an early stage of language development, even before the OT text had been committed to writing. Thus, the ho. could function as the passive of the qal for certain roots. This may be deduced from the fact that there are ho.-inf. which are related to the qal. Such would account for the merging

Root	Niph'al					Hoph'al				
	Total	Partic.	Perf.	Imperf.	Rest	Total	Partic.	Perf.	Imperf.	Rest
ḤBA	19	3	7	4	5	1	-	1	-	-
KWN	68	37	3	25	3	6	2	4	-	-
KLM	26	5	9	9	3	2	-	2	-	-
NGR	4	2	2	-	-	1	1	-	-	-
NDḤ	24	17	7	-	-	1	1	-	-	-
NKH	1	-	1	-	-	16	6	8	2	-
NṢB	51	43	8	-	-	3	2	1	-	-
NṢL	15	-	1	10	4	2	2	-	-	-
SBB	20	-	14	6	-	6	5	-	1	-
RAH	99	3	34	50	12	4	1	3	-	-
ŠḤT	6	1	3	2	-	2	2	-	-	-

of pass. qal imperf. and ho.-imperf. As for the pu. it is impossible to ascertain to what extent these forms could be distinguished at the times of classical Hebrew. The fact that for certain roots pu.-perf. and ho.-imperf. are the only remaining forms (e.g. **LQḤ**) appears to indicate that this may have been the case.

For other roots it is more difficult to come to a conclusion on this. The fact that ni. perfects and ho. imperfects occur side by side appear to indicate that the ho. replaced the ni.-imperf. The theory of the pass. qal does not exclude this possibility, yet possibly this concerns a later development.

It is remarkable, moreover, that, for the roots of which ni.-forms function as hi. passives, a counter development has occurred much like that of the pu.-stems. The ni. of these roots shows preference for usage of the imperf. whereas the ho. seems to favor usage of the perf.

In conclusion we may state that the passive qal-imperf. before or at the time of classical Hebrew functioned as the passive of niph'al, hoph'al and qal. For certain roots it is impossible to ascertain this accurately. For other roots it cannot be known with absolute certainty to what extent the passive qal-imperf. merged with the ho. in part or completely.

It may be observed, however, that apart from the replacement of the pass. qal by pu. and ho. a development occurred--as with the pu.--which is basically a merging of the 'passive' verbal stems (ni.-perf. and ho.-imperf. and vice versa). This finding is enhanced due to the Masoretic vocalization which represents the passive-imperf. as a ho.-imperf.

4.4 The relationship between the niph'al and the pass. qal-part.

4.4.1 Introduction and methodology

As was stated in 4.1.4, there are 119 roots of which both ni. forms as well as forms of the pass. qal-participle occur in the OT. It is remarkable that of those 119 roots there are 77 of which the ni. participle does not occur. Relatively speaking this is a high number. Now we should assert that for a number of roots in this group, in general, few forms of the ni. occur. For a few roots many ni.-forms occur, e.g. of **KRT** (72 ni. and 3 pass. qal-partic.), **PQD** (resp. 20 and 78), **ŠMR** (resp. 37 and 3), **ŠPK** (resp. 8 and 3), etc. It is possible that, for the roots of which no forms of the ni.-participle occur, the pass.-qal participle functions as the ni.-participle. It cannot be maintained with complete certainty because the number of forms is often relatively small and because the assessment criteria are lacking.

There are forty-four roots of which ni. participle and pass. qal-participle occur. Below, I will describe the relationship obtaining between these participial forms. We will examine whether they overlap in meaning or whether they are completely distinct. We have divided the roots into three groups, depending on the semantic relationship between the ni. and the active verbal stems (qal, pi. or pu.).

4.4.2 The relationship between the pass. qal-part. and the ni. part. for roots of which the ni. occurs in a semantic relationship to the qal: 36.

We present an overview of these roots including the numbers of ni.-participles and pass. qal-participles as distributed over the various genres:

	Niph'al-participle				Pass. qal-participle			
Root	Total	Prose	Poetry	Prophecy	Total	Prose	Poetry	Prophecy
AHB	1	-	1	-	5	4	-	1
AZR	1	-	1	-	1	1	-	-

Root	Niph'al-participle Total	Prose	Poetry	Prophecy	Pass. qal-participle Total	Prose	Poetry	Prophecy
ASP	4	2	-	2	1	1	-	-
ARR	1	-	-	1	40	32	1	7
BZH	10	2	2	6	4	1	1	2
BḤR	6	-	6	-	18	14	2	2
BNH	1	1	-	-	4	2	2	-
BRR	2	-	2	-	7	4	1	2
GLH	2	2	-	-	6	4	2	-
GR'	1	1	-	-	2	-	-	2
DGL	2	-	2	-	1	-	1	-
DRŠ	1	1	-	-	2	-	1	1
HPK	2	1	1	-	2	1	-	1
HRS	2	2	-	-	1	1	-	-
ZKR	1	1	-	-	1	-	1	-
Z'M	1	-	1	-	2	-	1	1
ḤMD	4	2	2	-	3	-	2	1
HRṢ	5	3	-	2	3	1	1	1
JD'	3	1	2	-	3	2	-	1
JLD	7	6	1	-	6	3	3	-
J'S	5	4	1	-	1	-	-	1
KTB	1	1	-	-	112	104	3	5
NSA	10	-	-	10	8	1	3	4
NTN	3	2	-	1	10	10	-	-
SWG	2	-	-	2	1	-	1	-
'ZB	3	1	1	1	12	4	1	7
'SR	1	1	-	-	12	10	1	1
'ŚH	4	4	-	-	16	14	2	-
PWS	4	3	-	1	1	-	-	1
PRS	1	1	-	-	4	3	1	-
PTH	1	-	-	1	13	10	2	1
QBṢ	1	1	-	-	1	1	-	-
QLH	1	-	1	-	2	2	-	-
QRA	4	2	-	2	7	1	-	6
RAH	3	3	-	-	1	1	-	-
SBR	11	5	3	3	2	1	1	-
Total	112	53	27	32	315	233	34	48

The figures for the different genres may be represented as follows:

	Total	Prose	Poetry	Prophecy
Ni. pt.	112	53	27	32
	26.2 %	18.5 %	44.3 %	40 %
Pass. qal	315	233	34	48
	73.8 %	81.5 %	55.7 %	60 %
Total	427	286	61	80

A fairly interesting aspect is that the pass. qal. participle occurs much more frequently than the ni.-participle. Even if the roots **ARR** and **KTB**, with 40 and 112 occurrences, are left out of consideration, the pass. qal-participle still remains at a relatively high percentage (60 %). When the figures for the various genres are compared in more detail it becomes clear that the high percentage of pass. qal-participles in prose is due to the great amount of occurrences of the roots **ARR** and **KTB.** Apart from these roots the percentage for the pass. qal is 65 %.

For the majority of these roots it is difficult to make an easy semantic distinction between the ni.-participle and the pass. qal-participle, e.g.

AZR : ni. (Ps. 65:7) and pass. qal (1Kin. 1:8) 'girded'
ASP : ni. (Isa. 13:4) and pass. qal (Ez. 34:29) 'assembled'
ARR : ni. (Mal. 3:9) and pass. qal (Jer. 11:3) 'cursed'
BNH : ni. (1Chron. 22:19) and pass. qal (Neh. 7:4) 'built'
KTB : ni. (Est. 8:8) and pass. qal (Est. 6:2; 10:2) 'written'
PTḤ : ni. (Zech. 13:1) and pass. qal (Jer. 5:16) 'opened' etc.

It is remarkable that the pass. qal-participle is often used as the adjective of a substantive. Likewise, the ni.-participle shows preference for a certain genre (e.g. **BḤR** ni. 6 x in Pro.).

4.4.3 The relationship between the pass. qal-participle and the ni.-participle for roots of which the ni. occurs in a semantic relationship to the pi: 2

The following roots are concerned:

	Niph'al-participle				Pass. qal-participle			
Root	Total	Prose	Poetry	Prophecy	Total	Prose	Poetry	Prophecy
DBR	1	1	-	-	1	-	1	-
ḤPH	1	-	1	-	2	2	-	-

The ni.-participle of **DBR** (Ez. 33:30) may be translated reciprocally: 'who speak about you amongst themselves'; the pass. qal-participle (Pro. 25:11) translates as a passive 'spoken'. It is remarkable that both the ni. as well as the pass. qal-participle are related to the pi. and not the qal (likewise for **BRK**)

The pass. qal-participle of the root **ḤPH** (2 Sam. 15:30) may also be related to the qal (also 2 Sam. 15:30) 'covering of the face'; the ni.-participle (Ps. 68:14) is related to the pi. (1 Chron. 3:5, 7 etc.) meaning 'covered with gold'.

4.4.4 The relationship between the pass. qal-participle and the ni.-participle for roots of which the ni. occurs in a semantic relationship to the hi.: 3.

	Niph'al-partic.				Pass. qal-partic.			
Root	Total	Prose	Poetry	Prophecy	Total	Prose	Poetry	Prophecy
'LM	4	2	1	1	1	-	1	-
PRD	3	2	1	-	1	1	-	-
ŠB'	11	1	1	9	1	1	-	-

The pass. qal-participle of **'LM** (Ps. 90:8) is used substantivally 'our secrets'. It is the only qal-form of this root in the OT. The ni.-participles (1 Kin. 10:3; Pro. 12:14) may also be translated as 'hidden'. It is possible that the ni.-participle (Ps. 26:4) differs: 'Those who hide themselves', i.e. 'hypocrites'. The form in Nah. 3:11 is unclear.

Moreover, only one pass. qal-participle occurs of the root **PRD** (Ez. 1:11) 'be spread' (of wings). The ni.-pt. may be translated as 'separated' (Judg. 4:11; Neh. 4:13 and Pro. 18:1).

The only qal-form of the root **ŠB'** is found in Ez. 21:28 in the expression **ŠeBŪ'Ē ŠeBŪ'ŌT**. The exact meaning of this expression is unclear. Possibly, we are dealing here with archaic remaining forms as in the case of the pass.-qals of the two roots discussed above. Another explanation is that it is a noun (**ŠeBŪ'ĀH**) with a masculine plural (cf. Ez. 13:20 where a masculine plural for the word **NPŠ** is used).

4.5 The niph'al-hitpa'el relationship

4.5.1 Introduction

According to traditional grammars, (such as GESENIUS-KAUTZSCH 1909, &54e-g and BERGSTRÄSSER, 1929, 1977, &18b), the hitp. serves first of all as a reflexive or reciprocal form of the pi. In certain cases, it may serve as a qal reflexive. In the latter instance, we may wonder whether or not these are remains of the Gt-stem of the qal. For it is remarkable that Hebrew has a pi. reflexive with a t-infix (the hitp.) yet, contrary to other Semitic languages, it does not have a qal-reflexive with a t-infix. It has been suggested, therefore, that these forms originally existed in Hebrew but that they have disappeared. Hence, attempts have been made to discover remains of this form in the OT text.[259]

The hitp. may receive a passive meaning only rarely. Bean, however, shows that the description 'reflexive' does not adequately fit the function definition of the hitp.[260] In chapter 2.5 we defined a reflexive verb form as follows: 'a verb form, of which the grammatical subject undergoes a certain action, (or, of which the grammatical subject is the object of the action), expressed by the verb and where the grammatical subject agrees with the agent, i.e. the person who performs or who causes the action'. According to this definition a reflexive verb may not receive an accusative object, whether or not it is marked by **AT** in Hebrew. Only rarely, ni. are constructed with an object.[261] However, the OT provides a number of examples of hitp. constructed with an accusative object.[262] Bean, in his description of hitp. syntactic usage, observes, with respect to the (rarely occurring) hitp. passive, that a marked increase in frequency occurs in post-exilic material; (post-exilic passive usage outnumbers that in pre-exilic material at a ratio of three to one).[263]

My research agrees with Bean's findings with respect to the reflexive function of the hitp. For a great number of roots a distinction can be made between the ni. and the hitp. The ni. expresses the undergoing of an action the agent of which needs not to be mentioned. That is why ni.-forms, depending on the context, may be translated passively as well as reflexively. Yet the hitp. expresses the active performance of an action or an emphasis which is placed more on the active action than on the undergoing of the action. The hitp. may be translated as active, reflexive or reciprocal, but rarely as passive.[264]

Here, I list a number of examples in the category prose of 'passive' ni.-forms and 'active' hitp.-forms, without taking into consideration the relationship of ni. and hitp. to the active verbal stems:

GNB : ni.-impf., Ex. 22:11, be stolen (cf. pu.); hitp.-impf. 2 x, 2 Sam. 19:4, 'steal into'

HPK : ni. 16 x, esp. pass. be changed (13 x); hitp. 2 x, Gen. 3:24, 'whirling around', active; Judg. 7:13, 'tumble into'.

ḤLQ : ni. 5 x, 'be distributed'; 'distribute oneself' hitp. 1 x, Josh. 18:5 (nb. plus obj.), 'distribute among one another', active.

ḤLH : ni. 3 x, 'be/become ill', passive; hitp. 3 x, 2 Sam. 13:2, 5, 6, 'keep o.s. ill' (i.e. 'pretend to be ill').

MDD : ni. 2 x, Jer. 31:37/33:22, passive; hitp. 1 x, 1 Kin. 17:21, 'stretch oneself', active.

MKR : ni. 16 x, passive/reflexive; hitp. 4 x, 'sell oneself' (figuratively), 1 Kin. 21:20, 25; 2 Kin. 17:17; cf. also Deut. 28:68 ('sell oneself to').

NQŠ : ni. 1 x, Deut. 12:30, passive; hitp. 1 x, 1 Sam. 28:9, 'lay a snare', active.

'LM : ni. 7 x, passive, 'be hidden' hitp. 3 x, Deut. 22:1, 3, 4, 'hide oneself for', active.

PRṢ : ni. 2 x, 1 Sam. 3:1, 1 Chron. 3:1(?), passive; hitp. 1 x, 1 Sam. 25:10, 'run away', active.

ṢDQ : ni. 1 x, Dan. 8:14, 'be restored', passive; hitp. 1 x, Gen. 44:16 'bring up as justification to someone else', active;

QŠR : ni. 2 x, 1 Sam. 18:1; Neh. 3:38, 'be bound', 'be joined together'; hitp. 3 x, 2 Chron. 24:25, 26; 2 Kin. 9:14, metaphorically: 'conspire against'.

RṢH : ni. 6 x, 'be accepted by'; hitp. 1 x, 1 Sam. 29:4, 'make oneself acceptable to', active.

RṢṢ : ni. 1 x, Ez. 29:7, 'be broken' hitp. 1 x, Gen. 25:22, 'press together', active.

From the examples supplied above it is evident that ni. and hitp. differ from one another in the following aspects:

1)The hitp. may be constructed with an accusative object (cf. Josh. 18:5 **ḤLQ**).

2) The hitp. can express a nuance in meaning that may best be described as 'to behave oneself in a certain way' (see e.g. **ḤLH**, **MKR**, **RṢH**, etc.). Therefore, these forms may at times adopt a metaphoric sense (e.g. **QŠR**, **MRR**). In this respect the hitp. differs from the qal.

3) For the hitp. of a number of roots lexicalization occurs (e.g. **GNB**, **HPK**, **QŠR**, etc.), much like the findings for e.g. Akka-

dian roots with a t-infix.

For a number of roots it is difficult to make a distinction between the meaning of the ni. and that of the hitp., e.g. of the roots **KRK** and **KAS** (ni. 2 Sam. 10:6 = hitp., 1 Chron. 19:6). It may well be possible that, for those roots of which the hitp. occurs in a refl./pass. relationship to the qal, it concerns original qal reflexives with a t-infix.[265] In my view it is impossible to determine to what extent these forms were recognizable at the time when the OT was put in writing, or whether Masoretic vocalization was misapplied.[266]

Below I will restrict myself to a discussion of the roots of which the ni. occurs in a semantic relationship to the pi. Since the hitp. serves as a pi. reflexive, the question raises itself what the formal and semantic distinctions are between the forms of the ni. and those of the hitp.

4.5.2 Certain specific problematic cases

Bergsträsser's grammar, (1929, &16d), asserts that for certain roots of which the ni. occurs in semantic relationship to the pi. the ni.-perfect and the hitp.-imperfect may supplement one another. It mentions the examples of the roots **ṬMA** and **JṢB.**[267] Although the root **ṬMA** functions as a striking example of such supplementation, there are more roots for which the phenomenon occurs.

The following roots are concerned:

Root	Niph'al					Hitpa'el				
	Total	Partic.	Perf.	Imperf.	Rest	Total	Partic.	Perf.	Imperf.	Rest
BRR	3	2	-	-	1	3	-	-	3	-
GAL	3	1	2	-	-	2	-	-	2	-
DKA	1	1	-	-	-	2	-	-	2	-[268]
ṬMA	18	2	16	-	-	15	-	-	15	-
KSH	2	-	1	-	1	9	3	-	6	-

In what way might this distribution over the verbal stems be explained? It is possible to vocalize the hitp.-imperf. of **ṬMA** as a pi. or ni.-imperf. Yet it does not explain why the Masoretes read this form as a hitp. Possibly, this phenomenon points to the fact that the process of 'merging' of verbal stems already occurred at the time when the OT was put in writing and that it may not exclusively be attributed to Masoretic vocalization.

It is also remarkable that other roots, of which the ni. occurs in a semantic relationship to the pi., the corresponding hitp. forms show a preference for the imperfect (e.g. **GLH**, **KWN**, **KḤŠ**, **MLṬ**, **NḤM**, **NKR**, and **'RH**). For these roots there is no supplementing process ni.-hitp. nor is there a cumulative preference. Moreover, it cannot be ascertained which semantic difference obtains between the hitp. and the ni. (cf. e.g. the root **BRK**, ni. Gen. 12:3/18:8/28:14 (perf.) vs. hitp. Gen. 22:18/26:4).[269]

We will not discuss the hitp. in detail here since in most cases it is easily distinguishable from other passive-reflexive verbal stems both in form as well as in meaning.

V Summary and Conclusions

5.1 The direction which Jenni chose for his research of the function of verbal stems was different from that selected by preceding grammarians. With respect to the function of the ni. his grammar differs in two ways from those of men such as Gesenius-Kautzsch and Lambert:

a) The ni. may only occur in direct opposition to the qal and not in direct opposition to the pi. or hi.
b) The ni. expresses a uniform category of meaning. His definition of the ni. justifies a passive as well as a reflexive and a tolerative translation of ni.-forms.

Jenni's views on the ni. have been based on the mutual relationship of the verbal stem. He assumes that in Biblical Hebrew these verbal stems fit into a system within which each verbal stem has its own well-defined function and meaning semantically distinct from the other ones.

5.2 The results of my research agree with those of Jenni's presuppositions and methodology in the following two respects:

a) In Biblical Hebrew the distinctive notions of reflexive-passive-tolerative, as applicable in European languages, do not apply. Within the ni. it is impossible to make a formal distinction between these categories of meaning. I have based my views on the assumption that the ni. expresses a uniform category of meaning.
b) The ni. may not be studied in isolation. Its study ought to include its relationship to other (seemingly equal) passive/-reflexive verbal stems (cf. Jenni's *Das Hebräische Pi'el* versus Bean).

5.3 My research differs from Jenni's presuppositions and methodology in the following three aspects:

a) A study of the ni. should not only comprise the ni.-forms conjugated according to the normal paradigm, but also forms which deviate from the paradigm and, in as much as possible, forms gleaned from epigraphic material. The latter sources do not provide anything for this study.
b) The textual material is divided into the three genres: prose, poetry, and prophecy. If possible or if necessary, these genres are subdivided in even greater detail.

c) The ni. may occur semantically in an oppositional relationship not only to the qal, but also to one of the other active verbal stems (pi. or hi.).

5.4 The classical grammars study and describe the passive/reflexive verbal stems in relationship to the active verbal stem. My research is aimed at describing and studying the passive/reflexive verbal stems and their mutual relationships.

5.5 Much can be said for the theory on the old passive of the qal, which was formulated as such by Williams and others (old passive qal forms exist though Masoretic vocalization regards them as pu.- and ho.-). However, the theory cannot be proven for a full 100 %.

5.6 In Masoretic Hebrew forms of the pu. may occur in a passive relationship not only to the pi. but also to the qal. The ni. shows a preference for usage of the imperfect whereas the pu. shows preference for usage of the perfect for those roots of which the ni. and pu. occur both in a passive relationship to the qal. For some roots it is possible that two complementary forms of a pattern are involved: pu.-perf. and ni.-imperf. This phenomenon applies especially for prose (cf. Ezekiel). The poetic books of Job and Proverbs deviate from this principle.

It is possible that this preference and the complementary aspects which are so obvious may be traced back to the fact that the Masoretes did not recognize these as pass. qal-forms. Therefore, they vocalized these forms as the ni.-imperf and pu.-perf. which, in form and meaning, are the most closely related. Otherwise, it appears that also in the *Vorlage* the semantic opposition between the various verbal stems has weakened. This is evident from e.g. the presence of overlaps of participles of ni., pu. and pass. qal. Also for those roots of which the ni. and pu. occur in a passive relationship to the pi. there may possibly be a case of complementary functions or cumulative preference. In this context the ni. shows preference for usage of the perf. whereas the pu. favors that of the imperf. Yet the material is too scarce to draw meaningful conclusions. Moreover, we note that the verb forms complement one another for a number of roots of which the hitp. and the ni. occur in a pass./refl. relationship to the pi. (ni.-perf. and hitp.-imperf). The above-mentioned phenomena cannot be explained from a mistaken Masoretic vocalization. Therefore it is possible that, under the influence of the disappearing pass. qal-verbal stem, even in the *Vorlage* the forms of this verbal stem had been replaced by the ni. and pu. forms respectively.

5.7 Moreover, the forms of the ho. may occur in a semantic relationship to the hi. but also to the qal in Masoretic Hebrew. Both for those roots of which the ni. occurs in relationship to the hi. and of which corresponding ho.-forms exist, as well as for the roots of which the ho. and ni. occur in a semantic relationship to the qal, the ho. shows preference for usage of the imperfect whilst the ni. favors usage of the perfect. For a number of roots it is possible that the ho.-imperf. has replaced the ni.-imperf. There does not appear to be a difference between prose, poetry and prophecy. Yet it must be noticed that the examined number of ho.-forms occurring in poetry is small.

Even for these forms it is possible that a number of them were not recognized as pass. qal-forms by the Masoretes. Therefore, they have been vocalized as ho.-imperfects. In agreement with our findings for the pu. this finding does not apply for all roots. The existence of ho.-infinitives, which may be related to the qal in meaning, points to the fact that, again, in the *Vorlage* semantic opposition has weakened.

For the roots of which the ni. occurs in a semantic relationship to the hi. a reverse development has occurred: the ni. shows a preference for usage of the imperf. whereas the pu. favors usage of the perf.

5.8 The resulting overall view of the relationships ni. versus pu. and ni. versus ho. is fairly complex. Since ni. as well as pu. and ho. may be related to more than one active verbal stem, various developments have occurred which cannot be traced back exclusively to Masoretic vocalization. It is evident that these developments were occurring in the period in which the OT texts were recorded. The presupposition, then, which maintains that the verbal stems in Biblical Hebrew form a closed system within which each verbal stem has its own well determined distinct semantic function and meaning, is incorrect. It is possible that such a situation existed in a very early stage of Hebrew, yet support for it is no longer evident in the (un-)vocalized OT text. In the OT text we can indicate a development, (due to the influence of the disappearance of the pass. qal), due to which the verbal stems are as it were telescoped into each other. It is striking that one verbal stem shows preference for usage of the perf. and another for the imperf. especially where two passive verbal stems (ni. and pu; ni. and ho.) are related to an active verbal stem. In this context perf. and imperf. are not tied to a certain verbal stem. This view is probably enhanced due to Masoretic vocalization. Yet in my opinion it may be traced back to developments occurring prior to that.

5.9 This research is a first attempt to the study of passive/reflexive verbal stems. Much research remains necessary yet. My study of the passive/reflexive verbal stems is especially geared towards the ni. It would be interesting to find out to what extent a study geared to the ho. or the pu. might yield new perspectives.

Notes

Chapter I

1. JENNI 1968.
2. In fact, Jenni was not the first to attempt the description of the verbal stem in a monograph. In this respect the doctoral thesis of Stuart A. Ryder II stands out, entitled *The D-stem in Western Semitic*, University Microfilms, Ann Arbor, Michigan, 1966, order no. 66-14.995. Jenni and many other scholars were not familiar with this. The study gained popularity when it was published as a book: RYDER 1974.
3. I use the terms 'perfect' and 'imperfect' instead of the terms 'afformative' and 'preformative conjugation', which are formally more appropriate, since almost all of the literature discussed below makes use of this terminology.
4. It would lead beyond the scope of this study to present an extensive bibliography of studies on the 'tenses' in Biblical Hebrew. That is why only the most important works will be referred to below. The complexity of the issue is such that, in spite of the great amount of research devoted to the question of the exact meaning of the perfect and the imperfect, it still has not been answered definitively. There are at least six different views on the function of the tenses:

   1) perfect and imperfect may express a tense aspect, BAUER 1910, SAWYER 1976;

   2) they may refer to an *Aktionsart*, which indicates whether an action is complete or incomplete, DRIVER 1892, WILLIAMS 1978;

   3) they may refer to an 'aspect', i.e. a subjective aspect by means of which the speaker wants to indicate how he regards the action expressed by the verbal form, studied according to various approaches, RUNDGREN 1961, MICHEL 1960, KUSTÁR 1972;

   4) some authors assume that there was a stage in the development of the 'form' of the verb in West-Semitic that was highly comparable to that of the verb form in Akkadian and Sumerian, (cf. MEYER 1972, or the school of Rössler, SIEDL 1971, BOBZIN 1973). Some describe the verb from a historical viewpoint as a mixture of idiom corresponding to Akkadian and a kind of West-Semitic in which every form of a closed func-

tion system was lost, as argued by DRIVER 1936. Others study the verb form in comparison with Egyptian forms, THACKER 1954;

5) scholars describe the perfect and the imperfect by means of linguistic theories developed by H. Weinrich which treat language as a means of communication, SCHNEIDER 1982;

6) it is assumed that there is no difference in function between the perfect and the imperfect, SPERBER 1966. MC.FALL 1982 presents an overview of the issue of the so called 'waw-consecutive'. For an overview of studies of the verb system since 1951 one may consult METTINGER 1973, FENSHAM 1978 and BOONSTRA 1982.

5. See PORGES 1875 and the various comparative Semitic grammars: WRIGHT 1890, 198-226; ZIMMERN 1898, 81-92; BROCKELMANN 1908, 504-544; O'LEARY 1923, 208-234; GRAY 1934, 76-85; MOSCATI 1959, 119-126; MOSCATI 1964, 1969, 122-130. GOSHEN-GOTTSTEIN 1969 presents an overview and a new approach to the study of Semitic verbal stem.
6. See on the ni.: RIEDER 1884; HALFMANN 1888, 1892; LAMBERT 1900 and for after 1968: 43ff. See for the hitp. STEIN 1893, YALON 1932, SPEISER 1955 and DOMBROWSKY 1962 and for the studies after 1968: ch. 1.6.
7. For a biography on Gesenius' life and work see: FELLMAN 1981 and MILLER 1927.
8. GESENIUS-KAUTZSCH 1909; EWALD 1870; BAUER-LEANDER 1922, 1965; JOÜON 1923, 1965. I consulted older editions of Gesenius' grammar in as far as it was possible for me to find them: the 1st edition GESENIUS 1813; the 2nd edition GESENIUS 1816 and GESENIUS 1817; the 8th edition GESENIUS 1826; the 20th edition GESENIUS-RODIGER 1866 and the 22nd edition GESENIUS-KAUTZSCH 1878. Moreover, I consulted the English translation of Gesenius: GESENIUS-KAUTZSCH-COWLEY 1910 and older impressions of Ewald: EWALD 1827; EWALD 1842 and EWALD 1863. See Appendix A for a full list of the consulted grammars.
9. JENNI 1967.
10. JENNI 1969.
11. JENNI 1978.
12. JENNI 1977.
13. The Hebrew word **QAL** means 'light', as contrasted with **KāḇēD** 'heavy', by means of which Jewish grammarians of old refer to the other verbal stem. Cf. GESENIUS-KAUTZSCH 1909, &39a: *Grundform*; JOÜON 1923, 1965, &40a: *la conjugaison simple*; LETTINGA 1976, &41: *grondstam* [= basic stem; transl.]
14. JENNI 1968, 12, 15ff., 275: first conclusion: "Das hebräische Pi'el ist nicht nur morphologisch, sondern auch in der bedeutungsmodifizierenden Funktion eine einheitliche Stammform, die innerhalb des hebräischen Verbalsystems zu den anderen Hauptstammformen in distinktiver Opposition steht." In fact this is not a conclusion but a presupposition of Jenni's.
15. JENNI 1969, 61ff.
16. GESENIUS-KAUTZSCH 1909, &30a.
17. GESENIUS-KAUTZSCH 1909, &30d.
18. GESENIUS-KAUTZSCH 1909, &30g wishes to preserve the purely historical concept 'root' for the bi-literal stems because the

three letters, the so-called 'trilitera', may be traced back to a basic form consisting of two letters, the so-called 'bilitera'. A biliteral stem may have formed the basis for various triliteral stems, e.g. **KR** as root for **KRH**, **KRR**, **KWR**, and **AKR**. However, other grammars do call the word stem a 'root', see e.g. STADE 1879, &139; BERGSTRäSSER 1929, &1b,c; JOüON 1923, 1965, &34a; LAMBERT 1946, 1972, &155, 158 and LETTINGA 1976, &40a.

19. GESENIUS-KAUTZSCH 1909, &30a; see also GESENIUS-RöDIGER 1866, 67, 77.
20. GESENIUS-KAUTZSCH 1909, &79a
21. GESENIUS-KAUTZSCH 1909, &38. This division is also found in the older grammars of Gesenius', see e.g.: GESENIUS 1816, 44; GESENIUS 1826, 50,51; GESENIUS-RöDIGER 1866, 89.
22. GESENIUS-KAUTZSCH 1909, &38d: "Hierbei ist nicht ausgeschlossen, dass zu Nominibus, von denen Verba denominativa abgeleitet sind, der entsprechende (ursprüngliche) Verbalstamm, sei es im Hebr. oder in den Dialekten, noch vorhanden ist". As an example Gesenius-Kautsch mentions among others the root **LBN** 'be white', which occurs in Biblical Hebrew only in the hitp. and the hi., from which is derived the noun **LeBeNaH** 'brick' from which the verb **LBN** (qal: 'make bricks') is derived.
23. GESENIUS-KAUTZSCH 1909, &39a: identical to the imper. sing. masc.
24. GESENIUS-KAUTZSCH 1909, &39c; see also GESENIUS 1817, 233.
25. See e.g. EWALD 1870, &126a; STADE 1879, &153b; BAUER-LEANDER 1922, 1965, 279ff.; BERGSTRäSSER 1929, &2a. Cf. also ORNAN 1972, 125ff. and JOüON 1923, 1965, &40a, in &43a, however, he states that: "Pour la commodité on énonce généralement la racine sous la forme de la 3e p. sg. m. du parfait,..."
26. GESENIUS-KAUTZSCH 1909, &52f.
27. GESENIUS-KAUTZSCH 1909, &52a,f.
28. GESENIUS-KAUTZSCH 1909, &52g,h. GESENIUS 1816, 61 and GESENIUS 1826, 70 ff. mention the causative as the first meaning of the pi.
29. JOüON 1923, 1965, &52d: *le sens fondamental*. Note that Joüon relates the doubling of the middle radical to the meaning: &52a: "L'intensité du sens est très naturellement exprimée par l'allongement de la consonne."
30. BAUER-LEANDER 1922, 1965, 290ff.: "Die intensiven Stammformen haben sich bei viel Verben schon im Ursem. kausative Bedeutung angeeignet, und diese tritt auch im Hebr. haüfig auf."
31. JENNI 1968, 9ff.
32. GOETZE 1942, cf. also GAG, &88.
33. GOETZE 1942, 2. Note how Goetze accepts that the Š-stem (comparable to hi.) and the N-stem (comparable to ni.) have a semantic relationship to the basic stem (p. 4). Earlier, Poebel had pointed out that the D-stem in Akkadian does not have an intensive meaning but that, in analogy to Sumerian, it represented plurality of transitive verbs and it carried a transitive-causative meaning in intransitive verbs. See POEBEL 1939,5, 65ff. Goetze does not agree with this conclusion.
34. GOETZE 1942, 6: "In conclusion it can be stated that in Akka-

dian all D-stems (with the exeption to be mentioned presently) are in parallelism with statives." The only exceptions are the quasi D-forms (e.g. *ruqqudum* 'dance'; *qubbum* 'complain').

35. The term 'stative' was used for the first time by the Assyriologist B. Landsberger. It is also called the permansive or the verbal adjective: GAG, &77d and p. 16xx; UNGNAD-MATOUŠ 1969, &54; see also KRAUS 1984 and, lastly, HUEHNERGARD 1986 and 1987.
36. GOETZE 1942, 5: e.g. *ṭāb* 'is good'; *arik* 'is long'; *ḫaliq* 'is lost'.
37. GOETZE 1942, 5ff. "it denotes 'put a person or a thing in the condition which the stative indicates'"; e.g. *ṭubbum* (make good), *urrukum* (make long, lengthen); *ḫulluqum* (make lost).
38. GOETZE 1942, 5: "it denotes a condition which results from the subject's own action with reference to a person or a thing", e.g. *aḫiz* (holds); *ṣabit* (possesses); *maḫer* (has received). When it is related to intransitive verbs it may indicate a 'rest after some movement'.
39. GOETZE 1942, 5: 'make somebody have something', e.g. *lubbušum* 'cause somebody to be clothed in some garment'; *lummudum* 'make someone instructed in something'; *ṭubbum* 'make that something is sunk'. Goetze is not very clear in this case. This group of statives might also be referred to as a factitive even though he does not refer to it in this way.
40. GOETZE 1942, 5: "It denotes a state of affairs which results from another person's action, but the agent remains unspecified", e.g. *aḫiz* (is being held), 'is held'; *ṣabit* (is being seized), 'is seized'; *maḫer* (is becoming received), 'is received'. Many statives may belong to the second as well as to the third group. This depends on whether they are intransitive or transitive.
41. GOETZE 1941, 6: *uḫḫuzum* 'make (somebody) hold (something)' and 'make (something) fitted'; *wulludum* 'make (a woman) give birth (to a child)', 'make (a child) borne' (sic).
42. GAG, &88f: e.g. *ṣabātum* 'grip'; *ṣubbutum* 'keep gripped'; *ṭaradum* 'chase away'; *ṭurrudum* 'chase away'.
43. GAG, &88c.
44. GAG, &88c, h; p. 18xx. He does not see a clear relationship between these and the factitive D-stems.
45. CAD, AHW and the grammars of LANCELOTTI 1962, &74; HECKER 1968, &83b; UNGNAD-MATOUŠ 1969, &64; RIEMSCHNEIDER 1973, &11.1; CAPLICE 1980, &52. Only FINET 1956, &95 and the unimportant grammars of RIJCKMANS 1960, 67 and LIPIN 1973, 129 maintain the intensive meaning of the D-stem.
46. GOETZE 1942, 8.
47. For the Hebrew grammars see notes 26-30 and for Arabic grammars: WRIGHT 1896, &40 and FISCHER 1972, &164. Notice what the Semitic comparative grammar of MOSCATI 1964, 1969, &16.4 says about the D-stem: "This stem, which is attested over the whole Semitic area, seems to have a primarily 'factitive' significance, i.e. as a causative in relation to a state or condition". He mentions examples from Akkadian and Syrian. However, he also includes the denominative and intensive meaning!

48. JENNI 1968, 15.
49. JENNI 1968, 275: "sondern es drückt das Bewirken des dem Grundstamm entsprechenden adjektivisch ausgesagten Zustandes aus." See also JENNI 1978, &13.3.1.2.
50. JENNI 1968, 26 (**ḤăKăM**), 29cf. (**GăDŏL**), 123-126; JENNI 1978, &13.3.1.2.
51. JENNI 1968, 275: "Es bezeichnet das Bewirken des adjektivischen Zustandes ohne Rücksicht auf den Hergang und als vom Objekt akzidentiell erlittene Handlung."
52. JENNI 1968, 275: "es bezeichnet das Bewirken des adjektivisch auszusagenden Ergebnisses der Handlung im Grundstamm ohne Rücksicht auf den aktuellen Hergang."
53. JENNI 1968, 124-126.
54. JENNI 1968, 276; JENNI 1978, &12.3.1.2.: "Das Hi. hat gegenüber dem Grundstamm kausative Bedeutung, d.h. das Subjekt veranlasst ein Objekt zu dem im Grundstamm ausgesagten Vorgang, bzw. zu der im Grundstamm ausgesagten Handlung"
55. JENNI 1968, 34-36. He describes it (p. 34) as follows: "Das Machen ist im Faktitiv ein direktes Bewirken, im Kausativ dagegen ein Objekt mit-aktivierendes und daher indirekteres Veranlassen." As a sample verb he mentions the root **QṢR.** In the pi. (Ps. 102:24) this form may be best translated as 'make short', 'shorten' and in the hi. (Ps. 89:46) as 'allow to be short', 'allow to last a short period of time'. The first case is an unfinished action which yet continues, the second a past completed action.
56. JENNI 1968, 38-40; VON SODEN 1970, 178, in his review of Jenni's book, wishes to postpone his judgment on the explanation until all verb forms are investigated for which the D- and Š-stems appear to have identical meanings. According to him this would only be possible after completion of the CAD and the A.Hw.
57. A few grammars mention a factitive meaning of the pi.: BAUER-LEANDER 1922, 1965, 292: &38r. Here, the factitive is regarded as an element of the causative. It occurs with so-called 'verbs of condition'. Cf. JENNI 1968, 33, who wants to restrict the concept *zustand* (condition) to nominal sentences. He has developed his views on the difference between nominal and verbal sentences in JENNI 1977; here he pleads for the abolition of the term *Zustandsverbum* (verb of condition). LAMBERT 1946, 1972, &649 also mentions the factitive: "Si le verbe exprime au qal le fait d'acquérir une qualité, le pi'el marque d'ordinaire le fait de donner cette qualité, action factitive, e.g. **ḤaZoQ**, *devenir fort*, **ḤiZZeQ**, *fortifier*." Lambert regards the declarative as a variant of the factitive. In his view the hi. may also have a factitive meaning (see &656). He gives the factitive a meaning different from that of Jenni's.
58. In the study of other grammatical topics of classical Hebrew others have made use of Akkadian grammar as well; see note 4, subheading 4.
59. GESENIUS-KAUTZSCH 1909, &51.
60. JENNI 1969, 63 and JENNI 1978, &11.3.1.2 and &11.4.9. In this

respect Jenni has opted for a different course from that of the previous editors of the Hollenberg grammar. See HOLLENBERG-BUDDE 1912, 20 and HOLLENBERG-BUDDE 1967, &16d. These grammars assert that the original (and the still frequently occurring) meaning of the ni. is that of the tolerative ("eine Handlung an sich vollziehen lassen") and that from this the ni. reflexive and passive use has evolved. However, earlier editions of the Hollenberg grammar have adopted Gesenius' approach; see e.g. HOLLENBERG 1899, 27.

61. JENNI 1969, 63: "Das hebräische Nif'al bezeichnet das Geschehen eines Vorgangs oder eine Handlung am Subject selber ohne Rücksicht auf die Art oder den Grad der Mitwirkung dieses Subjects am Geschehen".

62. JENNI 1969, 63. Jenni regards the ni.-forms of **MKR** as toleratives. BERGSTRÄSSER 1929, 89 quotes these as a rare case of a transitive verb and a '(one-)self' as accusative object.

63. GESENIUS 1816, &38; GESENIUS 1826, &38.

64. GESENIUS 1817, &68; GESENIUS-RODIGER 1866, &52. Compare to this EWALD 1827, &103 and GESENIUS-KAUTZSCH 1909, &51h.

65. For this, consult ch. 4.1.4.

66. The view, as found in GESENIUS 1817, &68, is rejected by the grammar of GESENIUS-KAUTZSCH 1909, &51h, which regards these as 'mixed forms' of the pu. and the ni. Yet OLSHAUSEN 1861, &275 treats these forms as the passive of the polel. MANDELKERN, 245 agrees with Gesenius. The lexicons of GESENIUS 1915 and HAL regard these as ni.- forms. KÖNIG (1897), &100b mentions other arguments for a reflexive original meaning of the ni. and the hitp.

67. BAUER-LEANDER 1929, 1965, &38c,d presents examples of this development from Swedish and Czech.

68. Below I present a list of the grammars which I consulted which agree with Gesenius in this respect (in chronological order until 1966, see for the more recent period note 110): EWALD 1827, &103 and later editions, EWALD 1870, &123; VETH 1852, &36; LUZATTO 1853, 149; THIERSCH 1858, &81; OLSHAUSEN 1861, 588; STADE 1879, 118, 126; KÖNIG 1881, 180f.; KÖNIG 1895, 383, 385; KÖNIG 1897, 33ff.; NOORDTZIJ 1907, &45; UNGNAD 1912, &282.3; STRACK 1917, &49; BERGSTRÄSSER 1929, 89; BAUER-LEANDER 1929, 1965, 279ff.; JOÜON 1923, 1965, &51c; PEDERSEN 1926, &28; LAMBERT 1946, 1972, &663; GRETHER 1951, &31k,l; NYBERG 1952, 118ff; GEMSER 1953, &97; BERTSCH 1956, &55; DAVIDSON-MAUCHLINE 1962, &22; GREENBERG 1965, &18 and MEYER (1969), 107.

69. LAMBERT 1900, 106: the ni. "a conservé son acception primitive de réfléchi."

70. Among the grammars which state that originally the ni. was a passive the following may be listed (also in chronological order up to 1966): SARCHI 1828, &181, 182. He states that the n-prefix of the ni. represents the passive. GROENEWOUD 1843, &34; NORDHEIMER 1838, &141; VOSEN-KAULEN 1874, &21 (However, later editions of this grammar agree with Gesenius, see e.g. VOSEN-KAULEN 1927, &26); SCHILLING 1943, &23; LEFEVRE 1945, 57, 65 and YOUNG 1951, 129. Other opinions on the original

function of the ni. are found in HOLLENBERG-BUDDE 1912, &16: the tolerative, see note 60. DE VRIES 1931, &61 asserts: "the meaning of **NP'L** is not at all primarily passive, but reciprocal. . .". From this the reflexive would have originated. Yet WEINGREEN 1939, &52 states in a footnote: "The significance of the Niphal thus oscillates between reflexive and passive." Finally, the view of CHRISTIAN 1953, 33, 78, 79 deserves to be mentioned: The deictic element -n indicated originally "the far and distant" and thus it became a modification of multiple meaning. Originally the ni. did not have a distributive meaning, i.e. "each individually", from which other meanings evolved.

71. NORDHEIMER 1838, 93-95, note x.

72. See for Arabic: WRIGHT 1896, &52. BOONSTRA 1982, 65ff. and 179f. discusses recent publications concerning the 7th verbal stem in Arabic, see also p. 59. Nordheimer assumes that the forms of the etpe'el, etpa'al and ettaf'al in Aramaic originally were passives; see contrary to this opinion with respect to Syrian: NÖLDEKE 1898, 1966, &159 and BROCKELMANN 1968, & 167; for Old-Aramaic in general: SEGERT 1975, &5.6.7.3; for Biblical Aramaic: BAUER-LEANDER 1927, &28 and &76o-x; ROSENTHAL 1961, &99.

73. JENNI 1969, 64 .

74. JENNI 1969, 63; LAMBERT 1900, 198ff., 209f.

75. THIERSCH 1858, &81; GESENIUS-KAUTZSCH 1909, &51f; BERGSTRÄSSER 1929, &16d; BAUER-LEANDER 1922, 1965, &38z'; JOÜON 1923, 1965, &51c; DE VRIES 1931, &96 and also the precursors of the grammar of Lettinga: NAT 1939, &41d and NAT-KOOPMANS 1945, & 41d; moreover: GRETHER 1951, &31 and MEYER 1966, &66,1a. See for grammars after 1968: ch. 1.6.

76. See note 75 for bibliographical references: GESENIUS-KAUTZSCH and also BAUER-LEANDER and DE VRIES.

77. See note 75 for the bibliographical references: BERGSTRÄSSER, JOÜON, GRETHER, NAT, NAT-KOOPMANS and MEYER.

78. LAMBERT (1900), 210ff. The grammars of BERGSTRÄSSER 1929, &16c, NAT 1939, &41d and GRETHER 1951, &31 subscribe to his opinion.

79. See chapter 3.4

80. GESENIUS-KAUTZSCH 1909, &51f: the root **ḤLH**, in both qal and ni. 'be ill', see also THIERSCH 1858, &81.

81. JENNI 1969, 63ff.: "Während das Qal den Zustand oder den Vorgang, in dem sich das Subject befindet, ganz allgemein ausdruckt, kommt es beim Nif'al in diesen Fallen jeweils auf das Eintreten, Manifest- Werden des Zustandes oder Vergangs am Subject an. Dabei betont das Nif'al nicht so sehr das Ingressive oder das Werden gegenüber dem Sein beim Qal, sondern das geschehnishafte *sich als etwas erweisen*, den Zustand oder Vorgang an sich manifest werden lassen".

82. JENNI 1969, 64: as other verb he mentions e.g.: **B'R**, qal: *dumm sein*, ni.: *sich als dumm erweisen*; **MWṬ**, qal: *wanken*, ni. *ins wanken gebracht werden*; **QDŠ**, qal: *heilig sein*, ni.: *sich als heilig erweisen*. This opinion shows some resemblance to that of EWALD 1863, &123, who states that the ni. may also express

a *selbsttätigkeit* (e.g. **NQRB** *sich nähern*).

83. GAG, &90e-g.

84. EDZARD 1965.

85. GAG, &90g: "Die Funktion des N-stamms von Zustandverben ist meist ingressiv (z.B. *ibašši*: *'ist'*; *ibbašši*: *'entsteht'*; *nadrum*: *'wütend'*: *annadir*: *'ich geriet in Wut'*; *ittakil*: *'er gewann Vertrauen'*)". See also the Ergänzungen zu GAG, &90g for more examples.

86. JENNI 1969, 67 says about the distinction between actual and resultative: "Im Qal wird die Handlung in ihrem Vollzug, in ihrem Hergang, in actu gesehen, im Pi'el dagegen nur von ihrem Ergebnis her, als Erreichen des Resultats, ohne Rücksicht auf den Hergang der Handlung."

87. Jenni mentions the distinction only with respect to the verb stems that are transitive in their basic stem (67), but his final conclusions appear to indicate that this applies as well for intransitive basic stems (68ff.) He does not mention the distinction in his grammar of 1978.

88. JENNI 1969, 66: "Während das Erleiden einer Zustandsänderung im Pu'al als etwas Definitives, Endgültiges erscheint, beinhaltet das Nif'al stärker etwas Vorgangsmässiges und damit Nicht-endgültiges". As an example verb, Jenni mentions the root **ḤLH**. In Dan. 8:27 the ni.-form indicates a passing disease, while the pu.-form in Isa. 14:10 indicates that the king of Babel who is in Sheol is 'weak', 'ill' and in a situation which does not pass away but which is his definitive destiny. See for other examples 68).

89. This applies as well for the infinitives, according to Jenni: 5 % of the ni. infinitives are attested but only 1 pu. form (Ps. 132:1), which is debated by text criticism, see DAHOOD 1970, 243 e.g. Jenni calls the pu. inf. a contradictio in adjecto. Please note the occurrence of an inf. abs of the pu. Gen. 40:15.

90. JENNI 1969, 68, 69.

91. JENNI 1978, &12.3.1.2: "Das Hi. hat gegenüber dem Grundstamm kausative Bedeutung, d.h. das Subjekt veranlässt ein Objekt zu dem im Grundstamm ausgesagten Vorgang bzw. zu der im Grundstamm ausgesagten Handlung."

92. JENNI 1969, 69; JENNI 1978, &12.3.1.3: "Das Subjekt wird (von einem nicht genannten Agens) zu einem aktiven (selten passiven) Vorgang veranlasst."

93. JENNI 1969, 70: "Es ist also der für die hebräische Syntax entscheidende Unterschied zwischen Verbalsatz und Nominalsatz, der sich letztlich im hebräischen Stammformensystem widerspiegelt." See also JENNI 1977; in this article he makes use of the verb **ZQN** to discuss more thoroughly the differences between nominal and verbal sentences.

94. GESENIUS-KAUTZSCH 1909, &39e,f.

95. GESENIUS-KAUTZSCH 1909, &51f.

96. GESENIUS-KAUTZSCH 1909, &51f, &54g; the ho. may also function as passive of the qal: &53h,u.

97. As in GESENIUS 1816, &29; GESENIUS 1826, &30 and later editions; BÖTTCHER 1868, 258ff., Table XXIX; STADE 1879, &152b;

LAMBERT 1946, 1972, &643.

98. LAMBERT 1946, 1972, &643: "A l'origine, chacune de ces conjugaisons avait un passif, mais le passif du qal et des réfléchis ne s'est pas developpé ou est tombé en désuétude."

99. Thus, e.g. NORDHEIMER 1838, &138 and WEINGREEN 1939, &51.

100. As in ROORDA 1831, &135; VETH 1852, &36 and ITALIE 1881, 20.

101. Roorda as well as Veth assume that Hebrew contains the remains of a passive of the ni. (the nepho'al) and of the reflexive of the hi. (tiph'il or hittaph'el). See also note 105.

102. JOÜON 1923, 1965, &40.

103. As by STIER 1881, &16 and also the 2nd expanded edition of STIER 1893, &16; BEER 1916, &60; STEUERNAGEL 1917, &29; NAT 1939, &41 and later editions; TOUZARD 1949, &65; NYBERG 1952, &33g; BERTSCH 1956, &55,7; DAVIDSON-MAUCHLINE 1962, &21 and GREENBERG 1965, &8.3. LEFEVRE 1945, 59 and YOUNG 1951, &2.3.1 offer this classification as well. However, the difference is that they regard the ni. to be the passive instead of the reflexive of the qal.

104. See e.g. JOÜON 1923, 1965, &58.

105. BLAU 1957, 378 suggests that there may be three forms of the refl. of the hi. in the OT: Ex. 2:4, 2Sam. 22:27 and Ez. 33:17. See also note 101.

106. EWALD 1870, 333.

107. BAUER-LEANDER 1922, 1965, &38.

108. GAG, &86; note that there is no evidence for the Nt-stem in Akkadian. As far as I know there is one grammar which wants to apply the classification system of Akkadian grammar to Hebrew as well, namely, UNGNAD 1912, &286, cf. also UNGNAD 1926, &286. UNGNAD 1906 defends this classification. On this see GOSHEN-GOTTSTEIN 1969, 78.

110. To my knowledge 19 reviews of Jenni's book have appeared in print. Although not all of them are important, (many reviews provide little more than a summary), I have listed them below for the sake of completeness: (in alphabetical order) BEYER 1970; BLAU 1970; BROCKINGTON 1969; CAQUOT 1970; CONRAD 1969; DEGEN 1970; EMERTON 1969; FOHRER 1969; FOKKELMAN 1969, 1970; HAMMERSHAIMB 1970*; HILLERS 1969, cf. HILLERS 1967; HOSPERS 1970; JACOB 1969; LAMBDIN 1969; METTINGER 1973; RINGGREN 1970; SAWYER 1969; V.SODEN 1970; SOGGIN 1968. Other important publications are: CLAASSEN 1971, which discusses JENNI 1967 in on **ABD** and CLAASSEN 1972; MARGAIN 1974; BOONSTRA 1982 and WEINGREEN 1983.
(* thanks to Mr. H.J. Rijks for his translation from Danish.)

111. LAMBDIN 1969, 437; see also note 126.

112. HOSPERS 1970, 56ff.

113. i.e. CONRAD 1969; JACOB 1969; CAQUOT 1970 and RINGGREN 1970.

114. DEGEN 1970, 55.

115. FOKKELMAN 1969, 1970, 301.

116. BROCKINGTON 1969, 563; DEGEN 1970, 47.

117. HOSPERS 1970, 56.

118. See chapter 1.5.3

119. HOSPERS 1970, 57.

120. CAQUOT 1970, 174ff.
121. BROCKINGTON 1969, 562.
122. KRINETZKI 1981, &4.1.1 mentions the intensive, causative, denominative, and privative as functions of the pi. LASOR 1980, 88, 104: "The fundamental idea in this root seems to be intensification, strengthening or repetition..".
123. SAWYER 1976, 63: "D-stems are often causative in meaning..."; 119: "D-stem- and H-stem-forms are very often causative in meaning (X), and correspond in many cases to English verb--forms in -en ('deaden', 'blacken'), -ize ('immortalize', 'immunize'), -ify ('justify', 'codify'), en- ('enliven', 'enslave') and the like". One should take into consideration that it is a school grammar. Therefore, a popular approach has been opted for instead of a more scientific one.
124. BLAU 1976, &25.1.
125. GESENIUS-KAUTZSCH 1909, &52f,h.
126. LETTINGA 1976, &41i: "Pi'el (...) primarily carries factitive meaning (...). Moreover, the doubling stem may be intensive, (...), iterative (...) and declarative (...). The denominatives of the pi. (...), often have a privative meaning (...)". Cf. also BOONSTRA 1982, 78. LAMBDIN 1973, &148: "a) Factitive (transitivizing) b) Denominative c) Intensive d) Unclassified".
127. WILLIAMS 1978, &140-146.
128. A possible explanation for this might be that the first edition of this syntaxis appeared in 1967, one year prior to the publication of *Das hebräische Pi'el*, and that the author had not been informed of Jenni's work in the 2nd revised edition.
129. RICHTER 1978, 77 presents a survey of Jenni's views. IRSIGLER 1981, 77, 90ff.; WELZEL 1981, 32.
130. SCHWEITZER 1981; SCHNEIDER 1982, &29.3.3 says that the intensive meaning is debatable. He also mentions e.g. the factitive meaning.
131. LEEMHUIS 1977.
132. RYDER 1974 devotes a chapter to the D-stem in Koranic Arabic, see also p. 40, where this book will be discussed.
133. LEEMHUIS 1977, 7.
134. LEEMHUIS 1977, 125.
135. FRAIZYNGER 1979, in his article on the R1R2R2 stems in the Semitic language area, mentions the factitive as one of the meanings of the doubled stem in Hamito-Semitic, but he bases himself on the works of Goetze and Ryder, without even mentioning Jenni. Cf. also BOONSTRA 1982, 137ff.
136. CLAASSEN 1971, 4.
137. CLAASSEN 1971, 5 calls it an 'untenable transfer of identity'.
138. CLAASSEN 1971, 4.
139. CLAASSEN 1971, 5-10 attempts to prove that it does not apply for a number of roots in Hebrew. FOKKELMAN 1969/1970, 300ff. does the same for Biblical Aramaic.
140. JENNI 1968, 15.
141. E.g. BEYER 1970, 193; BROCKINGTON 1969, 563; DEGEN 1970, 1971, 51; RINGGREN 1970, 217.

142. BRØNNO 1943, 65ff., 73, 78; SPERBER 1966, 119ff.
143. JENNI 1968, 17: "Aus methodischen und praktischen Grunden ist hier nur der Kanon des hebräischen Altes Testament in die Untersuchung einbezogen worden. Eine Nachprüfung der These an den hebräischen Sirach- fragmenten und an den Qumranteksten steht mithin noch aus", cf. also 18.
144. JENNI 1968, 93.
145. DEGEN 1970, 53ff., shows how the verbs **ḤKH** and **QWH** may have undergone change in the course of time. Cf. 51.
146. See e.g. JENNI 1968, 80, example 30: Jer. vs. Deut.; 98, example 40: Ex. vs. Hos.; 154, example. 83: Job vs. 2Ki., etc.
147. FOKKELMAN 1969/ 1970, 301; on this, see also BERLIN 1979, 24: Ps. 139:21 (pi.-qal) and 25: Mi. 6:14b (hi.- pi.).
148. JENNI 1968, 102, example 42: perf. consec. vs. imperf. +we; 103, example 44: imperf. consec. vs. inf. cs.; example 46: inf. cs. vs. partic.; 107, example 48: imperf. vs. perf. +we.
149. Not a single review dealt with this aspect.
150. JENNI 1968, 259: "Dieses Monopol des Hif'il auf die durativen Verbalformen Imperfekt und Partizip muss mit der Verbalbedeutung zusammenhängen..."; cf. FOKKELMAN 1969/1970, 301 notices that Jenni takes all imperf. as duratives without distinguishing between the narrative punctual (**WaJ**)**JiQṬoL** and other **JiQṬoL**-forms.
151. MEYER 1972, 40ff.; METTINGER 1973, 69.
152. Cf. JENNI 1968, 164, where he mentions this theory.
153. See note 14; RINGGREN 1970, 217, who agrees with Jenni in this respect, says: "Diese Frage ist aber nie ernstlich gestellt worden. Jenni stellt sie und geht dabei von der richtigen Voraussetzung aus, dass wenn eine Sprache zwei verschiedene Formen ausbildet, muss jede Form eine eigene Funktion haben."
154. See 1.5.3.3.c
155. It is remarkable that the forms of the pi. and hi. of this root often occur together in the same sentence structure, see Judg. 6:4, 5; Lam. 2:5-8. Cf. also 2Ki. 19:12 (pi. perf.) vs. Isa. 37:12 (hi. perf.)!
156. METTINGER (1973), 69. See for these concepts: LYONS (1968), 79ff., 126ff. and 415.
157. JENNI 1968, 22ff. and 123. This was pointed out esp. by HILLERS (1969) and METTINGER 1973, 69.
158. JENNI 1968, 22: "Die Bezeichnung dieser Verben als Intransitiva geht von der Grundbedeutung aus, die normalerweise kein Akkusativusobject zuläst".
159. JENNI 1968, 22: "Wenn es sich aber nun zeigt, dass lmd von Hause aus intransitiv ist (worauf auch der Imperfekt-vokal a hindeutet) und sich nach Ausweis der verwandten Sprachen von *gewohnt sein* (äth.) über *sich gewöhnen an etwas* (aram) zu *etwas lernen* entwickelt hat,...".
160. JENNI 1968, 23, cf. also 123.
161. JENNI 1968, 151, 154ff. HILLERS 1969, 212 mentions as example the root **ŚB'**. According to Jenni, this root is intransitive, yet Hillers uses it as evidence proving that Jenni's definition of transitivity and intransitivity is inadequate.

Jenni's book as a failure and as an old fashioned work. E.g. he states that: "He (i.e. Jenni) speaks, not so much of a verb being used intransitively in a given sentence, or of intransitive verbs, but of *intransitiven Grundbedeutung*, intransitive meaning"(212). I question whether he is doing justice to Jenni's opinions. By means of the notion *Grundbedeutung*, Jenni refers to the meaning of the basic stem qal. He does not use the term with reference to the so-called basic meaning of the stem in the manner in which it played a role in 19th century grammar.

164. CLAASSEN 1971, 5.
165. JENNI 1968, 17.
166. See 4.2 and further.
167. See e.g. BROCKINGTON 1969, DEGEN 1970, FOKKELMAN 1969/ 1970. CLAASSEN 1972 discusses the 'declarative- estimative' hi. and contests the opinions of Jenni's as well as of Hillers'. We were unable to consult the book of U. Ornan, *More on the meaning of the binyanim* (Hebrew), in Mincha le Qodesh, ed. by C. Rabin and B.Z. Fisher, Jerusalem 1979, quoted in the article of Y.T. Radday, "The spoils of Egypt", ASTI XII, 1983, 143. Ornan assumes that the pi. and hi. in Biblical Hebrew are identical in meaning.
168. RYDER 1974; see note 2. BOONSTRA 1982, 119ff. also discusses this work.
169. See chapter 1.2
170. RYDER 1974, 164.
171. RYDER 1974, 166f.; cf. JENNI 1968, 257 on this.
172. RYDER 1974, 92f.
173. RYDER 1974, 21ff.
174. RYDER 1974, 55ff., 97ff.
175. BOONSTRA 1982; WEINGREEN 1983.
176. BOONSTRA 1982, 74ff.; 104ff.;117f., etc.
177. WEINGREEN 1983, 22.
178. With reference to ORNAN 1972, who mentions e.g. the durative and the repetitive as functions of the pi. which may be described adequately as 'extensive' as well.
179. WEINGREEN 1983, 22; GESENIUS-KAUTZSCH-COWLEY 1910, &43a.
180. GESENIUS-KAUTZSCH-COWLEY 1910, &53f.
181. WEINGREEN 1983, 25.
182. See e.g. JOÜON 1923, 1965, &41; RICHTER 1978, 70 (contra JENNI 1968, 24f.); IRSIGLER 1981, 76; BLAU 1976, &22.1, etc.
183. JOÜON 1923, 1965, 97f. presents a list of the *verbes statifs*. Weingreen classifies some of these as action verbs. See also JENNI 1968, 24ff.
184. JENNI 1969 was published in 1973.
185. JENNI 1969 and JENNI 1978, discussed in ch. 1.3.
186. See for these grammars Appendix A.
187. (in chronological order) BLAU 1976, &23.1 and 24.1; LETTINGA 1976, &41d; WILLIAMS 1978, 27; LASOR 1979, 167; IRSIGLER 1981, 88; KRINETZKI 1981, 53 and SCHNEIDER 1982, &29.3.2. LAMBDIN 1973, 175f. presents a classification on the basis of the English translation and only says that the ni. has medio-passive meaning. SAWYER 1976, 64, states only that the ni. often has

88; KRINETZKI 1981, 53 and SCHNEIDER 1982, &29.3.2. LAMBDIN 1973, 175f. presents a classification on the basis of the English translation and only says that the ni. has medio-passive meaning. SAWYER 1976, 64, states only that the ni. often has passive meaning. BEYER 1969 and SCHWEITZER 1981 report nothing of importance about the ni.

188. RICHTER 1978, 77 mentions JENNI 1969 in a note, yet describes the functions of the N-stem as: *reflexiv, soziatif/ reziprok, passiv und tolerativ*. WELZEL 1981 refers to JENNI 1978 in his bibliography but states only that the N is *reflexiv/passiv gegenüber G*.

189. MARGAIN 1974; the MÜLLER 1985 article, on the ergative structure in Akkadian and Hebrew will not be dealt with here because his subject matter is completely different from mine.

190. MARGAIN 1974, 25: "Le piel et le hiphil expriment une nuance causative plus faible- le tolératif- que l'on traduira, soit par *laisser*, soit par *permettre*". On p. 26 he refers to this tolerative meaning as "une attenuation du causatif". Although he refers to JENNI 1968 in a note, Margain does not discuss a possible factitive function of the pi.

191. BERGSTRÄSSER 1929, &16b.

192. MARGAIN 1974, 26,27: "Le tolératif du niphal ne serait pas alors derive du sens passif, comme on l'admet généralement, mais du causatif."

193. BEAN 1976.

194. BEAN 1976 refers to JENNI 1968 in his bibliography, but he fails to include JENNI 1969, in which the hitp. is discussed.

195. BEAN 1976, viii.

196. GESENIUS-KAUTZSCH 1909, &54 lists the following meanings of the hitp.: a) refl. of the pi.; b) recipr. as ni.; c) "eine mehr mittelbare Rückwirkung auf das Subjekt an.."; d) passive (rarely).

197. BEAN 1976, VIII.

198. BEAN 1976, 36ff.

199. He is the first to acknowledge the fact. Therefore, he presents the following suggestion for further research: "This dissertation is meant to be the beginning of the study of the Hithpa'el: thus the focus is broad and the conclusions are only indicative and tentative. Much remains to be investigated in order to understand the Hithpa'el stem, but two areas of interest should be studied as the next step in mastery of the stem. First, the Hithpa'el must be studied diachronically . . .(p. 175)." (Thus, the author indicates the necessity of careful research into the function of this stem in the various stages of the Hebrew language; e.g. attention must be given to differences between the pre-exilic and the post-exilic material). "Secondly, the Hithpa'el must be studied vis-a-vis the other stems, especially the Niph'al and Pi'el stems . . .(ibid)."

200. LETTINGA 1976, &41, see also note 102, 103.

201. IRSIGLER 1981, 78.

202. JENNI 1978.

203. GOSHEN-GOTTSTEIN 1969; BOONSTRA 1982, 32ff. criticizes this classification.

Chapter II

204. GESENIUS-KAUTZSCH 1909, &51a.
205. See e.g. GESENIUS-KAUTZSCH 1909, &66ff.; BERGSTRäSSER 1929, &20ff.
206. KBL 1953; HAL 1967; HAL 1974; HAL 1983; GESENIUS 1915.
207. THAT, Band II, 542 reports a slightly different outcome: 4140 forms (rounded down) distributed over 435 verb roots. The difference between my calculation and THAT's may be accounted for by the fact that THAT distinguishes more homonymic roots for certain verb roots.
208. Cf. GESENIUS-KAUTZSCH (1909), &67t,u.
209. We consulted KAI, GIBSON 1971, and AHARONI 1975. No ni.-forms are to be found in the last-mentioned collection of texts from Arad.
210. KAI wants to read a proper name here.
211. HOFTIJZER 1981 a, 173.
212. BEAN 1976, 48. The ratio is changeable in the minor prophets: Amos and Zephaniah rate low, yet Jonah rates high.
213. BEAN 1976, 79ff.
214. See the various introductions to the OT, cf also BEAN 1976, 48ff. and the literature mentioned there.
215. HOFTIJZER 1965, 51ff; HOFTIJZER 1981, 2ff.
216. GESENIUS-KAUTZSCH 1909, &51.
217. JOüON 1923, 1965, &51: 113-115.
218. LAMBERT 1900, 196-214; BERGSTRäSSER 1929, &16
219. see note 61.
220. It is striking of Lambert that he fails to mention the root **QBR** in his lists.
221. This root is not mentioned in the grammars. Cf. as well Akkadian *lapatum*. N.B. Lambert regards Ruth 1:8 **HMM** as a reflexive of the qal and translates it as (197): *se troubler*. It might just as well be regarded as a passive.
222. See the thesis of BAUER 1912, 104ff. It is impossible to prove that the Na x -inf. originally was the proto-semitic pronoun of the 1st pers. pl. and that it served as the reflexive of this person.
223. JENNI 1969, 63: see chapter 1.3.
224. JENNI 1969, 64: see also chapter 1.3.

Chapter IV

225 See chapter 2.2
226 See chapter 2.2. and note 207; the difference between Jenni's calculations and mine may arise from the fact that the identification of pu.-forms is not always straightforward.
227 GESENIUS-KAUTZSCH 1909, & 50a.
228 See 4.2.1.1.
229 GESENIUS-KAUTZSCH 1909, & 50f.

230 BERGSTRäSSER 1929, & 15d
231 See for the bibliographical data note 6 and chapter 1.6.3.
232 BEAN 1976, 189: Deut. 2:5 must be imperf. **TTGRW** and not perf!
233 NB Micah 1:11 K: perf. 1st pers.
234 See e.g. BöTTCHER 1868, &904, 906; DEMBITZ 1886, 1887; BARTH 1890; LAMBERT 1900, 200 ff.; BAUER-LEANDER 1922, 1965, 285ff.; JOüON 1923, 1965, 125 ff.; BERGSTRäSSER 1929, &15 and WILLIAMS 1970. The grammar of GESENIUS-KAUTZSCH 1909, &52e, s mentions briefly BöTTCHER and BARTH's view.
235 WILLIAMS 1970, 46, 47. Many other authors present lists of ancient passive qal-forms, e.g. LAMBERT and BAUER-LEANDER. The lists show remarkable differences. LAMBERT provides more roots and forms than WILLIAMS.
236 WILLIAMS 1970, 45 ff."However ....the Niph'al theme, originally with reflexive or middle and reciprocal force, came to be used also to express the passive idea. Consequently the passive qal became increasingly less common, until by the time of biblical Hebrew it was obsolete".
237 According to WILLIAMS 1970, 49 there are 8 roots, of which the ni.- imperfects differ only in vocalization from the passive qal: **DḤH** (Pro. 14:32; Jer. 23:12); **HRG** (Lam. 2:20; Ez. 26:6); **ḤṢB** (Job 19:24); **ṬRP** (Ex. 22:12; Jer. 5:6); **MRṬ** (Lev. 13:40 ff.); **ŚRP** (Josh. 7:15; Pro. 6:27); **ŠGL** (Isa. 13:16; Zech. 14:2) and **ŠṬP** (Lev. 15:12; Dan. 11:22).
238 See e.g. KNUDTZON 1915 and RAINEY 1978 for the texts and also BOHL 1909, 60ff., EBELING 1912, 59, 60 and RAINEY 1976. In the last-mentioned article Rainey insists that a few forms in a letter from Amarna (KL 72:600) should be read as a passive of the D-stem.
239 Grammarians express different opinions as to which forms may or may not be counted among the remainders of the passive qal.
240 'M' refers to 'many', cf. 3.1ff.
241 32 pu.-forms occur in Ez., 15 forms of the perf. and 3 of the imperf.: Ez. 26:21 (**BQŠ**, pass. of pi.), Ez. 14:9 (**PTH**, pass. of pi.) and Ez. 15:3 (**LQḤ**).
242 WILLIAMS 1970, 49.
243 LAMBERT 1900, 202.
244 Hitp.-forms of the root **PQD** (Judg. 20:15 (2x), 17; 21:19) occur as well as 4 hotp.-forms (Num. 1:47; 2:33; 26:62 and 1 Kin. 20: 27), see on this GESENIUS-KAUTZSCH 1909, &54 who treat the hotp. as a pass of the hitp. Others, according to this grammar, regard the hitp. and hotp. of this root (without doubling of the **QOP̲**) as old reflexive forms of the qal (cf. 4.4.1).
245 See 4.3.2.1
246 Note that the roots **GLH** and **RAH** are mentioned under two groups in this overview (Ib and IIb, and Ib and III respectively).
247 WILLIAMS 1970, 46, 47, 49.
248 Possibly a noun, see chapter 4.2.2.1.
249 LAMBERT 1900, 201 regards this as a remains of the pass. qal.
250 It is hard to assess whether the ni. of **BQ'** occurs in a semantic relationship to the qal or to the pi.

251 Lambert mentions 5 other forms of which the pu.-perfects are possibly old pass. qal-forms (**ASP**, **GNB**, **SGR**, **SQL**, and **PQD**).

252 see esp. groups Ib

253 WILLIAMS 1970, 49.

254 For a number of other roots ni.-imperfects occur relatively frequently as opposed to an almost lack of occurrence of ni.-perfects (prose: **ASP**, **BQ'**, **JLD**, **MNH**, **SGR**, **QBṢ**; poetry: **JD'**, **MLA**.

255 Note that in poetry one, and in prophecy two, pu.-perfects occur.

256 GESENIUS-KAUTZSCH 1909, &153 h.

257 GESENIUS-KAUTZSCH 1909, &153 h,u.

258 Note that imperfect forms are lacking for the four roots that were left out of the discussion under prose.

259 GESENIUS-KAUTZSCH 1909, &541 and BERGSTRäSSER 1929, &18i mention as examples e.g. the hitp. of **PQD** and in the Moabitic inscription of Mesa the root **LḤM**. According to them many hitp.-forms should be regarded as t-reflexives of the qal and they have been vocalized wrongly by the Masoretes

260 BEAN 1976, 24ff.

261 BERGSTRäSSER 1929 &16b, mentions as the only example the root **MKR**, see note 62.

262 BEAN 1976, 24, note 75, mentions as examples the root **AWH** which occurs ten times with an object, and also Ex. 32:3; Isa. 52:2, Num. 6:19.

263 BEAN 1976, 151ff.: "With regard to the passive subject-orientation, the level of usage does increase after the Exile, and the increase is not a small one in terms of the total number of manifestly passive forms. The passive translation is indicated three times as often in post-exilic material as in pre-Exilic. Indeed, the passive sense is used almost as often in the relatively small number of Exilic usages as it is in pre-Exilic writings." Unfortunately this conclusion is not open to verification by the reader since examples of roots and textual references are lacking.

264 NORDHEIMER 1838, 93-95, note *, defended this view by means of the root **ḤBA**, of which a hitp. form occurs in Gen. 3:8 and a ni. in Gen. 3:10.

265 BERGSTRäSSER 1929, &18b, mentions examples of hitp.-forms, which, according to him, occur in a pass./refl. relationship to the qal: **NDB**, **NSA**, **RAH**.

266 See SPEISER 1955, who wants to treat the **HLK** hitp. as a qal with tan-infix.

267 See for the root **JṢB** 4.3.2.3: III.

268 When the root **DKH** is added to this, the numbers of occurrences of the ni. become as follows: total 3, participle 2 and perfect 1.

269 BEAN 1976, 139ff. does not classify the hitp.-forms, in as far as I can determine, as 'manifestly passive', yet as forms which may both be reflexive and passive. This cannot be ascertained with complete certainty, see note 263.

Appendix A:

List of Hebrew grammars

Below, we present a list of the grammars of classical Hebrew which I consulted in writing chapter II. I consciously restricted myself to the grammars which have appeared since 1813. In the year 1813 the publication of the first edition of Gesenius' *Hebräische Grammatik* occurred. With him, the period of modern grammatical research of Biblical Hebrew begins. Because of the enormous number of grammars published in the period 1813-1982, I have attempted to collect a most representative selection. It was impossible for me to consult all school grammars and all the editions of the grammars which appeared during this time. Moreover, those grammars which did not supply information on verbal stems have, at times, been passed by.

See for more grammars: HOSPERS 1973, 179, 180, and for a historical overview: KÖNIG 1881, 2-9; JOÜON 1923, 1965, 6-8; BAUER-LEANDER 1922, 1965, 42-49, LOEWE 1972, JE and the literature mentioned in RICHTER 1978, 36, note 81.

The titles of the grammars are represented in abbreviated form. We refer to the bibliography for the full titles. The grammars have been ordered chronologically, starting at 1813.

Gesenius, W. *Hebräische Grammatik*, 1st edn., 1813.
Gesenius, W. *Hebräische Grammatik*, 2nd edn., 1816.
Gesenius, W. *Ausführliches grammatisch-kritisches Lehrgebaüde...*, 1817.
Gesenius, W. *Hebräische Grammatik*, 8th edn., 1826.
Ewald, H. *Kritische Grammatik der hebräischen Sprache*, 1827.
Sarchi, M. *Grammaire Hébraique*, 1828.
Roorda, T. *Grammatica Hebraea*, 1831-33.
Groenewoud, I.C.Sw. *Institutio ad grammaticam Hebraicam*, 1834.
Nordheimer, I. *A Critical Grammar of the Hebrew Language*, 1838.
Ewald, H. *Hebräische Sprachlehre für Anfänger*, 1842.
Veth, P.J. *Beknopte Hebreeuwsche Spraakkunst*, 2nd edn. 1852.
Luzatto, S.D. *Grammatica della lingua ebraica*, 1853.
Thiersch, H.W.J. *Hebräische Grammatik*, 1858.
Olshausen, J. *Lehrbuch der Hebräischen Sprache*, 1861.
Ewald, H. *Ausführliches Lehrbuch der Hebräischen Sprache*, 7th edn. 1863.
Gesenius, W. and Rödiger, E. *Hebräische Grammatik*, 20th edn. 1866.

Böttcher, F. *Ausführliches Lehrbuch der Hebräischen Sprache*, 1868.
Bickell, G. *Grundriss der Hebräischen Grammatik*, 1869.
Ewald, H. *Ausführliches Lehrbuch der Hebräischen Sprache*, 8th edn. 1870.
Vosen, C.H. and Kaulen, F. *Kurze Anleitung zum Erlernen der Hebräischen Sprache*, 12th edn. 1874.
Gesenius, W. and Kautzsch, E. *Hebräische Grammatik*, 22nd edn. 1878.
Stade, B. *Lehrbuch der hebräischen Grammatik*, 1879.
Italie, H. *Beknopt leerboek der Hebreeuwse taal*, 1881.
König, Fr.E. *Historisch-Kritisches Lehrgebaüde der Hebräischen Sprache*, Vol. I, 1881.
Stier, G. *Kurzgefasste Hebräische Grammatik*, 1st edn. 1881.
Hollenberg, W. *Hebräisches Schulbuch*, 7th edn. 1889.
Strack, H.L. *Hebräische Grammatik*, 3rd edn. 1890.
Stier, G. *Kurzgefasste Hebräische Grammatik*, 2nd edn. 1893.
König, Fr.E. *Historisch-Kritisches Lehrgebaüde der Hebräischen Sprache*, Vol. II. 1895.
König, Fr.E. *Historisch-comparative Syntax der Hebräischen Sprache*, 1897.
Noordtzij, A. *Beknopte Hebreeuwsche Spraakkunst*, 1907.
Gesenius, W. and Kautzsch, E. *Hebräische Grammatik*, 28th edn. 1909.
Gesenius, W., Kautzsch, E. and Cowley A.E. *Hebrew Grammar*, 28th edn. 1910.
Hollenberg, W. and Budde, K. *Hebräisches Schulbuch*, 11th edn. 1912.
Ungnad, A. *Hebräische Grammatik*, 1912.
Beer, G. *Hebräische Grammatik*, 1916.
Steuernagel, C. *Hebräische Grammatik*, 5th edn. 1917.
Strack, H.L. *Hebräische Grammatik*, 12th, 13th edn. 1917.
Bauer, H. and Leander, P. *Historische Grammatik der Hebräischen Sprache*, 1922 (1965).
Joüon, P. *Grammaire de l'Hébreu biblique*, 1923 (1965).
Pedersen, J. *Hebraeisk Grammatik*, 1926.
Ungnad, A. *Hebräische Grammatik*, 2nd edn. 1926.
Vosen, C.H. and Kaulen, F. *Kurze Anleitung zum Erlernen der Hebräischen Sprache*, 22nd, 23rd edn. 1927.
Bergsträsser, G. *Hebräische Grammatik*, Vol. II. 1929.
Strack, H.L. and Jepsen, A. *Hebräische Grammatik*, 14th edn. 1930.
Vries, S.Ph. de *Leerboek der Hebreeuwsche taal*, 1931.
Nat, J. *Hebreeuwsche Grammatica*, 2nd edn. 1939.
Weingreen, J. *A Practical Grammar for Classical Hebrew*, 1939.
Schilling, D. *Grammaire Hébraique élémentaire*, 1943.
Lefevre, J. *Précis de grammaire hébraique*, 2nd edn. 1945.
Nat, J. and Koopmans, J.J. *Hebreeuwsche Grammatica*, 3rd edn. 1945.
Lambert, M. *Traité de grammaire hébraique*, 2nd edn. 1946. (1972).
Touzard, J. *Grammaire Hébraique*, 1949.
Grether, O. *Hebräische Grammatik*, 1951.
Young, G.D. *Grammar of the Hebrew Language*, 1951.
Nyberg, H.S. *Hebreisk Grammatik*, 1952.
Gemser, B. *Hebreeuse Spraakkuns*, 1953.
Bertsch, A. *Kurzgefasste Hebräische Sprachlehre*, 1956.
Brockelmann, C. *Hebräische Syntax*, 1956.
Davidson, A.B. and Mauchline, J. *An Introductory Hebrew Grammar*,

25th edn. 1962.
Greenberg, M. *Introduction to Hebrew*, 1956.
Johns, A.F. *A Short Grammar of Biblical Hebrew*, 1966.
Sperber, A. *A Historical Grammar of Biblical Hebrew*, 1966.
Hollenberg, W. and Budde, K. *Hebräisches Schulbuch*, 25th edn. 1967.
Beyer, Kl. *Althebräische Grammatik*, 1969.
Meyer, R. *Hebräische Grammatik*, Vol. II. 1969.
Meyer, R. *Hebräische Grammatik*, Vol. III. 1972.
Ornan, U. *Hebrew Grammar*, in E.J., Vol. 8, 1972.
Lambdin, Th.O. *Introduction to Biblical Hebrew*, 1973.
Blau, J. *A Grammar of Biblical Hebrew*, 1976.
Lettinga, J.P. *Grammatica van het Bijbels Hebreeuws*, 8th edn. 1976.
Sawyer, J.F.A. *A Modern Introduction to Biblical Hebrew*, 1976.
Jenni, E. *Lehrbuch der hebräischen Sprache*, 1978.
Richter, W. *Grundlagen einer althebräischen Grammatik*, I Vol. 1978.
Williams, R.J. *Hebrew Syntax*, 2nd edn. 1978.
LaSor, W.S. *Handbook of Biblical Hebrew*, Vol. II. 1979.
Irsigler, H. *Einführung in das Biblischen Hebräisch*, 1981.
Krinetzki, G. *Bibelhebräisch*, 1981.
Schweitzer, H. *Metaphorische Grammatik*, 1981.
Welzel, G. *Programmierte Grammatik des Hebräischen*, 1981.
Schneider, W. *Grammatik des Biblischen Hebräisch*, 5th edn. 1982.
Note: for a list of the comparative grammars of Semitic languages which I consulted in writing chapter 2, I refer to note 5, cf. HOSPERS 1966. An enumeration of the Akkadian grammars used for this dissertation may be found in notes 44 and 45.

Appendix B:

Criteria for determination of the semantic relationship of the ni. versus active verbal stems

Which criteria should be adopted for the determination of the semantic relationship between the ni. on the one hand and the qal, pi. or hi. on the other? Lambert does not discuss this question in his article on the ni. Yet reading between the lines one may find how he came to his classification of ni.-stems.

My list differs in a number of respects from that of Lambert. Thus, I do not distinguish between reflexivity and passivity (see 2.5). A number of different approaches with respect to Lambert's treatment are discussed in the notes in 3.3. Since these different approaches have been based not only on exegetical arguments but also on theoretical principles, we will present a short discussion below on the criteria which I used in the determination of the semantic relationship between the ni. and other verbal stems.

1) First, we base ourselves on the possibility that the ni.-form may occur in a semantic relationship to the qal; the ni.-form expresses the occurrence of an event or the undergoing of an action directed at the subject, as expressed by the qal (e.g. **QBR**, qal: 'bury' vs. ni: 'undergo the action of burying', i.e. 'be buried', or 'allow oneself to be buried').

2 A) If the qal of a certain root does not occur in the OT, we investigate whether the ni. may occur in a semantic relationship to the pi. or the hi. in as far as the forms of these verbal stems occur (e.g. **ŠMD**, hi: 'destroy', vs. ni. 'the undergoing of the action of destruction', i.e. 'be destroyed').

2 B) When the semantic meaning of the qal and the ni. differ from each other, and when they cannot be related, we examine whether the ni. may occur in a semantic relationship to the pi. or hi. (e.g. **Z'Q**, qal: 'call', 'shout'; hi.: 'call together', vs. ni.: 'undergo the action of calling together' i.e. 'be assembled').

3) In practice, it is not as easy as outlined above. For a number of roots it is difficult to determine the exact difference between the semantic value of the qal and the pi. (e.g. for the stem **PTH**, see note 323). For these roots we used the JENNI 1968 study and dictionaries to determine the difference between qal and pi.

4) Another problem in the OT is that for some roots the number of forms occurring of the various verbal stems is too limited. Is it permissible to determine the semantic relationship to the ni. on

the basis of a single pi.-form? Lambert does it regularly in his list (see e.g. note 45: **BRR**; 133: **JAŠ** and 329: **Ṣ'Q**). We do not follow Lambert in this respect unless a semantic relationship is quite evident when both forms occur in a single verse in an oppositional relationship. In doubtful cases we have always opted for the qal.

5) If the ni. of a certain root occurs in semantic relationship to the qal, the possibility may exist that some forms of the same root occur in semantic relationship to e.g. the pi. or the hi. It is only indicated in our list if this relationship is extremely clearly present as indicated by semantic characteristics or by opposition in a certain verse of scripture. In doubtful cases we have always opted for the qal (e.g. **QRA** II, see note 346; **RAH**, see note 353).

6) In the cases in which the meaning of the ni. seemingly agrees with that of the qal, pi. or hi. our list will indicate this by means of the symbol '='. In doubtful cases the symbol '=' is not included.

Appendix C:

List of KeTîB-QeRē variants

Below we include a list of **KeTîB-QeRē** variants in the OT which relate to a change in the respective verbal stem. Compare GORDIS 1971.

ROOT	KeTîB	QeRē	LOCATION
JLD	pu.	ni.	2 Sam. 3:2
KWN	ni.	hi.	2 Chr. 35:4
LWN	hi.	ni.	Ex. 16:2, 7/ Num. 14:36, 16:11
MWṬ	hi.	ni.	Ps. 140:11
MWT	qal	ho.	2 Kin. 14:6
MWT	ho.	qal	Pro. 19:16
NWN	qal	ni.	Ps. 72:17
NTN	ni.	pu.	2 Sam. 21:6
RWM	hi.	pu.	Dan. 8:11
ŚJM	hi.	ho.	Gen. 34:33

See also 2 Kin. 11:2, (**MWT**) and 2 Kin. 12:12 (**PQD**).

Register of quoted sources

Bibliography

AHW. v. Soden, W. (1965). *Akkadisches Handwörterbuch.* (And later editions), Wiesbaden.
Aharoni, Y. (1975). *Arad Inscriptions.* (in Hebrew), Jerusalem.
Barth, J. (1890). "Das passive Qal und seine Participien". In: *Jubelschrift, Dr. I.Hildesheimer,* 145-153. Berlin.
Bauer, H. (1910). *Die Tempora im Semitischen.* Berlin.
Bauer, H. (1912). "Mitteilungen zur semitischer Grammatik, Vol. II, Die Herkunft der Reflexivformen im Gemeinsemitischen". *ZDMG* 66, 104, 105.
Bauer, H. and Leander, P. (1922). *Historische Grammatik der Hebräischen Sprache des Alten Testaments.* Halle. (Hildesheim 1965).
Bauer, H. and Leander, P. (1927). *Grammatik des Biblischen Aramäisch.* Halle.
Bean, A.F. (1976). *A Phenomenological Study of the Hithpa'el Verbal Stem in the Hebrew Old Testament.* The Southern Baptist Theological Seminary, Ph.D.
Beer, G. (1916). *Hebräische Grammatik,* Vol. 2. Berlin and Leipzig.
Bergsträsser, G. (1929). *Hebräische Grammatik, Vol. II: Verbum.* Leipzig, (Hildesheim, 1962).
Berlin, A. (1979). "Grammatical Aspects of Biblical Parallellism". HUCA L (50), 1979, 17-43.
Bertsch, A. (1956). *Kurzgefasste Hebräische Sprachlehre.* Stuttgart.
Beyer, Kl. (1969). *Althebräische Grammatik.* Göttingen.
Beyer, Kl. (1970). "Review of Jenni, E., Das hebräische Pi'el". *ZDMG 120,* 1970, 192-195.
Bickell, G. (1869). *Grundriss der hebräischen Grammatik.* Leipzig.
Blau, J. (1957). "Über die t-Form des Hif'il im Bibelhebräisch". VT VII (7), 1957, 385-388.
Blau, J. (1970). "Review of Jenni, E., Das hebräische Pi'el". Lešonenu XXXIV (24), 1969-70, 228-233.
Blau, J. (1976). *A Grammar of biblical Hebrew.* Wiesbaden.
Bobzin, H. (1974). *Die 'Tempora' im Hiobdialog.* Marburg/Lahn.
Boonstra, F. (1982). *Nieuwere theorieën omtrent de verbaalstammen in de klassiek-semitische talen (oorsprong, relaties en functies),* dissertation. Meppel.
Böttcher, Fr. (1868). *Ausführliches Lehrbuch der Hebräischen Sprache,* Vol. II. Leipzig.
Brockelmann, C. (1908). *Grundriss der vergleichenden Grammatik der Semitischen Sprachen,* Vol. I. Berlin.
Brockelmann, C. (1956). *Hebräischen Syntax,* Neukirchen.
Brockelmann, C. (1968). *Syrische Grammatik.* Leipzig.

Brockington, L.H. (1969). "Review of Jenni, E., Das Hebräische Pi'el". JTS NS XX (20), 1969, 562-564.
Brønno, E. (1943). *Studien über hebräischen Morphologie und Vokalismus*, Leipzig.
Brown-Driver-Briggs-Gesenius. (1972). *A Hebrew and English Lexicon of the Old Testament, based on the Lexicon of W. Gesenius.* Oxford, (1951).
CAD. (1965). *The Assyrian Dictionary of the University of Chigago*, Chicago-Glückstadt. 1965, and later editions.
Caplice, R. (1980). *Introduction to Akkadian*. Rome.
Caquot, A. (1970). "Review of Jenni, E., *Das hebräische Pi'el*". Syria 47, 174-175.
Christian V. (1953). "Untersuchungen zur Laut- und Formenlehre des Hebräischen". *Österreichische Akademie der Wissenschaften*, Sitzungsberichte, Vol. 228, Proceeding 2, Wien.
Claassen, W.T. (1971). "On a recent proposal as to a distinction between Pi'el and Hiph'il". JNSL I, 3-10.
Claassen, W.T. (1972). "The declarative-estimative Hiph'il". JNSL 2, 5-16.
Conrad, J. (1969). "Review of Jenni, E., *Das hebräische Pi'el*". *TLZ* 94, 746-747.
Cooke, C.A. (1903). *Textbook of North-West-Semitic Inscriptions.*
Dahood, M. (1970). *The Psalms*, Vol. III. Anchor Bible, no. 17. Garden City.
Davidson, A.B. (1962). *An Introductory Hebrew Grammar.* Rev. throughout by J. Mauchline. 25th edn, Edinburgh.
Degen, R. (1970). "Zum neueren hebräistischen Forschung, I Das hebräische Pi'el". Wdo VI, 1970-71, 47-55.
Dembitz, L.N. (1886-87). "The passive of Qal". *Hebraica*, Vol. 39, 40.
Dhorme, E. (1967). *A Commentary on the Book of Job.* Nelson.
Dombrowsky, B.W.W. (1962). "Some remarks on the hebrew Hithpa'el and inversative -t in the semitic languages". JNES XXI, 1962, 220-223.
Driver, G.R. (1963). *Problems of the Hebrew Verbal System*, Edinburgh.
Driver, S.R. (1892). *A treatise of the Use of the Tenses in Hebrew and some other Syntactical Questions*, 3rd edn. Oxford.
Edzard, D.O. (1965). "Die Stämme des altbabylonischen Verbums in ihrem Oppositionssystem". In: *Studies in Honor of B. Landsberger*, AS 16, 111-120. Chicago.
Emerton, J.A. (1969). "Review of Jenni, E., *Das hebräische Pi'el*". In: *Booklist*, 65.
Ewald, H. (1827). *Kritische Grammatik der hebräischen Sprache.* Leipzig.
Ewald, H. (1842). *Hebräische Sprachlehre für Anfänger.* Leipzig.
Ewald, H. (1863). *Ausführliches Lehrbuch der Hebräischen Sprache des Alten Bundes*, 7th edn. Göttingen.
Ewald, H. (1870). *Ausführliches Lehrbuch der Hebräischen Sprache des Alten Bundes*, 8th edn. Göttingen.
Fellman, J. (1981). "Lines on the life and work of Heinrich Friedrich Wilhelm Gesenius". JNSL IX, 33-34.
Fensham, F.C. (1978). "The use of the suffix-conjugation and the

praefix-conjugation in a few old hebrew poems". JNSL VI, 9-18.
Fischer, W. (1972). *Grammatik des klassischen Arabisch*. Wiesbaden.
Fohrer, G. (1969). "Review of Jenni, E., *Das hebräische Pi'el*". ZAW 81, 135.
Fokkelman, J.P. (1969-70). "Review of Jenni, E., *Das hebräische Pi'el*". NTT 24, 299-301.
Frainzyngier, Z. (1979). "Notes on the R1R2R3 Stems in Semitic". JSS 24, (1-12).
GAG v. Soden, W., (1968). *Grundriss der Akkadischen Grammatik*. Samt Erganzungsheft zum GAG, AnOr 33/47. Rome.
Gemser, B. (1953). *Hebreese Spraakkuns*. Pretoria.
Gesenius, W. (1813). *Hebräische Grammatik*. 1st. edn. Halle.
Gesenius, W. (1816). *Hebräische Grammatik*. 2nd. edn. Halle.
Gesenius, W. (1817). *Ausführliches grammatisch-kritisches Lehrgebaüde der hebräischen Sprache*. Leipzig.
Gesenius, W. (1826). *Hebräische Grammatik*. 8th edn. Halle.
Gesenius, W. (1962). *Hebräisches und aramäisches Handwörterbuch über das Alte Testament*, 17th edn. Berlin.
Gesenius, W. and Kautzsch, E. (1878). *Hebräische Grammatik nach E. Rödiger*, reworked by E. Kautzsch, 22nd. edn. Leipzig.
Gesenius, W. and Kautzsch, E. (1909). *Hebräische Grammatik*. Completely reworked by E. Kautzsch, 28th edn. Leipzig.
Gesenius, W., Kautzsch E. and Cowley, A.E. (1910). *Gesenius' Hebrew Grammar*. as ed. and enlarged by the late E. Kautzsch, revised in accordance with the 28th German ed. (1909). Oxford.
Gesenius, W., Rödiger, E. (1866). *Hebräische Grammatik*. Republished by E. Rödiger, 20th. edn. Leipzig.
Gibson, J.C.L. (1971). *Textbook of Syrian Semitic Inscriptions, Vol. I. Hebrew and Moabite Inscriptions*. Oxford.
Goetze, A., (1942). "The so-called intensive of the semitic languages". JAOS 62. 1-8.
Gordis, R. (1969). "The root **DGL** in the Song of Songs". JBL LXXXVIII. 203, 20.
Gordis, R. (1978). *The Book of Job*. New York.
Goshen-Gottstein, M.H. (1969). "The system of verbal stems in the classical semitic languages". In: *Procedures of the International Conference on Semitic Studies, held in Jerusalem*. 70-91.
Goshen-Gottstein, M.H. (1985). "Problems of semitic verbal stems". A Review. Bi.Or XLII no.3/4, 278-283.
Gray, L.H. (1943). *Introduction to Semitic Comparative Linguistics*. New York.
Greenberg, M. (1965). *Introduction to Hebrew*. Englewood Cliffs, N.J.
Grether, O. (1951). *Hebräische Grammatik für den akademischen Unterricht*. München.
Groenewoud, (1843). Iac. Corn. Swijghuisen. *Institutio ad grammaticam Hebraicam*. . .. Trajecti ad Rhenum, (Utrecht).
Halfmann, M. (1888, 1892). "Beiträge zur Syntax der Hebräischen Sprache". Programm 1888, no.241. 1892 no. 256.
Hammershaimb, E. (1970). "Review of Jenni, E., *Das hebräische Pi'el*". 222-223.
Hillers, D.R. (1967). "Delocutive verbs in Biblical Hebrew". JBL

86, 320-32.
Hillers, D.R. (1969). "Review of Jenni, E., *Das hebräische Pi'el*". JBL 88, 212-214.
Hoftijzer, J. (1965). "Remarks concerning the use of the particle 't in Classical Hebrew". In: *Oudtestamentische Studiën*, XIV, 1-99. Leiden.
Hoftijzer, J. (1981). "Hebreeuws en Aramees als Bijbeltalen". In: *Bijbels Handboek*, Vol. I, 173-200. Kampen.
Hoftijzer, J. (1982). *A Search for Method*, Leiden.
Hollenberg, W. (1889). *Hebräisches Schulbuch* 7th edn. Berlin.
Hollenberg, W. and Budde, K. (1912). *Hebräisches Schulbuch*. revised by K. Budde, 11th. edn. Berlin.
Hollenberg, W. and Budde, K. (1967). *Hebräisches Schulbuch*. republished by W. Baumgartner, 25th. edn. Basel und Stuttgart.
Hospers, J.H. (1966). "A hundred years of semitic comparative linguistics". *Studia Biblica et Semitica- Th.Chr.Vriezen... dedicato*, 138-151. Wageningen.
Hospers, J.H. (1970). "Review of Jenni, E., *Das hebräische Pi'el*". BiOr XXVII (27), 56-57.
Hospers, J.H. (1973). *A Basic Bibliography for the Study of the Semitic Languages*. Vols. I and II, 1973-74. Leiden.
Huehnergard, J. (1978). "'Stative', Predicative Form, Pseudo-Verb". JNES 46, 215-232.
Huehnergard, J. (1986). "On Verbless Clauses in Akkadian". ZA 76. 218-249.
Irsigler, H. (1981). *Einführung in das Biblischen Hebräisch*. ATS 9, St. Ottilieën.
Italie, H. (1881). *Beknopt leerboek der Hebreeuwsche taal*. Utrecht.
Jacob, Ed. (1969). "Review of Jenni, E., *Das hebräische Pi'el*". RHPhR XLIX (49), 289.
Jastrow, M. (1975). *Dictionary of the Targumim, the Talmud Babli and Jerushalmi and the Midrashic Literature*. New York.
J.E. *Jewish Encyclopedia*, (1901 and later edn.), "Christian Hebraists", 300-30.
Jenni, E. (1967). "Faktitiv und kausitiv von **ABD** "zu grunde gehen" in Hebräische Wortforschung". *Festschrift zum 80. Geburtstag von W. Baumgartner*, 143-157. Leiden.
Jenni, E. (1968). *Das hebräische Pi'el*. Zürich.
Jenni, E. (1969). "Zur Funktion der Reflexiv-passiven Stammformen in Biblischen-Hebräischen". *Proceedings of the 5th World Congress of Jewish Studies.*, Vol. 4. 1973, 61-70. Jerusalem.
Jenni, E. (1977). "Zaqen, Bemerkungen zum Unterschied von Nominalsatz und Verbalsatz". In: *Beitrage zur Alttestamentlicher Theologie, Festschrift für W. Zimmerli zum 70. Geburtstag*, 185-195. Göttingen.
Jenni, E. (1978). *Lehrbuch der hebräischen Sprache des Alten Testaments*. Basel und Stuttgart.
Joüon, P. (1923, 1965). *Grammaire de l'Hébreu biblique*. Rome.
KAI. Donner, H. and Rollig, W. (1971). *Kanaanäische und Aramäische Inschriften*, 3rd edn. Wiesbaden.
Kapelrud, A.S. (1984). *Joel Studies*. Uppsala.
KBL. Kohler, L. and Baumgartner, W. (1958). *Lexicon in veteris*

testamenti libros. Leiden.
Kellerman, D. (1972). "**aašam**". In: TWzAT, 463-472.
Knierim, R. (1971). "**aašam**". In: THAT, 256.
König, Fr.E. (1881). *Historisch-Kritisches Lehrgebaüde der Hebräischen Sprache*, Vol. I. Leipzig.
König, Fr.E. (1895). *Historisch-Kritisches Lehrgebaüde der Hebräischen Sprache*, Vol. II. Leipzig.
König, Fr.E. (1897). *Historisch-comparative Syntax der Hebräischen Sprache*. Leipzig.
König, Fr.E. (1922). *Hebräisches und Aramäisches Wörterbuch zum Alten Testament*. Leipzig.
Kraus, F.R. (1984). "Nominalsatze in altbabylonischen Briefe und der Stativ". *Mededelingen der Koninklijke Nederlandse Akademie van Wetenschappen*, afdeling Letterkunde. N.R. 47/2, 21-71.
Krinetzki, G. (1981). *Bibelhebräisch*. In: Reihe Katholische Theologie, Vol. II. Passau.
Kustár, P. (1972). *Aspekt im Hebräischen*. Basel.
Lambdin, Th.O. (1969). "Review of Jenni, E., *Das hebräische Pi'el*", CBQ 31, 435-437.
Lambdin, Th.O. (1973). *Introduction to Biblical Hebrew*. London.
Lambert, M. (1900). "L'emploi du Nifal en Hébreu", REJ 41, 196-214.
Lambert, M. (1946, 1972). Traité de grammaire hébraique 2. Corrected and completed by G.E.Weil, Hildesheim 1972. (Paris 1946).
Lancellotti, A. (1973). *Grammatica della lingua Accadica*. Jerusalem.
LaSor, W.S. (1979). *Handbook of Biblical Hebrew, Vol. II: Grammar*. Grand Rapids.
Leemhuis, F. (1977). *The D and H Stems in Koranic Arabic, a Comparative Study of the Function and Meaning of the Fa''ala and 'af'ala Forms in Koranic Usage*. Doctoral Dissertation. Rijksuniversiteit Groningen 1977. Leiden.
Lefevre, J. (1945). *Précis de Grammaire Hébraique*. Paris.
Lettinga, J.P. (1976). *Grammatica van het Bijbels Hebreeuws*, 8th. edn. Leiden.
Lipin, L.A. (1973). *The Akkadian Language*. Moscow.
Loewe, R. (1972). "Hebraists, Christian". In: *Encyclopedia Judaica*, Vol. 8, 9-71.
Luzatto, S.D. (1853). *Grammatica della lingua ebraica*. Padua.
Lyons, J. (1968). *Introduction to Theoretical Linguistics*. Cambridge.
Mandelkern, S. (1925). *Veteris Testamenti Concordantiae Hébraique atque Chaldaicae*. Berlin.
Margain, J. (1974) "Causatif et toleratif en hébreu", *g.l.e.c.s.* XVIII-XXIII, 23-31. 1973-1979.
Mc.Fall, L. (1982). *The Enigma of the Hebrew Verbal Systems Solutions from Ewald to the Present Day*. Sheffield.
Mettinger, T.N.D. (1973). *The Hebrew Verb System, a Survey of Recent Research*, ASTI IX (1973), 64-84. Leiden 1974.
Meyer, R. (1969). *Hebräische Grammatik*, Vol. II. Berlin.
Meyer, R. (1972). *Hebräische Grammatik*, Vol. III. Berlin.
Michel, D. (1960). *Tempora und Satzstellung in den Psalmen*. Bonn.
Miller, E.F. (1927). *The Influence of Gesenius on Hebrew Lexico-*

graphy. New York.
Moscati, S. (1959). *Lezioni di Linguistica Semitica*. Roma.
Moscati, S. (1969). *An Introduction to the Comparative Grammar of the Semitic Languages*. 2nd. edn. Wiesbaden.
Müller, H.P. (1985). "Ergativelemente im akkadischen und althebräischen Verbalsystem", *Biblica* 66, 385-417.
Nat, J. (1939). *Hebreeuwsche Grammatica*. 2nd edn., Leiden.
Nat, J. and Koopmans, J.J. (1945). *Hebreeuwsche Grammatica*. 3rd edn. revised by J.J.Koopmans. Leiden.
Noldeke, Th. (1898). *Kurzgefasste Syrische Grammatik*. 2nd edn. Leipzig. (Republished, Darmstadt 1966).
Noordtzij, A. (1907). *Beknopte Hebreeuwsche Spraakkunst*. Kampen.
Nordheimer, I. (1838). *A Critical Grammar of the Hebrew Language*, Vol. I. New York.
Nyberg, H.S. (1952). *Hebreisk Grammatik*. Uppsala.
O'Leary, De Lacy (1923). *Comparative Grammar of the Semitic Languages*. Co-author: De Lacy. London.
Olshausen, J. (1861). *Lehrbuch der Hebräischen Sprache*. Braunschweig.
Ornan, U. (1972). "Hebrew Grammar", *Encyclopedia Judaica*, Vol. 8. Jerusalem. 124-128.
Ornan, U. (1979). "More on the meaning of the binyanim". (In Hebrew), *Mincha le qodesh*, ed. by C. Rabin and B.Z. Fischer. Jerusalem.
Pedersen, J. (1926). *Hebraeisk Grammatik*. Kopenhagen.
Poebel, A. (1938). "Studies in Akkadian Grammar", AS 9. Chicago.
Porges, N. (1875). "Ueber die Verbalstammbildung in den Semitischen Sprachen, *Sitzungsberichte der kaiserlichen Akademie der Wissenschaften*. Phil.-hist. Classe, 79th Vol., 281-354. Vienna.
Richter, W. (1978). *Grundlagen einer althebräischen Grammatik*, Vol. I, ATS 8, St. Ottilieën.
Rieder, A. (1844). "De lingua hebr. verbis, quae vocantur derivativa nif. et hitp.", Programm 1844, nr.4. Leipzig.
Riemschneider, K.K. (1973). *Lehrbuch des Akkadischen*, 2nd. edn. Leipzig.
Ringgren, H. (1970). "Review of Jenni, E., Das hebräische Pi'el". In: *Theologisch Zeitschrift von der Theologischen Fakultät Basel*, 26, 216-217.
Roorda, T. (1831). *Grammatica Hebraea*, Vol. I and II, Leiden.
Rosenthal, F. (1961). *A Grammar of Biblical Aramaic*. Wiesbaden.
Rudolf, W. (1971). "Joel". KAT XIII, 2. Gütersloh.
Rundgren, F. (1961). *Das Althebräische Verbum: Abriss der Aspektlehre*. Uppsala.
Ryckmans, G. (1960). *Grammaire Accadienne*, 4th edn. Revised by P. Nastier. Louvain.
Ryder, St.A. II. (1974). *The D-stem in Western Semitic, Janua Linguarum*, Series Practica 131. The Hague-Paris.
Sarchi, M. (1828). *Grammaire Hébraique*. Paris.
Sawyer, J.F.A. (1969). "Review of Jenni, E., *Das hebräische Pi'el*". In: JSS XIV (14), 1969, 260-262.
Sawyer, J.F.A. (1976). *A Modern Introduction to Biblical Hebrew*, Stocksfield.
Schilling, D. (1943). *Grammaire hébraique élémentaire*. Paris.

Schneider, W. (1982). *Grammatik des Biblischen Hebräisch*, 5th edn. München.
Schweitzer, H. (1981). *Metaphorische Grammatik*. ATS 15, St. Ottilieën.
Segert, S. (1975). *Altaramäische Grammatik mit Bibliographie, Chrestomathie und Glossar*, Leipzig.
Siedl, S.H. (1971). *Gedanken zum Tempussystem im Hebräischen und Akkadischen*. Wiesbaden.
v.Soden, W. (1970). "Review of Jenni, E., *Das hebräische Pi'el*". In: ZA 60, 176-178.
Soggin, J.A. (1968). "Review of Jenni, E., *Das hebräische Pi'el*", RSO XLIII, 311-313.
Speiser, E.A. (1955). "The durative Hithpa'el, a 'tan'-form", JAOS 75, 118-121.
Sperber, A. (1966). *A Historical Grammar of Biblical Hebrew*. Leiden.
Stade, B. (1879). *Lehrbuch der hebräischen Grammatik*, Vol. I. Leipzig.
Stein, A. (1893). *Der Stamm des Hithpa'el im Hebräischen*, Vol. I. Leipzig.
Steuernagel, C. (1917). *Hebräische Grammatik*, 5th edn. Berlin.
Stier, G. (1881). *Kurzgefasste hebräische Grammatik für Gymnasien*, 1st edn. Leipzig.
Stier, G. (1893). *Kurzgefasste hebräische Grammatik für Gymnasien*, 2nd edn. Halle a.S..
Strack, H.L. (1890). *Hebräische Grammatik*, 3rd edn. Berlin.
Strack, H.L. (1917). *Hebräische Grammatik*, 12th, 13th edn. München.
Thacker, T.W. (1954). *The Relationship of the Semitic and Egyptian Verbal Systems*. Oxford.
T.H.A.T. *Theologisches Handwörterbuch zum Alten Testament*, in 2 Vols. republished by E. Jenni, (1971). München/Zürich.
Thiersch, H.W. (1858). *Hebräische Grammatik für Anfänger....* Erlangen.
Touzard, J. (1949). *Grammaire Hébraique*, abrégée, Nouvelle ed. par A. Robert, Paris.
Ungnad, A. (1906). "Die Bezeichnung der Verbalstämme im Semitischen". OLZ 9, 45-47.
Ungnad, A. (1912). *Hebräische Grammatik*. Tübingen.
Ungnad, A. (1926). *Hebräische Grammatik*. Tübingen.
Ungnad, A. and Matous, L. (1969). *Grammatik des Akkadischen*. Fully revised by L. Matous, 5th. edn. München.
Veth, P.J. (1852). *Beknopte Hebreeuwsche Spraakkunst voor de gymnasieën*, 2nd edn. Amsterdam.
Vosen, C.H. and Kaulen, Fr. (1927). *Kurze Anleitung zum Erlernen der Hebräischen Sprache*, 12th edn. Freiburg im Breisgau.
Vosen, C.H. and Kaulen, Fr. (1927). *Kurze Anleitung zum Erlernen der Hebräischen Sprache*, 22nd and 23rd edn, revised by J.Schumacher. Freiburg im Breisgau.
de Vries, S.P. (1931). *Leerboek der Hebreeuwsche taal*. Haarlem.
Weingreen, J. (1939). *A Practical Grammar for Classical Hebrew*. Oxford.
Weingreen, J. (1983). "The Pi'el in Biblical Hebrew: a suggested

new concept", Henoch 5. 21-29.
Welzel, G. (1981). *Programmierte Grammatik des Hebräischen.* Heidelberg.
Williams, R. (1970). "The passive Qal theme in Hebrew". In: *Essays on the Ancient Semitic World*, 43-50. Toronto.
Williams, R.J. (1978). *Hebrew Syntax: An Outline*, 2nd. edn. Toronto.
Wolff, H.W. (1969). *Joel.* BKAt XIV, 2. Neukirchen-Vluyn.
Wright, W. (1890). *Lectures on the Comparative Grammar of the Semitic Languages.* Cambridge.
Wright, W. (1896). *A grammar of the Arabic language 3.* Vol.I. Cambridge.
Yalon, H. (1932). "Mitteilungen 2: Hithpa'elformen im Hebräischen". ZAW 50, 217-220.
Young, G.D. (1951). *Grammar of the Hebrew Language.* Grand Rapids.
Zimmern, H. (1898). *Vergleichende Grammatik der Semitischen Sprachen.* Berlin.

Published in the series STUDIA SEMITICA NEERLANDICA:

1. *Dr. C. van Leeuwen*, Le développement du sens social en Israel avent l'ère chrétienne.*
2. *Dr. M. Reisel*, The mysterious Name of Y.H.W.H.*
3. *Dr. A.S. van der Woude*, Die messianischen Vorstellungen der Gemeinde von Qumrân.*
4. *Dr. B. Jongeling*, Le rouleau de la guerre des manuscrits de Qumrân.
5. *Dr. N.A. van Uchelen*, Abraham de hebreeër.*
6. *Dr. H.J.W. Drijvers*, Bardaiṣan of Edessa.*
7. *Dr. J.H. Meesters*, Op zoek naar de oorsprong van de Sabbat.*
8. *Dr. A.G. van Daalen*, Simson.*
9. *Dr. Leon A. Feldman*, R. Abraham b. Isaac ha-Levi TaMaKh. Commentary on the Song of Songs.*
10. *Dr. W.A.M. Beuken*, Haggai-Sacharja 2-8.
11. *Dr. Curt Leviant*, King Artus, a Hebrew Arthurian Romance of 1279.*
12. *Dr. Gabriel H. Cohn*, Das Buch Jona.*
13. *Dr. G. van Driel*, The Cult of Aššur.*
14. *Dr. H. Jagersma*, Leviticus 19. Identiteit, bevrijding, gemeenschap.*
15. *Dr. Wilhelm Th. In der Smitten*, Esra. Quellen, Ueberlieferung und Geschichte.*
16. Travels in the world of the Old Testament. Studies presented to prof. M.A. Beek, on the occasion of his 65th birthday.*
17. *Dr. J.P. Fokkelman*, Narrative Art in Genesis. Specimens of stylistic and structural analysis.*
18. *Dr. C.H.J. de Geus*, The Tribes of Israel.
19. *Dr. M.D. Koster*, The Peshitta of Exodus. The Development of its Text in the Course of Fifteen Centuries.
20. *Dr. J.P. Fokkelman*, Narrative Art and Poetry in the Books of Samuel. A full interpretation based on stylistic and structural analyses. Volume I: King David (II Sam. 9.20 & I Kings 1.2).
21. *Prof.dr. J. Hoftijzer*. The Function and Use of the Imperfect Forms with Nun-Paragogicum in Classical Hebrew.
22. *Dr. K. van den Toorn*. Sin and Sanction in Israel and Mesopotamia.
23. *Dr. J.P. Fokkelman*, Narrative Art and Poetry in the Books of Samuel. A full interpretation based on stylistic and structural analyses. Volume II: The Crossing Fates (I Sam. 13-31 & II Sam. 1).
24. *Dr. L.J. de Regt*, A Parametric Model for Syntactic Studies of a Textual Corpus, Demonstrated on the Hebrew of Deuteronomy 1-30.
25. *Dr. E.J. van Wolde*, A Semiotic Analysis of Genesis 2-3. A Semiotic Theory and Method of Analysis Applied to the Story of the Garden of Eden.
26. *Dr. T.A.M. Fontaine*, In Defence of Judaism: Abraham Ibn Daud. Sources and Structures of ha-Emunah ha-Ramah.
27. *Dr. A.J.C. Verheij*, Verbs and Numbers. A Study of the Frequencies of the Hebrew Verbal Tense Forms in the Books of Samuel, Kings, and Chronicles.
28. *Dr. P.A. Siebesma*, The Function of the niph'al in Biblical Hebrew in relationship to other passive-reflexive verbal stems and to the pu'al and hoph'al in particular.

* = out of stock.

Reviews

R. Fuller, JBL 112/3 (1993) 508-10.

W. Watson, JJS 43/2 (1992) 563-64.

W.G.E. Watson, JSS 39/1 (1994) 107-8.

PAUL D. SANSONE, O.F.M.

940726 29.00 (23.20)